Walk Towards the Gallows

Walk Towards the Gallows

The Tragedy of Hilda Blake,
Hanged 1899

Reinhold Kramer and Tom Mitchell

UNIVERSITY OF TORONTO PRESS
Toronto   Buffalo   London

Originally published by
Oxford University Press Canada 2002
© University of Toronto Press Incorporated 2007
Toronto Buffalo London
Printed in Canada
ISBN 978-0-8020-9542-8 (paper)

Printed on acid-free paper

National Library of Canada Cataloguing in Publication Data

Kramer, Reinhold, 1959–
Walk towards the gallows: the tragedy of Hilda Blake,
hanged 1899 / Reinhold Kramer and Tom Mitchell.

Includes bibliographical references and index.
ISBN 978-0-8020-9542-8

1. Blake, Hilda, 1899-1899. 2. Murderers—Manitoba—
Brandon—Biography.   I. Mitchell, Tom, 1949– . II. Title.

HV6248.B543K73 2007   364.15'23'092   C2007–901388–0

Contents

Dedicated to
Paul and Helene Kramer,
and to 'Jozef Tomczak', who, though he never existed,
was forced to fend for himself at the age of 12 in 1945.

To Bonnie,
who stopped measuring the cost
long ago.

Acknowledgements

Thanks to Ron Godfrey and John Milne for allowing us to go through the house once inhabited by Robert Lane, Mary Lane, and Hilda Blake. Isobel Cotton, who several years ago put together a scrapbook on the Church of the Advent in Kola, helped with information about the Stewarts' role in the church. On a pleasant and companionable trip out to the Church of the Advent, Doug Freeman told us what he knew of the Stewart and Rex families. Jim and Elizabeth Wall of the South West Branch of the Manitoba Genealogical Society shared information about family histories. During evening walks, Chris Johnson, whose grandmother was the first person at Mary Lane's side on 5 July 1899, made numerous suggestions and offered his unique insight into the case.

Thanks to Don Hamilton for providing access to records of the former Brandon jail. Thanks also to Lorraine Thurston; Olive Andrews; Jean Scott; Chris Dunning of the Rural Municipality of Wallace; Val Hulbert of the Anglican Diocesan Office in Brandon; Jody Baltessen, Jackie Nicholls, Brian Hubner, Janelle Reynolds, and the late Michelle Fitzgerald of the Manitoba Provincial Archives. Loretta Barber, Lorraine Gadoury, and Tina Lloyd at the National Archives of Canada assisted with Ottawa files related to the Blake case. Alicja Brancewicz in the Brandon University library cheerfully arranged valuable interlibrary loans throughout this project. Ron Gonty helped with land titles, homestead records, and photographs of the Rex family; Edward Phelps of the University of Western Ontario searched the David Mills papers; and Jim Naylor of Brandon University suggested useful sources.

We also thank our British friends: Dianne Yeadon of the Norfolk Studies Library; Jean Kennedy of the Norfolk Record Office; Superintendent Kirkham of the Norfolk Constabulary. Dr John Alban, County Archivist at the Norfolk Record Office, arranged our access to records from the Heckingham Workhouse. Christina Crease and Carol Carpenter, who have published a little parish history called 'Langley-with-Hardley', enthusiastically answered many of our queries.

Bill Morrison, Paula Mallea, Rita Kramer, David Williams, Greg Kealey, an anonymous reviewer for Oxford University Press, and Richard Tallman read drafts of the manuscript at various stages and provided many useful comments. Phyllis Wilson suggested the title. And: without the unattainable targets of Peter Brown's *Augustine of Hippo* and Carlo Ginzburg's *The Cheese and the Worms: The Cosmos of a Sixteenth-Century Miller*, this book could not have been written in the form that it is.

Introduction:
The Murder of Mary Lane

Wednesday, 5 July 1899, was one of those pleasant afternoons that compensates for the plunging cold of the prairie winter. At 21° Celsius, the weather in Brandon, Manitoba, seemed perfect for an outdoor tea party. Not 30 feet from the back entrance to their home, the four children of Robert and Mary Lane—Thomas, Edith, Mary Jr, and possibly Evelyn—along with several friends—Kathleen and Helen Johnson, Georgina Hanley, and a girl whose surname was Henderson—sat on the lawn of a vacant lot, enjoying the party that Mary Lane, the mother, had promised them if they were good. Mary, 32 years old and pregnant, worked inside, hanging curtains on the parlour windows. Just after four o'clock, she ran screaming out the front door and onto the public sidewalk, took a few steps south on Tenth Street, and collapsed. Blood stained her dress. She had been shot in the back at close range—her skin and blouse singed by flames from the pistol—and the bullet had passed through the top of her lung, lodging finally just above her heart. In some apocryphal accounts a toddler, presumably Evelyn, was playing on the floor at the time of the shooting, and the dying Mary had snatched the child up in order to protect it before running out to the street.[1] Mrs Johnson, the next-door neighbour, was first to answer the screams. Another neighbour, Mr Sampson, ran to call for a doctor and for Mary's husband, Robert, while the Lane servant girl appeared on the scene to bathe Mary's face with water. When Sampson returned, Mary was still alive, but before the doctor or Lane could arrive, blood accumulated in her lungs and she suffocated. She died without saying who had shot her.

Within minutes of the shooting Mary's body was carried into the Lane house and laid on the parlour floor, while a teacher, Miss

1

Bawden, quickly spirited the children away.[2] Sampson alerted the police, and reports of the shooting sped through the city. The news of a lethal assault on a respectable middle-class woman in the sanctuary of her home in the middle of a July afternoon seemed unbelievable. 'Terrible news of a cruel murder committed in the heart of the city spread like wild-fire. Too horrible to be true seemed the tale which every tongue was telling . . . one of Brandon's women had been ruthlessly taken by an assassin's bullet.'[3] The *Western Sun* called the murder 'one of the most atrocious crimes in the annals of Manitoba's history and one of the most villainous that ever occurred in the Dominion of Canada'.[4]

There was one eyewitness. Emily Hilda Blake, the 21-year-old servant girl who had been employed by the Lanes since the summer of 1898, had been carrying out bread and butter to the children and ironing curtains for Mary. Despite the horrific events, Blake gave a precise and lucid account of the murder, complete with motive. She had first sensed the existence of an unknown man when she saw his shadow at the back door, but she didn't attend to him because she assumed that he was someone hired by Robert Lane to work on the lawn. When she eventually turned, she saw a tramp, stooping to place his bundle on the ground next to the door. She wasn't startled; the railway spur being just behind the house, such figures often appeared at the kitchen door. He wore a soiled white shirt and a new suit of blue overalls, his bundle a brown parcel or valise or perhaps a sack. Standing 5' 10" tall, he looked about 30 to 35 years old, with a well-tanned face, a light moustache, and a beard of probably two or three days' growth. 'His eyes were set far back in the head', she said. 'They did not appear very sharp, but had a vacant stare.' She was sure that she would know him if she saw him again; later she would be less sure.[5]

His tone inoffensive, the tramp asked, 'Could you give a fellow something to eat?' Blake did not respond, referring him to Mary, who stood on the parlour sofa hanging the drapes that Blake, a few steps away in the summer kitchen, had been ironing. Without turning, Lane said, 'Make him work for it before you give him anything.'[6] This seemed to anger the tramp. He responded under his breath in a foreign language, and, as Blake walked into the kitchen proper from the summer kitchen, he followed, his gait unusual. In the kitchen he stood behind her, facing towards Mary in the front parlour. Mary at that point sharply instructed Blake not to bother with him. Denied, the tramp advanced a few steps to stand in the passage between the kitchen and the parlour, brandished a revolver from under his coat, and shot Mary in the back. He shot twice. Thrusting her arm straight out at the inquest, Blake demonstrated how the man had levelled his gun to kill her mistress.

'Oh Hilda! . . . I'm on fire!' Mary cried, and ran through the front door onto Tenth Street, the tramp at the same time fleeing in the opposite direction out the back door.[7] He made no attempt on Blake's life, but for her part Blake also screamed. She did not know where the murder weapon was; she thought perhaps that the tramp had taken it with him. She assumed, as well, that he must have picked up his bundle, for it, too, had vanished.

Blake initially followed the dying Mary through the parlour, but she only got as far as the front hallway. There she collapsed, for how long she didn't know, but she never lost consciousness. On regaining her self-possession, she stumbled awkwardly out onto Tenth Street. 'Everything seemed black before my eyes and I felt dizzy when I came to the sidewalk.' She found Mary on the sidewalk in a pool of blood, Mrs Johnson crouching over her, others gathering. Blake went back inside for water and then returned to bathe Mary's face.

Within a few hours, the investigating officer, Police Chief James Kircaldy, doubted Blake's story. During the next days of manhunts and the near-lynching of a tramp, Kircaldy accumulated a number of circumstantial details that didn't fit her account, and he ultimately used those details to get a confession from her. After her arrest she admitted that she had killed Lane with a gun purchased in Winnipeg weeks before, and added that, notwithstanding ample evidence of premeditation, she had committed the murder because of a sudden and overwhelming fit of jealousy. She begged Kircaldy to shoot her on the spot. At the preliminary hearing she pled guilty and requested 'the most severe punishment possible', well knowing that she was requesting the gallows. She refused legal counsel, and despite a movement to have her sentence commuted, she was hanged four days before the end of the nineteenth century, the only woman to be executed in Manitoba, one of only two women executed in Canada between 1873 and 1922.

*

Our biography of Hilda Blake first took shape around a missing body. In 1985, when the *Brandon Sun* reported the excavation of the old Brandon jailyard to create the Rideau Park Personal Care Home, speculation abounded as to the location of the bodies of Blake, William Webb, and two other men executed at the old jail.[8] Information was sketchy, the only knowledge having been passed down from generation to generation of guards, and Bill Ryan, a retired guard, told the *Sun* that 'now just a handful of us old guards knows where [the graves] are.' During the 1960s, in the corner of what had once been the prison exercise yard, Ryan had discovered Blake's grave when he was assigned to fill in ground that had settled into the coffins. The area had been a courtyard back in 1899, but by the 1960s it was paved with tarmac. After the jail closed the grounds fell into disrepair, and by 1985 tall weeds and saplings poked through the tarmac where the unmarked graves lay. Ryan objected to the possibility of exhumation to make way for the seniors complex: 'I maintain that the ground where a body is laid when one dies belongs to God. Wherever you are put, that's where you remain as God's property.'[9] As he wished, the bodies were ultimately left in peace and the Rideau Park Home was constructed above the gravesites, with a shallow crawl space rather than a full basement at the building's northeast end.[10]

More important than any single absent body are the absent biographies of the lower classes. Chief Kircaldy's web of circumstantial details and Robert Lane's possible, but elusive, involvement in the events leading to the crime make interesting reading; nevertheless, the murder mystery is only one focus of this book. The 'history of housemaid's knee in Belleville in the 1890s',[11] a type of history that once so repelled J.L. Granatstein—that's what we wanted to write! Such a history could reach from the housemaid to a runaway child, adultery, and a potential prison break; even to the suffragette movement and Clifford Sifton's immigration policies; and back again to the housemaid still on her knees, unable to get the required shine onto her floor. Before the twentieth century, women typically left only scattered and incomplete records of their lives. Such reticence, at least in the Victorian era, was a mark of virtue: women were supposed to be selfless and anonymous in their devotion to family. To leave a public record of one's earthly existence bordered on the unseemly, and such strictures applied even more conclusively to lower-class domestic servants. Hilda Blake, though she might dream about the weapon-buying habits of Sir Walter Scott's heroines, was a solitary menial in a middle-class home. Anonymity was a requirement of the office.

But Hilda Blake was—sometimes unintentionally—an outrageously indiscreet witness to her own life and times. An abundance of records, both official and informal, bear directly on her journey from youngest child of a Norfolk police constable to convicted murderess standing on a scaffold in Brandon. They consist of personal correspondence, newspaper reports, Court of Queen's Bench court pockets, judges' notebooks, Norfolk workhouse records, and family stories. We have indicated where questions exist about the accuracy of the information, but the newspapers' probable main sources on Blake—Chief Kircaldy and Rev. C.C. McLaurin—seem reliable. If the two Conservative newspapers in Brandon—the *Brandon Times* and the *Independence*—had been caught in a clear error, the Liberal paper—the *Western Sun*—would have trumpeted the fact, and vice versa.

Although Blake's existence was in many respects a profoundly solitary one, the nature of her life as an orphan, as a domestic servant, as a woman, and, ultimately, as an emblem of victimized femininity, offers a rich field of inquiry. The best women's history cannot be 'ghettoized and partial', as Joan Sangster notes, but makes 'comparisons between women and men, relates women to men, and shows how women's lives were created by, within and sometimes in opposition to the world of men.'[12] A full biography of Blake thus requires a narrative that would move beyond the lurid and sensational details of her life, offering the kinds of thick cultural description that one finds in the work of Peter Brown and Carlo Ginzburg.[13] It is not our intention to glamorize the 'rogue female' in the way that the 'rogue male' has often been glamorized,[14] or to document some miscarriage of justice, nor (though women who murder are unusual even in the twentieth century) to emphasize only what is exotic about Blake. In the following pages, we simultaneously place Blake and her social order before the reader. Through Blake's grim progress the values, assumptions, and meanings central to the culture of late Victorian Canada present themselves, *in extremis*.

What did a late nineteenth-century domestic servant think about and fantasize about? As a biographical study as well as an exploration of late Victorian culture, gender, and class in Canada, the writing of this book posed a number of epistemological challenges. The contemporary debate in social history among advocates of the 'linguistic turn' and those committed to materialist approaches has influenced our approach, turning us towards the mediations of language.[15] Blake read *Jane Eyre*, Dickens, and Scott. Literature, as 'one of the most persuasive uses of language', influences how people 'grasp' themselves and how people interpret 'the real relations in which they live'.[16] We will attempt to show that literature played a crucial role in shaping Blake's subjectivity. In her story, melodramas of crime and punishment compete with romances of sudden elevations, social amelioration, and rehabilitation. Novels did not *cause* her to act in certain ways, but the *form* her actions took often depended on her reading. Although she probably didn't read Oscar Wilde, she intuited that her life must imitate art.

Yet simply to favour discursive analysis over materialism is to run
the danger of reducing the past to a series of competing discourses.[17]
The relationship of human consciousness, language, experience, and
action cannot finally be reduced to rhetoric. Power, class, and gender
show up not only as words, but as a kind of irreducible and sticky
matter adhering willy-nilly to individual lives. 'Men make history,'
the stickiest of economic philosophers has said, 'but they do not make
it just as they please. They do not make it under circumstances chosen
by themselves, but under circumstances directly found, given and
transmitted from the past.'[18]

*

'Like the doomed heroine in a Victorian novel'. . . . If such a phrase
never appears directly in this book, it is not because the phrase hasn't
been thought. Every biography, insists Roland Barthes, is a novel that
dare not speak its name. We tell a *story* because only a story can
expose the real workings of a culture, and only a story can express
our protest against time. The story that unfolds in these pages is constructed, not a 'found' narrative. Although contemporaneous sources
interpreted 'tragedy' very narrowly as 'pathos' when they spoke of
Mary Lane, tragedy in its fullness—especially the individual's breaking of taboos, the overpowering of the individual by larger social
forces, and the individual's eventual recognition of at least some of
the forces at play—still seemed to us the best trope for Hilda Blake's
story. Secondary debts have been paid to melodrama and romance,
since her contemporaries loved those genres, and she saw her own
life partly in those forms. Whatever distortions are created by our
effort at a coherent narrative, it is only through 'what happens next'
that Blake's subjectivity (and ours)—the human parabolic arc
towards death—can be felt.

We have tried to heed Leonore Davidoff's warning: 'Not only have
autobiographers but also historians have concealed their imaginations
and bridled their tongues so that "the past is . . . often presented as
idyllic—totally lacking in smells, urges and bodies".'[19] A debt to
present-day forms—to ironic and bodily forms that aren't always
nameable—cannot, of course, be safely ignored. Given the limits of
the historical record, however, we leave some smells and urges to the
novelist, since to be overly explicit about urges is often to drown the
historical subject in our own inner compulsions. While we cannot
help revealing some of our own urges, our goal is to allow Hilda
Blake (and her period) a purposive consciousness, instead of making
our own day and its conceits the nineteenth century's unconscious—

what the nineteenth century thinks without knowing it—as happens in Margaret Atwood's *Alias Grace*.

Like us, Atwood told the story of a domestic servant convicted of murder—the fictionalized Grace Marks, an Ontario woman convicted in 1843 of helping to murder her employer and his housekeeper.[20] While some areas of history seem closed to historians worried about documentation—the lyrical area, say, in which the alienist Simon Jordan dreams that only housemaids can swim—such areas are 'known' in profound ways by Atwood.[21] But at a cost. Atwood restages Grace's historical murder confession as a seance, during which Mary Whitney's lower-class voice explodes out of Grace, a wronged and murderous voice that has always been subliminally present in Grace's story, but which Grace has consistently repressed from her proper speech. Such an elegant ruse allows Atwood to keep her readers uncertain about Grace's guilt: Was Grace schizophrenic to the point that 'Mary', not 'Grace', committed murder? Was Grace split between 'inner' and 'outer' voices like everybody (according to Atwood, anyway) in the nineteenth century? Is the truth about the past ultimately unknowable?[22]

The overarching structure of Atwood's fictional double voicing (inner/outer, Grace/Mary, Simon/Grace) makes the novel suspiciously similar to Atwood's earlier poetic version of the nineteenth century, *The Journals of Susanna Moodie*. Evidently Atwood began her novel with a thesis about the nineteenth century and then shoehorned the historical Grace into that thesis.[23] Yet even if schizophrenia (the medical condition, not its literary image) were an appropriate diagnosis for the historical Grace, schizophrenia is much too simple as a diagnosis for an entire culture: the diagnosis never lets the nineteenth century mean what it says.[24] Like too many writers, Atwood punishes the nineteenth century for not being the twentieth. For a present day uneasy about its cardinal values—gender equality, freedom of speech, self-expression, skepticism towards religion, psychological explanations for just about everything—the bogeyman nineteenth century too often shows up as the ruthless cattle baron who must be shot by the present in the interests of liberty.

Certain nineteenth-century tropes—class struggle, the rise of female suffrage—persisted as coherent and believable 'stories' in the twentieth, but we will rely also on tropes that apologists for the present have dismissed—orphanhood, evangelicalism, romance, melodrama, and moral idiocy. We try to avoid both a too-harmonious account of Hilda Blake or an account that simply makes her a postmodern cipher. Out of a variety of feminist, medical, legal, and literary constructions

at the centre of a scandal that remains unresolved, Hilda Blake
emerges. Her story, never fully known, involves a complex interaction
between private pain—orphaned at nine, she never again felt at
home—and an inhospitable social order. Others in similar positions
did not murder their employers, yet the social order in which she stood
as an orphan and domestic servant strictly limited her opportunities. It
would be easy, but too simplistic, to parade Hilda Blake as an unconscious suffragette, or, conversely, as a moral fable. Hers was an individual life at the intersection of several social histories, a life often
opening out into broader issues, but she is no emblem, finally, of anything but herself.

Hilda Blake resisted the imposed social roles not in any public or
revolutionary way, but by roughly trying and failing to seize a position that was not hers. Attempting to unweave the many languages
surrounding her may give us some idea of what, in the late nineteenth
century, went into the making of the individual subject. At some point
that plurality achieves unity, if only to walk towards the gallows.

PART I

1

A Vulnerable and Isolated Virtue

In great families, when an advantageous place cannot be obtained either in possession, reversion, remainder, or expectancy, for the young man who is growing up, it is a very general custom to send him to sea.

—Charles Dickens, *Oliver Twist*

In 1888, at 10 years of age and accompanied by her 12-year-old brother Tommy, Emily Hilda Blake was sent to sea. Not to work on board ship, but to emigrate to Canada. The two children were orphans—recent inmates of the Heckingham Workhouse (Loddon and Clavering Union). Hilda had been born to Henry and Sarah Ann Blake in January 1878 at Chedgrave, 10 miles southeast of Norwich on the acres and acres of farmland and low marshes known as the 'Norfolk Broads', a large, rough triangle with the coast as the base and Norwich the apex. Chedgrave and environs belonged to Sir Reginald Proctor-Beauchamp. By 1879, when he was only 26 and Henry Blake 33, Beauchamp had already fought against the Turks at Shipka Pass, had travelled to China and Japan, and had inherited his father's, Sir Thomas Proctor-Beauchamp's, land. The young Beauchamp resided on an 800-acre estate with a large and elegant mansion, Langley Hall, 'a veritable treasure-house of art . . . filled with busts, paintings, and statues'.[1]

The Blakes' lives were much more circumscribed. Cottage tenants on the Beauchamp estate, they were religious and 'most respectable people'[2]—at least so Beauchamp later claimed—but poor, near the

9

bottom of a social structure dominated by landowner and parson. Fishing and farming were the region's principal industries, and as a young cottage tenant in the 1860s, Henry Blake worked as an agricultural labourer while Sir Reginald was being educated at Eton and at Trinity College, Cambridge. While late nineteenth-century fishing followed more or less traditional patterns, in agriculture the machine had replaced labour-intensive practices of the past. Threshing, winnowing, turnip-hoeing and cutting, sowing, haymaking, corn-cutting and binding, corn- and straw-stacking, and a score of other things were done by machine, to the exclusion of a great deal of manual labour. At 23, married and supporting two children, Blake graduated from tenant farming to become a police constable in the Norfolk Constabulary. His work may have included bailiff duties for Beauchamp vis-à-vis the other tenant farmers. After the oldest daughter, three sons—Henry Jr, Theodore, and Augustus—were born respectively in Grimston, Loddon, and Hickling.[3] Rev. Henry Alfred Barrett, Beauchamp's uncle and the Chedgrave parson ever since Henry Blake and Sir Reginald Beauchamp were children, would speak, after Henry's death, of him as 'a highly respected officer in the Police Force'.[4]

Barrett exaggerated. Although Blake had risen to constable second-class by 1870 and first-class by 1873, he was dismissed from his job the following year for drunkenness. The dismissal took place in August of 1874—the same year in which Reginald Beauchamp succeeded his father—and only one child, Tommy, was born to the Blakes in the next three years, a time during which they must have struggled financially. Unusually, Henry Blake was reappointed to the police at the end of December 1877,[5] and eventually rose again to constable first-class. Less than a month after the reappointment Hilda was born. It may be that Sir Reginald had a hand in Blake's reappointment and in his almost immediate promotion to constable second-class, because Henry and Sarah chose a Beauchamp name as a middle name for their new daughter: 'Hilda', after Hilda Beauchamp, Sir Reginald's sister. Whether the name was a thank-you, a hope of some future elevation, or simply an imitation of one's superiors cannot be said. In any case, the young girl went by 'Hilda', not by her first name, 'Emily'.

Another boy, Donald, was born in 1881. By 1883 the family had remained in Chedgrave on the banks of the leisurely Chet River for all of the five years of Hilda's life. But the seeming stability of the Chedgrave years proved illusory, as the 37-year-old Henry Blake became deathly ill in 1883 of 'phthisis pulmonalis, diarrhoea, and exhaustion': probably tuberculosis. His wife, Sarah, wasn't well either. When it was clear that Henry was in the final throes of his illness,

Rev. Barrett came to pray with the two parents that 'God would graciously fulfil his promise of being the Father of the fatherless.' Hilda's 'dying father and departing mother' confirmed the parson's wishes with 'deep toned, heartfelt Amens'.[6] After Henry Blake died, poverty must have descended—his widow receiving a gratuity of only £25—and the family remained for a short while in Sarah's sickly hands until she followed her husband to the grave a few years later. Hilda was orphaned at the age of nine.

Only working-class children like the Blakes became orphans in Victorian England. Middle- and upper-class children left parentless were usually absorbed into the families of close relatives or placed under the care of a guardian. Working-class children, however, were frequently left dispossessed, stranded, and completely dependent on the state or charitable organizations for their welfare. Few initiatives replaced the social structure of the family; the Adoption of Children Act, which provided for such children, was approved in Britain only in 1926. Although the material conditions confronting orphans were not necessarily more onerous than those facing the typical working-class child, it was nevertheless shattering to be isolated, alienated from the family setting, and placed in a poorhouse or sent as young agricultural labourers and domestics to strange homes in the colonies. Like state wards nowadays, who may be shunted from one foster home to another, working-class Victorian orphans usually knew the irrevocable loss of a permanent home. For a while the eldest sister looked after Tommy, Hilda, and six-year-old Donald, but the sister married, and was then either unwilling, or perhaps unable, to provide for them.[7] As winter closed in at the end of November 1887, Tommy was sent to live among 600 other paupers in the Heckingham Workhouse, where Rev. Barrett and Sir Reginald were Guardians. A month later, just before Christmas, the eldest sister sent Hilda and Donald to join Tommy. The Workhouse was only a few minutes' walk east from their former home, but in all other ways it was far from their earlier lives. The children's diet category was assigned and a number affixed to their clothes.

Although Donald remained in the Workhouse until at least 1891,[8] Hilda's stay was relatively short, since Sir Reginald, like Canada's future Governor-General, the Earl of Aberdeen, happened also to be on the board of the Self-Help Emigration Society, contributing £20 yearly to the cause.[9] On 16 April 1888 a motion was proposed by Sir Reginald, and confirmed by Rev. Barrett and the other Guardians, that the Workhouse master purchase outfits for Hilda and Tommy at a cost not to exceed £2 each, outfits suitable for a sea journey to

Heckingham Workhouse where Hilda, Tommy, and Donald Blake were sent after their parents' deaths. Constructed in 1763 as a House of Industry, it had been set ablaze in 1836 by an anti-Poor Law agitator. (Norfolk Research Centre, C 658844 Hal.)

Canada.[10]

About 80,000 pauper children arrived in Canada between 1869 and 1925.[11] The emigration of young destitutes had been provided for under the amendments made to the British Poor Law in 1850, which allowed for assisted emigration of children at the discretion of the Poor Law Guardians. This power was qualified in two ways: first, the emigration of each child had to be approved by the Poor Law Board; second, the child in question had to agree to the proposed emigration.[12] Their parents dead, Tommy and Hilda did not fight against emigration. Nevertheless, the wordings of the letters and of later court documents make it quite clear that the main consent came from Hilda's eldest sister and brother, who were probably 22 and 18 respectively.[13] As Joy Parr notes, the Guardians of workhouses and children's homes carefully managed parents or other relatives, suppressed information about emigration, and painted Canada in glowing terms to the children so that there was a minimum of resistance. In the Blakes' case, Beauchamp and the Heckingham Guardians had very little opposition to contend with, but it seems unlikely that Hilda and Tommy were capable of making a free and informed decision about their Canadian prospects.

The departure of the Blake children came as a result of correspondence initiated by Mrs Letitia Janet Stewart, the wife of a western Canadian farmer, Alfred Perry Stewart, who had emigrated from England in 1884. The marriage seems to have been Letitia's second, since she was 12 years older than her husband and was once known as Mrs Singer.[14] At 43, she was no longer at the safest child-bearing age, and in the spring of 1887 she had written to ask for 'a couple of poor orphan children to be brought up' on the Stewart farm.[15] The Honorary Secretary for the Immigration Department of the London-based YWCA, who replied to the Stewarts a year later, chanced to be Constance Beauchamp, sister of Sir Reginald Beauchamp and twin sister of Hilda Beauchamp. Constance wrote that two orphans brought to her attention by Reginald were willing to go to Canada through the Self-Help Emigration Society.

The Society's 1893 Report boasted to British taxpayers and philanthropists about the Canadian Dominion as a solution to British poverty—'throughout the vast extent of the Dominion a compulsory poor rate is unknown'—and the 1892 Report proudly quoted the *Nottingham Evening Post*: 'The Society has been instrumental in sending large numbers of people to Canada, who, but for its timely assistance, would in all probability have gone to swell the great body of helpless poor in this country.' Despite any incipient helplessness, emigrants were in theory expected to pay some part of their expenses, and the Society claimed to send out a physically, educationally, and financially 'superior class' of emigrant.[16] The Blakes could not have qualified under such conditions, but with the Beauchamps' personal interest in their cases, that didn't matter. The Beauchamps may have felt that they were obligated (albeit in the least expensive way possible) to see to their bailiff's family before washing their hands of the matter. Arrangements for sending orphans overseas and out of mind must have seemed providential. Merely for the price of postage the Beauchamps at once discharged their family obligations to a deceased employee, did their Christian duty by two young children who might after all rise materially in the colonies, and (felicitously) shortened the list of paupers dependent on their parish. 'Sailors', Constance Beauchamp called her young wards. Complaining of having to run the Self-Help Emigration Society without a manager, Beauchamp wrote, 'through God's goodness we have not had many sailors in but it is rather a trial yet the Lord is doing it so it is well.'[17] In the din of 'the

Lord is doing it,' perhaps the words 'saving of expenditure' and 'looked well in the accounts' were not as audible to young Hilda Blake before her sea-journey as they were to Oliver Twist when he left *his* workhouse,[18] but it would have been odd indeed if such thoughts did not cross the minds of the Beauchamps and the Guardians.

Not everyone rejoiced at such transportations. Back in 1845 the *History, and Gazetteer Directory of Norfolk* already noted that from June 1835 to July 1836 upwards of 3,000 paupers had emigrated from Norfolk at the expense of their parishes, mostly to Canada. The author of the *Directory*, favouring the language of economic utility rather than that of social amelioration, questioned the policy of sending away 'the bones and sinews of the nation, which might be beneficially employed at home in agricultural improvements'.[19] On the Canadian side of the Atlantic, the assisted emigration of orphans smacked a bit too much of the old British practice of transporting criminals to the colonies. In a town near Brandon at the time of Hilda's murder trial, 'Moralist' complained to the *Melita Enterprise* that 'It may seem uncharitable to refuse these hungry homeless waifs a seat at our fire-side and table . . . but . . . with the limitless wealth and intelligence of the British nation it seems incredible that a better solution of the slum question has not been found. . . . Why does not the British aristocracy adopt or assimilate or amalgamate this blood with the taint of Cain?'[20]

In a letter dated 5 May 1888, Constance Beauchamp, speaking as it were on behalf of the British aristocracy, thanked the Stewarts in the colonies for taking the children, and hoped that they would turn out to be nice children '& be the Lord's servants & so reward you for taking them.' She would have liked to have seen the children as they passed through London, she insisted, but the night they arrived would unfortunately be her 'night at Mrs. George Hollands [*sic*]', so Beauchamp promised to send her mother as proxy.

Whoever waved goodbye, Hilda and Tommy left Liverpool for Canada on 10 May 1888 aboard the s.s. *Lake Superior*. For six days by sea to Montreal under the supervision of Alfred Broadhurst, and then five more days alone to Elkhorn, Manitoba, depending on the kindness of successive CPR conductors, Hilda and Tommy travelled towards the unknown. Broadhurst telegraphed the Stewarts as soon as he had placed the children on the train from Montreal. He later said, 'I knew her as a quiet, well behaved and affectionate child, and she seemed greatly to appreciate the little benefits she was enabled to enjoy while under my immediate care during the voyage.'[21] The Stewarts would soon find reason to disagree, characterizing her as 'artful' and unco-operative.

*

The orphan was a figure of great pathos and yet also one of the most problematic social types in late Victorian society. Kimberly Reynolds and Nicola Humble estimate that more than 50 mainstream Victorian novels were constructed around the lives of fictional orphans, reflecting the widespread existence of actual orphans in British society. More importantly, the convention reflected and helped to shape society's emotional response to the problems of orphans. The 'real-life figure of the orphan . . . generated in the public a strong sense of guilt, unease, helplessness and resentment'[22]—a reaction largely rooted in the pathos of innocent and naïve children left to struggle through life alone without the guidance or support of parents or kin, all this in an age when the family was increasingly viewed as the heart of the social order. While orphans in real life might suffer through difficult, unattractive, and short lives on the street, in the factory, or in the field, orphans presented in fictional works were constructed to evoke a great deal of sympathy. That sympathy could, on the one hand, inspire social reform; on the other hand, fictive representations could also overshadow real lives to the extent that both orphan and the 'adopting' family might expect an idealized encounter between a grateful, hard-working child and a ready-made, loving family.

John Reed notes that 'to be a female and an orphan as well, was to be doubly disadvantaged. Hence female orphans of all ages came to represent, not surprisingly, a vulnerable and isolated virtue.' The conception of their vulnerability was rooted in the perceived fragility of their gender, their susceptibility to sexual temptation, and their isolation from parental influence. Attractive young girls left without parental protection had to fend off the sexual predations of employers and 'suitors'. Their struggle was first to survive; then, if possible, to regain a life of security and happiness through marriage. Failure could result in the lonely isolation of a single woman eking out a living through domestic service, or in the life of an outcast shamed by sexual disgrace. The fate of the Victorian literary orphan was determined in large part by her capacity to acquire personal discipline in the absence of parental guidance. The orphan must find her own way and shape her own identity in the face of adversity and temptation.[23]

Literary conventions help us to approach Hilda Blake on at least two levels. First, she had a reputation for reading novels, so we might anticipate that in her actions and language she might display a certain degree of self-consciousness about her roles. These novels would later influence her melodramatic self-presentation at the murder trial, a presentation forming what one might call the adult version of her childhood 'artfulness'. Second, and perhaps more importantly, literary conventions allow us to project models according to which a social phenomenon (such as orphanhood) was understood and spoken about—in other words, the expectations and limits attached to the particular story in which one found oneself. This second and more fundamental sense of the importance of narrative requires no self-consciousness: in fact, a narrative conveyed explicitly through fiction or more subliminally through prevailing social discourses is likely to be uncritically received and repeated by the child.

To Reed's narrative about a vulnerable and isolated virtue, which gained its most popular representation in *Jane Eyre*, Hilda's story adds other narratives, some focused mainly through the orphan's point of view and some mainly through the point of view of the caregiver: the orphan as an object of Christian charity; the orphan as grateful and inexpensive labour; the orphan as a representative of the ungrateful and scheming lower class (a representative like Becky Sharp, for example, in *Vanity Fair*). Hilda's story also hints at Michael McKeon's categories of *progressive* and *romance* narratives—*progressive* narrative tracing the upward-moving trajectory of a lower-class or non-conformist hero who is characterized by moral and economic industriousness, *romance* narrative turning upon the discovery of aristocratic birth.[24] Clearly, the various narratives often placed opposing constructions on identical events, but that in no way prevented individuals from simultaneously invoking opposed narratives. As narratives impinge on the real world of human action, they function variously: to reveal fantasies, to express unmet expectations about how an orphan or a caregiver should act, and, once in a while, to describe actual experience faithfully. Certainly, most fantasies and expectations find some echo in experience, and no faithful description leaves fantasy and expectation behind entirely.

The people who talked about Hilda's 'adoption' used an interesting mixture of orphan narratives. Letitia Stewart, by referring to 'poor orphan children to be brought up' on the Stewart farm, hinted at charity in the most neutral of ways. The Stewarts referred to their 'charitable intent' more directly in a later Surrogate Court document, but, early on, reticence was decorous in the family that stood to gain financially from orphan labour. Yet money did change hands. The Stewarts paid for the children to come to Canada, and evidently had sent a monetary gift to Mr Holland, who, it turned out, 'had no children suitable'.[25] Constance Beauchamp, whose economic interest was less clearly at stake (though her Society did receive bonuses for sending out children[26]), could be much more explicit about the Stewarts' gain. Her hope for the Stewarts—that the Blakes would turn out to be nice children 'and be the Lord's servants and so reward you for taking them'—appealed directly (in keeping with her YWCA affiliation) to the narrative of Christian charity and only slightly less directly to the narrative of inexpensive labour. Speaking of 'servants' and 'reward' to the caregiver was probably a well-understood euphemism for the economic exchange about to take place, quite in keeping with the Victorian tendency to spiritualize economic transactions. The Self-Help Emigration Society literature was more direct: Canada did not want clerks, professional men, or merchants; Canada wanted artisans to a limited degree, farmers, and, above all, domestic servants.[27]

This is not to accuse Beauchamp of hypocrisy in masking the economic element of the transaction. The dichotomy between 'the Lord's servants' and 'domestic' servants or between 'reward you spiritually' and 'reward you materially' was clearly less pronounced for an essentially pre-Marxian society than it is for a post-Marxian society. As Beauchamp conceived of it, the material reward would accrue mainly to the Stewarts, with the Blakes rewarded by becoming nice and industrious children—industriousness a good omen, of course, for the Blakes' future material prospects, especially if one put faith in a progressive narrative. But for Beauchamp, as presumably for the Stewarts, the progressive narrative (implied in the name of the Self-Help Emigration Society and in the agreement to educate) was probably less significant than the narrative of inexpensive labour. The apportionment of rewards tacitly acknowledged the initial financial outlay on the part of the Stewarts, who agreed to pay passage and to educate the children.[28] From the receiving end in the colonies, the Stewarts might have understood the material tropes, though perhaps not the elegiac tone, in the *History, and Gazetteer Directory of Norfolk* when the author spoke about the disappearing 'bones and sinews' of Great Britain.

*

If the Blake children departed for Canada under the sanction of Christian charity and inexpensive labour, these two conflicting narratives collided head-on shortly after the little sailors found land and began life on the Stewart farm at Kola, near Elkhorn and 80 miles west of Brandon, Manitoba. There the central paradigm of Hilda's exile in Canada emerged: the recurring motif of the literary orphan's confinement and escape.

A year and a half after Hilda and Tommy's arrival, Stewart wrote the following letter for the Canadian Immigration Service:

Burnside Farm, Elkhorn, 21st November, 1889.

Sir,—I think that any man that has a little capital to start can do very well in this country. I came out in the fall of 1883, and my wife and five children in the spring of 1884. What money we have invested in this country we have had a larger interest for than we ever got in the old country from the same amount, besides having a large house, stables, granary, horses, cattle, etc. Of course, this year the crops have been bad about this part, but we have 140 acres ready for wheat next year, when, if we have a good crop, it will put us straight a bit. It is a splendid country for cattle, and they can be kept at low cost. I have a half section here, and I bought a farm in the North-West, and the first year it half paid for itself. We are all contented with the country, and would not care to live in the old country, after living six years in this nice atmosphere. Of course, the winters are cold, but we never suffer from the cold, as we have a good tight house of twelve rooms, which two stoves will keep warm in the winter. I might mention the first ten acres I cropped I got 75 bushels of oats to the acre. This was in 1885. In fact, I got twice as much from 10 acres as I got this year from 120.

A.P. Stewart

P.S.—I might mention that my garden did better this year than it ever did before, and it was never watered. I had peas, beans, cabbages, broccoli, onions, carrots, corn, tomatoes, pumpkins, cucumbers, etc.—[29]

That the Stewarts were the ones who named Kola (after the English estate from which they emigrated)[30] and that the immigration agent turned to Stewart (among others) to write an encomium for Manitoba indicate that Stewart was a man of substance. Indeed, with a hint of the British affectation of class contrary to other farmers in the immigration report, A.P. attached his estate's name—'Burnside Farm'—to his report. In 1886 the Stewarts refused an offer to buy their property. They were clearly wealthier than their neighbour Mary Rex, with a 44- by 24-foot house valued at $2,000 compared to the 22- by 24-foot Rex house valued at $700.[31] Although the Stewarts had been on poor terms with the Rexes ever since A.P. had banished Mary from his house in 1886 'on account of unladylike conversation', the Stewart home was a centre of the community's social and religious life, especially for the area's bachelors. When Letitia Stewart died in 1899, it was affirmed that 'many a young fellow remembers today the many kindnesses received at her hand.'[32]

But A.P.'s story of unfailing material progress is more interesting—like his wife's reticent letter to Constance Beauchamp—for what it *doesn't* mention: his 'five children' include three stepsons (Archibald Charles Head, Joseph Singer, and Robert Burn Singer) as well as two stepdaughters (Evelyn and Fanny Singer), but he does not mention two Norfolk orphans living under his roof and working without pay alongside his family, even though earlier that same year in official court documents he called one of those orphans 'my adopted child'. He does not mention that the orphan had run away, that amid several bouts of litigation she was made to return, and that she finally ran off again, all in the eventful 18 months between Hilda's arrival and Stewart's cheery account of farming in the Northwest.

'I hope you say your prayers every night . . . and pray for the people who feed you, and take care of you, like a Christian', a gruff gentleman hectors the orphans in *Oliver Twist*.[33] Within a few months of the 10-year-old Hilda's arrival, high-minded advice of this sort was urgently needed, because her relationship with the Stewarts had deteriorated. The adoption of an older child typically initiates a family crisis, and it is not unusual for children who have not completed the work of mourning to be perceived as 'superficial, manipulative, and narcissistic'.[34] Such was the case with Hilda. Responding to complaints from the Stewarts about her 'falsehood and artfulness', Rev. Barrett wrote a letter in his capacity as one of the Guardians of the parishes in the Loddon and Clavering Union and as the clergyman of the parish in which the children had been born. Barrett explained that both children had been trained in the Chedgrave school, had demonstrated good abilities, had been obedient and well behaved. He regretted hearing of the complaints, but hesitated to pass them on to his nephew, Sir Reginald: 'I know it would annoy both him and his uncle Lord Dorchester who are both interested in the Society which seeks to give opportunities of emigration to fitting persons.' The project of exporting children, with its economic and feel-good benefits, was more important than two wayward children. (When, in the following year, matters grew worse and Beauchamp did discover what was happening on the Stewart farm, he proved even less inclined than Barrett to worry about the Blakes.) Nevertheless, Barrett advised the Stewarts that 'I shall . . . do whatever may be conducive to their interests and can only regret that any conduct on Hilda's part should have given trouble.'[35] Translated, this meant that Barrett was willing to write the children a letter filled with high-minded advice.

The letter that Barrett sent makes extensive use of the narrative of Christian charity. Referring to letters that Hilda and Tommy had previously written to their sister in Norfolk, Barrett said, 'I am rejoiced to hear that you can write of the great kindness you are receiving from Mrs. Stewart.' In Barrett's narrative, the Stewarts fulfil the providential intent of divine grace in caring for the fatherless: 'I am amazed at times at the wonderful way in which He has fulfilled His promise and answered the deep toned heartfelt Amens of your dying Father and departing Mother.' Barrett's distance from the actual situation and his interest in continuing to export workhouse children made it easier for him to idealize the Blakes' positions in the Stewart home and to speak of amazing answers to prayer. He reminded Hilda and Tommy that they had been baptized, that their parents had set them apart for 'God's service', and that they were little Jesuses:

> You are holy children, in the sense of the word holy, set apart for God, just as the Communion Table is called the Holy Table as a Table set apart for God's service—remember Jesus Christ died for you. He has taken you up, as it were, in His arms to bless you with the promise of the Holy Ghost that you may be like Jesus—now Jesus was truth—if you are not truthful you are unlike Jesus—all happiness is in being like Jesus.

'Jesus was thoughtful about His mother', Barrett added, and went on to insist that 'Mr & Mrs Stewart are doing to you a parent's part. . . . Study to be obedient—willing to do them service', he urged, using, in echo of Constance Beauchamp, that ambiguous word 'service'. He also admonished the Blakes to obey their teacher, Miss Randall, and hoped to hear good reports about the Blakes that he could pass on to Sir Reginald and the Guardians.[36] Beyond simply emphasizing truthfulness, Barrett invoked Pauline theology, in which human beings led by the spirit become God's children alongside the eldest son, Jesus. Barrett hinted that here the Stewarts' saving action had imitated Christ's divine grace, and that the Blakes should imitate the proper human response of submission and righteous living, although he wasn't ready to follow Pauline metaphors so far as to add: 'and if children, then heirs'.[37]

Barrett's letter to the children reflected, at least in part, the motivation of British child-savers in sending children like Hilda and Tommy Blake to Canada. Parr explains that 'helping children was an honour akin to sheltering the Christ-child himself. To turn away from a child in distress was to deny the Lord, who too had entered this world in lowly circumstances.' Yet simply placing such children in a poor house or orphanage was felt to be inadequate. Isolation on the street or in institutional settings tended to cause children to 'dread and hate those who ought to be nearest them', and to 'grow in evil, until the fruits of evil are prized as the best things in the world.'[38] As Barrett's letter reflected, child-savers wanted children to learn obedience and proper conduct through affection and respect, not through simple adherence to authority. The verse in Psalms 68 that follows Barrett's 'Father to the fatherless' phrase declares that 'God setteth the solitary in families', and most Victorians would have agreed that a family context was required for emotional maturity and the inculcation of moral values. Those responsible for the emigration of orphans hoped that the opportunity to live within a Canadian family would provide such a context. In this way, emigrant paupers would be introduced to the power of 'Christian love at work'.[39]

The Christian child-saving terms of Barrett's letter would have struck a responsive chord in the Stewarts. Letitia was called 'a most ardent worker in the cause of Christ's Church', because between 1884 and 1886 she had allowed her large house to be used for Anglican services and by 1886 she had donated land, raised funds in England, and thus founded the Church of the Advent (now Kola Anglican Church, no longer the site of regular services).[40] One of her older sons may have gone into the ministry, and when the Blakes joined the family, Letitia was still entertaining visiting clergy. In 1911, 12 years after her death, a brass cross would be unveiled, memorializing her central role in establishing the church.[41] Constance Beauchamp's frank expression of spiritual concerns to Stewart and the evangelical terms in which those concerns were articulated (low-church terms that would not have been out of place in Methodist holiness circles or among nascent Pentecostals) suggest that the sympathy between the two women was in large part religious: 'We are so thankful & glad to hear the good news of your son—may he be a mighty witness for the Lord. . . . Our brother in China . . . has just been *filled* with the Holy Ghost after many months of great depression—a real baptism so that he speaks Chinese easier than English & thinks in Chinese & can't hold back from speaking what the Lord is teaching him.' Evidently the shared religious discourse made it much easier for the sender of the two little exports to trust the receiver, and to feel that the economic aspect of the emigration was an insignificant addendum to what was a charitable, and therefore spiritual, transaction.

However, for many child immigrants—and it seems particularly so in the case of Hilda—the wrenching experience of being removed from kin at an early age proved highly traumatic, and the new family setting unconducive to moral growth. Her case wasn't unique, because a few years later the Self-Help Emigration Society was taken to task for failing to supervise wards such as Joseph Henry Adams, a 16-year-old who, weak-minded and prone to bed-wetting, wandered the country homeless and in semi-starvation after being fired from his place of service. To the Minister of the Interior, the Self-Help Emigration Society protested that it did not send children to Canada 'unless under the care of their parents or responsible friends with whom they would continue after arrival.'[42] The discrepancy between the 'artful' and unco-operative Hilda who called forth Barrett's letter and Alfred Broadhurst's description of a 'well-behaved' and 'affectionate' Hilda suggests that among the Stewarts she did not get whatever love and nurture she needed. She was not really adopted in 'the full sense of the word' (to use Rev. Barrett's phraseology). Summing up a constant theme in the autobiographies of the 'home children' (as these orphans were called), Phyllis Harrison suggests that, 'Having started from the premise that poverty-stricken children . . . were being given a much greater opportunity . . . some people accepted that these children were somehow not like other children—with the same needs for affection, love and understanding. . . . Many [farmers] deeply regretted their previous attitude to the children and tried to make up for it in later years.'[43] For Hilda and many others, the transportation experience 'clouded the childhood memories . . . with mystery and bitterness', shaping adult tendencies.[44] Both Hilda and the Stewarts carried idealized expectations of the orphan's position—the Stewarts expecting a tractable and grateful child whose labour would prove valuable, Hilda expecting quite a bit more than room, board, and an education.

2

A Workhouse Child, & You Know
What That Is!

*After a time it is possible you may be attacked by home sick-
ness, and you may want to come back again. The best remedy
is to buckle to hard and vigorous work; and if you do that,
I believe, after a time, you will be as keen and eager for
Canada as the Canadians themselves. If at times you do
not find things as you wish and expect, you must not
commence criticising, but try and look on the bright side.*

    —Lord Aberdeen to a group departing under the auspices
        of the Self-Help Emigration Society, 21 May 1892

*The English and Scotch people are the most wonderful
people in the world. . . . Although you may not think it, your
going out from this country is for the good of the world
at large, and in some indirect manner you may be moulding
its future history, for nobody knows what you may be doing
by starting new homes in a distant colony. The real way to
get on in a new country is to resolve never to grumble. You
will find hot days and cold days, but if you look only at the
sunny side, everything will be brighter and happier.*

    —Professor Drummond of Glasgow to the same group

'Study to be obedient', Rev. Barrett had urged, but his letter solved
nothing. Apart from a few vague words, such as Hilda's later reference
to her 'brother in the West',[1] Tommy Blake disappears from the historical record after Barrett's letter. Not so Hilda. On the cold morning

23

of 5 March 1889, about a year after her arrival in Canada, Hilda, now 11, followed the expedient that worked so providentially in *Oliver Twist* and *Jane Eyre*: she ran away from the Stewarts, apparently in a fit of temper after being disciplined by Letitia Stewart.

The bald Manitoba prairie was not quite the same as the mothering hamlets that appear in the fields of British fiction. Elkhorn, the closest settlement, was 11 miles to the northeast; Hilda, not knowing her way there, must have walked south across fields past the quarter-section farmed by Mary Rex, heading for nowhere. Rex was a 58-year-old widow—the only sort of woman who could acquire a homestead—and farmed with the help of her eldest son, Herbert (who already had a small shanty of his own), her 26-year-old daughter, Harriet, an 18-year-old son, Colin, and one hired man. She was on poor terms with the much younger Stewarts. As Hilda made her way past the Rex farmstead Mary saw her and feared that she could become lost wandering south on the prairie.[2] It being a cold day and Hilda poorly clad, Rex sent Lisle Carr, the hired man, on horseback to find the child. At about the same time, A.P. Stewart, discovering that Hilda had gone missing, sent his stepson, 17-year-old Archibald Head, to look for her. Head walked, following the traces of her footprints. When Carr and Head simultaneously spotted Hilda walking in the distance, Carr galloped past Head and, getting in front of Hilda, stopped her progress. Head caught up and grabbed hold of her, but Carr persuaded him to let go, and Hilda, unwilling to return to the Stewarts, eventually mounted Carr's horse.

After Head had been absent for a while, Stewart sent Joseph Singer, a slightly older stepson, out to find Head. When Singer encountered Head and Carr, another struggle ensued over Hilda. This time Herbert Rex arrived on the scene and threatened to ride over Singer and Head if they persisted in blocking the way. Singer and Head relented, following Carr, Herbert Rex, and Hilda to Mary Rex's farmhouse. There Singer told Mary Rex not to trust the girl:

> you can't believe a word she says. She is a liar thief a workhouse child, & you know what that is! . . . O she'll steal bread butter or anything she is a very naughty girl & is always quarreling with her brother and we are not going to keep her.

But Mary Rex refused to turn Hilda over to Singer and Head unless they produced evidence that Stewart was her guardian. Hilda looked 'more dead than alive' and needed feeding, according to Rex.

Once Singer and Head had left, Hilda told her story. She had run away because she was so miserable: 'Mrs Stewart said she wished [I] was dead she said I detest that child I loathe the very sight of her. She spoke kindly before strangers but at no time else.' A week before, Letitia had turned her out of the house and told her to go to Elkhorn, predicting that she would freeze to death on the way. Hilda implored Rex to keep her and not force a return to the Stewarts. A short time later, A.P. Stewart knocked on the door and demanded his ward, while Hilda watched 'in a perfect tremor'. He showed Rex correspondence relating to Hilda's status, but Rex maintained that the correspondence was inadequate.[3]

It was not unusual for 'home children', resisting the demands and abuses of their new families, to run away, though it was quite unusual for girls, especially one as young as Hilda, to do so.[4] The Self-Help Emigration Society had a visitation program in which 'honorary correspondents' would check up on the progress of the emigrants, but such visits were sporadic and more likely to occur if the emigrant lived in a major centre.[5] There is no evidence that any 'honorary correspondent' was ever involved in Hilda's case.

In the days after Hilda's departure, the Stewarts initiated legal steps to secure her return by charging Mary Rex with kidnapping. The Justice of the Peace found grounds for prosecution and had Rex confined to jail (probably a county jail in Virden) until she came up with $500 bail.[6] Her case was set for the County Judges Criminal Court in Brandon during the Spring Assizes. On 20 March Rex came to Brandon Provincial Court House, where Hilda would later come to trial and be jailed as an adult,[7] but the Crown offered no evidence against Rex and she was quickly acquitted.[8] At Hilda's request, Rex then took the necessary steps to become the child's legal guardian, and on 18 April 1889 the Surrogate Court of the Western Judicial District ruled in Rex's favour.[9]

Furious at her incarceration, Rex also began legal action against the Stewarts for malicious prosecution, saying that she had 'been injured in her reputation and suffered pain of body and mind and was prevented from attending to her business and incurred expense in defending herself.' Following a trial before Judge A.C. Killam during the Fall Assizes in Brandon, the court issued a small verdict for the plaintiff of $46, representing the costs incurred by Rex in defending herself against the kidnapping charge.[10] When cross-examined about why Hilda had left, A.P. Stewart and his two stepsons were unanimous: 'don't know why Hilda left'; 'don't know why child left'; 'know nothing why child left'. The events must have been particularly galling for the Stewarts because of their central roles in the Church of the Advent, to which Herbert Rex (and possibly Mary)

belonged. During the time of the 'child-stealing' affair, the Stewarts
were in the process of forming a parish around the church, and on
17 May 1889 the Bishop of Rupertsland arrived for the official founding of the parish. He probably stayed at the Stewart house.[11]

Although the matter of Hilda's legal guardianship was seemingly
resolved by 18 April 1889, the contest over physical possession of the
child continued. Late in the afternoon of 23 May, Hilda left the Rex
house to bring home the cattle from a nearby pasture. Once she
arrived in the pasture she recognized the cattle as belonging to the
Stewarts and turned back home. As she walked she saw Lisle Carr
coming towards her on horseback from one direction and two other
men, also on horseback, riding towards her from the direction of the
Stewart place. Expecting the worst, she ran towards Carr, but as she
tried to mount Carr's horse, Joseph Singer and Archibald Head
arrived, caught hold of her, and, after a successful tug-of-war while
she screamed, carried her back to A.P. Stewart.

Despite her resistance and her cries to be left with Carr, Hilda
shortly thereafter co-operated with the Stewarts in petitioning the
Surrogate Court to revoke the papers of guardianship issued to Rex.
The Stewarts provided the court with a letter from Sir Reginald
Beauchamp in which he reviewed the circumstances that had brought
the Blake children to the Stewart farm. Beauchamp concluded his letter by noting his 'great regret that we have heard of the girl having left
your house and I much hope that both for her sake and yours that
arrangements may be made for her return to your care.'[12] In addition,
A.P. Stewart now testified that when Hilda was returned to his home in
May she was in 'a wretched condition being then dirty and scantily
clad', testimony that threw Rex's previous accusations back at her.[13]
Hilda, in her 5 June submission to the court, less than two weeks after
her forced return, contradicted her own earlier statements that she had
been ill-treated by the Stewarts. She explained that she had been comfortably housed and clothed during her first tenure with them, and that
Mrs Stewart's disciplining of her had been well-deserved: 'I was
treated very kindly by Mrs Stewart . . . except when I was naughty
when she gave me a smack but that was my own fault.' Hilda also said
that unlike Mary Rex, the Stewarts had provided her with an opportunity to receive education and religious instruction. She now spoke crit-
ically of the treatment she had received from Rex:

> I was required to herd the cattle of Mrs Rex and in doing so would
> have to go sometimes five miles. I was also employed at digging
> and raking in Mrs Rex's garden and had to do other hard work

such as carrying two pails of water at a time and scrubbing the floor—and in fact during the whole period of my residence at Mrs Rex's I was treated and employed as an ordinary servant. I was during this time poorly clothed and never received a bath during the time I was at Mrs Rex's place.[14]

Her only reason for not returning to the Stewarts voluntarily, the statement said, had been fear of what awaited her upon her return. Rex had advised her that the Stewarts would surely mistreat her and send her to a reformatory. Further, Hilda asserted that the papers submitted to the Surrogate Court in May, seeking the appointment of Mary Rex as guardian, had not been prepared at her request and that she had been misled as to the details of these papers. Since her return to the Stewarts on 23 May she had received good treatment in every respect, and it was her desire to remain there with Tommy.[15]

Hilda's testimony to the Surrogate Court was contested by Brandon lawyer George Robson Coldwell, who had acted as legal counsel for Mary Rex during the earlier proceedings. Coldwell testified that at the time of the first custody case he had met privately with Hilda and in a lengthy conversation had set out the obligations and liabilities of both Mary and Hilda in the event that Mary was made guardian. Coldwell believed that the child understood and supported the steps being taken:

Hilda Blake expressed herself to me as being very much in fear of . . . Alfred P. Stewart and two young men who were living with him and desired that I should take such legal measures as would place Mary Rex in a position to protect her and it was entirely upon my advice and at the solicitation of . . . Blake that application was made for letters of Guardianship . . . to Mary Rex.[16]

Coldwell, the rising lawyer whose path would cross Hilda's again much later, had little reason to lie to the court, but Hilda's apparent desire to return to the Stewarts undermined the force of his testimony.

In contrast to Hilda's half-page statement during the proceedings that gave Mary Rex custody, her 5 June Surrogate Court statement about wishing to revoke Rex's custody ran to five foolscap pages of sophisticated periodic sentences and adult concerns. Reference is twice made to the money spent by A.P. Stewart to bring Hilda and Tommy to Canada, as well as to the fact that Hilda has 'no property' nor 'any expectation of having the possession of any by inheritance or otherwise'. Very obviously the statement was not a rephrasing of Hilda's testimony but a text authored by A.P. Stewart or his lawyers, a text that Hilda was then expected to sign. This 5 June statement elaborates on a more concise one-and-a-half-page statement of 29 May 1889 made to the County Criminal Court not by Hilda but by *A.P. Stewart*, during the prosecution of kidnapping charges against Joseph Singer and Archibald Head.

Nevertheless, the 29 May proceedings elsewhere include a summary of Hilda's testimony, in which the voice of the child does manage to enter the formal context of the court document:

> There were a great many papers one was read over to me but I don't know if it was the paper that was read over to me that I signed. I left Mrs Stewarts on the 5th of March and I was afraid to go back because I was in a temper and they might illtreat me.

Some of these phrasings are carried over into the 5 June statement— 'I then got into a temper'; 'Mrs Rex told me that they [Mr and Mrs Stewart] would surely illtreat me'—but generally the voice of the 5 June statement is clearly the voice of an adult who remembers very precisely the many costs incurred in the care of the orphan child, the particular arrangements made for the child's benefit, and the inexplicable ungratefulness of that child:

> I was also taught during this time every day by Miss Randall the governess employed at said Alfred P. Stewart's and benefited greatly by the opportunities of education there afforded. I also received during this time religious teaching every day from both said Miss Randall and Mrs Alfred P. Stewart. . . . During the time I was at Rex's the full extent of the education I received was four lessons in arithmetic and history, but I received no religious education nor instruction and I never heard the name of God mentioned except when it was taken in vain.
>
> One Lisle Carr lives at Mrs Rex's and he is not a believer in the Bible and claims that those who wrote it are idiots.

Interspersed among such descriptions of Hilda's education are explanations of why she did not return voluntarily to the Stewarts. Typically, those explanations begin not with references to fear of punishment or fear of being sent to the reformatory, but with references to her own bad behaviour: 'being afraid after my conduct to return to the Stewarts place I made up my mind at that time to remain with said Mrs Mary Rex'; 'I was afraid to go back to Mr Stewarts place as I knew I had been a bad girl.' Stewart's defence is a bit *too* thorough, since at the same time as Hilda denies her earlier claim that the Stewarts maltreated her, she also justifies the receiving of maltreatment as an appropriate response to her own bad conduct. Clearly Hilda signed the 5 June statement, but she could not have written or dictated it. Instead, the statement was a rhetorical performance on the part of A.P. Stewart and his lawyers, designed to defeat Mary Rex on several levels.

The 5 June statement fits a legal context in which the discourses of money and Christian orthodoxy are more to the point than discourses of Christian charity or divine grace. A.P. Stewart's 29 May Criminal Court statement, the original of 'Hilda's' 5 June statement, enumerates expenses: 'I paid for some clothing for said children and also for their passage money.' The court was supposed to conclude that it was only just for Stewart to expect some return on his investment. Stewart also referred to Herbert Rex's 'shanty', emphasizing his own wealth and precedence. While Rex had arrived from York, England, in November 1883 and had applied for land for his mother,[17] Stewart had arrived in the spring of 1884. Nevertheless, by the time of the litigation Stewart already boasted 'first class buildings and well up to 200 acres in cultivation', not to mention a good herd of cattle,[18] compared to the much smaller house and cultivated area on the Rex farm.[19] And the scarcity of press reports on what was later called 'the celebrated "Rex" case'[20] may have been connected to the Stewarts' pull in the community: by 13 June, even though the *Virden Advance* had carried few and brief reports, its Kola correspondent was already listing 'the child abduction case' under 'Things that weary us'.[21]

Stewart also called upon orthodoxy, explaining Rex's initial decision to keep Hilda as a vindictive response to his own uprightness: 'in the year 1886 I forbade said Mary Rex my house on account of unladylike conversation and have not been on speaking terms with her since then.'[22] Rex was trying 'to annoy' him, he said, and was not 'actuated by charitable motives'. Mary Rex, in her statement during the first trial, had said, 'What I did, I did out of sheer humanity with no other motive',[23] adopting a secularized version of the Christian charity narrative, but Stewart may have been right about the wish to annoy, since it was unusual for Canadians to side with a British orphan against their neighbours.[24] Rex's secular language suggests that she, despite also being listed (like A.P. Stewart) as Church of England in the 1901 census, did not share the intensity of the Stewarts' religious convictions, and it must have been humiliating for the Stewarts with their high profile in the local church to be involved in a child custody case. Stewart turned Rex's more lax religious attitudes to his own account by emphasizing that his neighbours profaned the name of God. He said that Rex was not 'a suitable and discreet person' to have the guardianship of Hilda. Although Mary Rex claimed that 'my position & character will bear the strictest investigation', Stewart wanted to persuade the court that she was irreligious.

Given subsequent events, it is clear that neither during the proceedings that gave custody to Mary Rex nor during the proceedings that confirmed Hilda's return to the Stewarts did Hilda tell the complete truth. Had she been happy with the Stewarts, she would not have run away in the first instance, nor would she have testified against the Stewarts in the first round of litigation. Mary Rex claimed to have taken in Hilda only after her 'frequent importunity'.[25] On the other hand, had she been happy with Mary Rex's treatment, Hilda seems to have been strong-willed enough to have asked the court to leave her with the Rex family. That physical or sexual intimidation by one or more of the men in the Stewart household led to Hilda's new testimony is unlikely, but cannot be completely discounted, given Coldwell's testimony about her fear of the men and given the rumour that after the murder trial she had, in a letter to Mrs Stewart, confessed to having shot one of Stewart's sons. The rumour was probably false; the death had been declared a suicide.[26] In any case, the first two legal victories for the Rex family, combined with Hilda's will, would surely have predisposed her to continue her legal escape from the Stewarts had her experience with the Stewarts been substantially worse than with the Rexes. The most convincing explanation for her about-face is that physical and emotional conditions were bad for her among the Stewarts but worse among the Rexes; that her praise of either home was a relative, not an absolute, assessment; and that such praise was designed, both times, to help her escape from what she saw as intolerable situations. Combined with Hilda's precarious emotional state, these difficult situations convinced her that she must change her status.

Her complaints about the workload and discipline contained deeper anxieties. Families like the Stewarts and Rexes relied on both their own children and adopted children for inexpensive labour. Head, Joseph Singer, and Robert Burn Singer were all 13–15 years younger than the 33-year-old A.P. Stewart and were not his biological children. Robert Burn Singer and Joseph were the children of Capt. R.B. Singer, probably Letitia's late husband: one source refers to Letitia as 'Mrs Singer', and beside her grave is that of Robert Burn Singer, who 'died at Burnside Farm' in 1894—'Burn' perhaps being a name handed down and thus the source of the farm's designation.[27] Joseph was born in Gibraltar and educated at Wellington College in England and then the Collegiate in Winnipeg; the distances are explicable in the context of Capt. Singer's military career.[28] By 1886, A.P. Stewart was already casting about for land for Joseph, the eldest stepson still at home. Stewart had his eye on a quarter-section that for two years running had not been cultivated by its owner, which was adjacent to Stewart's own property.[29] Joseph evidently did not get that quarter-section, yet by 1889 he had acquired two quarter-sections, just like his stepfather and clearly with his stepfather's help. Like Herbert Rex, he built a 12- by 12-foot shanty on the newly acquired land to fulfil the Dominion Lands Act requirements, but he often supplemented his income by working elsewhere (getting wood in winter, haying and harvesting in summer) and his real residence was evidently still with his mother and stepfather.[30] In return for food and board at the Stewarts, he probably worked part-time on the two Stewart quarter-sections and part-time on his own fields—that is, his relationship to Stewart was at once filial and economic. Head, who testified 'I live at Stewarts', and Joseph Singer, who testified 'I live at Mr. Stewart's House', spoke almost as if they were employees rather than stepchildren.[31]

Hilda and Tommy Blake did not even have the status of stepchildren. Farmers knew themselves to be the protagonists in a progressive narrative, and saw their 'adopted' children as one of the mechanisms to ensure that progress. To supplement the work of kin, Canadian families often assisted with the immigration of children like the Blakes who had been orphaned or whose parents could not provide for them. Thousands of children came to Canada under such arrangements to work in domestic or agricultural labour, and they became a valuable commodity in rural Manitoba where farming and household management were labour-intensive. Children in Hilda's situation were generally 'regarded as servants rather than as members of a family in which they were placed'.[32] Indeed, in the 1891 census A.P. Stewart declared that he 'employed' two people. We know who those people were, for under 'Relationship to Head of Household' the census lists both Tommy and Hilda as 'Dom.' (i.e., 'Domestic'), their professions as 'General Servant'.

Some home children were able to turn their ambiguous status to advantage.[33] For most female 'adoptees', however, the goal of changing one's status was elusive, and since only marriage could bring them something approximating their own land, they had little in the way of material improvement to look forward to during the repetitive daily round of hard work. Hilda was required not only to work hard, but also to accept the physical and social identity of the immigrant pauper—completely dependent for her well-being and happiness on strangers

The graves of Letitia Stewart and of her son Robert Burn Singer, who died by suicide in 1894, are located at Church of the Advent in Kola. To the left, just out of camera range, is the field across which Blake walked in her first bid to escape the Stewarts. (Authors' collection.)

interested mainly in her labour. As late as 1922, a survey conducted by the United Farm Women of Manitoba indicated that 176 of 307 farms lacked a system of running water. Only a handful had labour-saving devices such as electric irons and vacuum cleaners. Most farm women cleaned stoves, carried wood, and did a variety of other menial tasks, including milking cows, tending gardens, and taking care of the chicken coop. Only 15 women surveyed reported that they employed domestic help year-round.[34] Even farmwives, who, unlike their adoptee-servants, at least had a proprietary interest in their own labour, felt stifled and transformed into drudges by their work.[35]

That the Stewarts went so far as to educate their 'adopted children' may explain their 'surprise' when Hilda first ran away. Many home children complained that the education promised by their guardians never materialized. While English workhouses could not put a child to full-time work until the child could read, write, and do arithmetic,[36] compulsory school attendance was not introduced in western Canada until 1916, and bills to ensure that British immigrant children got an education were not passed until 1897; even then, the penalties for non-compliance were toothless.[37] Since Kola did not get its own school until probably 1890 and Arawana (even closer to the Rexes and Stewarts) not until 1897,[38] Mary Rex would have had to incur the salary of a governess, an expense the Stewarts paid to Miss Randall but that Rex was evidently unwilling to pay.

Hilda, at age 11, was in that ambiguous stage when her work should have been enough to feed and clothe her but would not have been enough to require wages. The work that Hilda did at the Rexes—herding cows, digging and raking the garden, fetching water, scrubbing floors—was not unusually onerous for farm children of Hilda's age, although scrubbing floors was generally assigned to the older 14–18 age group. Given the charges that Hilda levelled at Mary Rex, it seems likely that the Stewarts held to the British-Canadian convention that required boys, not girls, to do most of the work in the fields.[39] Working conditions for the farmer's biological children would probably have been similar to those of the 'adopted' children. However, Parr shows that since late-adopted children were not indebted for their first 10 years of food and shelter, did not usually receive the same perquisites as biological children, and would not inherit anything, the term 'adoption' covered up the fact that all the economic benefit accrued to the receiving family. As one Victorian adage put it, 'Service is no inheritance.'[40] Orphanages such as the Barnardo Homes therefore negotiated wages for wards who had been 'adopted' by families. Unlike the boys and girls sent out by Barnardo Homes, Hilda had no one to negotiate the terms and conditions of her 'adoption'. Rev. Barrett, relying exclusively on the narrative of Christian charity, certainly paid no attention to working conditions or remuneration. At the same time, differences in upbringing, speech, and manners made it unlikely that Hilda would ever truly become part of a Canadian family and kept her in what Davidoff calls the twilight zone between the family and the paid workforce.[41] The myth of belonging to a family was usually nothing more than the orphan's fantasy and the family's sentimental gloss. One of Parr's sources captures it best: 'Doption, sir, is when folks gets a girl to work without wages.'[42]

Reading between the lines of the quoted court documents, one may guess that the Stewarts, with their religious commitments, were more willing to fulfil 'adoption' obligations involving education, clothing, hygiene, and a reasonable limit on labour, but that they also made Hilda adhere to a strict behavioural code and punished her harshly when she broke the rules. Hilda would much later call A.P. Stewart 'unmoveable'.[43] For her part, Mary Rex probably allowed Hilda greater behavioural latitude but required more work and was unwilling to fulfil educational obligations. Like Mrs Joe in *Great Expectations,* 'she [weren't] over partial to having scholars on the premises.'[44] Hilda 'thought she was abused', said Rev. C.C. McLaurin in a later interview, adding, 'no doubt she was wilful, and did not take correction kindly.'[45] Keeping in mind that in the nineteenth century the word 'abuse' generally meant 'ill-used' (and did not have the contemporary connotation of physical or sexual abuse),[46] such an assessment conveys a dual assessment of responsibility: on the one hand was Hilda's personal insubordination; on the other, a lacerating social order for orphans.

The court accepted Hilda's testimony and, on 22 June 1889, Judge D.M. Walker removed Mary Rex from the position of guardian. On 17 October Judge Walker also acquitted Archibald Head and Joseph Singer of 'Child Stealing',[47] and the acquittal must have had a salutary effect, since Singer later become a Virden lawyer, offering to defend Hilda free of charge at the murder trial. Because the Stewarts had not been Hilda's legal guardians, the revocation of the letters of guardianship from Mary Rex left legal responsibility for Hilda with the Poor Law Guardians of the Loddon and Clavering Union back in Norfolk, and the girl herself in the hands of the Stewarts.

She did not stay long. Despite her testimony about the Stewarts' respectful and caring treatment, she soon fled again and took up residence further away with a family north of Elkhorn.[48] This time no effort was made to force her return.

*

By rejecting first the Stewarts, then the Rexes, and then the Stewarts again, Hilda rejected the discipline her adopters sought to impose, and, more fundamentally, she rejected the principal features of her new life as an orphan-labourer in Canada. While Rev. Barrett had written to both Hilda and Tommy, it seems evident that from the beginning Hilda was the principal focus of concern. In Victorian eyes, anger and rebellion were serious moral failings, and Victorian England's most famous orphan—Jane Eyre, whose story Hilda knew[49]—is advised how to behave towards those who pay for her keep: 'be humble and . . . try to make yourself agreeable to them.' According to Gilbert and Gubar's feminist interpretation of *Jane Eyre*, Charlotte Brontë departs radically from the narratives both of Christian charity and of the orphan as inexpensive labour. Helen Burns, the orphan in *Jane Eyre* who says 'it is weak and silly to say you *cannot bear* what it is your fate to be required to bear', dies, while Jane, the orphan who will not turn the other cheek, succeeds: 'If people were always kind and obedient to those who are cruel and unjust, the wicked people would have it all their own way.'[50] Elizabeth Rigby's 1848 tirade against Jane could easily have been a description of Hilda Blake:

> [She is] proud, and therefore she is ungrateful, too. It pleased God to make her an orphan, friendless, and penniless—yet she thanks nobody, and least of all Him, for the food and raiment, and the friends, companions, and instructors of her helpless youth. . . . On the contrary, she looks upon all that has been done for her not only as her undoubted right, but as falling far short of it.[51]

It seems hardly surprising that the vulnerable and isolated Hilda should, though less virtuously than in fiction, experience Jane's rage and rebel against the dispossession and exile that had transformed her into a Canadian agricultural servant.

But *Jane Eyre* is a romance narrative. In *Jane Eyre* the orphan's appalling material conditions are gradually transformed into ideal conditions, not simply through hard work and moral effort (which dominate progressive narratives), but also through the magical trope of discovered parentage. Hilda evidently felt the pull of such romances. It may be that Hilda, in reply to the menial position in which she found herself, was already subconsciously activating what her contemporary, Otto Rank, called 'the family romance of neurotics', a narrative in which children mentally attempt to replace the despised parents with an idealized couple of noble birth, a narrative in which the true hero is the ego.[52] In her 29 May testimony, Hilda spoke of having 'no mother or father in this country', as if she were not quite convinced that her orphanhood were final. In the same breath she also spoke of letters from England that 'said' that A.P. Stewart had the right to her guardianship—as if she acknowledged, but was not existentially convinced by, the Beauchamp letters.[53] Her later visitor in jail, Dr Amelia Yeomans, certainly found her to be full of 'a most irrational self-importance'.[54]

A great deal of Rank's Freudian terminology has fallen by the wayside, yet recent psychiatric studies of adopted children, such as Paul Steinhauer's *The Least Detrimental Alternative* (1991), still use Rank's account of the idealization of lost attachment figures.[55] The problem is exacerbated for the 'adopted' child, since the present despised parents are quite obviously not the 'true parents'.[56] For Hilda, named after Hilda Beauchamp but now called 'a workhouse child', the vulnerable and isolated ego had to be defended, not always virtuously, against the emotional and perhaps physical threat coming from one set of 'counterfeit' parents (the Stewarts), and against the drudgery and barrier to education inflicted by another 'counterfeit' parent (Mary Rex).

Like Jane, who long before her promotion thought herself 'quite a lady', and like Oliver Twist who, too delicate to be a bona fide street urchin, had noble blood and was eventually adopted by the rich Mr Brownlow,[57] Hilda as an adult would often act as if she were much more than a domestic servant. Rank's assessment was primarily designed to show how the child's imaginative psychology was prefigured in various mythologies, but Victorian fiction—from *Oliver Twist* (1837–8), *Jane Eyre* (1847), and *Little Lord Fauntleroy* (1886), which all use the family romance straightforwardly, to *Great Expectations* (1860–1) and *Tess of the D'Urbervilles* (1891), which use it ironically—often relied on the family romance as well, using it as a social, rather than psychological, indicator. In Victorian fiction, what is usually at stake is not just self-image but material advancement. According to one rumour, Hilda would later write to Letitia Stewart that she had become 'a full fledged nurse', having been trained at the Brandon Hospital, and that she was 'en route to the old country'.[58] If she did fantasize about nursing, such a fantasy would have surprised no one. Not many employment options were open to women, but respectable middle-class women could aspire to careers as teachers or nurses. Some of the nursing work—bathing and feeding patients, cleaning utensils, changing linen, bedclothes, and bedding—was not far removed from domestic service, but at least one did dispense medicine, the job had social prestige, the uniforms were attractive, and the pay—about $400 a year—was much better. Like domestic servants, nurses received room and board; unlike domestic servants, however, nurses had both privacy and regular hours, so that every evening and during a two-week vacation they were free to do as they pleased. And in one sense, Hilda could speak of herself as a 'nurse' without lying. A fair number of women, making $50–$80 a year, listed their occupations in the 1901 census as 'nurse'—in other words, *nursemaid* to the children of the middle class.

Hilda resisted the demands of the Stewarts and Rexes; she expected more than she was given; she lied; she ran away. After she was gone, the Rexes and Stewarts continued to farm in the Kola area, and tax rolls for the years 1899–1905 suggest that, materially, both families prospered. The skeptic Lisle Carr spent three months in jail after stealing a gold watch from Mary Rex.[59] A.P. Stewart ended up alone. By the time of Hilda's hanging in 1899 Stewart was, at 45, the sole resident of 'Burnside Farm', his wife dead, his stepchildren either dead or off the farm. Robert Burn Singer, 'aged 23, youngest of the late Capt. R.B. Singer 28th Regiment, 5th Fusiliers, and stepson of A.P. Stewart',[60] shot himself in 1894, bringing 'so great a sorrow' into his mother Letitia Stewart's life.[61] A tactful news report hinted at Robert's suicide: 'great sympathy is felt with the relatives of the late R.B. Singer. . . . Dr. Rolston coroner, was called out on day of death and after careful examination found that an inquest was unnecessary.'[62] 'Thy will be done' reads the tombstone.

After the marriage of her daughter, the Stewarts followed Joseph Singer, the older son, to Winnipeg, where he was completing law studies.[63] There Letitia was active in St George's Church and in the Hospital Aid Society. When Singer joined a law partnership in Virden, the Stewarts built a house in the town and lived in it for two years amid a 'large circle of friends'. Letitia joined the St Mary's Church Ladies' Aid and was the chief promoter in bringing a cottage hospital to Virden, but she died at the age of 55 in 1899, after going to Winnipeg to have a tumour removed. Virden was shocked, for both the tumour and the operation had been kept secret.[64] A.P. Stewart decided, shortly afterwards, to return alone to his farm.[65] Still grieving his wife's death (which occurred on 8 October, between Mary Lane's murder and Hilda's execution), he visited Hilda in jail, and may have attempted a reconciliation, since she refers to him in a letter: 'Even Mr. Stewart, who I thought quite unmoveable, has been particularly kind.'[66]

One need not conclude from all this that Hilda was simply an innocent and wronged child. Whether her disobedience and artfulness originated in the Stewarts' treatment of her, in the primary wound at the death of her parents, or even earlier, the evidence does not permit us to say.[67] The blow struck by the loss of one's parents occurs outside of language, outside of narrative, and is felt long after a particular narrative is worn out, yet orphanhood is also a *story*, and Hilda's personal difficulties were articulated through her rebellion against her social role. Narratives about orphanhood may, of course, be made use of by someone accused of murder, by others begging mercy for the accused, and by historians who seek to recover the trace of the past for present ends. Our skepticism ought not, on the one hand, to diminish for us either the real and alienating events of orphanhood and emigration in their personal effects upon Hilda; on the other hand, neither ought our skepticism to fog over individual criminal responsibility even when we concentrate on the social elements of Hilda's case. Nevertheless, the narrative of the orphan as inexpensive labour, a narrative shared by the Stewarts and Mary Rex, was bound to clash destructively with the idealized narrative of Christian charity under which the Blakes were shipped to Canada. Lord Aberdeen's 'bright side' proved rather elusive. Even if there are reasons for not fully conflating Hilda's story with *Jane Eyre*'s narrative of a vulnerable and isolated virtue, the position of the immigrant orphan child was still among the most difficult in late nineteenth-century Canada.

3

Garden of the Lord

*Fear and reverence Nature no longer; she is no mystery, for
she 'worketh by motion,' and Geometry . . . Geometry can
chart these motions. Feel, then, as if you lived in a world
which can be measured, weighed, and mastered; and
confront it with due audacity.*

—Thomas Hobbes, *Leviathan*

*The wilderness and the solitary place shall be glad for them;
and the desert shall rejoice, and blossom as the rose. It shall
blossom abundantly, and rejoice even with joy and singing . . .*

—Isaiah 35:1–2a

Sometime in the 1890s, Hilda Blake, not yet an adult but now alone,
arrived in Manitoba's second largest city. Brandon. The city, in which
Robert and Mary Lane already lived, was younger than Blake. As
recently as 1880, Brandon's resolutely (and beautifully) Victorian
cityscape had been open, though not unoccupied, prairie. For millen-
nia, southwestern Manitoba had been traversed by nomadic Aboriginal peoples. Beginning in the 1730s, fur traders and explorers had
travelled the Assiniboine River, and the Hudson's Bay Company had
established the trading post Brandon House in the 1790s at the junc-
tion of the Souris and Assiniboine (25 miles southeast of Brandon's
present location) to compete against the North West Company for the
prairie provisions required to carry traders to the Northwest. By the
1830s, buffalo hides and pemmican were the principal commodities

in the Plains economy, but the buffalo was hunted nearly to extinction, and in 1867 a bison herd appeared in the Souris River area for the last time.

Migrating bison were replaced by itinerant squatters, speculators, town promoters, and railway navvies—the 1870s advance guard of a new agricultural order. Construction of the Canadian Pacific Railway line west of Lake Superior in 1881 brought a flow of settlers, and in two short decades the landscape was transformed by the artifacts of progress: water tanks, loading platforms, warehouses, elevators, and passenger stations in town; the geometry of commercial agriculture in the countryside.[1] On 11 October 1881 the first CPR passenger train clattered into Brandon across the railway trestle spanning the Assiniboine, and as the steel rails advanced, Brandon, Oak Lake, Virden, and Elkhorn sprang up amid feverish speculation in already inflated land values. Settlement spread northward to Birtle and Russell, the latter town founded in 1883 by Major C.A. Boulton, who within two years would lead 'Boulton's Rangers' in the campaigns of the North-West Rebellion against disaffected Métis led by Louis Riel. In the railway's wake came the new order itself: farmers, job seekers, fortune hunters, professionals, and enterprising businessmen, among them young Robert Lane, a native of Woodstock, Ontario.[2]

The West into which the 16-year-old Lane came with his parents was first and foremost an imaginary place, fashioned by the narratives of evangelical Christianity, European romanticism, and Victorian progress. For expansionists, the West 'in its wild state was a region of secular and temporal darkness with little to redeem it.'[3] At the same time, Robert M. Ballantyne (an author once employed by the Hudson's Bay Company), gentlemen travellers like Capt. William Butler (author of *The Great Lone Land*), and several artists depicted the West as a vast territory at once wild and beautiful and fertile. Here in the 'garden of the world', in a pure new society more vital and decent than its eastern counterpart, 'one could live life close to the natural order as it had taken shape at the creation.'[4]

The myth of the new West placed man at the centre of a world created only for his use, and people like the early Baptist missionary, Robert McDougald, raised their voices in Utopian hymns: 'this moral wilderness will blossom as a rose, and this region of darkness and desolation will become as the garden of the Lord.'[5] McDougald's vision combined the Genesis creation narrative with a messianic narrative from Isaiah: one ought to approach the prairies as one would a wild garden to be tamed, a garden delivered by God to man to be possessed, made safe, civilized. Such sentiments were easily allied with

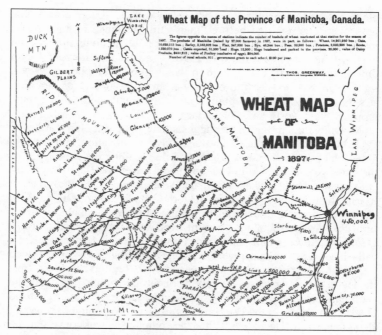

Wheat Map of Manitoba, 1897. Railways lines and the wheat frontier shaped 'the Garden of the Lord' in the late nineteenth century. (Provincial Archives of Manitoba, N6167.)

notions of racial and cultural superiority so central to late Victorian British imperialism, and post-1870 newcomers—mostly Ontario Protestants—thus felt justified in remaking the West into the image of their rural Ontario homeland. Enlightenment rationalism and its religious counterpart, the Great Awakening of the eighteenth century, gave moral sanction to man's dominion over nature and to the possessive individualism of the new settler society.[6] In other words, the expansionist carried to the West both the biblical rose and Hobbes's 'due audacity', the notion that nature had been designed by God to respond to the hand of man and, thus, should serve man.[7] The West was a 'heritage' given by God to be rationally claimed from nature, row upon row, section upon section, township upon township. Later, by the early 1900s, western historians like George Bryce would speak in Miltonic terms of nature corrupted by the East's technological order, and would long wistfully for the pre-1870s West, a time and place before the machine—in Bryce's words, a 'Utopia, an Eden, before sin entered, and before "man's disobedience brought death into the world and all our woe" '.[8] But for now the civilizing mission was ordained by the Creator. Progress must come inexorably, an unfolding of a pre-existing plan in which good triumphed over evil, light over darkness, virtue over vice, an ordered grid of Brandon streets over the desolate plains. Only men and women of robust morality were worthy of such a place.

McDougald's messianism suggests that this particular 'garden of the Lord' was not so much a new creation as a renovation, and not only a material but also a moral production. In recalling his experience of the early years, Rev. Colin Campbell McLaurin, the Baptist minister who became Hilda Blake's spiritual adviser, spoke of 'a determination to establish the Divine Will in Western Canada'.[9] The 'Divine Will' always purposed a moral transformation of the individual, not structural change to the economic system, even when times grew difficult.[10] Demonstrating the individualist resources of what Michael McKeon calls the progressive narrative, Rev. (Capt.) Wellington Bridgman (who rode the Methodist circuit from Brandon up to Regina) combined spiritual with material progress by relying on the stereotypical figure of the profligate but genial younger son as against the upright but too-stolid eldest: 'The men [in the West] were mostly of the younger son type', Bridgman wrote. He added: 'When the younger son was converted, the father and all the world like him the better of the two.'[11] In a country where younger sons like Robert Lane could indeed become wealthy even though they had started out with very little, one could easily maintain a faith in the power of individual action. 'The people of this great "West" . . . are ever a buoyant and a hopeful people . . . men and women of enterprise and of resource', said Jessie McEwen, the president of the Brandon Local Council of Women.[12]

From October 1898 through the summer of 1899, Brandon's *Western Sun* carried columns by the Rev. Thomas De Witt Talmage, an American Presbyterian clergyman who graduated from New Brunswick Theological Seminary. Talmage's themes ranged from the meaning of life's 'vicissitudes', the evils of intemperance (worse than any of the 10 plagues that befell Egypt), public schooling (thousands educated into 'imbecility'), and the feminine ideal, to the wages of temptation, shame, and pretension.[13] But the Victorian enthusiasm for conflating moral and material progress ensured that Utopian narratives about the West would also appear in secular dress, where land and wheat, not God and moral conduct, aroused the passions. Later, and with less moral complexity than McDougald, the *Winnipeg*

Morning Telegram incorporated Brandon's physical setting into the Genesis narrative, seamlessly translating the West from a bountiful yet undeveloped land, intermittently occupied by Cree and Dakotah, into an Edenic garden destined to be the breadbasket of the British Empire: 'from all time nature had marked this region with its vast undulating and fertile stretches of wood and plain, river and prairie, and its beauty of scenery, as the site of a city of consequence. The hand of nature specially endowed this Eden of beauty for the habitation of a contented and happy people given not to roam or wander, not to warfare, but to peace, not to hunting and destruction but pursuits of production and usefulness. . . . Here was the granary of the empire.'[14] This idyllic narrative suited Ontario businessmen, railway promoters, and land-hungry farmers.

By depicting the prairie as uncultivated and the wandering Aboriginals as spiritually and culturally inadequate, the expansionist narrative provided a justification for land titles and for the attempted transformation of Aboriginals into sedentary wards of the state. Sedentary agriculture was interpreted as a mark of civilization; people were encouraged to *move* west, but then to *settle*. Western employers soon began to complain bitterly about the new wanderers: domestic servants such as Blake, who had been encouraged to move west but who were driving up wages because they kept moving from one employer to the next.

While hope of material prosperity drew Robert Lane's Methodist parents to Canada, it was ultimately the 'healthful' climate that drew them to the West. Scottish they were: Thomas Lane's was a family of weavers from Bonnybridge (near Stirling); his fiancée Elizabeth Brydon's family hailed from the vicinity of Hawick (just north of the English border). Like so many Scots in mid-century, they emigrated to Canada to better their prospects, first Thomas on a rough Atlantic passage, during which the animals aboard had to be slaughtered for food. Elizabeth booked a fare on the first steamboat, which sank before it got to Scotland, forcing her to go by sail. The two married in Ingersoll, Ontario, settled for a time in Waterton, on the north side of the St Lawrence, and then moved to Woodstock, where they operated a store. Robert was born on 21 September 1863, younger than his brother John and older than his four sisters. But Elizabeth was arthritic. Her physician may have seen CPR pamphlets extolling the West's healthful climate, another more tangible benefit than morality, for he prescribed the drier air of the West. Rev. Bridgman retrospectively enunciated the prevailing wisdom: 'A person who was a dyspeptic in old Ontario was free from his trouble here.' Others, Bridgman claimed, drew their last

asthmatic breaths in the East, or left behind rheumatism.[15] James
McCann, a farmer, thought so too: 'I have enjoyed better health since
I came to Manitoba than I ever had in Ontario.'[16]
Manitoba beckoned. In November 1879, William Gerrond wrote:

There's as gude land at Birdtail Creek
As e'er gaed work to pleuch or harrow,
as fertile soil as man need seek
Among the rolling plains of Arrow.[17]

On the physician's advice, the Lanes came to the Birdtail among a
group of Ontario settlers in 1880, when Hilda Blake was still a two-
year-old living with her alcoholic father in Norfolk. From Hamilton
they took the American train to Chicago, St Paul, Pembina, and the
CPR branch line to St Boniface. Elizabeth (and probably her four
daughters) then travelled by steamboat up the Assiniboine from Winnipeg through Brandon to Fort Ellice. Every night the boat was
stopped and tied up because of the many sandbars. Meanwhile
Thomas Lane, John, and Robert made the two-week 200-odd-mile
journey by land, herding horses, oxen, and purebred cattle to Birtle.
The Lanes travelled with Joseph Dutton and George Walley, while
Joseph's cousin, Ben Dutton, who eventually married Robert's sister,
Agnes, went on ahead. It was Ben and Agnes Dutton's home that
became a gathering place for 'games, taffy pulls, and sing songs'.[18]
    Speaking of the elder Lane, one descendant said, 'Grandpa Lane
was the most Godly man I ever knew. He had family prayers.'[19] It is
likely that Rev. A. Sutherland, a Methodist minister passing through
Birtle, was referring to Robert's father when he reported: 'On Sunday
morning a good congregation gathered in the house of a Mr. Lane, to
which I preached with much comfort.'[20] By coming west, the elder
Lane was fulfilling the Canadian Methodist Magazine's call, in 1881,
to 'lay deep and strong the foundations of a noble Christian state' in
the West,[21] and at the same time laying the foundations for Robert's
future wealth. John and Robert were 19 and 17 respectively when
they, like their father, took up homesteads.
    When the North-West Rebellion arose four years later and Major
C.A. Boulton sought to raise local companies in Birtle, Robert Lane, 21
years old, joined the #2 Birtle Troop of Boulton's Mounted Infantry.
The volunteers, attached to the 'A' Battery of the Royal Canadian
Artillery, marched west in early April 1885, taking their equipment
through rivers and along muddy trails not yet dried out by the sun. River
crossings sometimes took two days. Some nights the temperature

Boulton's Mounted Infantry, c. 1885. Although the Métis Provisional Government in 1869 condemned Major C.A. Boulton to death, Louis Riel spared him. With Robert Lane as a member of the troop, Boulton lived to fight against Riel in 1885. (Provincial Archives of Manitoba, N10169.)

dropped to 15° below zero. It is likely that in the Rebellion the future drayman Lane got his first sense of the difficulties involved in transport, and also of the skills that he possessed to overcome those difficulties. He was a handsome man and ideally suited for the hardships of the transport business: a big and muscular man who, it was said, could lift a piano by himself.

At Fish Creek the volunteers encountered their first resistance, as Métis snipers pinned them down from a ravine. Major Boulton, fearing that the horses would be slaughtered, ordered his men to free them. Several Birtle men lost their lives in the skirmish before supporting troops could turn the battle. Afterwards, Militia Commander Frederick Middleton read the funeral service and rallied the troops: 'Your comrades did their duty and have nothing to regret.' Lane and the rest of Boulton's men pushed on to Batoche, where they formed Middleton's right flank in the battle of 12 May 1885, cleaning out Métis rifle pits. Victory did not end Lane's service. Boulton was ordered to scour the countryside for Louis Riel, Gabriel Dumont, and Poundmaker. Although Dumont escaped and Riel turned himself in elsewhere, Boulton's men did participate in the arrest of Poundmaker when the Cree chief gave himself up at Battleford. There Lane witnessed his first and only pow-wow: chiefs and braves arrayed on one side; Middleton, his officers, and 'the largest camp of soldiers that had ever visited the North-West territories' on the other, in grim imitation of earlier treaty signings when such displays of force had not yet been required. Middleton warned Poundmaker to avoid flowery language, offered him no terms, and scolded him for the rebellion, adding words that echoed the 'Garden' narrative: 'I am only a soldier, and I do not know what the Government will do in the matter, but I have no doubt you will be helped to live in the future by the cultivation of the land as in the past.'

Next, Boulton's men were assigned to catch Big Bear. They trailed him, but he managed to stay ahead of them and turned himself in at Fort Carlton before they arrived. Lane and the volunteers did, however, see one member of Big Bear's band, a crippled woman who, unable to keep up with the flight, had hanged herself beside the trail rather than fall into the hands of the volunteers. With the surrender of Big Bear, Lane and the rest of the troops returned home to fetes and to a formal welcome from the mayor of Birtle:

> We fully recognized the subtlety and fighting ability of the foes you were to engage; but we cherished a fond hope and a lively expectation, knowing that the prayers of the Christian church and the Christian people of the Dominion were constantly presented to the God of battles for your preservation, and remembering that you were young Canadians—that you inherited in a direct line the blood, the bravery, the pluck and endurance of the defenders of our flag in the brave days of old. . . . Canadians are worthy sons of the worthy sires who defended the old flag in the days gone by, and secure to us the character of a self-reliant and prosperous young nation.[22]

'The foundations of a noble Christian state' were thus laid in blood. Both rhetorically in speeches such as the mayor's, and in the lives of new westerners like the Lanes, the 'Garden of the Lord' narrative and the 'Christian state' were constantly being translated into a story of secular progress.[23] And no wonder. In the fall of 1887 a bumper harvest of wheat resulted in such a flood of grain-filled wagons streaming along Brandon's Pacific Avenue that the boom town came to be known as 'The Wheat City'. In spite of a depressed market, such harvests did much to inspire farmers. A.P. Stewart's 1889 letter for the Canadian Immigration Service came out of Brandon's hinterland to celebrate a now tangible and materially productive garden. Despite English cavils about the 'worship of mammon',[24] western settlement, it was affirmed, would complete the construction of

Canada and mark another step in global human progress. Settlement would bring thousands of fertile acres of land into production, open a new agricultural frontier for Canada, and reaffirm, against doubters, the deep Victorian conviction in the virtue of man's transcendence over the physical world.[25] Settlement would provide opportunity for those with ambition and energy, and would sustain national prosperity through massive investment in new railways, construction, and agriculture. Brandon was becoming an increasingly garden-like place where streets—at least those south of the tracks—were safe and women and children lived free of fear. By 1896, the population had swelled to 4,431.

If the West disappointed some of its first permanent European settlers, it did not disappoint Robert Lane. After the frenzy of development attendant upon the arrival of the CPR, a long and painful recession set in that stretched into the 1890s. Land values, crop prices, commercial transactions, and rates of settlement all fell. Disillusionment grew from contradictions between the promise of a prosperous garden and the reality of western life, and from the disparity between glorious bumper crops and falling grain prices. Moral explanations for this state of affairs came easily. Many blamed the greed of grain traders, elevator companies, railways, and banks, as well as the incompetence and venality of federal politicians; it seemed reasonable that a conspiracy of eastern interests was undermining the region's destiny. Only in the mid-1890s did the bleak economic prospects of the mid-1880s ease and modest growth return. The tide of change grew to historic proportions after 1896 when the worldwide depression vanished in an epoch of unprecedented prosperity, and the most intemperate of the early Utopian prophecies began, once again, to sound prophetic.

*

Robert Lane did very well in the 1890s. At the about the same time that the Stewarts and the Rexes fought over Hilda Blake in the late 1880s, Lane sold out in Birtle and moved, this time alone—like the proverbial 'man who rose from nothing'[26]—to Brandon. He worked as a drayman. Carrying mainly coal and wood at first, he soon began to cut Assiniboine River ice, store it, and sell it once the days grew hot, allowing him to employ four men even during the summer when the fuel business was light.[27] His horse teams ran all day and into the night.[28] Well on the path to success, he wed Mary Robinson of the Binscarth area; he also took on a business partner, Alexander McIlvride, a young man whom Lane had known in Ontario and who had recently moved west. For a time, McIlvride and his wife Sarah shared the house of the newlyweds Robert and Mary.[29]

Devoutly Anglican and about three years younger than Robert, Mary had come with her parents, John Robinson and Annie Jane Callander Robinson, in 1889 from Durham, England, to the General Wilkinson farm east of Birtle. The marriage seems to have been a step up in class for Robert, since the Robinsons, like the Stewarts, set great store by country estates and English connections: John Robinson's gravestone announces that he was 'late of Hill House, Aylcliffe, England'. Like the Thomas Lanes, the Robinsons had been drawn to Canada by the hope of material prosperity, and John was well enough off to employ a salaried worker on his farm in 1891.[30] Robinson farmed near Birtle for 10 years before retiring to Brandon to live with the Lanes, either just before or just after the murder in 1899.[31] A short seven months after the murder of his daughter, John died too. No hopeful motto adorns his grave, just the simple, 'At Rest'.

There were early setbacks for the newlyweds. A fire swept through one of the McIlvride & Lane warehouses in 1891, killing 12 horses;[32] and in September 1892 Annie, the Lanes' first child, named after Mary's mother, died at 13 months of cholera infantum. Dr McDiarmid, who would later testify about Mary's death, certified that of Annie. Her gravestone says, 'Gone Home . . . Closed are thy sweet eyes/from this world of pain/But we trust in God/to meet thee again.' The Lanes evidently could not agree about where to go to church, because their next child, Thomas, born in 1893, was not baptized at St Matthew's Anglican until a year after his birth, and the rest of the children were not baptized there at all.[33] In 1901 Robert listed his own and his children's religion as Methodist.

Nevertheless, by 1898 the young Lanes had four children: Thomas, Edith (born in 1894), Mary (1896), and Evelyn (1898). Their father couldn't always be home. After the Klondike gold rush began, two enterprising Brandon businessmen—W.J. Burchill and J.A. Howie—realized that miners, no matter how close they were to striking the motherlode, must eat, and do so at inflated prices. With difficulty but profitably, Howie transported 100 four-year-old cows through Vancouver and Skagway, drove them over the Chilcoot Pass, and slaughtered them. Robert Lane assisted in the venture. He went ahead, three months after Evelyn's birth, to build three large scows on the banks of the Lewes River and ferry the meat to Dawson City.[34] By means of such enterprises, he laid the foundation of his wealth. In September of the same year, before 'scores' of admirers, McIlvride & Lane showed off a new dray: 'the best manufactured today . . . capable of sustaining

Robert and Mary Lane, c. 1895. This formal portrait emphasizes Victorian ideals of marriage and domesticity, deceptively so, if Blake's account is accurate.

immense loads without any perceptible effect'.[35] Lane already boasted a home, a business property on Rosser, and a lot on Tenth, which he used to store cordwood.[36] By 1899, McIlvride & Lane was overwhelmingly the largest transfer firm in the city, owning 25 to 30 horse teams, as well as a large coal and wood yard, and controlling the city's ice trade.[37] McIlvride even named his first son Robert after his partner. After the events of the murder, it was McIlvride's sister, Jessie, who married Lane, though perhaps without her brother's blessing. Jessie arrived in Brandon in 1898, but there is no hint of a close relationship with Lane until 1900.

While Alexander McIlvride joined the Conservatives and sat as an alderman on city council from 1896 to 1901, Lane joined and became treasurer of the Brandon Gun Club,[38] a position that indicated both his upper-class hopes and, to some degree, his arrival. In 1889, officers of the Brandon County Rifle Association (the Gun Club's predecessor) had included such powerful men as Brandon's first mayor, T. Mayne Daly, and men of growing influence, such as the lawyer and future Minister of the Interior, Clifford Sifton. Gun Club members organized fox hunts, in imitation of the British aristocracy,[39] though the more usual practice was to hunt the plentiful but elusive prairie chickens using 'chicken dogs'. Members protested loudly when their pleasures were endangered by suggestions that 1899 be a closed season on prairie chickens.[40]

The Lane residence was a comfortable yet not pretentious two-storey house, still standing today at 333 Tenth Street. To the north the next lot remained vacant; to the south lay other upper-class houses, the Northern Pacific roundhouse, and then open prairie. During weekdays, Tenth Street was full of traffic going to and from downtown. It seems likely that the Lanes had electric lighting, since Brandon in 1889 was 'the first city in the Northwest to be lighted by the incandescent lamp' and the most prominent light on the first night belonged to a private home.[41] The house was heated by a coal furnace; as well, Tenth was one of the few streets to boast running water and a connection to the city's sewage system.

With their new-found wealth, Lane could easily afford to keep a domestic servant. Domestics were employed not only to ease the burden of household work carried by wives and mothers but also to convey the social standing of the family—since only 10–20 per cent of households had servants[42] and since a servant transformed the wife into a figure of leisure. Such was the case of the Lanes: Mary had four young children, with a fifth on the way, so her workload was heavy; she was also the wife of an up-and-coming young businessman.

Despite all this, the personalities of Robert and Mary Lane remain indistinct. 'My Downfall', a poem written by Hilda Blake in jail, refers to 'the devil, in the form of a man', and we will later argue that she was speaking of Robert Lane. At the same time, Lane's obituary in 1924 describes him as 'a man of quiet demeanor and a good-hearted fellow', a description with which descendants agreed. The references to Mary Lane are even more sketchy, with most newspaper reports characterizing her simply as a domestic angel, her family again concurring.

*

The Lanes' milieu can be reconstructed with more certainty. On 10 May 1899, two months before Mary Lane's murder, 4,000 of Brandon's 5,000 people clogged the streets leading to the corner of Lorne Avenue and Eighth Street. After three or four days 'of the bleakest kind', the sun lit up the heavens—clearly a smile of divine favour upon the event that was about to occur. Traffic was stopped, the roofs of the neighbourhood houses were transformed into vantage points, and some of the curious even clung to telegraph and telephone poles. They came to witness the laying of the cornerstone of First Methodist Church and, more than that, to certify the temporal and spiritual transformation of the prairie as Brandon reached its age of majority. For the *Western Sun*, the construction of First Methodist heralded a new era: 'The old-timer, and there were a few of them privileged to gaze upon the scene, could scarcely realize that only a span of a little over a decade and a half has passed since there was nothing but the open prairie.'

The laying of the cornerstone was no simple sectarian triumph. On the platform were dignitaries from Brandon and points east as far as Ottawa. Rev. E.A. Henry, the Presbyterian minister, and Rev. C.C. McLaurin of First Baptist were on hand to congratulate the Methodists on their progress. But the leading figure on the platform was Elizabeth Sifton. Her father-in-law, J.W. Sifton, had been a railway contractor, a force in the Methodist community, the abstemious principal behind the Methodist-inspired Brandon Sons of Temperance, and a member of the legislature. In the 1880s, J.W.'s son Clifford had helped to breathe life into Manitoba's Liberals. By 1899 Clifford had five sons and a legal career, was an occasional lay preacher in the church, and already cut a national political figure as Brandon's MP and the powerful Minister of the Interior. Since he needed to be in Ottawa that May, it was his wife who laid the cornerstone.

Cornerstone-laying, First Methodist Church, 10 May 1899. The broad public appeal of this event showed the prestige and power of Brandon's Methodists in shaping the city's moral ethos, if not always the private behaviour of Methodists like Robert Lane. (Brandon Sun Souvenir Collection, 1901. Daly House Museum, Brandon, Manitoba.)

Even as all eyes 'centred on [Mrs Sifton] in her new avocation'[43] and Brandon celebrated the successful transplanting of Ontario Protestant civilization, the West was already in flux, prodded by Clifford Sifton. Four train cars were about to fill with Doukhobor immigrants and head towards Manitoba; 400 'Galicians' had already passed through Ottawa a month earlier on their way west.[44] In the first decade after 1900 Brandon's population jumped from 5,000 to nearly 12,000; by 1911, one-quarter of the city's population claimed a non-British lineage. Not surprisingly, the rise of western nativism was a by-product of such demographic novelty. But in the transitional year 1899, 4,000 Brandonites—no doubt mostly the same 4,000 who witnessed the cornerstone ceremony—could still trace their roots to Ontario or directly to the British Isles. Victorian evangelical Christians—Methodists, Presbyterians, and Baptists—still defined the city's social ideals and served as social exemplars, frowning when newcomers did not bend to the customs of the land: 'some of the Jews were noticed yesterday taking advantage of the last snow, and were busily engaged in hauling straw into the city in spite of the fact that it was Sunday.'[45]

The Siftons were the ideal emblems of Brandon's British respectability—he the model of industrious Methodist masculinity;

and she, on the podium that cloudless day, the model of virtuous femininity. The domestic ideal represented by a stable Christian family
such as the Siftons was rooted in the evangelical revolution of the
eighteenth century, a middle-class ideal representing 'an expression of
self-confidence, both against the immoral aristocracy, and against the
masses, thought also to be prone to sexual immodesty and vice'.[46] The
ideal exerted a broad influence over society in British colonies. In very
English Brandon, the powerful legacy of evangelical Christianity, and
particularly Methodism, the city's largest Christian denomination and
the faith in which Robert Lane was raised, permeated every aspect of
social life in the city. In evangelical discourse, the family was the cornerstone of the social order, for 'the family nurtured all moral
impulses, sustained order and respect and lightened the burden of isolated individualism.'[47] A writer in the Methodist *Christian Guardian*
set out this foundational canon early in the nineteenth century:

> The first, most natural, and most ardent of all social affections, are
> found among those of the same blood, or between members of
> one family united under one common parent or head. All society,
> civil, political, and moral originates in and receives its character
> from this.[48]

The private worlds of middle-class families (and respectable
working-class families) were idealized as centres of domestic tranquility and moral sanctuary from the rough and tumble of the street.
In the spring of 1899, the Children's Aid Society—created in Toronto
by social reformer John Kelso—also spread to Brandon, to bring
homeless, neglected, and destitute children into families.[49] The CAS
sought to become these children's 'friend and protector', to find
homes for them with 'intelligent Christian families', and to protect
society 'from its enemies, ignorance, vice, and crime by guaranteeing
Christian home training to neglected and exposed children who otherwise would swell the ranks of the "dangerous class"'. The CAS manifesto asserted that 'many a helpless child will be lifted by the strong
arm of the law from its unwholesome surroundings and will be given
an opportunity to develop into a useful citizen.'[50] At the same time
that Hilda Blake's tragedy was approaching its climax, Canadian
child-savers were working towards local solutions for the problem of
child neglect, in contrast to the British model of workhouse and emigration. Yet in Canada, too, the domestic ideal, while accepting the
regrettable existence of moral failing as a feature of the human condition, made it improbable that any respectable middle-class home
could be seen as a place of sexual or emotional danger.

Marriage—for women the only gateway to respectability and social stability in Victorian Brandon—stood at the centre of the domestic ideal. Victorians endorsed marriage only when one could afford to maintain a family and a home—as Lane of course could—for the stable home was a foundation of society against 'an unstable and rapidly changing society'.[51] Other conditions for respectable marriage also existed: marriage must not be a social convenience but must be rooted in the sanctity of the vows and in a clear understanding of the relative roles of men and women. Sex outside marriage was lethal for a woman's reputation, but maternal feminists also criticized the tolerance of male promiscuity, demanding, in the language of the Woman's Christian Temperance Union, 'a white life for two'.

'Each gender had separate territory—male space and female space. Men moved in one world of work, power, and associations, women moved in another.'[52] Like most middle-class businessmen, Robert Lane kept his office separate from his residence. His main office was on Ninth Street and Rosser Avenue, Brandon's main street, three blocks away from his home. Nevertheless, although Brandon men of every class were the dominant partners in marriage, and although the domestic ideal may have constrained women in obvious ways, the ideal also set a standard against which the public and private behaviour of men was assessed. The idealized view of the good husband, given early expression by the Methodist *Christian Guardian,* typified the emotional orthodoxy to which all respectable men were expected to assent, even if the flesh was occasionally weak:

> The good husband is . . . constant as well from inclination as from principle: he treats his wife with delicacy as a woman, with tenderness as a friend; he attributes her folly to her weakness, her imprudence to her inadvertency . . . and pardons them with indulgence: all his care and industry are employed for her welfare; all his strength and power are exerted for her support and protection.[53]

The male head of the family and household was expected to provide a model of conduct and morality, to govern the family and household with 'wisdom, charity, order and purity'.[54] As a teamster, Robert Lane did not quite have the same status as Sifton did, but as a successful businessman he was headed in Sifton's direction. As the father of four small children and the husband of Mary Lane, his morality was to be relied upon.

A respectable Methodist woman, in the feminine sphere, had an even more idealized image to live up to:[55]

> The good wife is . . . ever mindful of the solemn contract she hath entered into, is strictly and conscientiously virtuous, constant, and faithful to her husband and . . she is humble and modest from reason and conviction, submissive from choice and obedient from inclination. . . . she makes it her business to serve, and her pleasure to oblige her husband . . . her tenderness relieves his cares, her affection softens his distress, her good humour and complacency lessen and subdue his afflictions.[56]

Social respectability and personal happiness—if Victorian doctors were to be believed—depended on a woman's ability to make a good marriage and to bear children.[57] An 1874 article entitled 'Women's Sphere' suggests the domestic and maternal content of the idealization:

> Woman's first and only place is her home. Within its sanctuary she will find her mission. . . . She is destined by Providence to make her home a blissful spot to those around her. It should be full of the merry sunshine of happiness—a cloister wherein one may seek calm and joyful repose from the busy, heartless world. . . . Her kingdom is not of this world, worldly. The land she governs is a bright oasis in the desert of the world's selfishness.[58]

Rev. Talmage, in a *Western Sun* article just before the murder, was quick to defend wives, especially the 'Marthas' who toiled at home— 'O man of business, if you had as many cares . . . you would be a fit candidate for an insane asylum'—and he defended the right of bereaved mothers like Mary Lane to brood over their deceased children. Nevertheless, he, too, idealized the wife's role: 'Romance and novelty will do for a little while', he said, but the 'loaf of domestic happiness' required 'ingredients from heaven. It is the self-sacrificing people that are happy.'[59]

Such idealization of women and men privileged the domestic sphere and, by implication, the religious sphere as most suited to woman's nature and attributes. It is therefore not surprising that Elizabeth Sifton, and not some other proxy for her husband, was chosen to lay the cornerstone at First Methodist and to receive a sterling silver trowel for her labour. She provided the climax of the proceedings when she stepped forward, watched the stone being placed, and said:

> In the name of the Father and of the Son and of the Holy Ghost, I lay this corner stone for the foundation of a house to be built and consecrated to the service of Almighty God according to the order and usages of the Methodist Church. Amen.

In the Brandon equivalent of *noblesse oblige* at the ceremony's close, she held an informal reception. 'Older people pressed forward to grasp her hand and way was made for the boys and girls of the city who were not to be deprived of getting near the lady that Brandon people are so proud of and possibly securing a word of recognition.'[60] Sifton's role suggested that women could exercise some control in the home,[61] the 'citadel of respectability',[62] and in the church, where women's capacity for social purity and moral virtue allowed them a growing authority. The role of Letitia Stewart, who was more significant than her husband in the founding of the Kola Church of the Advent, suggests this as well.

Mary Lane, a conventional middle-class woman, lived within the public sphere of the church and the private sphere of the home. On the day she was murdered, she had been presiding over her children's tea party and had been putting up curtains. Contrary to Mary Rex or Hilda Blake, Mary Lane embodied the ideal of the domestic angel. A.P. Stewart, criticizing Rex for 'unladylike conversation', had been able to use that ideal against her, partly because she was not overly careful about the distinction between private skepticism and public affirmation of Christian belief, but also because Rex, a widow in charge of a farm, was uncertainly poised between the private home and the potentially demoralizing sphere of work.[63] The emphasis on feminine moral perfection would also reappear later when the newspapers frowned upon the kinds of songs that Hilda Blake sang in jail. Mary Lane, however, fulfilled the external requirements for domestic angel, since she was a stay-at-home mother who sewed and went to church.[64] She would not be difficult to idealize after her death, as the *Winnipeg Daily Tribune* did: 'Mrs Lane was a favorite in a large circle, all who knew her described her as a lady of high personal character, of a quiet, reserved disposition.'[65] Brandon's *Western Sun* went one better, calling Lane 'the most devoted of wives, and the fondest of mothers'.[66] The medical details of the assault on her body helped retrospectively to idealize her further and gave her death a greater pathos.

Other things being equal, even the very fact that she had a servant could aid in her idealization, for, as Leonore Davidoff argues, 'in the nineteenth and early twentieth centuries, women who had servants were perceived as more pure, more feminine, more ladylike.'[67] That Blake's employment helped to idealize Mary was more prosaic than ironic: in Canada, even more than in Britain, the establishment of a class system based on wealth and sensibility required external markers other than birth.

Of course, as in all social orders—and this was particularly so in the closing years of the Victorian epoch—a space existed between the ideal promulgated by those in positions to define orthodoxy and the reality of everyday life. Everyday life was suffused with 'anxiety, accommodation, and resistance'. As Andrée Lévesque has observed, 'This margin can only be mapped through a study of actual behaviours, and these can often only be perceived through the social and judicial consequences that ensued from them.'[68] Thomas Lane's late baptismal date (not unusual for country people far from church, but unusual for city people) gives us teasing hints of a contest of wills between Mary and Robert, Mary wishing to raise her children as Anglicans and Robert evidently arguing contra. The fact that the rest of the children were not baptized at St Matthew's Anglican implies that Robert held power even in domestic and religious matters.

Yet like Letitia Stewart and Elizabeth Sifton, Mary Lane was active in church and did not simply obey her husband's wishes. Despite the lost argument about where to baptize the children, she herself did not change denominations to please Robert, and she continued to be part of St Matthew's, as her funeral would later indicate. At St Matthew's the vigorous Rev. Macadam Harding—the sort of man who made things happen[69]—helped raise $14,000 for a new church building and pushed for religious instruction in public schools.[70] Although we do not know how directly Mary was involved in church activities, the parish women had a progressive reputation: the St Matthew's Ladies Aid not only raised money for the new church, but also, along with the Woman's Christian Temperance Union and the Women's Hospital Aid Society, helped found the Brandon Local Council of Women in 1895. Lady Aberdeen, the Governor-General's wife and the first president (in 1893) of the National Council of Women, explained to Brandon women that the Council's purpose was 'the welfare of the community, the betterment of Canada as a whole, and the betterment of conditions affecting women and children'. That Lady Aberdeen, an obvious and powerful model for the middle-class woman's entry into the public sphere, identified with the role of social reformer and social purifier gave the role legitimacy. The NCW expressed itself as operating within traditional feminine concerns, yet attempted to widen those concerns into politics: 'the N.C. takes a deep and intelligent interest in all matters connected with true home-making', but to this was added the will to assist 'those seeking to secure the welfare of women and children, to broaden our sympathies, enlarge our views of responsibilities to others and help us to overcome narrow prejudices.' Therefore, during the late 1890s, in addition to such charitable endeavours as Education of the Blind, the Victorian Order of Nurses, the Custodial Care of the Feeble-minded, and Traveller's Aid, the Council took political positions favouring curfew law and pushing to raise the age of consent from 16 to 18.[71]

Such a renovation of the role of women showed the continued influence of the doctrine of separate spheres, for philanthropy and social work were seen as extensions of the natural capacities of women to nurture and to uplift morally. Not all Canadian women were satisfied with the patriarchal character of the social order. Increasingly, the Victorian exclusion of women from the public sphere, including politics, was under attack. The vigour of gender-orthodoxy advocates seemed to increase as the grip of the orthodoxy weakened. In the wake of the outbreak of the Boer War in the fall of 1899 a writer in the *Canadian Magazine* reasserted the discourse of separate spheres with a vengeance:

> The voice of the woman was heard everywhere, and little was denied her during the years immediately preceding 1899; but during that year the call to arms shut out all other sounds. The voice of the female agitator was hushed. War brought back the knowledge that she was but the weaker vessel. It reaffirmed, what the race had almost forgotten, that man is the guardian, the defender, the fighter, the ruler; that woman is but the mother and the comforter of voters, warriors and rulers, the nurse of the wounded, the chief mourner for the slain.[72]

Why *voters* would need to be comforted remains a mystery, but such sentiments could gain a sympathetic response in Brandon, a socially conservative town.

Although the evidence is limited, it seems that Mary Lane embraced a conventional female role and that she was her home's moral centre. If deviation from the norms of respectability and morality occurred within the Lane household she was likely not privy to the straying. Charles Adams, a Liberal member of the provincial legislature from Brandon who knew her personally, called her, just after her death, 'a woman of most genial character and highly respected by everybody'.[73] At a moment when eulogy is called for, one might not want to put too much weight on the words of a politician up for re-election, or the words of someone who, since he owned a leather and harness business, probably did business with Robert Lane.[74] Yet others—a Mr Rea and the lawyer R.G. MacDonald—agreed, calling her 'estimable' and 'one of Brandon's most respected citizens'.[75] According to family stories, she was a kind person, and the family didn't for

a minute believe Hilda Blake's 'tramp' story because, even if it had
been 4 a.m., Mary would have given the tramp food. Later, the apocryphal story that 'the poor woman's first thought when the shot was
fired was the protection of her children' and that she snatched up her
youngest child[76] may have been based on ideas about Mary's character. One daughter in the next generation was named in Mary's memory, and of her eldest son Thomas it is said that he neither spoke ill of
anyone nor used foul language of any kind. Even Blake idealized
Mary, by confessing that she first kissed and then shot her—'Judas
like', as the *Elkhorn Advocate* was quick to point out.[77]

We will argue later that there may have been other, more complex
reasons for saying that she had kissed Mary, but if Hilda Blake
wanted sympathy, she would have been well advised to characterize
Mary as a harsh or insidious mistress rather than as a betrayed Christ.
The *Birtle Eye-Witness*, Mary's hometown newspaper, asserted that
'a bomb came when the girl confessed she had quarrelled with her
mistress' and then had taken revenge,[78] but such a direct motive
appears nowhere else, suggesting that the *Eye-Witness* relied on a
reporter's unsubstantiated guess or a family invention. It seems probable, instead, that the kiss, in part, tells the truth: that Mary was a
genial woman and employer; that the conflict was no simple tale of a
victimized servant; that even if the kiss was Hilda Blake's prior apol-
ogy for the act she was about to commit, the act would be committed,
no matter how genial Mary was, because in the role of wife and
mother she stood between Hilda Blake and her hopes.

4

A Good and Faithful Servant

A servant's 'character' is her most important possession,
as losing it could mean economic ruin. A good servant is
clean, celibate, obedient, respectable, hard working,
and an early riser.

—Genevieve Leslie, 'Domestic Service in Canada'

Well done, thou good and faithful servant: thou hast been
faithful over a few things, I will make thee ruler over many
things: enter thou into the joy of thy lord.

—Matthew 25:21

While the Lanes rose through the social circles in Brandon, Hilda Blake made her solitary way—probably since the age of 12 or 13—as a domestic servant. According to Joseph Singer, she lived for less than a year at a farm north of Elkhorn, spent the next seven or eight years in Winnipeg, and then in 1897 or 1898 came to Brandon.[1] Other evidence, however, suggests that while she certainly worked as a domestic in Winnipeg,[2] she came to the 'Garden of the Lord' earlier: she had been employed at 'points west', including Aikenside (near Chater) where she worked for Robert and Mary Crozier,[3] and then at Brandon for Mrs Frank Merritt, a member of the Woman's Christian Temperance Union; and for Mary Lane's friend, Charles Adams, the leather and harness merchant who had been an alderman, mayor of Brandon, and Liberal MPP but who by 1899 was spending much of his time in Toronto, where his wife lived.[4]

*Looking west on the south side of Brandon's main street—Rosser Avenue—near 9th Street, c. 1901. The office of Lane & Elviss Coal, Wood, Ice and Transfer was across the street at 909 Rosser. (*Brandon Sun* Souvenir Collection, 1901. Daly House Museum, Brandon, Manitoba.)*

Employers repeatedly counselled servants to find a good place and to stay there instead of casting about for higher wages. But servants, Blake included, declined to take such self-serving advice and moved often, both to increase their meagre salaries and to improve their conditions of employment. Farmwives like Lavinia Jeffery of Minnedosa complained, with some justification, that servant girls gravitated towards the towns and cities: 'few girls will accommodate themselves to the work of a N.W. farm and the towns and cities are at present over supplied.'[5] City wives disagreed, of course, claiming to feel the shortage just as keenly. The 'restlessness' of servants became proverbial: 'as soon as they have acquired some considerable skill and proficiency they will want to change their employer in order to play off Miss Wiseacre to a new mistress.'[6]

Because of the Stewart/Rex custody battle, Hilda Blake had learned early on that a move could change her material conditions. If she was not quite one of the 'masterless men' upon whom the English Revolution has been blamed,[7] growing cities such as Winnipeg and

Brandon provided some measure of anonymity and freedom. At some point in her travels, Blake began to use the alias 'Hilda Clarke',[8] perhaps to distance herself from the custody case in Elkhorn or to cover up difficulties in other places. A move to a larger centre would have allowed her some distance from a past that could shame her. She was ambitious. Despite her employment she must have spent some time in high school, because, even though she left the Stewarts at age 12, reporters at the trial judged that 'in appearance and education she was quite above the average servant girl.'[9] In other words, although home girls were less likely than home boys to attend school,[10] she must have negotiated conditions of employment that allowed her to continue to be educated as she had been at the Stewarts.

She kept up a correspondence with her sister, but no longer had ties to a specific place or to certain people, and for her, Brandon's increasing prosperity meant the possibility of easier work and better pay than in a farm household. By running away from her first two homes, she had rebelled against the feudal position of an indentured labourer, and by changing positions often she entered into capitalistic relations, whereby she sold her labour to the highest bidder. But a young teenager had limited bargaining power. Pay increases were small, and domestic service held little promise of economic or social advancement. While the social identity and accessible public terrain of middle-class women were broadening, Hilda Blake, like most lower-class women who remained socially and economically segregated, continued in narrow circumstances.

It was humiliating to be known as a servant.[11] Service was 'an occupation of last resort' when there were no other jobs open,[12] or for those who had only household skills and not much education.[13] A young woman like Blake, who had no relatives to find a place for her and who must either work or starve, would have found service all but inescapable. By the time she was 16 she was already contemplating suicide.[14] Her later behaviour would add a theatrical dimension to her despair and suggest that she never really planned to kill herself, but there is no reason to doubt that she, like other home girls,[15] wanted her life to end.

Blake's experience of isolation as a domestic servant was, of course, far from unique. Service was the single most common form of paid employment for women in Canada, comprising 41 per cent of the female workforce in 1891, and yet domestics were constantly in short supply all over Canada. Employers like Mrs Lawrence of Clearwater complained, 'The great trouble in this country is there are not enough girls to do the work, and I often wonder, if there is such a lot of girls in England out of work, why they don't come here, as here a good girl would not be one day without a place.'[16] Brandonites like Jessie McEwen echoed such sentiments—'We trust that a satisfactory way may be found of bringing the surplus supply of trained house servants in older lands into touch with the pressing need and the great demand for it here'[17]—as did the Department of the Interior's Winnipeg immigration agent: 'Good general servants are still at a premium here, being very scarce; in fact, there is not one to be found.' Although he must have been aware of orphan transportation projects such as the one that brought Hilda Blake to Canada, even such projects could not fill the many open positions:

> It is a great pity that some scheme cannot be devised whereby five hundred strong, healthy, young girls and women, of fourteen years of age upwards, might be sent annually to Manitoba, as no greater boon could be conferred upon the toil-worn lady, in either city or country, than the much-needed and now craved-for help of a good servant.

Such an arrangement, it was insisted, would benefit more than just those who needed servants. The theory went thus: in a Canadian West full of single men and lacking marriageable women, immigrant domestics would soon become immigrant wives with their own comfortable homes. The Winnipeg agent concluded that 'The society or government giving effect to such a scheme, would earn for themselves the lasting gratitude of twenty-thousand ladies in Manitoba, while the young man's dread of bachelordom on a prairie farm would be a thing of the past.'[18]

The state did respond to the much discussed 'servant problem'. According to Marilyn Barber, 'domestics were the only unaccompanied female immigrants so solicited and they were treated as preferred immigrants along with farm families and single male farm labourers.'[19] The Self-Help Emigration Society, through which the Blakes came, reported 'The Bitter Cry of Manitoba' for more female servants: 'The girls do not need to be trained; if of good character and able to do hard work, they will prove invaluable.'[20] Still, from 1870 to at least 1930, domestic servants remained in short supply because the work was difficult and the hours were long. Despite all the rhetoric of 'much-needed', 'craved-for', and 'at a premium', the pay was poor.

In the 1890s, 10 per cent of the female population (age 10 and up) had entered the labour force, and most of those women remained isolated in gendered workplace ghettos. Men could earn good wages in Brandon. The superintendent of Methodist missionary work in the

West, Rev. James Woodsworth (J.S. Woodsworth's father), made $1,600 a year, while Police Chief Kircaldy made $1,000. Employers like 'drayman' Robert Lane and 'teamster' Ekiel Bronfman (patriarch of the Seagram's clan) could clear $1,200 after salaries, expenses, and reinvestments (though Bronfman, being a Jew, could not expect wealth to bring him into Brandon's leading stratum). In the working class, a carpenter could make $250–$350, as could a farm labourer, a locomotive fireman, or a painter, while a postal clerk, a mason, or a drayman working for Lane could get $400–$500, and a CPR foreman could take home as much as $600. For women, the opportunities were much more limited. Nurses, at $400–$500, were paid a reasonable wage, and teachers too, though they started at lower wages, could aspire to $450 a year. A dressmaker could make anywhere from $150 to $500, depending on how much time she wanted to put in and how much demand there was for her fashions. A female crockery clerk or cashier could make $240–$300, a stenographer $200–$400, and a telephone operator $65, though whether the latter wage represented full-time or part-time work is not clear. At the very bottom, no matter how much they made, were prostitutes, and one step above prostitutes, making between $72 and $180 a year, usually $120, were the largest group of women in the paid labour force: domestic servants working in middle-class homes. From what Hilda Blake's successor earned in 1901, we may infer that Blake's rate of pay by 1899 was slightly less than $150 a year.[21] And judging both from the statistics around illegitimate births and from Blake's case, domestics were more likely to be propositioned than to be proposed to.

*

In Winnipeg and Brandon, Hilda Blake earned a reputation as a hard-working and conscientious employee.[22] There were, and still are, rumours that when she was in Aikenside she was somehow involved in the 1896 death of an 11-month-old infant, Clifford Ward Crozier. Afterwards the mother, Mary Crozier, apparently had a nervous breakdown. In Crozier family stories, Clifford died when Blake was caring for him, Robert and Mary Crozier having gone to town. They returned to find Clifford dead in his crib, with a mark on his head and a piece of firewood next to the crib.[23] But this version of events seems unreliable. The rumours were reported and discounted in 1899 by the *Western Sun*, and there is no substantial reason to doubt the death certificate, filled out by Dr J.W. Runions, which cites 'La grippe few days' under 'Cause of death and duration of illness'.[24] Not until two days after it occurred was the death registered, so it is possible, but unlikely, that the family decided to cover up Blake's role. More probably, the parents in hindsight felt guilty about going to town when their child was sick, and after his death they cast about for someone to blame. The little boy was buried in a homemade coffin of spare lumber and soft white cloth; on his gravestone was written, 'Our short lived flower returned again to God'.[25]

Since coming to Brandon, Blake had been given a good character,[26] and one employer claimed that he never knew a better girl 'or one so affectionate and careful with children'. His children 'almost worshipped her, she was so kind to them.'[27] She worked for Adams, then Merritt, and, on 15 July 1898, a year before the murder, was hired by Robert Lane. He gave her an 8 by 12-foot room with a little closet, at the top of the stairs so that she could be the first one down in the morning. The room contained everything in the world that she owned. Judging by the inventories of servants' rooms, she would almost certainly have had an iron bed and a washstand. Half of domestic servants also had a table or chair, a small mirror, and a worn bit of carpet. Almost none had blinds, clocks, or lamps.[28]

For a servant such as Blake, the day would begin at 6:30 a.m. Like many upper middle-class families, the Lanes had only one 'maid-of-all-work', who would be expected to do everything: make meals; do laundry; scrub floors (often resulting in 'housemaid's knee'!), grates, and stoves; wash dishes; care for and babysit the four Lane children, including the one-year-old toddler, Evelyn. Carpets, furniture, and staircases had to be kept clean, and the least pleasant tasks were predictably assigned to the servants.[29] The day could end by 8:00 p.m., once the kitchen had been cleaned up after supper—unless the employer was in the habit of entertaining, in which case the servant could be kept working until two in the morning. The day done, one still had to put coal in the furnace, clean out the stove, and lay a fire in it for the next day.[30] A domestic could hope for one evening a week and part of Sunday off,[31] and, if she was sick too often on workdays, she could be fired.[32] Rheumatism, varicose veins, and neuritis were common among servants, while their rates of mental illness and mortality were higher than those of the general population.[33] The *Virden Advance* professed to be deeply puzzled as to why women would rather work in factories than become domestic servants. To the masculine mind it was incomprehensible, insisted the *Advance*, how housework could possibly be considered degrading.[34] Indeed, to observers raised on British practices, servants in Canada seemed amazingly free, because, for example, they didn't have to ask the employer's permission to mail a letter.[35] Employers who maintained

British notions of caste were generally harder to serve than Canadians were.[36] Even the genial Mary Lane would have retained some of the caste notions from her British background.

Although Dickens might satirize employers for being utterly incompetent and leaving every single practical matter to the hired help,[37] the 'laziness' and lack of consideration of servants was nonetheless legendary, at least from an employer's point of view:

> In the second half of the 19th century it was commonly accepted that people were experiencing a period of poor-quality domestic service because, it was thought, in times gone by, service had been marked by faithfulness, perseverance, and devotion, and in addition had been the prerogative of a very large number of families. This attitude closely resembles that of previous generations; all had considered themselves less well served than those who had preceded them.[38]

An employer such as Annie Swan, who confessed that she had never been a domestic servant, and therefore could not quite see things from a servant's point of view, was nevertheless ready to quote the Sermon on the Mount to her domestics, reminding them that 'service is the highest form of praise, and that nothing is really small or mean or despicable, except sin.'[39] The best employers, such as Aline Raymond, were paternalistic, decorating the servants' rooms, being generous with little extras, allowing them to partake of the best dishes, caring for them when they were ill, and allowing the servants leeway in the servants' areas of expertise, but on no account brooking pretension or idleness:

> the true practical, Christian way to act with [the servant] will always be to treat him as a child, to educate him and continue thus indefinitely, based on the same system we apply to our own children's education; by being as indulgent and patient in the little things as we are immovable on questions of principle.[40]

Maids-of-all-work such as Blake were often lonely, despite being at the centre of a bustling household. One maid, who loved her employer, described it this way: 'Ladies wonder how their girls can complain of loneliness in a house full of people, but oh! it is the worst kind of loneliness—their share is but the work of the house, they do not share in the pleasures and delights of a home. . . . I belong to the same church as my employer, yet have no share in the social life of the church.'[41] These conditions prevailed in the towns more than in the country.[42] Laura Goodman Salverson, working for some time as a maid, lamented: 'For girls like us the dice were loaded from the start. The ensign of the mop and the dustbin hung over our cradles. No wonder thousands of us married any old fool! Bed and board! Was that the answer? Was that all of life? Just to eat and sleep, propagate your misery, and die!'[43] In contrast to British employers, many Canadian employers allowed the help to eat with the family, but few employers were eager for their domestics to tie up the parlour entertaining friends, and so the domestic's own visitors were usually restricted: 'Who wants a dozen strange girls running in and out of one's back door?' asked one employer.[44]

Rev. Colin Campbell McLaurin became Hilda Blake's only close contact outside of her work. He visited her, and her only escape socially from the Lane household appears to have been the Sunday afternoon Bible classes that she attended at his First Baptist Church, a fairly large church of 277 members.[45] In the Northwest, clergymen often acted as intermediaries between employers seeking domestics and girls newly arrived in town. Writers from Rapid City, Birtle, and Turtle Mountain echo the advice of Mrs G. Roddick of Brandon: 'Bring a note of introduction to some minister, and there will be no difficulty.'[46] Blake, however, seems to have first met McLaurin two years prior to the murder, when she came to First Baptist with the children of one of her earlier employers, Frank Merritt.[47] McLaurin was about 43 years old when he and Blake first met. He had been married and a minister for 22 of those years, and had four children, his two oldest daughters, Bessie and Anna, on the verge of adulthood. He had already built a church while a student in Woodstock, Ontario. As a youth he told his father that he wanted to go to Bible college, so his father gave him a colt and a stand of trees where he could cut pine logs for his tuition. He couldn't sell them until the following spring, but Stephen Tucker, a Baptist lumberman, gave him four new ten-dollar bills anyway.[48] McLaurin's tenure in Brandon coincided with the two years of Blake's attendance, and he remained there for two years after her hanging, leaving in 1901 to superintend the Baptist missions in Alberta. His responsibilities he took seriously, preaching three times and conducting two Bible classes each Sunday. He said, 'I never had a sleepless Sunday night or a blue Monday. Monday was always my best day. From then on the burden grew until I was relieved on Sunday night. Perhaps all this is not to my credit, but it is a frank admission.'

McLaurin felt that it was a minister's duty, despite his own reluctance, not to wait for an invitation but to visit people in their homes:

A 1935 photograph of Rev. C.C. McLaurin, who in 1899 pastored First Baptist Church in Brandon. Blake's spiritual confidant, McLaurin took what he knew about the case to his grave. (Rev. C.C. McLaurin, *Pioneering in Western Canada: A Story of the Baptists*, [1939]. Published by the author, first leaf.)

When a young minister, it was a hardship to go into homes to which I had not been invited; but duty bid me go. Often I would pass a door two or three times in an afternoon, making an effort each time to overcome my timidity, but my courage failed me and I passed and repassed without knocking at the door. I would reason: perhaps they do not want me. Then I would wonder: what can I say if I do go in, etc., etc. But I became convinced that I could not preach effectively to people whom I did not know. Eventually I conquered all timidity in visiting homes, any home, to bring to them some spiritual help and become acquainted.

Early in his ministry he had scolded some of his congregation and had been taken aside by a wise deacon, who said, 'Scolding never does any good; when you talk to us about our failings before the whole congregation, it just makes it harder to do what you want us to do.' The young McLaurin went home, had a good cry, prayed, and purposed then 'never to scold again no matter how indifferent folks might seem.' With Blake he evidently pursued such a course—visiting her occasionally, befriending her, and hoping thereby to exhort her to salvation and to good deeds without scolding.

He was also a prohibitionist[49] and a patriot with an evangelical passion for souls:

There is no country in the world which presents to the immigrant finer prospects than the Dominion of Canada with its millions of square miles of the most fertile lands, abundantly watered by streams, rivers and lakes, with a climate not to be surpassed in salubrity, anywhere in America, and with a constitution and laws which are the finest in the world.

Canadian Baptists' first mission, he said, should be to fellow Canadians, and he had entered the West because he saw it as the great Canadian mission field.[50] His highest satisfaction in the ministry came from seeing 'a soul won for Christ', either through a sermon or through a pastoral visit. His faith was intensely personal: 'God watched over me constantly; observed my conduct; heard my every word; knew my thoughts; was pleased or displeased with my actions.' During his visits to Hilda Blake he would have tried to arouse similar personal convictions in her. Yet because of his own experience, he distrusted 'feeling' and 'the Spirit's voice' as a guide for Christian conduct: 'I have never been able to be sure of the Spirit's guidance from a mere impression. Sometimes it was right, sometimes wrong. Only by a knowledge of duty from the teaching of God's Word, and by a knowledge of myself and the demands made upon me, am I sure that the Holy Spirit is leading me.'

Blake's escape to McLaurin and First Baptist was rather limited, literally—for at that time the church was located on 10th and Princess, only a block from the Lane house—and metaphorically—for McLaurin was not in the habit of suggesting worldly remedies for women who did not want to be domestic servants.[51] Not a highly imaginative person, he was eulogized as a man who did not have extraordinary gifts, but who made 'faithful, consistent and consecrated use of the gifts which were his'. In later years, at the same time as he claimed that the Bible gave better knowledge of God and man than 'all books of history, science and philosophy, if piled sky high', he also lamented that his constant duties had prevented him from reading much: 'To be widely informed in literature is a source of strength to a preacher. In this I failed and have deeply regretted it.'[52] In some ways, his circle of thought was more consistent and more narrow than Blake's. She found an emotional support in him, but not a kindred spirit. He must have been puzzled by her remark, as the hanging drew near, that she wished she were a Hindu who believed in reincarnation.[53]

Although she never became a member of First Baptist,[54] the church seems to have been the locus for the existential questions that troubled Blake. The presence of religious tracts in her room and the 'religious disposition' that she showed suggest that her church attendance was not simply a formality to establish her 'character' in the eyes of potential employers, but that in spite of her 'artfulness' and crime she maintained a lifelong desire for spiritual revelation. What is most striking, of course, is how much her piety was at odds with her economic, emotional, and (perhaps) sexual ambitions. McLaurin's great ideals—'each church-member should be wholly given to Christ. . . . each member should be a living witness of Christ's passion, and a deep sympathizer in the work of saving souls'[55]—she would have had difficulty living up to. Instead, she would have fit better (surreptitiously so) among the penitents that Virden's Rev. Bridgman described at a Methodist testimony service: 'Some had not entirely broken away from sin, but they served notice on the devil that when conditions got right he could expect a jolt at any time.'[56] In the days leading up to her execution, Blake said, 'I seem to be possessed of two natures, one good and one very bad, and they seem to control me at different times. I am either good or very bad.'[57] Her counselling with McLaurin suggests that she was trying to understand and perhaps balance her contradictory and pathological impulses. She had, McLaurin would later say, no friends.[58]

Blake's case also shows that, despite the matchmaking optimism of the Winnipeg immigration agent and the repeated complaints of employers, domestic service did not lead, like a destiny, into marriage. There were a number of reasons for this, principally the domestic's high degree of isolation and lack of freedom. Employers were astonished when, as often happened, a woman left service for another trade.[59] Yet even when the new trade paid less, at least the woman had her evenings to herself, the privacy of her own home, and freedom from direct supervision for at least part of the day; the domestic's 'home', in contrast, was at all times her place of employment. She could not compromise her 'character' or her role with the children by inviting men into her room. Women who still lived with their parents were likely to be given much more freedom than the domestic—the freedom of the kitchen or parlour later in the evening, perhaps, while they were being courted.[60] Privacy, while not essential for courting, certainly helped, especially since employers of domestics tended to discourage marriage for fear that the servant, in setting up her own home, would abandon service.[61] Women in other trades also had greater opportunities for social contact with both sexes on the job, while a domestic's social contacts were often limited to her employer's children and his wife. Finally, women in other trades could hope for promotion and did not suffer the social stigma of being branded a 'servant', particularly galling to a woman as attuned to class difference as Blake later showed herself to be.[62] Increasingly, domestic service—because it created social and economic dependence—was the lowest-status occupation, apart from prostitution, in which a woman could work.[63]

Yet, while domestics such as Hilda Blake had reason to be unhappy with their lives, their social and economic oppression rarely shaped a political consciousness leading to group resentment or revolt.[64] This should not be surprising. Servants had virtually no opportunity to acquire a consciousness other than one leading to social conformity. Their education tended to be rudimentary, and domestic manuals reminded them that the order of human society reflected the divine pleasure: 'Had God seen that it would have been better for your external [earthly] good that you should be great and rich He would have made you so; but He gives to all the places and duties best fitted to them.'[65] Most servants worked alone within a controlled environment. Their daily responsibilities created few opportunities for reflection. Solidarity and resistance, typically communal values shaped in response to a common foe, were alien to the lonely domestic. The acceptance of conventional Victorian notions about femininity and of the socio-political order was arguably even a psychological necessity for success. Personal self-worth and vocational success came easier if one demonstrated palpable loyalty and devotion, even servility, to employers, while disloyalty or signs of resentment could mean dismissal.

Working-class culture provided little alternative. Respectable Anglo-Canadian working-class families in the city's east and south ends tried hard to replicate middle-class notions of respectability. Of course, financial realities made the lives of working-class women far more burdensome than the life experienced by those of the middle class. Many working-class women, after all, were required to work outside the home or take work or boarders into the home to bolster the family income. Although a farm labourers' union was formed in Brandon during the spring of 1899,[66] working-class men neither counted female domestic servants as fellow workers nor showed concern for the socio-economic oppression suffered by women (and immigrants). Labourite analysis did not include a critique of the productive relations in the home, where men assumed a patriarchal role. Until well after the turn of the century the public influence of workers was restricted to voting for middle-class candidates. The experience of the city's workers did shape a class pride—a badge of self-reliance—but that lay side by side with a general acceptance of capitalist economic relations, at least until the transformations triggered by World War I.

For many domestics, their condition of moral and political passivity was also rooted in their deeply conventional views of the place of women in society. In the late nineteenth century, women could pursue few respectable avenues besides nursing, teaching, and stenography, all of which required some form of higher education.[67] Hilda Blake would eventually be torn between the desire to act in aggressive ways and the wish to behave as a 'proper' woman, but if she had more benign fantasies of learning to nurse, she had no opportunity. The social and economic position of domestics was, for the most part, beyond their power to address; and for many the acceptance of the paternalistic order and the sense of attachment to a particular family tended to assuage the worst features of the position. In short, domestic servants were improbable rebels against middle-class values, capitalist relations of production, or their constrained social identity.

Among those domestics who did harbour resentment towards the existing order,[68] the problem was invariably how to escape. That domestics should accept their station and not give themselves so many airs was repeated again and again by employers, including Mrs A.M.

Duensing of Emerson, Manitoba, who advised newcomers 'not to follow the example of the majority of the Canadian girls, to think that they are ladies and that work is a disgrace.'[69] Rebellion tended to be expressed in private ways, as Blake's was. The only way a domestic could go on strike was to refuse certain chores or, when all else failed, to give notice, hoping for better luck in the next place.[70] Generally, domestics yearned for success *within* the system, wishing for their own families, homes, and the economic and social independence that one usually associated with marriage. Most home girls left service as soon as they could.[71]

At the inquest, Blake claimed that her relations with the Lane family had always been harmonious, and others agreed. Neighbours said that 'she was passionately fond of the Lane children, and the kindness with which she always treated them went very far towards increasing the favor in which she was held.'[72] Evidently she had attained, at least outwardly, the kind of submission that the Rev. Barrett had earlier wished for her in urging that she be willing to do 'service'. McLaurin said that 'she was a good and faithful servant, made few acquaintances, and was not in the habit of being out at night or absent from the city. The fact is that all who knew her most intimately—neighbors—were the last to give credence to the report that she was the party who committed the awful deed.'[73] A clergyman like Rev. McLaurin might be expected to place a literal moral interpretation on Christ's parable of three unsupervised servants, two of whom faithfully invest their master's capital, but McLaurin, like Rev. Barrett before him, understood his society well enough not to allude to the master's practical responsibilities. The parable's mystical meaning is lost in McLaurin's Victorian moral emphasis, so that any allegory about the kingdom of God disappears under literal suggestions about how domestic servants, rather than Christians generally, ought to behave. Yet at the same time, in the turn-of-the-century labour market, there was little chance that such practical readings would be carried through to the parable's end, at which point the master says to the good and faithful servant, 'I will make thee ruler over many things.' Instead, good employers gave Christmas bonuses;[74] others presumably felt that the servant's full reward should more properly come in the next world. Blake was in the position of those who, as Ngaire Naffine puts it, had been 'taught to want the goals of their culture but denied access to them.'[75]

The hope of some working-class parents that service might lead to upward mobility in *this* world would later find a plaintive echo in Blake's adoption of a higher-class persona during the trial, but her more immediate and unidealized sense of what it meant to be a domestic servant was best expressed by McLaurin: 'she always seemed thoughtful, though given to despondency at times, and often said to me with feelings of regret that had she not been so willful, she might have been in a different position.' Blake likely meant that obedience in her first placement (at the Stewarts) could have had material rewards. Given the education of Joseph Singer at the Collegiate in Winnipeg and his ascent into the legal profession, she may have been right, particularly with respect to education. The experience of most domestic servants, however, suggests otherwise—economic and social conditions, not wilfulness, generally dictated their mode of employment. Unlike Singer, she wasn't even a stepchild, and only 1–3 per cent of servants ever inherited anything from their masters.[76]

Several days before her execution, Blake wrote, 'I feel as if I could sit quietly down and await my fate. I have never felt the like before, although I have pretended to be submissive.'[77] That this fatalism was unusual for her suggests that Blake was never as submissive or as oriented towards middle-class values as she pretended to be. At some point in her employment she learned the racist 'coon songs' that were so popular in the 1890s, and that she would later sing in jail, confounding the earnest visitors worried about the health of her soul.

At some point, too, Blake had begun to read novels, preferring Scott, Dickens, and what the *Manitoba Morning Free Press* termed, with some irony, 'other high class novels'.[78] Scott and Dickens were popular everywhere, but it is not difficult to see why Hilda Blake, in particular, felt their attraction. The title of an 1892 article in the *Western Sun*, 'The Mother's Part in Fiction', may well have caught the 14-year-old orphan's eye:

> No fact is more distinctly impressed upon the reader of romance than that the mother is a superfluous and troublesome creature with whom the novelist will have nothing to do. . . . Walter Scott, canny with the wisdom of his race, made the same discovery at the beginning of his literary career, and his heroines are almost without exception motherless from an early age. . . . Dickens, foremost and greatest of novelists . . . rarely drew a mother except to caricature her; and not one of his more notable heroines but was either an orphan or possessed only of a father.[79]

If Blake didn't read the article, it can, nevertheless, explain to us something of what made Scott and Dickens so interesting to her. The heroines in novels provided models (both conventional and unconventional) for female behaviour under pressure, and often, we will

later argue, Blake acted in ways that imitated the actions of specific
Dickens and Scott characters. To argue that novel-reading leads to
crime would be to accept, uncritically, nineteenth-century complaints
about the malicious effects of prurient fiction;[80] still, Scott and Dickens would not have helped reconcile her to her station. The murder of
Mary Lane, against whom Blake seems to have borne no personal
malice and in whose house Blake claimed to have been comfortable,
suggests quite forcefully that Blake did not accept her station.
Although she had become much wiser than when she was among the
Stewarts, having learned to imitate the kind of good character sought
by employers—'clean, celibate, obedient, respectable, hard-working
and an early riser'[81]—Blake clearly felt insignificant and oppressed
by her life as a domestic. She was profoundly unhappy.[82]

PART II

5

My Downfall

It does good to no woman to be flattered by her superior,
who cannot possibly intend to marry her; and it is madness
in all women to let a secret love kindle within them, which,
if unreturned and unknown, must devour the life that feeds it;
and if discovered and responded to, must lead, ignis-fatuus-
like, into miry wilds whence there is no extrication.

—Charlotte Brontë, *Jane Eyre*

But one day the devil, in the form of a man,
  Came smiling towards me; said he "You can
  Know more, if you'll take them,
  Of joy and pleasures," I heard him say,
"Than e'er you have dreamed of; I'll show you the way."

—Hilda Blake, 'My Downfall'

There may have been another equally important reason for Hilda
Blake's despondency. Despite the obstacles intended to keep domestics from marriage, many did marry. Why not Blake? The answer
may be found in the circumstance that, ministers of the gospel
notwithstanding, a domestic's most constant male contact was her
employer. Whereas the domestic could not invite courting men to
her room without loss of character, she was often alone in the house
with her employer. In many cases and, so the evidence suggests, in
Blake's case, the employer made the domestic his sexual partner,
an entanglement also likely to discourage 'exogamy'. According to

76

Alison Prentice and to many other historians, 'perhaps the most serious problem of the domestic servant, if she was far from the protection of friends and family, was her vulnerability to sexual exploitation', particularly by her employer or her employer's sons.[1] Blake, who had no family but had a 'prepossessing appearance',[2] was doubly vulnerable.

The climax of her probable affair with Robert Lane proved extraordinary, but not so the events leading up to that climax. A late nineteenth-century woman subject to repeated sexual advances had few options. Pregnancy would be a desperate circumstance: to be a single woman with a young child raised questions about one's character and undermined chances for marriage, for further employment, and sometimes even for lodgings. Infanticide was sometimes a last resort in such cases:

> the bodies of newborn infants were found buried in the snow, ·
> inside hollow trees, at the bottom of wells, under floor boards, in
> privies and stovepipes, and floating down rivers. The mothers who
> were caught were usually destitute, unmarried, working-class
> women with no family to share the burden of their shame or help
> them raise a child.[3]

On the other hand, the seducer was unlikely to divorce his wife. The divorce rate in the 1890s remained very low, as popular opinion lined up against divorce.[4] Blake could leave, but economic dependency made that difficult, since to resign her job was to lose her residence as well. It was indeed better to leave than to be fired, but since a servant depended on her reputation for employment, leaving could mean a poor reference. Many domestics left anyway. Many others were made pregnant by their seducers,[5] the difficulties of survival then leading some of the pregnant into prostitution.

*

Two cases involving domestics, sexual exploitation, and murder in Ontario show us what a servant could expect before Canadian courts. The cases of Maria McCabe, sentenced to death in 1883 for murdering her illegitimate child, and of Carrie Davies, tried in 1915 for the murder of Charles Massey, a prominent member of the Massey family of Toronto, show what working-class domestics were up against. Like Blake, McCabe and Davies were young immigrant women whose employment as domestics had led directly to their being charged with murder. Both acted in ways that were out of character.

Maria McCabe was sent from Dublin to Canada as a pauper in 1880 at the age of 14. Her mother had died when Maria was very young, and her blind father was unable to provide for her. She sold matches and papers on the streets of Dublin to support herself and her father, then lived in a convent for three years—until the South Union of the City of Dublin sent her, along with 42 other girls, to Canada as a domestic. Within a few months she was seduced by her employer, Lewis Jones of Hamilton. McCabe testified that when Jones's wife was absent in London, 'he took the upper hand of me.' Seven months later McCabe informed Jones that she was pregnant, but he refused to take any responsibility for the baby and dismissed her, sending her out into the Hamilton streets to fend for herself. She was 15.

After the birth of her child, McCabe was evicted from her lodgings, and, since she had a baby, no one would employ her. The next part of her story sounds like the parable of the Good Samaritan—minus the title character. Penniless and homeless, she sought help from a priest and from the mayor of Hamilton. They refused. She roamed the streets with her baby in her arms until—chilled, hungry, and desperate—she finally threw the baby into an open cistern of water.

Four months later, the baby's remains were discovered. The police arrested McCabe and she readily admitted her guilt, telling the Hamilton chief of police that she was 'glad it was off her mind', that she 'hadn't had a minute of peace of mind since she had committed the murder.'[6] She was charged and, as Blake would later do, pled guilty, refusing to defend herself even though she knew that a guilty plea would mean the death sentence. During the 1883 Fall Assizes, the judge reluctantly sentenced her to death but recommended mercy.

A broadly based campaign to have her sentence commuted arose quickly in Hamilton. One appeal to the federal cabinet stressed her vulnerability as a young woman and the guilt of the man who had fathered her child:

> Remember that when a young girl has a child out of wedlock, that when she fell, it was an unmanly and cruel outrage upon woman whom as the weaker vessel every good man ought if he be capable of the slightest feeling to give aid and protect not to cruelly wrong. Remember when a poor girl is brought to shame the untold agony with which she looks forward to a blighted life; if the heartless man, who wronged her prove false and do not as he ought to marry her.[7]

The cabinet commuted her sentence to 14 years in Kingston Penitentiary.[8] An unsuccessful appeal was made in 1887 to grant her early release, but a further appeal in 1889 was successful. Both appeals insisted that she had been in a state of despair and drew attention to her exemplary conduct in prison. The deputy minister advised Minister of Justice J.H. Thompson that the 'term of imprisonment served by the prisoner has been sufficient to vindicate the law, and that the exercise of clemency would not now be detrimental to the administration of justice.'⁹ The McCabe case, 16 years before Mary Lane's murder, showed that although a pregnant domestic could expect some sympathy and her male employer would feel the community's moral indignation, the sympathy would probably arrive only after a death sentence and the indignation would include no legal remedy.

The case of Carrie Davies provides a later variation on the same theme. Early on the evening of 8 February 1915, Charles Albert Massey (son of the former vice-president of the Massey Manufacturing company, the late C. Albert Massey) was shot dead on the steps of his own Toronto home. He had been shot by Davies, an 18-year-old domestic servant from Bedfordshire, England, who had been employed by the Masseys since she arrived in Canada two years previously. Massey, a 32-year-old salesman for the York Motor Car company, was just about to enter his house when Davies confronted him at the doorway, pistol in hand. She fired two shots: the first missed, the second wounded Massey in the chest. He fled, but collapsed near the house next door, and died without making any statement. Davies alleged that the murder was 'in revenge for . . . approaches made to her by the victim'.¹⁰

A press report of the preliminary hearing described her appearance as full of contradictions:

She has soft, fair hair and blue eyes and the pink and white skin of the English girl, but her eyelids are heavy and droop narrowly at the corners, resembling the Slavic type more than the English. Her mouth is strong showing a capacity for resentment out of all keeping with her round childish chin. She was dressed modestly and appeared strangely out of place with the persons around her.¹¹

When confronted with the charge of murder, Davies sobbed convulsively and collapsed into her chair. No one appeared at the hearing to act for her, and she was remanded in custody. In the press, Davies's sister, Mrs Edmund Fairchilds, who also lived in Toronto, recounted how Davies had complained that Massey had kissed her and that she had had to run away from him. Fairchilds had told Davies 'to lock her bedroom at night, and if he tried again to bother her to run to the neighbours' house no matter how she happened to be attired.'¹²

Davies herself explained to the subsequent inquest that twice on the day before the shooting Massey had attempted to take advantage of her. She had killed him in self-defence: 'When I saw him I seemed to lose control of myself, and ran and got the revolver and shot at him.' At the time of her arrest, Davies told police 'I shot him; take me away from here; he ruined my life.'[13]

The trial, presided over by Chief Justice William Mulock (who had played a role in Blake's case), began two and a half weeks later. After presenting evidence to show that Davies shot Massey, the Crown prosecutor asked:

> Did she have justification? A woman in a house, who fears for her life at the hands of a strong, violent, lustful man, and kills him, may have a good defense. But in this case how much was danger and how much was imagination. The prisoner says that Massey kissed her twice. That is not a serious matter.[14]

At the time of the murder, the Masseys had contended that Davies must have murdered Charles in a fit of temporary insanity. Press reports appeared to support this line of analysis, indicating that she was under a lot of stress because she had come from a poor family and was expected to help to support three younger sisters and a nearly blind mother still in England. The trial, however, turned out to be 'much less a struggle to determine the guilt or innocence of a defendant than a gentlemen's agreement to recognize a heroine'.[15] The jury acquitted her. When the foreman announced the verdict, the courtroom resounded with shouts and cheers, and in a concluding statement, Judge Mulock told Davies:

> you have had a strict bringing up, and the influence of your parents upon you has fallen upon good ground. You have the highest regard for morality and honor. These qualities caused you to take a strong view of the things Mr. Massey did, so from the highest motives you did a thing which you will regret all your life.[16]

Clearly, a domestic could expect some measure of justice, but only if her 'character' was unimpeachable. The Davies case occurred 15 years after the Lane murder, but nevertheless shows what was already becoming a common feeling in late nineteenth-century Canada: if a gentleman seduced a 'girl', he ought to maintain the child, but if he found 'a woman already spoiled, he did not do her any harm, poor creature!'[17] In other words, once a woman entered any sexual relationship outside of marriage, she could not rely on the law to protect her from sexual assault, but if she had a reputation for chastity she might be able to defend herself on the spur of the moment. A woman in the mould of Carrie Davies could expect justice; a woman such as Maria McCabe could not.[18]

*

According to one local legend, Hilda Blake was pregnant at the time of her execution. *The Voice*, a Winnipeg labour newspaper, only reported this legend some 10 years after the event,[19] and since there are no hints of Blake's pregnancy in either the trial documents or the media reports (even though she would have begun to show by the end of 1899), the rumour must be false. Nevertheless, it may elaborate other, more credible, rumours of sexual misconduct. Two weeks before her execution, Blake wrote an autobiography for Chief Kircaldy and a stylized poem for publication, both of which—the first explicitly, the second by implication—placed the responsibility for her fall in the hands of Robert Lane. While Blake is not the most reliable source, her evidence, as we shall see, cannot easily be discounted. The autobiography no longer exists, but extant references disclose that in it she claims to have committed murder because Robert had promised to marry her if he were free.

Blake's reading of *Rob Roy* and *Jane Eyre* told her that socially improbable marriages could occur—for example, the marriages of the Protestant Hanoverian, Frank Osbaldistone, to the 'orphaned' Catholic Jacobite, Diana (Beauchamp) Vernon; of the bailie (i.e., alderman) Nicol Jarvie to his maidservant; and of the high-born Mr Rochester to his orphaned governess, Jane Eyre.[20] One could receive, as did Jane, early intimations of one's hope to rise in class: 'Bessie Leaven had said I was quite a lady: and she spoke truth—I was a lady. And now I looked much better than I did when Bessie saw me.'[21] If one were not as scrupulous as Jane in avoiding the temptation or compulsion to become a rich man's mistress, such hopes could easily betray one.

At the same time as she wrote the autobiography, Blake also wrote 'My Downfall', a much less explicit poem which *is* still extant, and which frames the murder inside a melodramatic struggle between good and evil. She gave the poem to her spiritual adviser, Rev. McLaurin, who passed it along to the *Western Sun*. While it is possible that McLaurin either suggested themes or helped edit the poem, Charlotte Brontë probably had more influence over the poem than did McLaurin, who was the circumstantial and not overly imaginative author of *Pioneering in Western Canada: A Story of the Baptists.*

Published on the front page of the *Western Sun* on 14 December 1899,
'My Downfall' suggests that Blake was a victim of male predation:

Once I was innocent, light hearted and gay,
        And sang while I worked through all the long day;
A stranger to sorrow, not a care had I,
        A laugh on my lip, but never a sigh.

But one day the devil, in the form of a man,
        Came smiling towards me; said he "You can
    Know more, if you'll take them,
        Of joy and pleasures," I heard him say,
"Than e'er you have dreamed of; I'll show you the way."

I followed the tempter, along the smooth track,
        I'd gone a long distance 'fore e'er I looked back,
        Or thought of returning—
When I turned, the way back seemed so lonely and dreary,
        E'er I'd gone many steps I grew footsore and weary,
That down by the roadside, to rest and to weep,
        My strength was exhausted, I soon fell asleep.

I awakened refreshed, my exhaustion all gone,
        Saw the phantom of Pleasure, still beckoning me on;
    Then I made up my mind
To leave Prudence behind,
        And pursue my perilous way.

As I journeyed along my heart lost its song,
        For the path grew stony and dark;
Each step that I took tore the flesh off my feet,
        And the track was a blood-stained mark.

I looked at the tempter, in his eye was a gleam;
    I saw he was standing beside a dark stream;
He cried, "Come along, take a few steps more
    And your struggle is ended, your journey is o'er."

As I stood on the brink of that river,
    My heart grew faint and sick;
What I saw only made me shiver—
    I thought Fortune had played me a trick.

"As I look across I see only the dead,
    Neither joy, nor pleasure," to Satan, I said:
"But pleasures there are, though hidden from view,
They only wait to be claimed by you."

I thought as he spoke, he moved his hand
    And I saw I was standing on sinking sand.
As I leaped across, a frantic yell
    Reached my ear
When too late, I saw I had leaped into hell;
I tried to go back, but an awful wall
Loomed up, and separated me from all
    My youth and innocence.

Forsaken by friendship, kith, and kin
    I lie in my lonely cell;
    It seems but a dream that I've crossed that dark stream
    And descended from heaven to hell.

You hypocrites, pleading religion,
    You inquisitive seekers of fame,
Ready now with your good advice
    When I've drunk of the sorrow and shame;
You gave me no timely warning,
    You held out no helping hand,—
Why didn't you see me sinking
    As I stepped on this treacherous sand?

Oh Friend of all Friends who rules earth and sea,
    Look down with a pitying eye upon me;
    Thou'll forgive my transgressions, says the book that is best—
Come ye that are weary, and I'll give you rest.

Blake apparently found herself in a position not so different from
that of McCabe or Davies. Considered within the context of those two
cases, 'My Downfall' takes on the appearance of an authentic, if cryptic, portrayal of Blake's relationship with Robert Lane—a conventional story of seduction and betrayal. The poem can bear three main
lines of interpretation: the 'devil, in the form of a man', could simply
be 'Satan' and the poem a vague allegory about orphanhood, sin, and
punishment; the 'devil' could refer to a man who early in her life had
lured Blake into sexual impropriety; the 'devil' could refer to Robert

Lane. The three interpretations need not be mutually exclusive, however, since sexual impropriety could have begun elsewhere and continued with Lane, and since a general allegory does not preclude a particular sexual allegory about identifiable people.

In certain significant ways, Blake's whole culture helped to compose 'My Downfall'. A ballad that appears in *Jane Eyre*, and to which the orphaned Jane shows a strong emotional reaction, may have been a partial source for Blake's image of herself. Stanza 3 in 'My Downfall' uses the ideas, and partly the language, of the first stanza in Brontë's ballad:

> My feet they are sore, and my limbs they are weary;
>   Long is the way, and the mountains are wild;
> Soon will the twilight close moonless and dreary
>   Over the path of the poor orphan child.

The inconsistent metre in Blake's poem (especially in stanzas 2 and 10) does not have the lithe rhythm of such lines, but Blake's attempt to create the anapests in Brontë's manner can be seen often in 'My Downfall', particularly in the last stanza. Even though the orphaned speaker of the *Jane Eyre* ballad, unlike Blake, has no sexual sins over which to grieve, she, too, dreads entrapments and watery death, fearing that she will 'fall o'er the broken bridge passing,/Or stray in the marshes, by false lights beguiled', as Blake does in stanza 7. Those who in Blake's poem hold out no helping hand seem to be adapted from the assertion by Brontë's speaker that 'Men are hard-hearted.' Stanzas 11 and 13 of 'My Downfall' close the journey with a hope for rest and a conventional appeal to God as the orphan's friend. Brontë's ballad closes in a similar way:

> There is a thought that for strength should avail me;
>   Though both of shelter and kindred despoiled;
> Heaven is a home, and a rest will not fail me;
>   God is a friend to the poor orphan child.[22]

Such sentiments about orphanhood are conventional and Blake could have gotten them from other sources, but the echoes are close enough to suggest that Blake had read *Jane Eyre*[23] and had adapted Brontë's romantic melodrama to a Christian allegory about sin and punishment—conventional in Blake's culture, though not quite so appealing to Brontë (who satirizes exaggerated notions of sin and presents a fundamentally innocent heroine). The emphasis in 'My Downfall' on sexual prohibition, sin, responsibility, and forgiveness follows the Christian ethos that Blake likely would have learned from her parents and had confirmed for her not only by the Stewarts, McLaurin, and Baptist Sunday school tracts, but also by the civil order and even by Brontë's insistence on sexual purity. In the poem's central themes, at least, Blake had neither the independence of mind nor the skepticism necessary to modify substantially the framework into which the events of lives such as hers were conventionally put: a conventional nineteenth-century Christian perspective on women's place. Perhaps Blake's tragedy was that she read *Jane Eyre* instead of *Moll Flanders*!

Because Blake interpreted her life melodramatically, she concealed many of the social circumstances that led to the murder and instead looked for the source of her disgrace in the ethos of the morality play. In the process of creating a symbolic universe to make life understandable and tolerable, women like Blake may have shared 'a kind of half-conscious complicity in their own victimization'.[24] What could be important for her psychological health—a moral interpretation—could also keep her from explicitly raising wider social issues; yet, at the same time, what she desired—to erase Mary Lane and to afford a better social position—makes the speaker's moral interpretation of her life less convincing.

Following the conventions suggested by her culture, Blake thus relies on romantic psychology and melodrama, while ignoring, except unconsciously, the moral-banal narratives of class or gender struggle. In its emphasis on the central tragic heroine, the poem approaches the romantic mythos of the ego and its sensibility. The 'high-class' novels that Blake read usually owed a debt to melodrama but complicated its Christian moral dimension by presenting fallen heroines in a sympathetic—a Romantic—way. A broadly popular genre in the nineteenth century, romantic melodrama relied on characters highly exaggerated in their goodness or evil and plots that displayed 'virtue as a perpetually embattled ideal'. The villains—generally male—were diabolical in the extreme, and the protagonists—generally female—were endangered innocents. Scott's Effie Deans, Eliot's Hetty Sorrel, and Hardy's Tess 'each succumbed to illicit passion, each was abandoned by her lover, each bore a bastard as proof of her transgression, and ultimately each suffered grievously because of her lapse.'[25] We might add that each was treated sympathetically. Tess, who murdered the man who had dishonoured her, was greeted with outrage because Hardy treated her sexual vice sympathetically.

'My Downfall' likewise hedges about responsibility, wavering between a Romantic and a Christian sensibility, linking Blake to the general movement in which analysis of social circumstance was beginning to weigh more heavily than the emphasis on individual sin. The heroine of 'My Downfall' is robbed of her childhood innocence by a demonic lover who seduces her into evil pleasures. To the extent that 'My Downfall' is nebulous about the speaker's degree of responsibility, the poem portrays Blake as the embattled, melodramatic victim of Satan's seduction and betrayal, as a naïve, even if not quite an overpowered, woman. This moral apologia of Hilda Blake—a Romantic moralist as it were—may be contrasted with William Thackeray's more traditional satire in *Vanity Fair*, where the reader is distanced from Becky Sharp in exact proportion to her departure from conventional morality.

Although in some ways merely quoting the cultural discourses available to her—romantic psychology, Christian morality, and melodrama—Blake of course chose *which* cultural forms to draw upon. Melodrama appealed particularly to women because 'it foregrounded issues of gender and power and highlighted the role of the heroine, however passive and suffering she might be.'[26] The central tension in melodramatic plots was rooted in the plight of the heroine 'made desperate by the insensitivity, deceitfulness or even villainy of men.' Popular songs of the period—'There Are no Angel Men' (1890), for example—also cast men as devilish.[27] While the Christian narrative could make ontological sense of her suffering, it was her romantic sympathy for the sexually transgressing woman and her melodramatic focus on gender that could articulate the experience of a servant who felt that she had been ill-used.

The poem goes further, commenting implicitly on the specific events of Blake's life. She would have known that in a city that for several months had been blitzed with details and analyses of Mary Lane's murder, 'My Downfall' could never be received abstractly as a general allegory, and it's not surprising, therefore, that the allegory of sin and punishment shades implicitly yet surely into a sexual allegory. Tacit in the poem's language is the notion of sexual seduction and betrayal, even though the implied love affair is dealt with only vaguely. The reference to 'Prudence' as the abandoned virtue, the need to describe the devil as a man (instead of assuming that the identification was self-evident), the connection between pleasure and physical exhaustion, and the *bodily* nature of the suffering all imply a sexual seduction. The scene of desire clearly dominates the poem's world. Everything after the first stanza seems post-coital, and only in death can the hypersensitive speaker hope for, but not show, release—as if pleasure and its dark companion were the world's main facts. Like *Wuthering Heights*, 'My Downfall' emphasizes romantic abjection in love, a close knot of sexuality, hidden pleasure, and death. Sir Walter Scott and Charlotte Brontë had taught Blake that love was an effect of 'nature'; one defied 'nature' at one's peril.[28] It's not surprising, either, that *Jane Eyre* would come to mind in Blake's effort to describe such a seduction: Mr Rochester once kept a mistress, and he very nearly seduces his servant, Jane, too.

At the level of a particular sexual seduction, the allegory in 'My Downfall' still derives from a particular cultural discourse. Both the emphasis on sexuality as dangerous and the appropriate use of euphemism (especially on the part of women) were dictated to Blake by her society. That the sexual elements of her story were not expressed openly is one of the fundamental ways in which Blake conforms to her Victorian tradition, since Victorian literature often hints at sexual dilemmas but very rarely makes such dilemmas explicit.[29]

Nor is 'My Downfall' autobiographical merely with respect to Blake's sexual life. The staging of her orphanhood is clear enough in the line 'Forsaken by friendship, kith, and kin' and in the nostalgic evocation of childhood at the beginning of the poem. While 'kith and kin' was a cliché, the phrase may connect Blake's forsaken position in the jail cell with her much earlier abandonment at the age of nine. As a result, and consistent with the experience of many home children, the 'lonely cell' may refer not only to jail but also to her initial isolated position in Canada, as well as to the small room that she, a domestic, had in each house where she served. It is even possible that the 'dark stream', the image least likely to have a historical referent, captures her childhood memory of crossing the Atlantic. In the image of the 'Friend of all Friends' she echoes Rev. Barrett's conventional depiction of God as the orphan's succour, although for Blake (perhaps with a realistic understanding of the orphan's true position) that God is 'Friend', not 'Father'. At the same time she condemns society for its religious hypocrisy. Only when the orphaned domestic has descended to 'hell' do people truly take an interest in her life and fate.

Not quite as clear, but still distinguishable, is the moment of the murder. The speaker's cataclysmic leap into hell obviously occurs before death, since she still expects to be forgiven at the end of the poem. Apart from the murder, it is difficult to think of an event that in one blow would put Blake into hell or wall up the path back to innocence. Unlike her sexual transgressions, this 'wall' is literal, including as it does the legal interdiction that in the following stanza has placed her in a 'cell'.

But Blake's description of the murder is problematic for a couple of reasons. First, even though by the time the poem appeared the

whole city knew her as a murderer, Blake portrays herself as an inex-
perienced victim: it is her own flesh, not Mary Lane's, that leaves 'a
blood-stained mark'. Yet despite such repression, perhaps Mary is not
effaced completely. The 'frantic yell', which is unmotivated and has
no source in the poem, is best explained as coming from outside the
poem, Blake hearing again Mary's last cry of 'Oh Hilda!' Therefore
we might say that in one breath Blake (probably unconsciously) artic-
ulates two narratives, the Christian narrative in which she must
inevitably take responsibility for the murder and the more Romantic
autobiographical melodrama that still allows her to present herself as
a sensitive and suffering victim.

The murder is problematic, second, because Blake seems to pre-
dict it: 'As I look across I see only the dead'. This sin-as-death motif
could perhaps refer to Blake's suicidal thoughts, but more likely
refers to a literal murder. This by itself is not astounding, for the
poem was written after the murder and, as the Crown implied at the
preliminary hearing, the buying of the gun indicated Blake's malice
aforethought. More puzzling, rather, is the nature of the 'pleasure . . .
hidden from view' that the tempter promises, even *while* she sees the
dead before her. Because the speaker asserts that the way back from
pleasure would be 'so lonely and dreary', because Blake claimed that
she was 'jealous' of Mary Lane, and because the autobiography mentions Robert Lane's promise of marriage, the most likely explanation
is that the hidden pleasure was Blake's expected marriage to Robert
after his wife's death. Not knowing the consequences of his actions,
Robert may have used the seduction line that was almost proverbial in
the nineteenth century: 'If I *were* free, I *would* marry you!' Or, at the
very least, Blake fantasized that a widowed Robert, unaware of who
caused his wife's death, would be attracted to her. Could Blake have
gotten her cue on how to feel from Jane Eyre's fear that her beloved
master Mr Rochester would wed the talented Miss Ingram? 'If Miss
Ingram had been a good and noble woman, endowed with force, fer-
vour, kindness, sense,' says Jane, 'I should have had one vital struggle
with two tigers—jealousy and despair.'[30]

The status quo, for Blake, was intolerable. For any servant, no
good could come from indulging the master's (and possibly her own)
sexual pleasure: at best she could receive small perquisites; at worst,
she could become pregnant, losing both her job and her love. A marriage, whatever the psychological or moral cost to attain it, could
erase those hazards connected with her servanthood—sexual danger,
loneliness, economic insecurity, low community status, rootlessness—and replace them, if all went well, with security of person,

material comfort, status, an intimate and nearly balanced companionship, a home. If we grant that the retrospective speaker's foresight of
the dead gives us at least some indication of Blake's mental state at
the time she was contemplating the murder and not just her mental
state afterwards in jail, then in her eyes the murder seems unlikely to
have been the product either of mental disease or of some personal
conflict between servant and master; instead, the murder seems like a
reasoned, though misguided, response to social inequity.

Based on evidence inside and outside of the poem, we can reconstruct several plausible scenarios of Blake's sexual history. In the first
scenario she would have been sexually initiated at a young age. The
initiation would probably not have been a rape in which physical force
was used, since the speaker of the poem makes a decision to 'follow'
the tempter, yet Blake's youth (she could have been as young as 12)
suggests what we now call sexual abuse. In other words, given the
moral teachings of the day, she felt that she had made a sinful choice,
but in fact she had been manipulated, her free will more apparent than
real. Her job as a maid exposed her to the sexual predations of a few
employers who, like medieval lords, often expected that among the
many duties of the domestic was included the employer's sexual recre-
ation. Alone as a young teenager in Winnipeg, and without the protection of kin, she would have been an easy target. By the 1890s condoms
were being mass-produced in Britain and the United States,[31] so that
employers more careful than Lewis Jones was with Maria McCabe
could guard against the maid's pregnancy.

If she was sexually initiated at a young age, Blake was 'damaged
goods' in the Victorian understanding.[32] She had made no allegations
at the time of her first sexual experience; the courts would therefore
offer no help at a later stage, and men on the lookout for such women
could expect safety from prosecution. Since the law that protected
women from seduction applied just to those women of previously
chaste character,[33] the only alternative was simply to leave and to find
a new situation; Blake's use of the alias 'Hilda Clarke' may possibly
have helped to shield her against gossip arising from such an incident.
In this scenario, once Robert Lane's attentions began she decided that
in order to extricate herself from her precarious position and to take
the honourable role of wife, she must make a very aggressive gambit
against Mary Lane.

It must immediately be admitted that there is no direct evidence
for the first scenario. The scenario may explain Blake's tendency to
run away, but we have no way of even guessing at names (other than
Robert Lane's). Her occasional nostalgia for the Stewarts can be

interpreted as the victim's attachment to the pleasure and attention given by the perpetrator; conversely, the nostalgia may also be interpreted as a recognition that, despite Mr Stewart's inflexibility and harsh punishment, the Stewart home was better than Blake's subsequent placements. The length of the speaker's journey in 'My Downfall' suggests that the seductions did not begin with Lane, but such evidence is very indirect and vague. Nevertheless, the scenario must be cited to avoid the great hazard that, by agreeing to the Victorian prohibition on sexual discourse, we erase the abuse experiences of women in general and of domestic servants in particular.[34] Middleclass patriarchs in Canada were virtually inoculated against guilt for sexual offences committed against domestic servants. Women who faced the courts soon discovered that they were on trial not only for allegedly breaking the law but also for challenging the moral boundaries of respectable womanly conduct—triggering images of 'fast, immoral, petulant, bad women telling lies and laying traps for stalwart, hearty men'.[35] 'From 1880 to 1930, not a single Toronto domestic who laid a complaint of indecent assault or rape against her master saw him punished', a statistic that Carolyn Strange attributes to 'the belief that only an unchaste woman could induce a man to make sexual advances'.[36] Parr, too, notes that the rape of home girls was not likely to meet with a conviction.[37]

At the same time, data from the work of the Order of Sisters of Misericordia, who worked with unwed mothers in Montreal, show that domestic servants were among the *most likely* to become unwed mothers. Fully 50 per cent of the young women who came to the Sisters of Misericordia for help in the years 1885–1900 were domestic servants.[38] While the most dangerous terrain for young women was believed to be in the factories, streets, and offices of Canada's metropolises, the preoccupation with the 'sins of city life' obscured the sexual danger that menaced women in rural areas and those who worked alone in the homes of the apparently respectable middle class. Karen Dubinsky reports that in Ontario between 1880 and 1929, 'domestic servants accounted for over one-half of the victims of workplace assault.'[39] Most of these assaults were committed by employers, not fellow servants. Blake, in short, belonged to a social group frequently exploited not only for labour, but also for sex.

The second scenario of Blake's sexual history takes part of its evidence from the same statistics and stories, but in this scenario Lane is the main culprit as Blake's first seducer. Blake came to the Lanes relatively friendless, with many fantasies of social improvement but no potential roads towards it. Even though her power of choice was greater at the age of 20 than at 11, she was still Lane's servant, and, as such, 'seduction' (whether resisted or welcomed) cannot easily be ruled out, even though it was not the sort of thing that Lane would have found in *Heroes of Methodism*.[40] In an intercepted note from jail, Blake addresses the receiver:

> Now I feel ashamed of myself to be obliged to confess that even that little note has comforted me. You have a strong influence over me knowing as I do how wicked and dishonorable you can be to allow myself to be comforted by the thought that you have taken the trouble to be worried about me.[41]

Police Chief Kircaldy allowed the correspondence to go on, evidently hoping (in vain) that the outside party—and no name other than Lane's came up in the evidence—would incriminate himself.

In *Jane Eyre*, Blake knew, Mr Rochester had said to Jane, 'you have neither relatives nor acquaintances whom you need fear to offend by living with me', but Blake also knew that, according to Jane herself, 'Hiring a mistress is the next worse thing to buying a slave: both are often by nature, and always by position, inferior.'[42] Of course, Blake was already in a position that Jane would never have let herself get into. When Blake's sense of a conflict between her illicit sexual relationship with Lane and her religious beliefs increased, or when for more material reasons she became disillusioned with the relationship, Lane may have shifted his language to the romantic and socially productive promise that if circumstances were different (that staple of romantic fiction) he would marry her. This ploy may have meant very little to Lane, but for Blake it may well have amounted to a vow upon which she was prepared to act.

This *roman à clef* interpretation equates Lane with the poem's devil, and here, admittedly, there are problems, not just because Lane was never publicly accused, but because, as Dubinsky notes, in cases that involved sexuality the behaviour of the woman was scrutinized more intensively than that of the man.[43] Alan Hustak, who has written very briefly about Blake in a popular forum, has argued that Lane did not have sexual relations with his servant, but Hustak gives a surprising inflection to Blake's statement that she was 'jealous' of Mary. Quite implausibly, he suggests that the kiss before the murder marked the denouement of Blake's failed homosexual pursuit of Mary.[44] The sensational claim is easy enough to make, given its exotic cachet and given the Victorian proscription against naming homosexuality, but Hustak has no evidence of same-sex desire. Since kisses were (and still are) commonly used to show affection between heterosexual women, a kiss is a rather small nail upon which to hang an interpretation of Blake's sexuality. The murder, clearly premeditated as we will see, was committed when Robert was at work: no suspicion could possibly fall on him. Later, when events began to make her less reticent, she identified her lover. In 'My Downfall', the tempter is clearly male, and in her autobiography she named him: Robert Lane.

A more plausible counter-argument against Robert Lane's guilt or explicit involvement with Hilda Blake comes from Lane and Robinson family oral histories. According to these stories, Lane was not at all the kind of person to involve himself sexually with a servant; rather, Blake's hard past, her fantasies about Lane, and/or her misinterpretation of Lane's kindness, and/or *her* unwanted sexual advances to *him* combined to create the tragedy.[45] Blake was highly thought of, it is said, and was hired because the family felt sorry for her, believing her to be a Barnardo girl. The day of the murder, she and Mary were busy hanging curtains, but when Mary requested that she pass up a curtain, Blake instead pulled out a gun hidden under the curtain and shot her. 'You wicked woman!' Mary is said to have cried. These stories either give no real motive or suggest that Blake had been caught stealing for a criminal boyfriend (the receiver, it is then argued, of Blake's letters), even though no whisper of theft sounded in the media or in the legal documents, and even though curtain-hanging seems a rather quotidian postscript to a theft accusation. The most plausible family story suggests that Robert was a great tease, and that, in front of Mary, he liked to kid the maids, 'If I hadn't wed Mary, I would have married you.' Certainly the Robinson family did not afterwards hold Lane responsible for the murder or even think him guilty of infidelity; rather, they closed ranks, allowing Mary's father, John, to be buried in the Lane plot the following January and maintaining close relationships with the Lanes afterwards. Lucy Murdoch (Mary's older sister and godparent to the eldest Lane boy, Thomas) thought Robert was a wonderful father. Robert paid for music lessons for Lil Robinson (Mary's cousin) and always had his pockets full of candy for his Robinson nieces and nephews.

Despite the counter-arguments from the Robinsons and Lanes, the evidence suggests that Robert Lane and Hilda Blake likely did have a sexual relationship. The strongest support comes from Governor-General Minto, who became involved in the matter as a consequence of last-minute petitions for clemency. Referring to Blake's autobiography, Lord Minto wrote: 'if her story against herself is true it is completely intertwined with the story of Lane. . . . it was Lane's influence that was answerable to the murder and it seems to have been a shabby mean influence evidently intended to save himself, while she is bent on saving him.'[46] One cannot rely completely on the missing autobiography, however, since Blake lied about events on a number of occasions and could have easily authored a deceptive account. But the letters to a man outside of the jail, the authorities' (especially Minto's) belief that there might be a case against Lane, and Kircaldy's continuing investigation all suggest that Blake's autobiography was to some degree reliable. That there is only one devil in 'My Downfall' implies that Blake's sexual misconduct began with Lane; certainly she must have been aware that Brandon would so interpret the poem. Blake probably refused to incriminate Lane publicly not because he was innocent of adultery, but because she, like other tragic romantic heroines, separated the person Lane from his allegorical role as devil in her psychomachia; or because she knew that the law and public opinion would favour the businessman over the domestic; or, most likely, because she had consented to their relationship and Lane could never have guessed that she would act as ruthlessly as she did.

The devil proved to be a faithless lover. Social subordination effectively undermined the credibility of servants who claimed sexual misconduct by their employers. That public mores were slowly changing is evidenced by the recent introduction of laws making it an offence to seduce girls between the ages of 12 and 16, women under 21 who had been promised marriage, and women under 21 who (except for domestic servants) were wards or employees of their seducers. To prosecute, the offended woman must have been of 'previously chaste character'.[47] Stories of sexual predators corrupting innocent females, who were victimized by male calculation and their own feminine weakness, became increasingly common in late Victorian Canada, but, in practice, only those with deeply entrenched social status could accuse powerful men.[48] Despite pleas to include servants in the legislation, MPs felt that such an inclusion would open employers to blackmail.[49] Amazingly, A.R. Dickey told the National Council of Women in 1896 that the Department of Justice was not aware of a single case in which a servant needed such protection.[50] As in Ontario, so in Manitoba: 'both rural communities and families were understood to be zones of moral safety, "havens" ruled by benevolent but unquestioned patriarchs.'[51] The moral climate made it offensive to consider seriously, at least publicly, claims that middle-class homes could be sites of sexual abuse. Respectable men, seen as the guarantors of civility and law and order, were thus insulated from scandal.

A domestic servant who might claim mistreatment at the hands of a prominent man was instead likely to find her own moral character the focus of scrutiny, since she must have led him on or was intent on blackmail. Exact behavioural codes were endorsed: 'No lady or gentleman will flirt', Grandma Nichols, an authority on manners and housekeeping, said generally, but when Nichols described the behaviour it soon became clear that the onus for correctness was on the woman: 'A true lady will avoid familiarity in her deportment toward gentlemen. A young lady should not permit her gentlemen friends to address her by her home name, and the reverse is true.'[52] Women, it was felt in many quarters, were responsible for guarding their own honour and chastity.[53]

Lawyers defending men against criminal seduction charges could and did bring up not only sexual history, but also church or school attendance, employment history, and even the moral conduct of the complainant's parents[54]—her class position, in other words. In rape trials, too, 'race, ethnicity, and class shaped men's credibility as much as it did women's "rapability".'[55] The practice of Ontario criminal courts suggests that no matter how compelling Blake's story of betrayal was, it was not likely to be acted upon by the Crown because her character was assessed in a sexual climate wherein 'any woman who admitted to sexual relations outside prescribed boundaries was suspect.'[56]

Civil courts gave better odds than did criminal courts. Between 1820 and 1900 in Ontario, seduction cases were the most litigated cases concerning women, and 90 per cent of the cases went to the plaintiffs, partly because the burden of proof was less, but also partly, Dubinsky argues, because the actions had to be brought by the complainant's father—the contest therefore becoming a more equal contest between two men.[57] Blake, of course, had neither a father who could be wronged nor any expectation that either A.P. Stewart or the Guardians of the Heckingham Workhouse would still be much interested in her difficulties, particularly if she had not been chaste previously. Opponents of the seduction laws and prosecuted men were fond of citing the possibility that women were liable to make claims against men of property, while the real seducer might actually be 'a young man of buoyant expectations but no substance'.[58] But the point was moot anyway: by the time Blake had been in the Lane household for half a year, she turned 21 and fell outside of the Criminal Code provisions.

In both the first and second scenarios, we have emphasized Lane's role as seducer. There is a third plausible scenario in which he plays a less controlling part. This scenario is suggested by Dubinsky's argument that despite good intentions, seduction laws served to control female sexuality, since the laws posited (in a sophisticated way) the 'doctrine of female purity and passionlessness' and the understanding that 'only men have an active sexuality.'[59] In the third scenario, Blake could have become sexually active of her own volition. Despite her good character as a servant, she may have broken with the nineteenth-century stereotype of the passive woman not only in her final aggression against Mary Lane, but also in her sexuality, perhaps wanting, in the interminable round of domestic work, to make something *happen*. At some point she may have learned that sexuality could be used to shape male desires to her own ends. Her goal was to change her class position, and in Lane—whose obituary (albeit 25 years later) would describe him as 'a man of quiet demeanor and a good hearted fellow'[60]—she may have found a potentially malleable man, but one unlikely to divorce his wife.

As in the first scenario, the evidence is purely indirect. Although the sympathetic reading of 'My Downfall' by some of Blake's defenders shows how Victorian-feminist and social-purity discourses de-emphasized the possibility of female sexual urges and agency, the poem's speaker nevertheless shows a sense of agency: she is deceived, but she chooses. To the extent that the narrator is active in her own deception and makes a clear moral choice, the poem presents a more self-conscious moral agent (rather than a naïve victim) and therefore a tragic (rather than melodramatic) Hilda Blake, a young woman torn between the collective will and her own various desires. The second stanza of 'My Downfall' mentions 'joy and pleasure' as the motives for the speaker's initial fall. Also, Chief Kircaldy never brought charges of any sort against Lane, and just before Blake's execution, Kircaldy asked her to retract anything that might injure others, as if in the end he (unlike Governor-General Minto) had doubts about her veracity and about the contents of her autobiography.

In one variant of this scenario one could even argue that Blake had some sort of mental illness that drove her to fantasize and then act upon an affair that never took place. As we will later see in more detail, Dr Amelia Yeomans of the Woman's Christian Temperance Union visited Blake in jail and reported that Blake was 'a moral idiot'—in other words, that she was amoral, unable to discern properly between good and evil. Yeomans argued not only that Blake lacked 'concentration of thought' and 'logical sequence in her ideas', but also that her moral faculties were far below her intellectual faculties, and that her moral faculties exerted 'little or no inhibitory power over conduct'.[61] Joseph Singer, who had been involved in Blake's 1889 child abduction case, told the *Advocate* in Elkhorn that 'as to the girl's character and whether or not she was in her right mind or whether she is mutinous and vicious by disposition none of us would like to hazard an opinion under the circumstances.'[62]

But a diagnosis of mental illness (discussed more fully in Chapter 12) does not necessarily exonerate Lane of adultery. One cannot always separate 'amorality'—so-called because the subject will not adhere to her society's sexual mores—from a more serious kind of amorality in which the murderer has no sympathy for her victim. *Any* murder could suggest that the perpetrator is unable to identify sympathetically with the victim, but the praise Blake received as a servant before and after the murder suggests that she was not, in contemporary terms, a psychopath. Certainly she was able to function without difficulty in her day-to-day life. If we grant that Yeomans's diagnosis is based not just on an outdated model of the psyche but also on her experience of Blake, then perhaps Yeomans (like Singer and the Stewarts) did see something more disturbing in Blake than the refusal to adhere to conventional moral platitudes. Paul Steinhauer's linking of 'defects' in conscience and impulse control with a failure to complete the work of mourning suggests one possible contemporary explanation for Blake's psychological state,[63] though one might hesitate before calling it 'mental illness'. On the other hand, social explanations of her state must be given at least as much weight as psychological explanations. Doctors and reformers in the Victorian age noted the role of poverty and economic anxiety in causing 'madness', and female delinquency has been associated with the offender's perception of blocked opportunities.[64] In any case, Yeomans's diagnosis suggests that if psychopathology is the proper language with which to approach Blake, that pathology was of a moral, not of a hallucinatory or fantastic, nature. Her correspondence with a man outside the jail makes a solipsistic Blake fantasy highly unlikely.

The problem with the third scenario—of a Blake who was free and who initiated the sexual relationship—is that it may too easily invert the stereotype of the 'passive woman', replacing it with another nineteenth-century stereotype: the 'designing woman' who uses sexuality to entrap men of position. To call the 'designing woman' a stereotype is not the same, of course, as to argue that Blake *was not* a designing woman, yet it does seem too convenient to say that in a patriarchal society a woman's sexual licence should correspond so neatly to the wayward desires of men and to a larger social disorder signified by murder. Some variant of the second scenario, in which Blake had only partial control over her own sexuality, seems the more probable scenario, but given the tenuous nature of the evidence, no final determination can be made about either the time of Blake's sexual initiation or about the extent of Robert Lane's culpability. What we can be sure of is this: that if Blake had a sexual relationship with Lane in the months leading up to the murder, whatever their personal power relations and whatever his degree of culpability, his culture had given him a social ascendancy over Blake; and she thought that the murder might put her in a better position.

What were her options? She could have had Lane charged with seduction, she could have left for another situation, or she could have sought ways to move the relationship towards legality and respectability. Each option presented practical problems. Blake would have been unsuccessful in having the charge of seduction carry through to a conviction. As Karen Dubinsky has shown, male 'seducers' occupied a privileged position in the Victorian system of sexual exchange. Men had power 'because they were men, in a society . . . which . . . punished pre- or extra-marital sexual activity on the part of women.'[65] If the relationship with Lane was only the most recent of a series of affairs for her, Blake may have despaired not only at her economic, but also at her sexual, role. It is not surprising then that, as Anne-Louise Shapiro argues, women's exalted and melodramatic stories of passion should constitute a socio-economic polemic against unequal practices and give evidence of women's hopes, dreams, and illusions.[66] Despite the magical removal of Mr Rochester's wife in *Jane Eyre*, middle-class Brandon women were not in the habit of leaping to their deaths to make way for aspiring servants. If Blake was attached to Lane, then either charging him or leaving him was out of the question.

Only Mary Lane's death could activate the third option, potentially allowing Blake a relationship with Lane on the terrain of respectability, the terrain marked by marriage. Blake's aspirations were defined within this conventional boundary: she wanted to be a wife; instead of being at the mercy of chance, she wanted a safe, upper middle-class lifestyle. Although it's always more hazardous to argue from what doesn't appear in a text than from what does, it seems noteworthy that Blake made no mention of her domestic position in 'My Downfall'. This silence could mean either that she saw her social position as insignificant compared to her existential position within the Christian drama, or it could mean that in her self-fashioning she resisted the moral-banal identification of herself as a servant—that the murder was intended precisely to give the lie to such a pedestrian identification.

*

Around 11 May 1899, the day after Elizabeth Sifton laid First Methodist's cornerstone, and not quite two months before the murder,

Mary Lane left for a few weeks' visit to Birtle.[67] For a few weeks it is possible that the two lovers had free rein. For a few weeks, Blake must have felt that she was very nearly the mistress of the house. Yet her intimate relationship with Lane was socially unacceptable—both illegal and contrary to conventional moral standards. Revelation of Blake's sexual misconduct would instantly explode her reputation, and the domestic angel on the moral pedestal would quickly be replaced by a fallen woman, a sexual succubus.

The return of Mary from Birtle, probably near the end of May, must have been intolerable for Blake. Blocked aspirations in education and employment have generally been better predictors of female delinquency than of male: after a short time of relative freedom and an expanded place in the Lane home, Blake was again a domestic, the maid-of-all-work, her space in the house again reduced to the 8 × 12 of her little room. Then in June, three weeks before the murder, one of Blake's former employers—Mrs Frank Merritt, a 37-year-old mother of four—died of pneumonia after a five-week illness,[68] reminding Blake that wives did not necessarily live forever.

At about the same time Blake read sensational newspaper accounts that put a human face on statistics relating to domestics, seduction, and unwed motherhood. Agnes Glendenning, a 35-year-old domestic who had once served a jail term in Regina for arson and who worked on a farm close to Elkhorn (very near Kola, where Blake had lived with the Stewarts), left her six-month-old, illegitimate child on the prairie to die of starvation and exposure under the May sun.[69] She had named the child after her employer, George Taylor, and swore that he was the father. Taylor denied paternity at the preliminary hearing in Brandon: 'I am not the father of the child. She never said so to me. . . . She told me someone else was the father of it.' Over the course of two days near the end of May, Taylor convinced Glendenning to search for the abandoned infant, and, when they found it, he ordered her to nurse it. It died; and many people believed that Taylor, who had a wife and family in the East, was more guilty than Glendenning. Nevertheless, even though the police initially held him as an accessory, he was never put on trial. He had, after all, reported the dead child to the authorities and according to the letter of the law was not responsible for the child's welfare. Glendenning eventually entered a guilty plea and, pending trial, was put in the same Brandon Provincial Gaol to which Blake would shortly come.[70]

Blake must have read about the case. She clearly had access to the *Manitoba Morning Free Press Bulletin*, since her gun and one of her brooches were wrapped in the 7 June edition of that newspaper.[71] In fact, the *Free Press* with its large 'Situation Vacant' section was essential reading for any servant. She would probably have had access to Brandon's only daily newspaper, the *Western Sun*, as well. On 8 June, the *Sun*'s Part II front page carried the headline 'CHARGED WITH MURDER . . . Young Girl from the West is Charged with Murder'. A short précis of Glendenning's deed followed, and local gossip would have filled in the salacious details. More importantly, the *Free Press* on 13 June devoted a large section of its front page to the story, under the headline 'MURDER CASE AT BRANDON'. Glendenning was mistakenly described as a young woman of 23, an error that would have made Blake identify even more closely with Glendenning's situation. Of 'rather respectable appearance', Glendenning was 'little moved' in court, 'only once showing signs of weakness', according to the *Free Press*; the newspaper also reported in detail the claim that Taylor was the child's father.

Taylor's response to Glendenning's pregnancy showed Blake her own possible future: the hazards of continuing in a sexual affair with a man whose wife was still alive. Blake was confronted with the vulnerability and isolation of domestic servants, even domestics like Glendenning who had family nearby. If they opted in favour of sexual pleasure and companionship, they could not, upon pregnancy, count on the willing or socially mandated support of the child's father. Europeans were already raising serious moral questions with respect to cases such as Glendenning's: 'Where is the seducer, the cause of the pregnancy? Why isn't he with the accused? . . . Responsibility belongs to both.'[72] Residents of Glendenning's hometown had similar intuitions: 'Much dissatisfaction was expressed by residents of the Fleming district over the fact that . . . they believe she was more sinned against than sinning.'[73] But such discourses had not yet filtered into Canadian law.

Seven days after the *Free Press* report on Glendenning, Hilda Blake bought a gun. On 20 June she paid a flying visit to Winnipeg—in on one train and out on the next. At a gun shop only a few blocks from the Seymour Hotel, where she registered for dinner, she asked to buy a cheap gun and left the details up to the clerk, who suggested a 32-calibre American bulldog revolver for $3 and a 60¢ box of bullets. She only wanted a few bullets, not the whole box, she said, but the clerk refused to break up the box.[74] Later she claimed that the bullets were intended to kill herself, and that the murder of Mary Lane arose from an unpremeditated fit of jealousy. However, even though Blake had suicidal thoughts, both statements are implausible, since she had already secreted enough laudanum (a solution composed of alcohol,

*Hilda Blake, c. 1899. This was almost certainly the photograph shown to Walter Sutton, the clerk at the Winnipeg gun shop who identified Blake as the purchaser of a gun and shells. (*Western Sun, *Thursday, 13 July 1899. Authors' collection.)*

water, and opium) in her room at the Lanes' to kill herself if she really meant to. As well, every chamber in Blake's weapon contained a bullet. Most importantly, only premeditation can explain why, minutes after the shooting, Blake was able to provide a detailed fictional account of how the murder took place, complete with dialogue and a description of the murderer.

In all likelihood, Blake hoped to deal more pre-emptively with her situation than Glendenning had done.[75] By going to the larger city, she naïvely hoped to remain anonymous in her weapon purchase. But she was hugely conspicuous, not just because she wanted only a few cartridges and had to be shown how the revolver worked. She was conspicuous because women simply did not buy guns: Walter Sutton, the clerk at the Hingston-Smith Arms Company, had sold guns to only two other women in his 15 years of business, one during boom times in 1883 to a woman who, it later came out, intended to shoot a man. She practised with the gun in a 'ghosting gallery' until she knew how to handle it, 'but at the critical moment her heart failed her and she broke down.'[76]

Where did Blake get the unconventional and masculine idea of buying a gun? One probable source, since she was a reader of Sir Walter Scott, is *Rob Roy*. It would be easy for a woman of Blake's mentality to pass over Scott's depiction of the self-serving servant, Andrew Fairservice, and to concentrate instead on the novel's romantic interest, the upper-class Diana Vernon. Late in the novel Diana is revealed as 'Diana Vernon Beauchamp'—a surname with unforgettable associations for Hilda Blake, who herself had been named after Hilda Beauchamp. For much of the novel Diana is, as she calls herself, 'a dependent orphan . . . a creature motherless, friendless', until her father's identity is revealed in the last pages. She is condemned to live among people who do not have her best interests at heart, her only protection a frank nature and a gun. Indeed, she can 'fire a gun without blinking', and lists among her prize possessions a 'light fowling-piece, with an improved fire-lock'. Because of her 'orphanhood', she does not have the advantage of a feminine upbringing, and her masculine attitudes often prove a debility vis-à-vis Frank Osbaldistone, the novel's hero and Diana's love interest. Through Rob Roy's wife, Helen Campbell, who takes up arms like a man, Scott does show a darker side of (and thus his uneasiness about) masculine women. Helen becomes more cruel and more culpable than the male Jacobites, yet Scott allows even Helen to win a sneaking admiration from Osbaldistone. And the relatively more feminine Diana's attractiveness easily surmounts the social handicap that her 'masculine' habits bring. It would not be surprising if her masculine sense of agency appealed to Blake.

Blake could not have known that while Scott was celebrating the exploits of outlaws, Jacobites, and masculine women, he was also, in his capacity as gamekeeper to the Duke of Buccleuch, making examples of 'little blackguards' who dared to poach in the Duke's estates.[77] Outside of novels, too, women who bought firearms immediately triggered suspicions, quite correctly in Blake's case, about both their character and their intentions.

It would be naïve to argue that media (in this case novelistic) images of guns cause readers to pull triggers, but media images do help to determine the *form* that individual actions take. In the late

'A drama in a church', from Le Petit Parisien*'s Literary Supplement, 1893. In the late nineteenth century, women brandishing revolvers became prominent in fiction, though in actuality women rarely bought guns and almost never shot anyone. (Ann-Louise Shapiro, Breaking the Codes: Female Criminality in Fin-de-Siecle Paris [Stanford, Calif.: Stanford University Press, 1996], 146.)*

nineteenth century, women with revolvers were becoming prominent in fiction.[78] It may well be that Blake saw in Diana a model who combined conventional femininity with more assertive elements. Diana was an orphan who sometimes behaved with 'unrepressed tenderness', and who, though hedged about, did not wait passively to be defeated by life: 'Everything is possible for him who possesses courage and activity', says Diana to Osbaldistone, fixing him 'with a look resembling one of those heroines of the age of chivalry'.[79] And, significantly, *Rob Roy* gave Blake the Mattie/Nicol Jarvie model for the promotion of a servant to the status of wife.

Not all hungry people riot; some are consumed by hopelessness. Desperation only triggers action when accompanied by the resources needed to plan and to act. Most importantly, there must be a will, a calculus of future prospects, a visceral determination to grasp one's chance.[80] Maria McCabe and Agnes Glendenning had acted defensively, with an overwhelming sense of their limited social positions, but Blake had a stronger will, a more heroic self-conception, and Robert Lane had given her some hope for the future.

On 23 June, three days after Blake bought the gun, Lane's team of 'bronchos' became unmanageable at a CPR crossing, turning his dray around quickly, throwing him onto his side upon the tracks, and fracturing one of his ribs.[81] Lane's was the second accident to befall McIlvride & Lane in June. Lightning had struck Alexander McIlvride's house three weeks earlier, while the family was at dinner. Although the bolt demolished the chimney and stovepipe and tore plaster from the ceiling, 'the family miraculously escaped.'[82] Did Lane, recalling his father's devout Methodism, see divine warnings in the two potentially fatal accidents and therefore draw back from Blake? Did Blake, now that she had a weapon concealed in her room, more forcefully importune Lane with estranging demands? We don't know. The gun hidden in Blake's room and Lane's convalescence in bed must have changed their relationship, but *how* we don't know. Certainly Blake's plan to use the gun had to be shelved until Lane was clear of the house.

School closed for the summer on 30 June, giving Blake the six-year-old Tommy to take care of, in addition to a four-year-old, a three-year-old, a one-year-old, a pregnant mistress, and an indisposed master. By 5 July Robert was back at work, and, since a picnic was planned for the afternoon, Blake would be alone with Mary. With Glendenning's case creating a sense of urgency and Mrs Frank Merritt's death demonstrating that a man's marital status could be changed in the blink of an eye, Blake felt that she must usurp Mary's place now. Now, or not at all.

For one unattentive to the nuances of class behaviour, the fact that Jane Eyre first inherited £20,000 and only then, as an independent woman and class equal, married her former employer might have seemed like an unremarkable, minor detail. The escapes Blake had attempted earlier in life had not appreciably injured anyone, and, even if she never quite got to the Promised Land, neither had running away harmed her. In the bolder and lethal escape that Blake would now attempt, the consequences would be more extreme, both for herself and for others. Mary Lane occupied that respectable position which Blake wanted to claim. Going beyond her literary models, Blake thus took highly unusual steps for a woman at the same time as she sought out a destiny quite within the conventions of female domesticity. Everything is possible for her who possesses courage and activity. A Cinderella in a sexually charged world, she was not ready to wait passively for her apotheosis.

6

One of the Most Atrocious Crimes

One of the most atrocious crimes in the annals of Manitoba's history and one of the most villainous that ever occurred in the Dominion of Canada took place in Brandon a few minutes after four o'clock this afternoon.

—*Western Sun*, 6 July 1899

7

He Fears Not God, Neither
Regards Man

*The most appalling tragedy that has ever been heard of
in the west was committed . . . yesterday by a member of the
tramp fraternity, the victim being Mrs. Robert Lane.*

—*Winnipeg Daily Tribune,* 6 July 1899

After Hilda Blake hid her smoking gun in the kitchen and then moved
it, later that Wednesday night, to a spot under a lime barrel in the
backyard, Brandon went through two very different stages of dealing
with the murder. The two stages tell us much about the ethos of late
nineteenth-century Canada and about Blake's liminal place in
Canada's unsettled class system. During the first stage, while the
revolver and Blake's role remained hidden, most of the town believed
Blake's melodramatic story about the tramp, circled the wagons, and
mobilized itself against this external threat. As we will see in subsequent chapters, the second stage—when the revolver came to light
and an attractive British-born domestic stood accused of murder—
was marked by class and gender puzzlement, and eventually by argument about whether or not Blake should be pardoned.

During the first stage, the wanderer outside the city's social ethos
and the baleful foreigner combined into one fearful image of disorder.
That image issued in straightforward melodrama. Melodrama, Peter
Brooks asserts:

> starts from and expresses the anxiety brought by a frightening new
> world in which the traditional patterns of moral order no longer
> provide the necessary social glue. It plays out the force of that

anxiety with the apparent triumph of villainy, and dissipates it with the eventual victory of virtue. It demonstrates over and over that the signs of ethical forces can be discovered and can be made legible.

In its social dimension the ritual of melodrama involves the confrontation of good and evil on a temporal plane, requiring 'the expulsion of one of them'. The melodramatic mode offers 'no terminal reconciliation, for there is no longer a clear transcendent value to be reconciled to. There is, rather, a social order to be purged, a set of ethical imperatives to be made clear.'[1] Emerging in the early nineteenth century as a working-class cultural form, melodrama was rooted in the understanding that life was violent and irrational and that, as in the attack on Mary Lane, tragedy could erupt at any time. Lane's murder, apparently with only a minimal motive, seemed to show that the violence and irrationality existing among tramps and non-Anglo foreigners at the edge of the imagined city could easily penetrate its heart.

In the narratives of Canadian expansionists, the West's destiny would be shaped in the struggle of the virtuous against the forces of evil. As in the biblical Garden of Eden, so in the new West, matters of morality and virtue turned partially on the conduct of women. The state of civilization in the prairie West after 1870 was assumed to rely on the willingness of cultivated and moral middle-class women to sacrifice themselves in the interests of Canada and Empire: 'Women in the West were polarized . . . into those who were regarded as the virtuous and pure agents of the salvation of (white) men and civilizers of the new region of the nation, and those regarded as the promiscuous agents of the ruin of the same.'[2] The social purity and innocence of white, middle-class women such as Mary Lane left them vulnerable to a coarse and threatening world for which they provided poignant victims. To protect middle-class women from danger and moral contamination, they must be socially and physically isolated from the lower orders and the corruption of the street. They were insulated from dirt and tramps and fates worse than death by domestic servants like Blake, who aspired to the middle class but whose present station put them, practically and metaphorically, elbows deep in filth.

The narrative of 'civilization triumphant' implicitly posed its opposite: a sudden and melodramatic outbreak of immorality and disorder, threatening women and children. Melodrama had informed Brandon's collective response to the Riel Rebellion of 1885. Brandon—that 'Eden of beauty for the habitation of a contented happy people, given not to roam or wander; not to warfare but peace, not to hunting and destruction, but pursuits of production and usefulness'[3]—rushed

Western Sun, 6 July 1899. Breathless reports of Mary Lane's murder showed that at the centre of Brandon's popular aesthetic lay melodrama. (Authors' collection.)

volunteers to the front against the non-agricultural, nomadic Aboriginals and turned itself into an armed camp. As we have seen, among the volunteers who had gone to Batoche was the 21-year-old Robert Lane of Birtle. Although at its the nearest point the 'flame of rebellion' burned 350 miles away, Brandonites viewed their city as a 'strategic point' in the line of communications with the front, a point that the enemy, by a well-executed flank movement, 'might attempt [to] capture'.[4] Will White, editor of the *Brandon Sun* in 1885, recalled that the district was rife with, and considerably alarmed by, rumours of premeditated attacks by Indians. The Rebellion disclosed the wisdom of segregating the Aboriginal population on reserves distant from communities such as Brandon, in which Aboriginal men might threaten the safety of white women. Home guards were speedily organized and steps were taken to ensure the protection of the population: 'every house became an arsenal.' White felt that 'while the city was never in danger, there always existed the dread, and the precautions taken were justifiable.'[5]

Afterwards, the Rebellion was turned quite literally into melodrama. Mr Murdock of Robert Lane's town, Birtle, wrote a poem in praise of a dead volunteer, Darcy Baker, also from Birtle. The villainy is barbarous and nearly spectral:

> By winding streams 'far o'er the plain we go,
> Where dark ravines and woody bluffs appear,
> Where'er a swarthy, treacherous Indian foe
> May hide, to burst upon our flashing rear.

After Baker is wounded, he shows the heroic Canadian imperative to struggle to the last breath against the barbarian evil:

> With shattered heart, the stricken soldier lies,
> The fatal wound has almost ceased to bleed;
> The dying warrior vainly seeks to rise,
> And begs once more, his rifle and his steed.[6]

The soldiers who returned to Brandon staged a drunken mock-battle at Judge Walker's house, 'where Brandon's B Company, advancing as war-whooping Indians, surrendered after a hard fight to the equally noisy Ninetieth. . . . The crowds loved it all.'[7] If soldiers weren't precisely the best representatives of a peaceful agricultural ethic, no matter.

In 1887 another panic, this time non-military, erupted around the Sisters Faithful Companions of Jesus, who taught at St Joseph's Catholic school in Brandon. Leading Protestant families had been in the habit of sending their children to St Joseph's, but the decision of a young Methodist teenager, Emma Clement, to become a nun transformed the Sisters of St Joseph's into folk devils who allegedly had betrayed the trust of the community and threatened to erode the moral fibre of the city's youth. The Sisters spoke of Emma as a 'Poor child, surrounded by so many dangers', and prayed 'for the realization of her desires and ours!'[8] Yet, innuendo about Catholic cabals and perversions helped to cut enrolments at St Joseph's from over 110 to about 50 as most Protestants withdrew their children. A few years later, in the deepening crisis of the Manitoba Schools Question, St Joseph's was forced to close for a time. Even Catholic nuns could seem to be a melodramatic danger to Brandon's women and children, and could provide an occasion for the city to clarify its Protestant ethic.

*

By 1899, the Aboriginal and Catholic villains had lost their roar, but new monsters threatened. Tramps, who seemed to display the most contemporary wandering resistance to regular work and to the settled order, became the latest danger to white Protestant women and to Canadian society. Tramps were outsiders at best, at worst an immediate and active evil. This was especially true of non-Anglophone Eastern European tramps, the new post-Rebellion underside to the 'Garden of the Lord'.

Preoccupation with vagrants and tramps was a growing social feature of late nineteenth-century life in North America, first emerging in the United States in the 1870s. The contempt in which such figures were held is evident in the following comments made in 1877 by the Rev. Francis Wayland, Dean of the Yale Law School:

> And as we utter the word 'tramp,' there arises straightway before us the spectacle of a lazy, shiftless, sauntering or swaggering, ill-conditioned, irreclaimable, incorrigible, cowardly, utterly depraved savage. He fears not God, neither regards man. Indeed he seems to have wholly lost all the better instincts and attitudes of manhood. He will outrage an unprotected female, or rob a defenseless child, or burn an isolated barn, or girdle fruit trees, or wreck a railway train, or set fire to a railway bridge, or murder a cripple, or pilfer an umbrella, with equal indifference, if reasonably sure of equal impunity. Having no moral sense, he knows no gradation of crime. . . . Practically he has come to consider himself at war with society and with all social institutions.[9]

Prostitutes and gamblers might trigger moral anger, and Provincial Constable John Foster, who was a former Brandon Police Chief and who helped Kircaldy in the investigation of Blake, had several times evicted prostitutes from their homes, saying 'Brandon shall not be a harbour for that class of people.'[10] But the spectre of the tramp—a figure who stood in a more mysterious kind of counterpoint to the imagined community of the respectable—drew upon more unconscious fears to become a powerful symbol of disorder, as the wide-ranging nature of Rev. Wayland's invective and the emotional response to Blake's story suggest. The image of the drifting tramp served as a charged 'other' against which to define the middle-class respectability and decorum at the centre of the city's public culture. If middle-class men strayed from their wedding vows or misused their employees with poor wages[11] and yet at the same time contributed to the community's economic growth, the tramp bore no such ambiguous relation to evil.

Some historians have argued that the 'tramp menace' really had more to do with disciplining a pre-industrial workforce than it did with any threat of violent crime. The tramp problem was a matter of growing concern in late nineteenth-century Canada not because tramps had caused an actual rise in crime but because, in their rootlessness and irresponsibility, they seemed to symbolize 'rejection of the work ethic and middle-class values'.[12] Nevertheless, Toronto newspapers in the 1880s and 1890s condemned the presence of tramps, claiming, like Wayland, that tramps 'terrorized neighborhoods, intimidated defenceless women, and committed "murders, burglaries, incendiaries, and highway robberies."'[13] Although the ethical imperatives at stake were economic, not transcendent, talk of rape and murder raised the tramp out of the mundane workplace and up into the rarefied air of ultimate good and ultimate evil. Some commentators spoke less melodramatically: tramps 'loaf and drink and beg and steal, and in the low dens and dives have a real good time. Work is their aversion.' Occasionally the lash was recommended for 'foul-mouthed tramps, who will not work, but are ever-ready to abuse, berate, swear at and threaten those who will decline to give them food.'[14]

In one of its earliest editions in 1882, the *Brandon Mail* had noted with deep sarcasm that something must have been lost on the northwest corner of Sixth and Bridges Avenue, judging from the number of inactive persons who were to be found assembled in that vicinity during mid-day. The *Mail* suggested that 'our cops should order these automata to move on as such masterly inactivity in a western town is wholly against the code.'[15] Other reports of tramp activity were less benign. In 1884, the *Brandon Sun* headlined 'The Fiendish Work of Tramps near Duluth. A Woman Killed and Horribly Mutilated'. The story that followed certainly described a fiendish mutilation, but the only evidence that tramps were responsible was a tramp fire in the vicinity.[16]

If the *Brandon Mail* could afford to be ironic in 1882, there was no such leisure after 5 July 1899. Drifters looking like the intruder described by Blake had long been a frequent sight on and near 10th Street because a spur of the Northern Pacific Railway ran behind the Lane house. Some would beg for food; in fact, the Wednesday of the murder several people had seen tramps, lending Blake's story a specious circumstantiality. The children at the tea party thought that they had seen a man run from the Lane backyard.[17] And many of Brandon's citizens, able to catch a glimpse of Mary Lane's bloodied body, had witnessed and could speak with authority about the sort of outrage that an amoral tramp was capable of committing.

In framing the story of the tramp, Blake was not very circumstantially adept, describing him so that he looked rather too much like the man who periodically mowed the Lanes' grass. However, she well knew that although domestics were low on the class scale there were others who were lower, more alien, and that by catering to Canadian prejudices she could deflect attention from herself. The insulating servant, not the virtuous middle-class woman, first encountered the tramp, Blake said, and she set the rest of the encounter into the terms suggested by her society. Mary Lane spoke *down* to the mythical tramp from the couch upon which she was standing, and Blake gave her a speech full of disdain and moral sanction for a member of the lower orders: 'Make him work for it before you give him anything.' Materially above the tramp, Mary was a middle-class philanthropist, Blake implied, but a conscientious philanthropist—not in the habit of giving handouts, but quite reasonably demanding work for food. Those terms the tramp refused; speaking a foreign word, he rejected the entire Canadian system of rational economic exchange. The social distance between Mary Lane—icon of virtue and civilization—and the shiftless and irreclaimable tramp marked the crime as one directed against the social order. While Blake underestimated the circumstantial mindset so important already in nineteenth-century police work, she correctly intuited the popular imagination: her story infuriated Brandonites and they demanded that justice be immediately visited upon the diabolical tramp.

The press quickly embraced Blake's fearsome narrative. Without question the murder was the most fiendish and cold-blooded killing ever committed in the West and the most villainous ever to occur in the Dominion of Canada;[18] only 'a member of the tramp fraternity',[19] a social outcast of the most depraved kind, could account for such a pitiless slaughter. Fearful images of a deadly tramp loose, armed, and menacing somewhere nearby terrorized the city. Explanations of the murder were framed in a narrative of invasion and of strange and anonymous danger. There was even speculation that an organized gang of tramps was moving through the province leaving a trail of mayhem in its wake.[20] Middle-class women could be victims of indiscriminate violence in their own parlours in the middle of the afternoon. Who was safe?

Blake's memory that the assailant had spoken with a foreign accent and muttered a few words in a foreign language added to the murderous wandering tramp the equally incendiary image of the foreigner—of the tramp as a racial threat. It was common knowledge that immigrants to North America came here without proper gratitude or civility.[21] Nativist anger at non-British immigrants filling the city's North End contributed to the instant credibility granted to Blake's story. The North End consisted, almost exclusively, of the primitive and overcrowded homes of working-class immigrants recently arrived, transplanted from the small towns and steppes of Eastern and Central Europe. In the city's 'imagined' community, the North End's cultural particularism stood as a kind of affront to the dominant public culture—Anglo-Protestant and Victorian—south of the tracks. The foreigners were literally hidden from view on the river flats behind the noise, dust, smell, and industrial landscape of the Canadian Pacific Railway, with its attendant livestock yards and warehouses.[22] In 1902 a headline in the *Brandon Sun* would call the North End 'Brandon's Ghetto': 'It would hardly be imagined that in the clean, little city of Brandon there would be such a class of dwellings, but nevertheless there are many houses on the flats, the interior of which would make an uptown resident wonder for the time being if he lived in Brandon.'[23] Physical separation and linguistic barriers, so latent with menace in Blake's story, ensured mistrust and social alienation. Some Brandonites dismissed Eastern European immigrants as completely unworthy of Canadian citizenship.[24]

Earlier in the year of the murder, a group of 400 Doukhobors had been welcomed with song into Brandon, and they had replied with psalms in their own language. But the *Brandon Independence*, a maverick conservative newspaper devoted to attacking Brandon's Liberal MP Clifford Sifton and his federal immigration policy, was not impressed.[25] As recently as 1 June 1899 the *Independence* had attacked the Doukhobors in editorials:

[These people cannot] live in this country on potatoes and they cultivate little else, neither can they be employed as farm labourers because of their ignorance of our language; and consequently they will fester in their squalid villages and perpetuate to future years the ignorance, the superstition, and the laziness that they have brought with them.[26]

Attacks on the immigrants also appeared in the newspaper in February and November of 1899, so Blake's eventual confession evidently did nothing to temper the *Independence*'s rhetoric. Virden's Rev. (Capt.) Wellington Bridgman would later complain that it was very costly to civilize immigrants, and that although Canadian ladies expected Eastern Europeans to solve the maid situation, the new arrivals didn't know about brooms, churns, beds, or baths. Domestic science, Bridgman noted, took 300 years to evolve in Britain.[27] He was not alone in his assessment: many Canadians believed that Scandinavians might do in a pinch, but British domestics were preferred.[28] British servants are, said Arthur Copping, 'used to nice ways in the Old Country', so 'they're more careful to keep the place clean.'[29] Presumably Bridgman and Copping would have been quite contented with Hilda Blake.[30]

After Blake announced that a foreign tramp had committed the murder, Mr Sampson called both the doctor and Robert Lane and then gave the general alarm. The city fire bell began to ring. Hundreds of armed vigilantes, people of every class stirring to a communal solidarity, assembled at City Hall to join the search for the assailant, and in echo of the North-West Rebellion to surround the city, so as to prevent the murderer's escape. As the *Western Sun* noted the next day, 'The intensest excitement prevailed.'[31] Alderman Fleming read a description of the fugitive and Chief Kircaldy organized the search, sending carriages to all parts of the city to capture the assailant dead or alive. Within minutes of the murder, the searchers swarmed the bush along the Assiniboine River north of the city. Brandon was galvanized, transformed once again into an armed garrison. R.G. MacDonald, an Anglican lawyer, offered a $100 reward for the capture of the tramp. Hardware merchants furnished guns and revolvers to any who wished. Men went in every direction, carrying shotguns and revolvers, while women and children closeted themselves at home. Armed citizens searched the trains passing through the city. After tea, the Brandon Infantry was called out, and its leader, Captain Machaffie, was sworn in as a special constable.[32] Even Winnipeg was not immune to the hysteria. Provincial Attorney General J.D. Cameron, determined to bring the culprit to justice, stayed at his office until late in the night receiv-

City Hall, c. 1901. From the steps of City Hall armed search parties were dispatched to find the imaginary tramp of Blake's story, the menacing foreigner who threatened the lives of Brandon's innocent. (*Brandon Sun* Souvenir Collection, 1901. Daly House Museum, Brandon, Manitoba.)

ing messages and issuing orders.[33] Constable A. Munro and Detective McKenzie were dispatched to Brandon from Winnipeg on a special freight train at 1:35 a.m.; the train wasn't due to leave until 4:00 a.m. but the CPR detached part of it and sent the detached cars ahead, carrying the detectives.[34]

That the anonymous murderer was a tramp and came from some unidentifiable foreign place made him doubly an alien, perfectly cast to replace Riel as melodramatic villain. The *Western Sun*, controlled by Sifton and the Liberals (and therefore least susceptible to a fear of the immigrant), found the tramp story compelling enough to describe the tramp's 'Asyrian' [*sic*] accent and to quote Mr Vinning, a farmer from near Kemnay, who had given a ride to a tramp matching Blake's description: 'He told me that he was an Asyrian. I let him out of the rig when I got to 18th street, and he said that he was going to hunt up some grub. He looked a dangerous character, and I felt much more at ease after he got out of the buggy.'[35] The *Virden Advance*, another Liberal paper, said, 'These parasites of humanity are again much in evidence in this country, and a menace to unprotected women and property wherever they are. They should be hounded out of the country at the point of the bayonet if necessary.'[36]

It is understandable that Hilda Blake—wrenched out of childhood and home by the death of her parents, cast into a difficult role on Canada's western frontier, and sensing the dangerous discrepancies between accepted mores and her own sexual experiences—should turn to melodrama. If Blake interpreted her life melodramatically in her stories of a murderous tramp and later of a 'devil, in the shape of a man', the city's reactions to the North-West Rebellion, to a Protestant girl becoming a nun, and to the tramp story suggest that melodrama was part of Brandon's, not just of Blake's, aesthetic criteria, awaiting only particular actors. This, too, is understandable. According to Judith Walkowitz, melodrama not only 'acted arbitrarily, in its very structure calling into question the operation of law and justice', but also 'evoked the instability and vulnerability of . . . life in the unstable market culture of the early nineteenth century, where traditional patterns of deference and paternalism had been eroded.'[37] If justice operated fairly consistently in the Northwest (at least for the middle class), the image of Aboriginal violence could still touch residual fears, and the volatility of a market based almost exclusively on wheat could quickly destroy one's sense of security. Blake's melodramatic fiction was attractive because it drew the town together again in the face of a perceived external threat and suggested that something could be done to resist the vulnerability of frontier life. Perhaps more importantly, traditional patterns of deference and paternalism were not readily available in the West, where self-made men abounded and a contingent class system had to be cobbled together out of money, education, moral standing, and nerve, a system that often seemed more arbitrary than natural. For an unsettled class system, melodrama was an appropriate artistic form since it emphasized moral position over heredity. That a dramatic adaptation of *Lady Audley's Secret* played to appreciative audiences in Virden in 1899 is no surprise,[38] and an immediate attack on Brandon's demonic enemy was an appropriate way for citizens to clarify their own places in the West's social order.

It did not take long for the anonymous villain to receive a name. Rumours of tramps answering Blake's description were reported not only in Brandon, but also in Douglas, Wawanesa, Sewell, Treesbank, Sidney, Carberry, Virden, and elsewhere. A number of immigrant men, such as Thomas Woycheshen, whose family had to come and translate into English the charges he faced, were detained and eventually released.[39] By Wednesday evening the most likely suspect, Peter German, a migrant worker on his way through Brandon, was captured near the CPR stockyards in the North End by Ed Field and 'a dozen stalwart men'.[40] German's Galician origins turned out to be close enough to 'Asyrian'. When he was brought to the police station, shouts of 'The rope', 'Hang him', and 'Lynch the wretch' came from the large crowd assembled there.[41] It proved difficult getting him to a cell without harm. George Hanbury, the 14-year-old son of John Hanbury, one of Brandon's richest manufacturers, claimed to have spoken to German early in the morning, and many others suddenly remembered the suspicions they had harboured about him. The power of the tramp narrative showed itself most clearly among four other boys who had been playing on the corner of Princess Avenue and 15th Street that morning. Eleven-year-old Ed Harland, one of their number, told police, 'I saw the tramp who is now in jail, sitting on the side of the road . . . putting on his boots. . . . He had a sack, and I am almost certain he put a revolver, one about eight or ten inches long, it looked to be, in his sack.'[42]

Despite his accent and clothing, however, German turned out not to fit the image of the lazy, anti-social tramp very well. A *Free Press* correspondent managed to speak briefly with him through a cell window until police put an end to the interview. German farmed near Stonewall, had a wife and two children, and was on his way home from CPR section work near Medicine Hat, having stopped for supper with a friend who lived in Brandon's North End.[43] Brought face to face with German in his cell, Blake either was not prepared to add another murder to her first crime or feared that a strong alibi on his part would call her story into question. He was not the man, she told Kircaldy. Nevertheless, perhaps he should speak, Blake suggested, in case his voice and accent were recognizable. Kircaldy asked German some questions, and after he responded in broken English, Blake declared conclusively that he could not have been the murderer. But with two boys still sure that German was the one they saw running from the direction of the Lanes' house, Kircaldy detained him and, for good measure, all the other tramps.[44]

Once the crowd that filled the market square received the news that German might be innocent, search parties were again sent out in all directions, chasing other rumours. Early in the evening 200 men left for the Iron Bridge east of the city in response to claims that a tramp matching Blake's description of the assailant had been seen there. By midnight, most of the searchers returned home, tired, but through the night the local militia patrolled the streets. The *Sun* speculated that the fugitive must be hidden in the thick brush east of the city, towards which a tramp-like figure had been seen walking and running. Some little girls out picking strawberries on the prairie had seen him, as had two men. The fugitive disappeared into the heavy, impenetrable bush, and although the men had followed and searched, they could not locate him in bush so thick that one could scarcely force one's way through: uncultivated and wild, such a landscape, like the assailant it must harbour, challenged the city's moral order. Some boys herding cattle down by the river reported a man matching the description. The search for the tramp spread along the CPR and Northern Pacific rail lines to the east, west, and even south to the United States border, but despite an ever-widening dragnet and an ever-increasing list of tramps fitting the description, no one could be definitely linked to the murder.

For Hilda Blake, worried about the gun under the barrel but still going each night to her room in the Lane house, the trade-off in lowering the status of tramps and raising her own found a brief success. She had disposed of her immediate superior and had seemingly been able to exploit the city's prejudices to blame the murder on the class below her. Not until five days after the murder were German and the other tramps released.[45] The *Morning Telegram* from cosmopolitan Winnipeg allowed itself some irony at the expense of Brandon's provincial xenophobia:

> The unfortunate foreigner did not realize his awful close call and wondered much at the rough treatment he had received in Mr. Sifton's own town. The good hearted chief [Kircaldy] bought him a ticket to Winnipeg, and sent him on his way rejoicing, and murmuring to himself something in his own language, which if interpreted . . . would mean, 'I was a stranger and they took me in.'[46]

8

I Am Guilty!

Foul deeds have been done under the most hospitable roofs,
terrible crimes have been committed amid the fairest scenes,
and have left no trace upon the spot they were done. . . .
I believe that we may look into the smiling face of a murderer
and admire its tranquil beauty.

—M.E. Braddon, *Lady Audley's Secret*

For a moment, Hilda Blake stood in the sun. Despite her low status, she was suddenly thrust onto centre stage and could almost hope to inherit Mary Lane's former position in due time. To the powerful and arbitrary and evil force at work in Brandon she had given the names 'tramp' and 'foreigner', but she knew that the names were false. Soon other people, spurred by the failure of authorities to capture the assailant and by word of police investigations into Blake's claims, began slowly to mistrust the neatness of the tramp story.

The second stage in the reaction to the murder was initiated by Police Chief Kircaldy, whose duty it was to exonerate the harried tramps fleeing Brandon and to accuse a British-born, live-in domestic of murder. Kircaldy was a handsome man in his early thirties, raised in Fifeshire, Scotland, on 'oatmeal, the Shorter Catechism and the Ten Commandments'. As a boy, he was apprenticed to a horticulturist but wanted to join the military, so he knotted a piece of string at 34 inches, and when he could expand his chest to that span 'he threw aside his gardening tools.' After a stint in the famous Black Watch regiment and a time as a staff instructor at the Hythe School of

Police Chief James Kircaldy, c. 1899. Using Occam's razor, Kircaldy solved the Lane murder case, but kept the investigation open even after Blake's arrest. (Western Sun, 13 July 1899. Authors' collection.)

Musketry in Kent, he came to Brandon in 1891, working in John Hanbury's sawmill for $1.50 a day. A year later he had applied for, and got, the job of chief constable, his police force consisting of one man. By 1899 he and his wife Rosina had three young children, and he was about to sponsor his parents' immigration to Brandon. He was also the vice-president of the Brandon branch of the Western Canada Kennel Club; his work with the Kennel Club, which gave out prizes for 'best sporting dog or bitch', must have brought him into contact with Robert Lane, secretary of the Gun Club and just the sort of man to appreciate a good chicken dog.[1] Or Kircaldy may have come into contact with Lane more directly: Kircaldy was also a sharpshooter who won a fine shooting coat in an 1897 gun competition, presumably sponsored by the Gun Club.[2]

One imagines Kircaldy a little sad-eyed at having to silence the mythic resonance that so galvanized the city's collective will. Kircaldy was no particular friend of tramps—in 1897, for example, he had arrested seven tramps who had camped just east of the city[3]—but within a few hours of the murder in 1899 he had already begun to doubt both Blake's description of the murder and her allegation that a tramp was responsible. The skin surrounding the entrance of the bullet into Lane's body was discoloured, indicating that, despite Blake's statement, the weapon used to fire the bullet had been discharged at very close range. Darkening the Lane house, Kircaldy shone a lamp from upstairs back through the first bullet-hole, and the angle of the beam proved that despite Blake's claim, the shot could not have been fired from the kitchen. Since Blake was the only other person in the house at the time of the slaying, Kircaldy began to watch her closely. On Thursday morning a 'Mr. Talbot'[4] led a few men in combing the premises and back lane in a search for the revolver. Blake, not the most careful fugitive from justice, came outside and asked one of the party, a Northern Pacific brakeman named Landsboro, if he had looked under the barrels in the backyard. It was Blake who then rolled back a lime barrel, lifted up its broken bottom, and screamed. Behold, wrapped in newspaper, a revolver and a small box of shells.[5] Perhaps she believed that assisting the investigation would in some way insulate her from suspicion, or, more likely, the 'discovery' of the revolver, like her subsequent clothing at the preliminary hearing, simply revealed another facet of her aspirations: she not only wished to move up, but also to be noticed, to be significant.

In contrast to the abrupt simplicity of the tramp story, the second stage formed slowly and opened much room for speculation. The *Brandon Times* provided a sense of the extent of the talk:

> many stories that have been going the rounds are mere conjecture. Rumours of all kinds have been circulated, enlarged upon, and woven together until a dozen or more stories of the terrible tragedy have been told. The most improbable yarns have been manufactured

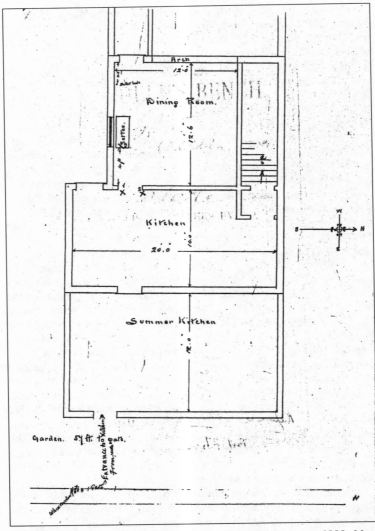

Floor plan of the Robert Lane residence, 333 10th Street, c. 1899. Mea-surements made by Kircaldy undermined Blake's story of a murderous tramp. The words at top left read 'Bullet hole'; those at the bottom left read 'Where revolver fd. +'. (Queen v. Blake [1899], Court of Queen's Bench Records, Brandon, Provincial Archives of Manitoba.)

and given out as facts to be hurriedly discussed and as quickly believed or discredited.[6]

The *Western Sun*, controlled by Sifton and therefore uncomfortable with Conservative anti-immigration hysteria, observed by Friday that even the hungriest tramp would not instantly shoot down a woman for simply denying him food—unless he had been enraged by repeated refusals elsewhere. Strangely, noted the *Sun*, the tramp had not called at any other house in the Lane neighbourhood. The revolver discovered on Thursday was new, as was the box of cartridges from which the shell had come. The average tramp in possession of a gun usually carried one that was well used, the *Sun* reasoned, while a new revolver and a fresh box of cartridges suggested that the weapon had been bought for a specific purpose. It also seemed unlikely that a tramp, after boldly firing two shots and killing Mary Lane, would leave Blake as a witness to his crime. He had had additional bullets in his gun and could have easily dispatched her.

'The housemaid', whispered the rumours, 'the housemaid'. Yet, given the prevailing stereotype of women as generally lacking the capacity for murder, those speculating about the case guessed that the maid could not be solely responsible. Many of the women convicted of murder in the deaths of their husbands were convicted on the basis of circumstantial evidence that linked them romantically with an accomplice who had committed the actual killing. The logic of such murders persuaded the police and the courts that women rarely did the killing, but usually knew of the lethal intentions of their lovers. The same logic was expected to apply to the Lane murder—someone else must have pulled the trigger or at least abetted Blake's deed.

Blake, of course, heard the rumours, and said that if she were accused of murder she would 'do something', a cryptic statement that the police interpreted as a suicide threat.[7] However, even as speculation tightened around her and Robert, and even as Mary Lane's relatives from the Binscarth area arrived in town for the funeral, Blake continued with her duties in the Lane home, while upstairs in a second-floor bedroom the body of Mary Lane lay, awaiting Saturday burial.[8]

Suddenly, and by the grace of the tramp story, Blake was, precariously, in the position that she had sought. She knew that in her beloved Scott's *Rob Roy*, when Mattie had been promoted from servant to Mrs Jarvie, she had 'behaved excellently in her exaltation'.[9] Now Blake, too, could seem to be the mistress of the home where she had once served: not just cooking but presiding over meals, not just watching the children but mothering and comforting them and Robert in their loss. Did a sexual relationship with Robert continue, furthering the illusion? Was he fooled by Blake's tramp story? Did he wilfully blind himself to what was happening? Whatever the case, Robert continued to entrust himself and his children to Blake.

On Friday evening the inquest into Mary Lane's death brought Blake back to the same courthouse where 10 years ago she had been the centre of a custody battle. Before a capacity audience and aware that people viewed her testimony with growing skepticism, she repeated her tramp story in great detail, her manner self-controlled and unfaltering.

At the very time that she lied to the inquest, a provincial detective and a doctor were busily searching her room.[10] The investigators found Sunday school tracts and a container of laudanum—for which they substituted port wine to prevent Blake from committing suicide and thus cheating justice. They left just enough laudanum to let the mixture retain its characteristic smell. Apparently Blake didn't read detective novels, since police also found a piece of the *Evening Free Press Bulletin* wrapped around a brooch, the bit of newspaper fitting exactly the one that had been found wrapped around the murder weapon. Finding that the cartridges used in the killing were not stocked by any Brandon business, Kircaldy dispatched Detective McKenzie to Winnipeg, where he discovered that both the murder weapon and the cartridges had been bought at the Hingston-Smith Arms Company a month ago. The clerk, Walter Sutton, confirmed, on the basis of a photograph, that it was Blake who had bought the gun.

Rather than make an immediate arrest, Kircaldy decided to confront Blake with Sutton. The police chief reasoned that by confronting her before she was formally aware of his suspicions, he could surprise an indication of guilt from her. He and McKenzie planned an 'accidental' meeting between Blake and Sutton. On Saturday Kircaldy asked Blake to accompany him to the police station in order to identify a suspect, and, as they walked, they encountered McKenzie and Sutton. It was apparent at once that Blake recognized the clerk: she riveted her gaze on him and spoke wildly. For his part Sutton confirmed that Blake was the woman to whom he had sold a revolver and ammunition.[11]

Still no arrest was made. Evidently Kircaldy expected to uncover an accomplice by waiting. On Saturday morning at 11:00 a.m., Mary Lane's funeral was held at St Matthew's Anglican Church, one of the largest funerals in the city's short history. Robinsons and Lanes came in from Birtle, with Tom Lane (Robert's brother) and Mr and Mrs B.

Dutton (Robert's younger sister, a convenor of Birtle's Woman's Christian Temperance Union) planning to stay in Brandon to aid Robert.[12] The Rev. McAdam Harding, assisted by the curate, Rev. Ryall, read the service:

> We brought nothing into this world,
> and it is certain we can carry nothing out. . . .
>
> Thou turnest man back to dust,
> and thou sayest, 'Return ye children of men.'
>
> . . . in the morning they are like grass that groweth up.
> In the morning it is green and groweth up,
> but in the evening it is cut down and withered.

As Mary's coffin was removed from the church, the choir sang the traditional canticle 'Nunc Dimittis', the words mostly from the Song of Simeon:

> Lord, now lettest thou thy servant depart in peace,
>   according to thy word.
> For mine eyes have seen thy salvation,
> which thou hast prepared before the face of all people;
> A light to lighten the Gentiles, and to be the glory of
>   thy people Israel.
> Glory be to the Father, and to the Son, and to the Holy Ghost.
> As it was in the beginning, is now, and ever shall be world
>   without end.
> Amen.

Meanwhile, Blake was at home, trying, according to one report, to end her life by drinking the laudanum she had bought. Its potency diluted, she did not succeed.[13]

After the service, a long cortege—the hearse, carriages containing the immediate family, and 75 private carriages containing 'citizens of all classes'[14]—wound its way south from St Matthew's to the cemetery outside the city. The mourners, shocked by the death of one so young, felt the resonance of the minister's words, 'In the midst of life we are in death.' At the graveside, earth was cast upon Mary Lane's coffin, and a last appeal made to the hope of the resurrection. Robert Lane eventually purchased a magnificent tombstone to stand over the grave, whether in keeping with his social position or out of guilt or in true grief is not clear. The stone reads, 'In Memory of Mary Robinson, Beloved Wife of Robert Lane, Died July 5 1899, Aged 32 Years. In life, in death, O Lord/Abide with me.'

The monument to Mary Lane at the Brandon cemetery made a public state-
ment about the unity of the Lane and Robinson families after the murder.
Below left, a small cross marks the infant Annie Lane's grave. (Authors'
collection.)

The next morning, Sunday, Blake apparently drew Robert's attention to reports in Saturday's *Free Press Evening Bulletin* that contained details of the police effort to identify the purchaser of the murder weapon.[15] Just before noon, while Blake was busy caring for the children and getting the mid-day meal, Kircaldy finally came to arrest her.

*

In contrast to the way that several tramps were roughly detained, the arrest of Blake was a study in chivalry on Kircaldy's part, sensibility and upper-class appropriation on Blake's part. Accounts of citizens arresting innocent tramps show the treatment that a foreign man could expect. Ed Field described how he and his companions arrested Peter German:

> As soon as I learned of the murder I went after the man. When I found him, I said to him, 'I want you.' His reply was, 'I don't think you do.' I then told him, 'Yes, you are wanted at the police station.' This was all that was said, and we took him.[16]

The arrest of a different tramp by Thomas Reid and several other men had happened with similar abruptness:

> When we were approaching near him he tried to run across a field. I got up to him, and told him I wanted him, and he replied in broken English that he would not go back to Brandon, and also said 'I am not the man.' We tried to persuade him to come with us, but we finally had to throw him in the rig.

Kircaldy soon decided that Reid's tramp was in no way connected with the murder, but kept him in jail for a few days anyway, 'as he is a suspicious character'.[17]

Blake's arrest, however, began with Kircaldy asking her to accompany him to his office. There he said, 'I have something to tell you and hardly know how to do so', before informing her that her statements could be used against her.[18] Perhaps Kircaldy, too, had read his Sir Walter Scott;[19] certainly, as one who would soon have his $5 donation to the needy Ramsden family published in the *Sun*, Kircaldy knew how a man of character ought to behave.[20] Blake, meanwhile, knew that heroines in novels, unlike the tramps who ran away or put up a fight, did not adopt lower-class methods of resistance. Instead, she broke down and begged Kircaldy to shoot her on the spot; failing that, she requested permission to poison herself with laudanum. He refused, of course. Months later, while in jail, she managed to obtain laudanum but did not use it, suggesting that her suicide requests were becoming literary and symbolic rather than real threats to be acted upon.

At the police station, she turned hysterical when Kircaldy told her that she could not return to the Lane residence to see the children one last time. She implored Kircaldy to let her bid them goodbye, and when he refused, she promised that if he allowed such a liberty, she would reciprocate with a complete confession. To this offer he agreed.

At the Lane house, Blake tearfully embraced the children. Weeping violently, she kissed each several times. According to one report, she lifted the 15-month-old Evelyn into her arms 'with most touching tenderness and sobbed over it for some time. The scene was most affecting. The children were weeping and even the police officers, with the greatest difficulty, maintained their composure, and a few tears trickled down the cheeks of the chief himself.' It was very much a theatrical scene, with Blake in the leading role, because when Kircaldy finally told her it was time to return to the police station, she was limber enough to shift roles. She shot him a wicked glance, saying, 'Oh, you cruel, cruel man; how could you do it?' Interpreting the scene's ending, the *Free Press* said, 'a little of the other spirit flashed out.'[21]

Before they returned to the station, the former police chief and leader of the Baptist Church choir—Detective John Foster[22]—concealed himself in Kircaldy's office to witness the confession. Blake gave Kircaldy and Foster what she had promised. She had shopped for a revolver with which to kill herself, she said, but then shot Mary Lane in an unpremeditated fit. Exhibiting 'some little feeling'—Kircaldy's polite way of saying that 'she completely broke down'—Blake wept and confessed that she had been overcome by jealousy over the relationship of Mrs Lane with her children and with Mr Lane:

> I went upstairs and got the revolver. When I came down I went into the kitchen. Then I went to Mrs. Lane and kissed her. She wondered what was the matter with me. Then I pulled the revolver from my pocket and fired at her head. She started to run, and I put the gun close to her back and fired again. She ran outside and fell in the hall. I hid the revolver in the kitchen and that night about eleven o'clock I put it under the barrel, where I afterwards showed the detectives where it was.[23]

The circumstantial details were thus definitively solved: both the first shot, which missed, and the second shot, which killed, had been fired at close range, not from the kitchen. The 'tramp' had appeared at no other houses, had spared Blake, and could not be found because he did not exist; the unlikely motive of refusing food was not the true motive; the gun was new because it had not been on the road with a tramp; Blake found the gun under the barrel because she had put it there herself. Occam's razor was still sharp.

*

The newly revealed style of Mary Lane's murder was not unheard of, at least in literature and among cynical wags in European metropolises:

> when you wanted to break with a woman . . . [you would] simply take the train without making a song and dance of it and allow 24 hours for her to get over wanting to shoot you. During these 48 hours she shrieks, she storms, she buys laudanum, she poisons herself, she makes a mess of it. As in all things, she doubles the dose, but when you return, you have been replaced. But today, *les revolveriennes* are no longer so nice; the 24 hours of the revolver has elongated considerably; they no longer buy laudanum but the latest model pistol and wait patiently.[24]

The modernity of Blake's style suggests a certain amount of melodramatic self-consciousness—she had been seduced by a pleasing upper-class devil and felt obliged to act the way that heroines in novels did. Many women who wounded former lovers and spouses claimed that they, like Blake, had originally wanted to kill themselves. 'An exalted language that encouraged extreme, stylized behaviors had become generally available' as a way of talking about the abjection that love was thought to bring about, and jealousy was considered to be a normal component of love.[25]

Yet Brandon remained confused. If circumstantial details and Blake's style were intelligible, the motive was emphatically *not* solved. Why did she shoot her mistress rather than her lover? And what did Hilda Blake mean by an 'insane fit of jealousy' at 'the affection between Mr. and Mrs. Lane and the children'?[26]

9

In Purple and Fine Linen

I knew I was common, and . . . I wished I was not common.

—Pip in Dickens, *Great Expectations*

Don't overdress yourself. . . . The street dress of a lady should be simple and without display. To dress conspicuously or in brilliant colors for the street is a sign of bad breeding.

—Grandma Nichols,
The Great Nineteenth Century Household Guide

That sexual jealousy was partly to blame for the murder we have already argued; but also important were motives related to social class and femininity. Hilda Blake's tears shed over the Lane children were probably genuine—she does seem to have loved the children sincerely—but tears also allowed her to downplay sexual jealousy and to emphasize her own maternal sensibility: 'If the man whom you take as your husband has children,' advised Letitia Youmans, 'be sure there is room in your heart for them, as well as for him.'[1] How much more so, if the man were of a higher class. Blake's claim that she was jealous of the children hints that she wanted not only Robert's exclusive love but also Mary's *role*—wife of a prominent citizen and mother of his children. The second stage after the killing—the revelation of the tramp's innocence—was in many ways more confusing than his guilt had been, not because citizens of Brandon suddenly had to revise the events and details of a story they thought they knew—a relatively easy task—but because the story now threatened to break through conceptual frameworks that had seemed more stable a week ago: class boundaries and (as we will see in Chapter 10) the 'feminine' personality. Blake occupied a liminal position in Brandon's Victorian order, between the family and the paid workforce. With her arrest, the causes for social disorder suddenly appeared to be inside rather than outside the garrison, and the melodrama took a more complex twist. Both the social context of Blake's preliminary hearing and the city's perception of her were freighted with notions of her standing vis-à-vis the other occupants of the Lane household, and with notions of what a domestic servant should or shouldn't do.

*

In Victorian Brandon, power and class privilege were measured neither by one person's ability simply to subordinate others to his or her will nor by one class's ability simply to control the state and the means of production. While capital, the ownership of land, and the ability to purchase the labour of others were prerequisites of class status, social position was also shaped discursively: by economic and political liberalism, by notions of respectability circulated in press and pulpit, by gendered divisions of private and public space. The entrepreneurial middle class was a class 'in continuous movement, capable of absorbing the entire society, assimilating it to its own cultural and economic level'.[2] Working through temperance unions, fraternal clubs, churches, and political parties, the middle class disseminated the values of thrift, deferral of immediate gratification, self-reliance, piety, and sobriety. These values broadened out from socio-religious discourse to areas as divergent as dress, street planning, politics, architecture, and literature. Through such contingencies Brandonites were bound to one another in an 'imagined community' of varied relationships—both reciprocal and subordinate.[3]

Within this order, the true subjects of history, those who possessed the confidence to shape it, were upper middle-class Victorian men. This class was itself divided, though not by first principles. Political partisanship, regional claims, and personal advancement could bring about vicious competition, but such conflicts were over spoils, not over first principles. There was no *one* middle class. The middle class was, like the classes below, structured hierarchically. The leading stratum was composed of families led by wealthy and powerful men, the indisputable élites of Canada's major urban centres. Mostly commercial capitalist in orientation, this stratum by the late nineteenth century increasingly drew its wealth from large industrial ventures, and after 1867 the first item on its agenda had been the acquisition of the prairie West.

Brandon of the 1890s contained families from this leading stratum: the Siftons and the Hanburys, for example. While only a few families achieved social prominence of a national character, members of Brandon's middle class—from prominent businessmen to corner grocers—embraced values and aspirations virtually indistinguishable from their social superiors. Theirs was a common sense of civic boosterism and economic expansion drawn from the currents of liberalism and evangelical Christianity. Both liberalism and Christianity legitimated the capitalist labour market, private property, the application of science and technology to the production of wealth, and notions of progress through unremitting physical labour—the labour of others, preferably. In a world where ever more systematically men employed other men and women to advance personal interests, the cardinal virtues were innovation, industriousness, decisiveness, and the dogged pursuit of success. In such ways—man or woman—one rose in society.

The belief that anyone could rise in social position also combined in Canada with an expectation that, at least on the farm frontier of Manitoba and the Northwest, British aristocrats were particularly unsuitable. 'It's a place where little is thought of wealth', reported Joseph Smith to the English Tenant Farmers, 'and more of men and character.'[4] Prosperity was better judged by landholdings than by fashionable clothing, and the clothes in which Blake had dressed the malignant tramp could not always so easily typecast their wearer: 'Donald', a man who has risen from nothing, says Arthur Copping, 'is surrounded by equally prosperous neighbours, who wear slouch hats and shabby overalls, looking to English eyes like men open to earn twopence by holding a horse.'[5] An 1895 sketch, 'The La-de-dah from London', by Kate Hayes, shows the kind of satire one could expect on the prairies: satire directed not at the rising middle class but at the falling English gentry. 'Dick Workman' escorts the English gentleman, 'D.G. Periwinkle-Brown', through a series of farming misadventures during which Periwinkle-Brown demonstrates not only the aristocracy's inability to deal with the practical matters of farming but also the aristocracy's legendary 'laziness'. An exchange between Periwinkle-Brown and Workman, just after Periwinkle-Brown has been the butt of a joke in a Winnipeg opera house, is instructive:

'Why did'nt you tell me it was'nt a place for—gentlemen?' said the La-de-dah.

Lane & Elviss, c. 1901, formerly McIlvride& Lane. The rise of Robert Lane's transfer company in the 1890s was built not only on coal, wood, and ice, but also on his ability to handle men and horses. (Brandon Sun Souvenir Collection, 1901. Daly House Museum, Brandon, Manitoba.)

'What do you mean?' asked Dick, feeling greater and stronger than ever the desire to punch this elegant young man.

'Why—er—of course—I—I mean—it was only the artisan clawse were thaw—er—and common people.'

'The Mayor of the city sat just behind you,' said Dick with asperity, 'and there were men there to-night sir, that could buy and sell both you and me out and out, and then write a cheque for twice our value in—common sense.'[6]

Men and women brave enough to put British notions of class behind themselves could succeed.[7] Those who spoke in the voices of the aristocracy had, of course, an assessment very different from that of Hayes. Mrs Cecil Hall complains, 'It would horrify our [British] farmers to have to do what gentlemen do out here. They are all their own servants.' Hall is dismayed by a servant who quits his employment rather than tend a fire in the evening so that his masters can have a kettle of hot water when they go to bed. After peeling potatoes she worries that she will never get her hands a decent colour again, yet, like Susanna Moodie victorious in the epic struggle to milk a cow, Hall twice boasts of undertaking 'the ménage' for *a whole day* when her maid-of-all-work takes holiday! Not surprisingly, Hall lasted only part of one summer in Manitoba.[8]

Some commentators celebrated 'the absence in Canada of rigid caste regulations', but others cautioned, 'England acknowledged [class] distinctions and Canada *pretended* to ignore them.'[9] According to Copping, there were only two classes in Canada: one (ranging from Barnardo boy to baronet) that made good, and one that avoided work.[10] To believe that moral behaviour and hard work rather than birth were the true mark of the individual's social value of course favoured the middle class.[11] Breaking with aristocratic notions of breeding, the rising middle class approached social position pragmatically. Status remained insecure, since a change in fortune or in behaviour could change one's status, but as long as one had some measure of economic power through which to demonstrate hard work and to exert social power, one could count oneself among those who had 'made good'.

John Hanbury, for example, had 'made good' since coming to Brandon in 1882. With only five years of education, he started in Markham, Ontario, as a farmer's chore boy. But he learned plastering, masonry, and bricklaying, so that when he arrived in Brandon he immediately began a career as a contractor and builder. He accumulated capital and 'established . . . a reputation for honesty and reliability, which formed the first round in that ladder of success.' 'Still rapidly climbing', he diversified in 1889. He acquired a planing mill (where he gave future Police Chief James Kircaldy his first Brandon job) and then entered the retail and wholesale lumber business. In the Duck Mountains he was hated because his timber crews denuded vast areas, but in mushrooming Brandon the wood was snapped up. By the late 1890s he was the 'lumber king of Manitoba', with over 150 men working under him in forest operations and in the mill, a lumberyard, and a warehouse. In 1900 the *Western Sun* reprinted a celebratory *Canadian Lumberman* article, lauding the president of The Hanbury Manufacturing Company, who 'unquestionably' stood 'in the front rank of Brandon's enterprising and successful businessmen'. Neither luck nor the abundance of opportunity was cited as being responsible for his success; rather, the article praised his ability to recognize opportunities, his 'fearlessness in attempting promising enterprises and [in] pushing them to their fullest extent . . . his keen business management and excellent executive ability; and lastly, though by no

John Hanbury residence, c. 1901. Domestic architecture expressed the position of Brandon's leading class and framed the subordinate lives of servants. (Brandon Sun Souvenir Collection, 1901. Daly House Museum, Brandon, Manitoba.)

means least important, his business sympathy or capacity to appreciate that others are at the same time alongside of himself for a place.'[12]

Hanbury's route into Brandon's leading stratum illuminated a trail that aspiring young businessmen like Robert Lane could follow. Like Hanbury, Lane diversified his operations (from coal and wood to the ice trade) and thus increased the number of men labouring under him. Like Hanbury, he also appreciated that other businessmen were 'alongside of himself'; in 1893 he praised Hanbury's products and received the following advertisement-reply in the *Brandon Times*:

> Thank you to Messrs. McIlvride and Lane for the very kind notices about our coal.
>
> —Hanbury and McNea, Agents.[13]

Enacting his growing social status, and proving that he did belong among men like Hanbury, Lane bought an impressive brick house, hired a domestic servant, went hunting with his chicken dog and his fellows in the Gun Club. The Gun Club in turn treated him with deference, cancelling its 13 July shoot out of respect for his bereavement.[14] Since in Canada there were few counterweights—few aristocrats to laugh at self-investiture[15]—middle-class attempts to rise went largely unopposed, and the hard-working Lane would have had no trouble including himself in the vaguely inclusive class that 'makes good'.

A beachhead for the expanding Anglo-British social order, the Canadian West nevertheless complicated that order by the promise of the frontier as a terrain of opportunity. The Canadian nineteenth-century context shows what is probably also true in other contexts: that 'class' was in a constant state of flux, renewing and reinterpreting itself daily, based on how people acted towards one another. If class is a series of events, then it is appropriate to speak at times as if there were many gradations between, for example, the British working class, 'live-out' domestics, live-in domestics like Hilda Blake, the Eastern European working class, tramps; at other times as if there were, broadly defined, only an upper and a lower class.[16]

The city's emergent residential pattern reflected a two-tiered social stratification in the most direct way possible. Along quiet, treed avenues named Princess, Louise, Lorne, and Victoria in homage to the British royal family's idealized domesticity stood the two- and three-storey houses of the city's élite, including that of the Lanes. The Lanes faced west towards their social equals. Through a careful mixture of initiative, ruthlessness, and philanthropy, combined with the prestige and authority derived from its position in the world of production, the city's élite, into which the Lanes were slowly merging, asserted community leadership and ensured that Brandon's most visible cultural landscape was unmistakably middle-class, Protestant, and Anglo-Canadian. Like any built environment, Brandon's ordered streets, Victorian nomenclature, intersections of private and public space, architecture of the workplace, and separation of neighbourhoods provided a sophisticated set of material contingencies that maintained class differentiation, so that Helen Campbell in her 1898 treatise *Home Economics* was perhaps not far off when she declared, 'the house is not only the result of character, but it also determines the character.'[17] To struggle against existing social roles or relationships would be to struggle against the city landscape itself.[18]

Domestic servants were *in*, but not *of*, the middle-class house. They were required to follow the behavioural and moral codes of the middle class, but their jobs did not give them middle-class status. While labour legislation and contract law increasingly shaped relations between capital and labour in the paid workforce, domestic servants remained, as Davidoff has suggested, 'closer to the age-old common law doctrine of *potestas*: children, wives and servants are under the protection and wing of the Master.'[19] Blake's relationship with Robert Lane was, in the first instance, a customary paternal one rather than a contractual one, though it is almost certain that a contract for her services existed. The process of 'making good' required first of all that one extricate oneself from the bonds of service. For Robert to 'make good' and then for the Lanes to pretend to higher status was perceived as natural, but for a servant girl to get ideas above her station was unseemly: a middle-class woman who employed a servant was thereby raised above the worst household tasks; and the servant who took them on was, by definition, lower-class. Even Cecil Logsdail, who argued that moral degeneracy increased as women entered the industrial workforce, admitted that it was housework that poorly paid female clerks fled: 'No doubt a large number of these female clerks undertake such work for no other reason than to avoid domestic duties, which they deem to be irksome.'[20]

*

From behind the Lanes' summer kitchen, one could see, distantly, the outlines of a world not created by the middle class: the East End. Increasingly, Brandon had the social geography of an industrial city, and outside the emergent middle-class residential region, the settled areas of Brandon were filling with workers' homes, including those of servants who could afford their own homes and who were thus a step above live-in domestics. The CPR main line, a block-and-a-half north of Rosser, divided both the Rosser business area (including Robert Lane's office) and the main residential area from the poor North End. Less abruptly, First Street marked the beginning of the East End, another poor, but at least Anglo-Celtic, neighbourhood. Skilled and unskilled workers of Canadian and British origin employed in the city's expanding transportation, construction, and manufacturing industries spread to the East End and a few to the far south of the city centre; these workers formed the top end of the working class, while Eastern and Central European workers in the North End formed the bottom. When an attempt was made in 1899 to unionize agricultural workers, demands were heard that 'all foreigners [be] debarred from joining', while one speaker, in more specific terms, 'objected to the Doukhobors and Galicians being admitted to the union.' Ethnic bias was joined by regional bias when other speakers argued that even Ontario farm workers be excluded.[21]   .

For Brandonites of all classes south of the CPR line, the North End represented a shoal of pauperism and vice. 'Brandon's Ghetto—Life Among the Lowly', the 1902 *Brandon Sun* story, told readers that a single house in the North End could contain three to five families: 'It would be hard to estimate the number of souls the four old walls and leaky ceiling sheltered.'[22] It was well understood that crime and violence belonged first to the North and then to the East End, that generally it would be North and East Enders who would stand in the court docket. The Canadian West was never quite a frontier in the idiom of the American West, and in most Canadian cities in the late nineteenth century, lawbreakers were typically incarcerated for minor crimes against persons and property. The records of the Brandon jail list larceny, vagrancy, assault, arson, theft, drunkenness, and forgery as the principal offences committed in Brandon in 1899. No arrests for prostitution or the tell-tale charge (if against women) of vagrancy appear in 1899. One woman was jailed for reasons of insanity, two—Agnes Glendenning and Hilda Blake—for murder, and one—Emma Stripp, whom we will shortly meet—for assisting a prisoner to escape.[23]

Lethal violence was very rare in Brandon. Before Mary Lane's murder, only two residents of the city had been shot to death, and only one of those had been murdered. In the first case the victim shot himself. During a visit to a Rosser Avenue gun shop in 1885, the city's first Chief of Police accidentally killed himself when a gun discharged while he was examining it. The other death was the only homicide since Brandon's founding. In 1888, William Webb, an East Ender, shot his wife, Mary Jane, while she stood at her ironing board and while their young son watched.

The murder occasioned no scandal or confusion, fitting directly into class preconceptions about deviance. The Webbs had lived a pauperized existence on the meagre earnings of Mary Jane's sewing and cleaning. Besides being poor, working-class, and often unemployed, William was also liable to binge on drink and had a reputation for violence. When he killed his wife, it was the second time in two years that he had shot at her. Webb's letter of confession, almost blackly comic in its simplicity, would have confirmed middle- and upper-class beliefs that the working classes lacked self-control: he 'had shot her for nagging. . . . He said it was a continual jawing day after day and week after week and that he got tired of it. It was ended now.' Interest in the case was predictably short-lived, since it only disclosed what the city already knew: that alcohol destroyed families and that there was good reason why lives lived on a more elevated terrain should run the city. Webb had been executed; a deeply flawed and guilty man had paid for his crime. Any significance to Webb's crime lay not in its challenge to conventional wisdom, but in the growing feeling that something ought to be done about the increasing urban blight.[24]

The early influence of the social gospel, which called into question Brandon's social stratification, did not appear until an 1899 *Western Sun* report of a speech by Professor Albion W. Small, professor of sociology at the University of Chicago. Small said that 'the social system in which we live and move and have our being is so bad that nobody can tell the full measure of its iniquity. . . . Socialistic indictments of our civilization are essentially sound.'[25] Later, such Utopian reinterpretations of the Christian mission would inspire western populist versions of the social gospel calling for a new social order, and animate men like J.S. Woodsworth, whose father James brought the Woodsworths to Brandon in 1885, and Rev. A.E. Smith, who studied with Woodsworth and who, during the 1919 labour revolt, would be driven from the First Methodist pulpit. But in September 1899 the *Western Sun* complained that quietist Brandon failed to honour the spirit of Labour Day.[26] 'There are no trade unions in this city, other than the railway Organizations, i.e., the Engineers, Firemen and Trainmen's Union',[27] the *Labour Gazette* reported in 1901. Generally, deference to authority, respect for hierarchy, and acceptance of subordination were still fundamental assumptions in Brandon's social order.

*

'Keep to your caste', Jane Eyre rebukes herself early on,[28] but romances such as *Rob Roy* and *Jane Eyre* seemed to tell Hilda Blake that it was possible and ideologically plausible to change one's class even in settled British society—'I have as much soul as you', Jane eventually says to the aristocratic Mr Rochester[29]—so why not in the fluidities of Manitoba? 'I call upon people here who would not have taken notice of me in England', said one successful working-class woman in Canada.[30] In Dickens's *Our Mutual Friend*, Eugene Wrayburn must be nearly murdered to do it, but eventually he braves the ridicule of 'Society' to marry the low-born but heroic Lizzie Hexam. Even *Great Expectations*, with all of its ironies against the wish to rise above one's class, depicts in visceral and sympathetic detail Pip's inability to be happy in his caste once he falls in love with the upper-class Estella. In fact, Dickens shows that there is no surer way to become dissatisfied with one's place than to serve in an upper-class house.[31]

Because western Canadian society was in flux, Blake could have expected that if she managed to marry Robert Lane, she would be able to leave her identity as a domestic behind fairly quickly. Within a few years people would owe her deference. But as long as she remained a servant, the case was different: 'No one seems to think a girl who works out good enough to associate with, except those who are in domestic service themselves.'[32] As a servant, Blake belonged to Webb's class of person, but as a Briton and a *live-in* servant, her position was more ambiguous: according to the fiction that helped keep pay low, domestics, despite their status, were minor ex officio members of the families in which they served. Blake was not 'respectable', but neither was she physically among the working class. The unsettled nature of the prairie class system, too, along with her upper-class role-playing, helped make Blake an ambiguous figure who seemed to belong nowhere.

In some quarters, of course, the choice of where to class Blake seemed easy, the rhetoric fitting a pre-existing political agenda. Press reports of her arrest all included brief summaries of Blake's remarkable journey from orphan, to poor house in England, to domestic service in western Canada at the age of 10, to apparent murderess at 21. In the letter from 'Moralist' to the editor of the *Melita Enterprise*, cited in Chapter 1, Blake's social origin—her 'blood with the taint of Cain'—explained her crime: 'Another victim has been added to the long list of unfortunates whose "tabernacle of life" has been broken into by an assassin, the output of an English slum.' The letter writer spoke of a danger to 'the lives of respected citizens and the purity of our homes'.[33] Even though Blake came from rural Britain, it is not surprising that 'Moralist' should make a rough equation between Blake and the 'draining' of 'Europen [sic] slums'.[34] And it would also not be surprising that Blake should fantasize about, or that her society should impute to her the fantasy of, becoming a nurse and putting her lower-class past behind her.

On the other hand, the kind of studied chivalry with which Kircaldy treated Blake suggests that in some quarters she *was* treated as something more than the common run of criminals, as someone nearly approximating a lady—that Blake was, improbably, having some success in her struggle against the social order. The decorous treatment may have occurred partly because Blake was British and could trace her lineage socially, if not biologically, back to the Beauchamp family. More likely, the decorous treatment had more to do with the men around her trying to demonstrate their own honour than with her actual status.

Blake's preliminary hearing took place before Brandon Police Magistrate K. Campbell on the Monday following her arrest. The Brandon courthouse in which the hearing and, later, the trial were held was an integral sign of the class landscape, showing, in a physical way, the state authority that required submission not only to a code of law but also to a code of personal deportment. Situated on four acres of property east of the city's East End, the courthouse had been constructed in 1884, following the designation of Brandon as the head-quarters for the Western Judicial District. It was an imposing structure of brick and stone, Italianate in architecture. A handsome vestibule, judge's quarters, and the offices of various state functionaries, jailer among them, comprised most of the ground floor. A wide stairway with oak steps and a walnut rail led to the second floor, where the jailer and other officials had bedrooms. The second floor also contained the grand jury room, witness room, petit jury room, judge's retiring room, and rooms for barristers. But the showpiece was the courtroom: 40 feet by 29 feet, it had a lofty ceiling with a fine skylight in the middle. The room was panelled all round, stained and grained to look like oak. Aside from space required for the dock, legal and jury sitting areas, and judge's bench, the room could accommodate 100 people. Each floor of the courthouse also contained cells, and far away from the courtroom, among heating boilers and closets in the basement, was a cell with its own kitchen, washroom, bathroom, and laundry: the 'condemned cell' into which Blake was never put.

Well before the beginning of proceedings, the vestibule on the main floor and the hall and stairway leading to the courtroom were a solid mass of people. Trials that held the promise of disclosures about sex-ual crime were enormously popular: 'Always well publicized and well attended, such trials unfolded as miniature morality plays, complete with heroes, villains, and audience.'[35] The crowd at Blake's prelimi-nary hearing was the greatest ever and, unusually, included a number of women. Inside the courtroom every seat was occupied, with some men perched on doors, and even the semi-circular fan-windows above the doors were full of faces.[36] Those in attendance had come to see the spectacle of a young murderess at the centre of a story, which, unlike the mundane events and working-class flavour of the Webb case, was as sensational and mysterious as any contained in fiction. The solem-nity of the courtroom and the earnestness of the proceedings promised judicial scrutiny of a case riven with questions of Blake's motive, of Robert Lane's role, and of relations between the classes.[37]

Yet the hearing took almost no time, since Blake didn't contest the charge. When the court was called to order, Dr J. McDiarmid testified that Mary Lane had died from hemorrhaging caused by a bullet that had pierced her left lung. He concluded that she had succumbed within minutes of the assault. The bullet—a blunt, battered piece of lead removed from Lane's body—was entered as evidence. Chief Kircaldy then testified that he had arrived at the scene shortly after Lane had been shot. An inspection of her clothing suggested to him that the murder weapon must have been held within six inches of her when it was fired, for her clothes and skin under the left shoulder blade had been burned at the point of the bullet's entry. It would have been impossible, he said, for an assailant to have inflicted the wound from the distance originally claimed by Blake. The person who fired the murder weapon had to have been standing immediately behind and slightly to the left of Lane. Kircaldy went on to describe Blake's confession, and Detective Foster confirmed his story.

What to spectators and to the newspapers produced more of a stir than the details of the murder was Blake's attempt to create a dignified courtroom appearance in both apparel and behaviour. Her clothing and demeanour revealed both her own social hopes and, ultimately, her society's attitude towards those hopes. Neatly dressed in a black cashmere skirt and a blue-and-white striped cotton blouse, she also wore a checked Windsor silk tie and black cashmere gloves. Dramatically topping off the effect was a white sailor hat with a purple band. She entered the courtroom with her head erect, her person 'calm and fully possessed'.[38] When Magistrate Campbell invited her to put questions to the witnesses, she told him that she had no intention of putting any questions to anyone. She could not, under the circumstances, escape responsibility. At best, she could implicate others, but this she was not willing to do, at least not at that time. Emulating the heroines of ballads who preferred 'death before dishonour', she refused to present any evidence in defence, and declared, 'I want to say that I am guilty, and I want you to inflict the severest punishment upon me that is all.'[39] She struggled for composure, 'but her lips trembled and the short statement ended in a sob. The scene was affecting and the magistrate was suddenly very busy with his papers', while Kircaldy looked down and the jail governor, Richard Noxon, used his handkerchief vigorously. Even Crown prosecutor R.M. Matheson covered his face with his hands.[40]

She was no menial, her outfit and behaviour said, but an honourable lady in tragic circumstances. For her, the danger was that being a friendless orphan, she might also seem one, like the dishevelled Biddy in Dickens's *Great Expectations*[41] or Oliver in *Oliver Twist*:

What an excellent example of the power of dress young Oliver Twist was! Wrapped in the blanket which had hitherto formed his only covering, he might have been the child of a nobleman or a beggar. . . . But now that he was enveloped in the old calico robes, which had grown yellow in the same service, he was badged and ticketed, and fell into his place at once—a parish child—the orphan of a workhouse—the humble, half-starved drudge—to be cuffed and buffeted through the world,—despised by all, and pitied by none.[42]

If she had read *Oliver Twist* and *Great Expectations* by this time, they would have confirmed for her that although a well-to-do farmer might go to town in a slouch hat, a lady in court must make a good impression. In *Great Expectations*, Magwitch, who looks like 'a common sort of a wretch', is condemned while the evil but aristocratic Compeyson goes free.[43]

The theatrical character of the event and Blake's role as the central dramatis persona were not lost on newspaper reporters eager to portray the scene in the language of sensation. Under the headline 'The Menial Attires herself in Purple and Fine Linen', the conservative *Winnipeg Morning Telegram* gave Blake's dress and demeanour a third of its trial reportage, insinuating that she was an overreacher, one who dangerously presumed to be higher than she was.

Such pretensions were, of course, unacceptable. It was not just the murder that was wrong, but also the wearing of purple and fine linen. Women in general, not just those of humble status, were enjoined by manners books to dress themselves with decorum: 'Don't overdress yourself', said Grandma Nichols in the etiquette portion of her 1894 homemaking guide. 'The street dress of a lady should be simple and without display. To dress conspicuously or in brilliant colors for the street is a sign of bad breeding.'[44] If even 'ladies' (Nichols appropriating for her North American middle-class audience the language of aristocracy) ought to be moderate in dress, then servants who gave themselves airs or who loved finery could only be regarded as ridiculous or insolent or simply as engaging in pursuits that a servant ought to have no time for.[45] 'Do not give a chambermaid clothes above her station, do not encourage pretension or idleness in any way', wrote a Canadian lady.[46] French commentators of the period argued that a woman who gave herself airs above her condition would not be a suitable spouse for a working-class man and would be easy prey for upper-class philanderers.[47] Until the early nineteenth century the betrayal of the authority of one's employer by killing him, his wife, or his children had not been 'murder' but 'petty treason', and the reaction in some quarters to Blake's overreaching may have owed its flavour to a revulsion that added to murder the social revulsion against a servant who was opening the road to anarchy.[48]

Raymond Williams has observed that 'no mode of production, and therefore no dominant society or order of society, and therefore no dominant culture, in reality exhausts human practice, human energy, human intention.'[49] Dialectically, the existence of conventional social roles, relationships, and meanings posed the possibility of the alternative, putting the hegemony of the naturally ordained, the virtuous, and the respectable under perpetual siege. While Blake did not pose an alternative to the dominant culture, her appropriation of élite roles put those roles under question. The style in which she appeared in the courtroom, along with the problematic motive she gave for the killing, indicates that the *Telegram* got it right: she refused to accept the identity of servant-girl-of-questionable-character that the *Telegram*, among others, was eager to impose on her.

Yet Blake, like other live-in servants, had to deal with an unbearable social ambivalence. If she dressed and behaved in a way beneath middle-class standards, she would be classed as an unregenerate person not deserving of courtesy or sympathy. If, however, she presumed to dress and act the lady, as she did at the preliminary hearing, certain quarters of society would quickly and roughly remind her of her place. *Theoretically*, Blake's hard work as a servant should have identified her as one (in the class structure) who was in the process of 'making good'. *Practically*, however, while unremarkable immigrants were turning into fuel and transfer merchants, 'timeless' forms were maintained beside rapid change. Since domestics were wanted for menial tasks and could display no measuring sticks of power, wealth, advanced education, or moral superiority, theory proved deceptive and the 'timeless' European distinctions between gentry and commoner were transposed, *mutatis mutandis*, into the distinction between the successful and the poor.

Of course, neither purple and fine linen nor an acceptance of responsibility could alter the crime that Blake had committed. The evidence presented at the preliminary hearing was clear enough to put her in the docket, and a trial date was set for late November. Until then she was to be held in the Brandon Provincial Gaol. Her stay there proved eventful.

10

Now I Feel Ashamed

If she had been faultless, she could not have been the heroine
of this story; for has not some wise man of old remarked, that
the perfect women are those who leave no histories behind
them, but who go through life upon such a tranquil course of
quiet well-doing as leave no footprints on the sands of time;
only mute records hidden here and there, deep in grateful
hearts of those who have been blest by them.

—M.E. Braddon, *Lady Audley's Secret*

As puzzling as questions about Hilda Blake's place in the class order
were questions about her femininity. Tramps, everyone knew, could
be violent and potentially murderous, but women outside of fiction
did not buy guns, never mind shoot other women in the back. When
the Brandon Collegiate Literary Society debated 'Women's influence
for good is greater than man's', the affirmatives won hands down.[1] In
The Female Offender (1895), the influential nineteenth-century
criminologists Cesare Lombroso and Guglielmo Ferrero had codified
what everyone knew: the '*occasional* [female] criminal' did her deed
remorsefully, only in great extremity; or reluctantly, only at the suggestion of a heartless lover; and her femininity could even be admired
if she later shaped her testimony to defend that heartless lover in
court. On the other hand, the radically different '*born* [female] criminal' showed neither altruism nor self-sacrifice, and 'a strong proof' of
her 'degeneration' was 'the want of maternal affection'.[2] Some of the
events during Blake's jail stay—notably the fear she raised in the

prison matron and Blake's 'escape' attempt—joined with the original crime against Mary Lane to make Blake seem very different from those abject women who remorsefully aborted their fetuses or lashed out in revenge against lost honour. Yet at the same time she appeared within the sphere of conventional femininity—claiming that she had kissed Mary Lane before the murder, bidding a tearful and maternal farewell to the Lane children, placing herself at Kircaldy's mercy, and, above all, refusing (sacrificially it seemed) to implicate Robert Lane at the trial.

Just as Lombroso and Ferrero maintained, it was indeed unusual for women to engage in violent crime; women who murdered contradicted generally held beliefs that women were inherently passive and necessarily moral. In Canada from 1867 to 1899, of the 274 individuals convicted of murder, only 13 were women.[3] Violent women were understood to be pathologically abnormal, and it is not surprising that the terms 'moral insanity' and 'monomania' were used, respectively, to characterize Blake and Susan Kennedy (who also killed a woman), or that the Canadian state used an insanity diagnosis to stop the execution of women much more regularly than the execution of men.[4] Despite what was depicted in novels and in *au fait* French magazines, those few women who did murder other women almost never used guns. The doctrine of separate spheres and the cult of domesticity framed the conventional boundaries of femininity in nurturing and domestic roles, making a woman such as Blake—who didn't seem to fit prevailing stereotypes—newsworthy.[5]

Yet in Britain from at least the 1880s, not only feminists but also muckraking journalists and novelists challenged conventional portrayals of gender and class. Scandal involving sexuality and gender became a recurring public theme. The rapidly growing popular press ensured that the public rendering of these 'scandals, causes célèbres, and exposés' permitted struggles over the meaning of sex and sexual danger.[6] Internationally, the celebrated case of Florence Maybrick, and in Canada, the cases of Olive Sternaman and Cordelia Viau, all accused of murdering their husbands, remained before the public.

The new and troubling images of women challenging conventional boundaries of femininity were to be found as well in the fiction published in newspapers, monthly magazines, and cheap mass-produced American editions of novels ranging from pulp fiction to Eliot, Hardy, and Dickens. In the British 'Sensation novels' of the 1860s and 1870s, the heroine typically displayed 'vulnerability, rage, violence, lust and vengeance as part of the range of female emotions'.[7] Murder was within her repertoire. Women who shot and poisoned their way through Victorian fiction introduced 'the revolutionary idea that women [were] . . . capable of committing almost any crime to achieve their personal goals', even though their goals were 'almost always highly conventional: romantic happiness and financial security through marriage'.[8] While fiction retained the Victorian idiom of women as saintly, yielding, forgiving, and moral—or, conversely, as passionate, wilful, violent, and seductive—nevertheless, by exploring and expanding the frontiers of femininity, these fictional accounts of violent women popularized a new sense of female agency.

Crime statistics suggest that women did not directly imitate the criminality of the heroines, but women did come to identify with the heroines' sense of freedom, and part of the reaction against Thomas Hardy, for example, reflected the fear that his work was dangerous to feminine morality. Hardy's *Tess of the D'Urbervilles* (1891), the sympathetic portrait of a working-class girl executed because she had stabbed a man who had exploited her for sexual ends, was rejected by three publishers. Its content was deemed unsuitable for Victorian audiences, and when it was finally published it was received with hostility as 'an extremely disagreeable story'. One reviewer dismissed the tragic heroine as nothing more than a 'little harlot'. Indeed, much of late nineteenth-century fiction was condemned by moralists for allegedly making vice appear attractive and violence natural.

Such reactions led Hardy to argue, in 'Candour in English Fiction', that the 'great bulk of English fiction of the present day is characterized by its lack of sincerity.' Novelists must, he said, deal candidly with 'the position of man and woman in nature, and the position of belief in the minds of man and woman—things which everybody is thinking about but nobody is saying.'[9] Nevertheless, or perhaps because of the reaction, Tess sold rapidly. Second, third, and fourth editions sold in a matter of months. In Canada, Hardy was both praised—'Tess may have a warm corner in many hearts'[10]—and criticized: 'Even Mr. Hardy, great writer as he is, has been led away by this dangerous gift [of depicting actual life with an unsparing hand]—witness his "Tess of the D'Urbervilles"—into unpleasant paths which he hitherto knew not, and to the depicting of unsavory details.'[11]

Hardy went further in *Jude the Obscure* (1896), depicting a woman who reacted rationally, not instinctively, against the structures of conventional marriage. In his postscript to the 1912 edition, Hardy noted approvingly the assertion of a German critic who had concluded that Sue Bridehead, the heroine of the novel, was:

the first delineation in fiction of the woman who was coming into notice in her thousands every year—the woman of the feminist movement—the 'bachelor' girl—the intellectualized, emancipated bundle of nerves that modern conditions were producing, mainly in cities as yet; who does not recognize the necessity for most of her sex to follow marriage as a profession, and boast themselves as superior people because they are licensed to be loved on the premises.[12]

Largely because of the hostile reaction to Sue Bridehead and to *Jude the Obscure*, Hardy wrote no more fiction for the last 30 years of his life. In Canada, too, Sue was perceived as a danger, because 'any treatise on hysteria which is thrown into a captivating popular form, and makes hysteria look like an interesting and romantic thing, will spread the malady.'[13] The fear of the New Woman was felt strongly:

Now, any average man looking at women, as, thank heaven! most of them are, recognizes in them beings more refined than himself; more merciful than himself; naturally and instinctively purer than himself; and altogether having less of the brute, if less of the demigod, in their natures than he has. But this debased type, now known as the 'new woman,' has always endeavored to show him and now has triumphantly done so, that a woman can be as coarse and vulgar in soul as a London costermonger.

'Truly' advanced women, on the other hand—Elizabeth Browning, Charlotte Brontë, George Eliot, Olive Schreiner—were worthy of praise.[14]

However, 'behind the paternalistic Victorian dogma that women were morally superior to men lay the age-old image of women as wild and degraded or evil and therefore capable of the most awful deeds.' Because she was the repository of emotion rather than reason, woman's sensibility could easily turn into its opposite, disordered mania. The notion that women who committed violent crimes 'acted from individual rather than environmentally produced motives and that there was something wrong with them . . . ran as a constant theme through the journal articles, charges to juries, and crime histories of the century.'[15] H.L. Adam's characterization of women in *Women and Crime* was typical of turn-of-the-century thinking about women's capacity for evil:

One of the most staggering and repugnant attributes . . . exhibited by bad women is their perfectly fiendish cruelty. It is all the more startling by being displayed by one who is supposed to be gentle by nature. It is certainly a matter for meditation that the cruelest forms of crime are invariably committed by women. Some of them indeed are so terrible, both in conception and execution, as scarcely to be credited to human agency.[16]

Adam's analysis reflected both traditional notions of the potentially evil character of women and newer biologically based notions that violent women were simply reflecting a greater capacity for atavistic behaviour than men, whose reason had evolved further. In the emerging discourse of medicine, unbridled women were portrayed as pathologically abnormal, an evolutionary throwback to an earlier, less rational stage in human development.

*

Portrayals of Hilda Blake both by herself and by others reflected the expanding range of identities and meanings that shaped popular versions of femininity. If particular character types rose out of particular moral frameworks, it became difficult to place Blake. The hints about Robert Lane's possible involvement not yet public knowledge, Blake did not fit into any particular image of female degradation, including that of the anarchistic New Woman. She had killed her mistress, but she also seemed to be hard-working, trustworthy, and proper in speech—not intellectualized or emancipated or vulgar.[17] Commentators on the Lane murder puzzled over whether to give greater weight to the deed itself or to the feminine attitudes Blake displayed before and after. The journalistic depiction of Blake as a woman consumed by social pretensions resonated with that of the destructive woman of Victorian literature who was 'generally motivated by pride or physical passion',[18] but there were unspoken questions that reached farther. Was the murder an insane and momentary departure from the norms of gender? Or was irrational and reprehensible female violence simply the flip side of an admirable but still irrational female devotion? More problematically, were there perhaps women who existed outside of the bounds of femininity?

Because of the aggressiveness of the murder, many people felt that Blake must forfeit the sympathy usually granted to women in tight circumstances. In Winnipeg the *Manitoba Morning Free Press* responded to Blake's confession by hyperbolically refusing to call her a woman: 'the details of the deed are most dreadful, showing a diabolic coolness and more cursed malevolence than could be expected from the most depraved member of her sex.'[19] If the *Free Press* did not exactly call her 'masculine', the rhetoric nevertheless corresponds with those nineteenth-century experts who said that individuals with inverted gender roles—'masculine' women and 'feminine' men—were susceptible to criminality,[20] a susceptibility that contemporary studies do not verify.[21]

'Moralist' in the *Melita Enterprise* also dismissed Blake's spurious female sensitivity, but without denying her femininity as such:

> The press tells us that the assassin 'clasped to her breast and repeatedly kissed' her victim's children, while 'strong men' looked and were deeply affected by it. The spectacle of a murderess, reeking with the mother's life-blood, slobbering over that mother's helpless, innocent children is truly a pitiable sight, and one that might well move 'strong men.' When those children arrive at years of understanding and know that, that thing was? [*sic*].
>
> We had grown accustomed to the rotation of female buzzards swooping down with bouquets and dainty deserts [*sic*] upon male criminals, but who shall classify those 'strong men' who dropped the chaste tear of sympathy into the lap of female crime?[22]

By thinking of the murderess as a particular kind of person and by adhering to the category of 'female crime', 'Moralist' discounts both the 'momentary departure' theory and the 'masculine woman' theory, and implicitly makes Blake's violence the atavistic and demonic parody of feminine love, its flip side.

Yet many of Blake's actions did not fit her comfortably into masculine or feminine stereotypes and thus confirmed neither the *Free Press* nor 'Moralist'. Blake's requests to be allowed to kill herself and, failing that, to bid goodbye to her young wards were the 'correct' and melodramatically feminine responses to her arrest, since they emphasized her remorse, her honour, and her place in the sphere of idealized femininity. Her 'confession' that she had kissed Mary Lane before killing her and her scolding of that 'cruel, cruel man', Chief Kircaldy, who pulled her away from the Lane children, also emphasized her femininity. It is significant that recent studies do show greater delinquency in women who advocate traditional feminine roles but who feel unfeminine themselves.[23] We have no way of knowing whether Blake actually kissed Lane, but by *saying* it had happened Blake could obviously do more than simply declare Mary Lane's goodness. Blake felt keenly that the murder had banished her from the sphere of the feminine, and she wanted to recuperate that sphere.[24] By publicizing the kiss, Blake would in some measure qualify the 'masculine' acts of buying a gun and shooting her mistress, qualify them by demonstrating her essential femininity—though, as 'Moralist' knew, there were logical convolutions required if one wanted to accept that a kiss *before* a murder could demonstrate remorse!

One late Victorian solution to the masculinity/femininity problem in crime was the 'love-mad' woman, and here the illogic of Blake's confession would not necessarily have damned her. Love-mad women in fiction date back to Ophelia, Dido, and Medea, but nineteenth-century authors found such figures particularly compelling.[25] According to Lombroso and Ferrero, love-mad women existed in reality. They belonged to the 'Crimes of Passion' category of young offenders, 18–27 years old: 'Strangers to the coldness of the normal woman, they love with all the intensity of Heloise, and take a real delight in sacrificing themselves for the man they adore, and for whom they are ready to violate prejudices, custom, and even social laws.'[26] Blake, who was orphaned at a young age and who had, according to reports, wanted to kill herself with laudanum, could be so explained. The rumours that someone else was involved in Blake's fall contributed to such an image, and later, when Blake's letter to a person outside the jail became public knowledge, the image took on fuller substance. It may even be that by claiming to have had a sudden fit of jealousy, Blake was invoking the traditional female disease of 'hysteria' as a possible explanation for her actions.[27]

One would naturally expect that little sympathy would arise for someone who had murdered her mistress and who pretended not to be a servant. But in fact Blake generated a great deal of sympathy, despite 'Moralist' and the *Free Press*. Blake's courtroom persona as a self-confessed and remorseful murderess who demanded the gallows touched the emotions of many spectators. 'The girl feels her position keenly and is anxious that her death should take place as soon as possible', said the *Western Sun*.[28] The generally unsympathetic *Brandon Independence* reported that, following Blake's confession at the preliminary hearing, 'she stood seemingly beyond all feeling; whilst there was hardly a dry eye in the court; and sympathy, in spite of her awful crime, was actually felt for the prisoner.'[29] Even the unsympathetic *Brandon Times* called the scene one of the 'most touching ever enacted in a Brandon court room'. Blake's face, reported the *Times*, 'was livid and drawn showing the unutterable pangs of remorse for her terrible crime. Every head in the court room was bowed and tears were on the faces of strong men who on Wednesday last were calling for vengeance.'[30] Blake, fully feminine, was paying now for a moment of insanity.

Brandon men, too—despite any journalistic satire about 'purple and fine linen' or 'strong men' dropping 'chaste tears'—knew that a

Southwest view of Brandon Courthouse and Gaol, c. 1901. Blake was eventually buried in the northeast corner of the prison courtyard. The courthouse is now part of Rideau Park Personal Care Home. (Brandon Sun Souvenir Collection, 1901. Daly House Museum, Brandon, Manitoba.)

woman, particularly a woman with a bit of a patrician air, could not be treated as one treated a male hobo. Although Blake had committed the same crime as the hypothetical tramp did, what was important afterwards was not the crime but the enactment of class and gender roles. 'I have something to tell you and hardly know how to do so',[31] Kircaldy had begun when he arrested Blake. The chivalrous police chief, the papers agreed, was not merely a shrewd detective, but the right sort of man: 'The extreme humanity he displayed towards the unfortunate woman has won everybody's approbation.'[32]

*

Instead of placing Blake into the Dickensian condemned cell or elsewhere in the basement of the Provincial Gaol, Governor Noxon furnished the jail's chapel for her into something that approximated a woman's sitting room or parlour. When Blake arrived in jail on 10 July, Agnes Glendenning (the domestic who had left her infant child to die on the prairie) was already there, having come on 27 May, and staying until her sentencing on 22 November, after which she was transferred briefly to Stony Mountain Penitentiary and then further afield.[33] A report shows that in mid-November 1899 there were seven men and two women confined in the Provincial Gaol.[34] The men were housed in the basement and Blake got the chapel. Although we don't know for certain where Glendenning stayed, it seems that no special arrangements were made for her.

Blake's chapel/cell, located on the main floor of the courthouse, was large. Besides a mattress, the room contained a few benches, a large table, an organ, a reclining chair and several arm chairs for entertaining visitors, while the walls were adorned with scenes from the life of Christ. A number of plants added a domestic touch, and through the large, barred windows Blake could look down on the prison garden. The *Brandon Times* spoke of the 'cheerfulness of the room' and of 'comforts not usually found in a prison cell'.[35] Needless to say, the 35- by 15-foot chapel[36] was not typical of the circumstances in which most prisoners found themselves; and indeed, it was probably the largest, most luxurious room that Blake had inhabited in her entire life.

Blake's youth, beauty, bearing, and lack of previous convictions probably influenced the creation of such a feminine place, although these factors would ultimately not mitigate her sentence. Agnes Glendenning—'plain-looking', almost middle-aged, clearly lower-class, convicted once already for arson, and called 'a natural born thief'— was not the object of such solicitousness, though in her case, too, such factors did not prejudice the sentencing.[37] At the time of sentencing, the actual crimes of Blake and Glendenning would loom much larger, but in the choice to transform the prison chapel into a sitting room, Blake's youthful femininity and her often patrician demeanour fit well into notions of the family and of 'separate spheres' that were beginning to influence attitudes towards female imprisonment.[38] What Naffine calls 'the nice girl construct'[39] was operative: Blake's criminality was viewed as an aberration, and informal controls were now coming into play to bring her back to feminine standards. Her behaviour in the 'cell', however, suggests that she could not be disciplined quite so easily.

*

While Robert Lane's sister, Mrs B. Dutton, returned to Birtle and sent her daughter Bella in her place to help Robert with the children,[40] Blake's main visitors in the chapel were Chief Kircaldy—still not completely convinced that Blake had acted alone—and Rev. McLaurin, whose presence Blake had requested immediately after she was first arrested. Despite the luxurious cell, Blake knew what the future held, and for a time she refused to eat, declaring, with high drama, that she intended to starve herself to death. By 10 August the 'suicidal' mood had passed and she began to partake of 'Mrs. Noxon's delicacies' again.[41] The *Virden Advance* could thus report that 'the Brandon murderess takes her confinement to jail very coolly and does not waste her time in tears or lamentations. She eats well and is most of the time quite light hearted.' Besides hunger, two things may have reconciled her to jail. Although the *Advance* claimed that she listened to McLaurin's ministrations 'with comparative indifference',[42] she nevertheless planned, at McLaurin's urging, to write an autobiography;[43] second, on 1 August, three weeks after Blake was first incarcerated and under special instructions from the Attorney General's department,[44] Noxon had hired Emma Jane Stripp, 'an aged lady',[45] to serve as a prison matron for Blake.

The logic behind Stripp's hiring was the same as that behind the chapel/cell and that behind Canada's first adult reformatory, the Andrew Mercer Ontario Reformatory for Females. This institution, first opened in 1880, was to be 'as free as possible from prison appearance, while possessing the solidity necessary to it'; inside, a female superintendent and an all-female staff would 'mother' their charges 'into respectable womanhood'.[46] Similarly, Noxon ordered Stripp to keep Blake under close observation, to prevent anything being brought to her in jail, and, above all, to prevent any suicide bid. Every night, Stripp was locked into the chapel with her ward, while a male guard settled down to sleep outside the door.

Stripp ran a restaurant on 8th Street near the train station: 'The right place for meals. Hot supper is always ready when No. 1 arrives whether late or not. Fried oysters a specialty.'[47] But she must have had trouble making ends meet and so took on the matron job. Her credentials were similar to those required at the Mercer Reformatory: 'any respectable woman possessing motherly virtues', to quote Carolyn Strange.[48] Kircaldy had known Stripp for eight years and thought her a law-abiding citizen, as did Noxon.[49] Others agreed, even after the events that would eventually lead Stripp into a criminal conviction and a jail term. A.C. Fraser, who had boarded with her in Wingham, Ontario, in 1878 and was now a successful merchant in Brandon, called her 'a law-abiding woman, an industrious well meaning woman'. Another friend from back in the 1870s, Mary Jane Jobb, was a bit more specific about what 'well meaning' meant; Jobb said that Stripp allowed herself to be imposed upon: 'She was a large hearted woman, a good kind hearted woman. She worked hard and gave it all away I often said.'[50] Yet as a lower-class woman both easily convinced by appeals to mercy and easily brow-beaten by those around her, Stripp was especially unqualified to manage a young woman of spirit and of no little cunning.

The Stripp family had come to Brandon after residing in Chicago, Toronto, and Wingham. Emma, with her two children, was already in

NOW I FEEL ASHAMED   155

Brandon by 1891 and running a restaurant, though her husband Frederick, a sometime carpenter, worked elsewhere.[51] In 1899 the family
lived in a poor area on Pacific Avenue. The Stripps had not thought it
important to have their children, Ella and Fred Jr, baptized at birth, and
in 1891 Stripp listed her religion as Baptist. But in 1892 and 1894, at
the ages of 15 and 23 respectively, the two children were baptized at
Mary Lane's church, St Matthew's Anglican—perhaps in the hope of
rising in class—and the children both married there, in 1897 and 1898.
Jail records for January 1900 list Emma Stripp's religion as Church of
England, too.[52] It may have been Stripp's connection with St
Matthew's that got her the matron job. G.R. Coldwell, the prominent
Brandon lawyer who had acted as Mary Rex's solicitor and who
would later be offered to Hilda Blake as court-appointed counsel, wor-
shipped at St Matthew's.

What exactly happened between Blake and Stripp on those nights is
subject for conjecture, but we know that in early September, Stripp, of
previously good character, smuggled into jail a file and some laudanum
(watered down, Stripp said),[53] and began to carry notes from Blake to
another person outside the jail. Evidently Blake realized, having read
Dickens, that the first order of business for any prisoner was to get a
file. In the opening pages of *Great Expectations* the convict Magwitch
binds little Pip with curses, and demands, 'You get me a file. . . . And
you get me wittles.'[54] Having succumbed to Mrs Noxon's delicacies,
Blake didn't need 'wittles', but she convinced Stripp to get a three-cor-
nered file from Fred Jr's tool box and enclose it inside a volume of
Dickens (whether this was an appropriate use or not of Dickens's work
we will not presume to say). With the file, Blake sawed partway
through one of the iron bars of her window—three-quarters of the way
through at the top and about one-quarter at the bottom. She carefully
concealed her work with a mixture of bread dough and stove blacking.

Such intrigue suggests a masculine sense of agency, yet the filing
could not have been a serious attempt to escape, because Blake was at
it for weeks and used more than one file. Rather, the 'escape' attempt
was a pastime, a bit of social theatre that Blake, once so perpetually
busy as a domestic, would play until discovered, a melodramatic fantasy interesting enough to beguile the hours, feasible in the pages of
Rob Roy but not, as she knew, in provincial and quotidian Brandon.
Unlike her running away from the Stewarts or her killing of Mary
Lane, Blake went less hopefully about this final attempt to escape her
condition, going through the motions and then playing up to Kircaldy,
as if she no longer had much faith in her own agency, no longer knew
where to go once she broke through the window.

Why did Stripp help? She claimed that she did not intend to aid Blake's escape. One explanation that Stripp tried out in court was that she was attempting to extract a confession. Such an explanation bordered on the ludicrous, since it would have been hard for Stripp to fool even herself (never mind the court) that a confession was needed when Blake had already confessed—though perhaps Stripp, like Kircaldy, yearned to discover that a man, and not Blake, was the principal culprit in the murder.[55] One Lane family story extrapolated rather boldly (not to mention anachronistically) upon the evidence, suggesting that Stripp was allied to a woman's liberation group trying to break Hilda out of jail.

It is possible that Stripp did sympathize with Blake, but any full explanation must include Stripp's statement that she *feared* Blake. At least once during her matronship, Stripp reported to Noxon that Blake was hysterical and unruly during the night.[56] Two women alone together in a cell must form their own small society, and it seems nearly inevitable that one would eventually begin to defer to the other. That Stripp was the one to defer is not surprising. She was evidently a timid person, since both her supervisor, Noxon, and her son rudely ordered her about with impunity. During Stripp's trial, Noxon reported that 'Fred was present when she and I were having some conversation in my office, & he told her when she was speaking to keep her mouth shut & I told her so too.' In the evening of the same day, Stripp apologized for her conduct. She said, 'I . . . asked Fred if it was any harm for me to take Mr. Stripp up there.' According to Noxon, 'Fred then said to her to keep her mouth shut. She didn't excuse herself except that she was sorry.'[57] The *Sun* later blamed Stripp's undoing on Blake, noting that it was generally understood that Stripp was 'under the influence of Hilda Blake whose superior will power was strong enough to command the woman now in jail.'[58]

In jail, through a combination of Stripp's fear and sympathy, Blake salvaged, again briefly, the position of mistress. Blake complained of a toothache; Stripp brought laudanum for relief. Blake required that certain letters be delivered; Stripp delivered them. Blake asked Stripp to secure a file; Stripp did so.

In the latter half of September maintenance workers preparing the jail windows for winter discovered Blake's filing. Noxon took out the blackened dough but then thought better and replaced it. Believing that the filing was being done from the outside, he sat up through 14 nights, hidden outside the jail, watching Blake's cell and hoping to catch whoever was trying to aid her escape. No one appeared. When Noxon subsequently confronted her with the charge that she had filed the bars in an escape attempt, Blake was at her playful best. Yes, she said, she had filed the bars, but no longer possessed the file. Who brought the file? he wanted to know. A mysterious stranger had come to her cell window, she replied, and stuck a fishing pole through it. On the end of the pole hung a banana that concealed, goodness gracious, a file.

She became somewhat less playful after reading a *Brandon Independence* article claiming that she had confessed to having shot R.B. Singer, who had been declared a suicide in 1894.[59] On Kircaldy's next visit, Blake gave him the file. He, unaware that a bar in the cell had been nearly filed through, passed the item on to Noxon, who disclosed the 'escape' attempt. But Blake's serious mood passed. Within a short time she was again playing at escape, requesting and receiving another file from Stripp.

There was more. Blake had been allowed to keep up some correspondence outside the jail, and on the floor of the cell Kircaldy found a rather puzzling note, apparently written by her. She often asked McLaurin to mail her letters, but it's not clear whether she intended to give the note to him or whether she intended to have Stripp carry it more surreptitiously. It certainly did not contain the sort of thing that McLaurin would have found edifying:

> Now I feel ashamed of myself to be obliged to confess that even that little note has comforted me. You have a strong influence over me knowing as I do how wicked and dishonorable you can be to allow myself to be comforted by the thought that you have taken the trouble to be worried about me. How I do wish I could see your face. But I knew you were near and endangering yourself for my sake. Now I shall be comparatively happy for a time longer. I feel quite resigned again. I felt that I could almost welcome the gallows today. I hope I shall feel like this when the time really comes, but the trouble is these moods last such a short time.[60]

The letter suggests a romantic relationship between Blake and someone outside the jail. Although she despaired of her own agency, Blake still fantasized about the sort of conventional femininity and miraculous loves she found in novels. There, the heroine's ideal femininity inspired the hero's daring. 'Affection can (now and then) withstand very severe storms of rigour, but not a long polar frost of downright indifference', said Sir Walter Scott's Flora Mac-Ivor, and for Blake it was enough at this point that her correspondent was risking his reputation either by sending letters or by attempting to see her. Kircaldy saw and was mystified by at least one letter 'sd [said] to have come from Winnipeg'. Stripp refused to shed any light. When confronted, she at first claimed, 'I don't remember the names now.' A few minutes later she returned to Kircaldy's office. 'About that letter,' she said, 'I wrote myself to myself because I was afraid of Hilda.' Kircaldy, of course, did not believe her, and proceeded 'to find out who the parties were that were writing these letters',[61] but he never made public what he discovered.

Given the content of the autobiography Blake finally wrote in December, the intended receiver of her epistle (and perhaps the author of the 'Winnipeg' letters) was probably Robert Lane. Blake framed her plight in conventionally feminine terms—feeling that she had been sexually dishonoured, but wishing, as long as Lane showed some tokens of affection, to bear much for the sake of love. While others called her occasional departure from female roles shameful, what shamed and yet energized Blake herself was her abjection in love. Theories suggesting that crime is symbolically masculine and that the 'feminine' woman will therefore not break the law[62] do not find ready support in the details of Blake's life. From the time she was arrested until her death, she wore a photograph around her neck,[63] and the note of melodrama in her letter, with its display of a long-suffering woman, is unmistakable. She displayed a male sense of agency in beginning to file her bars, yet, like other women in jail, her emotional life revolved around love and religion.[64] If it was too much now to expect to rise in class, she still hoped, as an attractive young woman, for the feminine consolations of romance and chivalry. Blake, the inveterate passer of notes, clearly hoped that she would receive something more than 'that little note', hoped, perhaps, that like Rebecca in Sir Walter Scott's *Ivanhoe* she would receive a slip of parchment upon which was written *'Demand a Champion!'*[65] She wanted a knight to come riding by. No knight came.

While Canada was in an uproar in early October about the possibility of sending troops to the Boer War, and the Brandon Council of Women joined their imperial sisters to create a Red Cross Society for the Canadians who would become sick and wounded fighting in South Africa,[66] Kircaldy waited for more evidence. But in the middle of October he and Noxon visited Stripp at her home to press her for explanations about the appearance of the file and note in Blake's cell. Stripp denied everything. She denied that she had given Blake a file and rejected accusations that she was conveying messages. Then, at the end of October, Blake handed Kircaldy a second file and a bottle of laudanum, which he took to a chemist for examination. On the basis of this evidence, Noxon concluded that at best Stripp was not performing her duties properly; at worst, she had smuggled the files and the laudanum into jail. Stripp's term of employment was originally supposed to run only until the end of October, but now she had begun talking as if she wanted to stay on longer.

Noxon was far from happy. Kircaldy had not divulged all that he knew, and apparently had no immediate intention of charging Stripp, for he still hoped that she would somehow prove of use in his continuing investigation of the murder. Noxon, however, feared that some aspersion might be cast on his own character:[67] it was not unknown for jailers to barter with their inmates for sexual favours, and the Criminal Code was in the process of being amended so that a jailer could himself be jailed for a year if his failure to perform a legal duty resulted in an escape.[68] Although he had only circumstantial evidence and pressed no charges at first, Noxon dismissed Stripp from her position on 1 November and barred her from the jail.

After hearing about the sudden dismissal, Blake asked Kircaldy, during an evening visit, to convey a note to Stripp. The envelope was not sealed, so Kircaldy instead kept the note and read it:

> Dear Mrs Strippe
>   Do not you be a bit uneasy
> everything is all right. I have <u>those things</u>
> where no one is ever likely to find them.
>   Everything is going on all right. I will
>   get the minister to mail this.
> There is no need to caution you to be silent
>   Hilda.[69]

To ask Kircaldy to deliver such a note was absurd if Blake's intention was really to cover her own and Stripp's tracks. The note must have had another purpose or complex of purposes. It was probably written to prolong the game of escape, Blake's bit of theatre. With its tone of a captain calming an anxious soldier or the stronger vessel encouraging the weaker, the note also prolonged the little society in which Blake was the upper class and Stripp the pliant lower.

Most of all, the note invited renewed attention to Blake. There is a kind of coyness about giving Kircaldy the note, a coyness that invited the young and (with his handlebar moustache) rather dashing Kircaldy again to declare for or against her, to aid or to expose her; but, either way, to pay her again the kind of intense attention that he had accorded during her first notoriety. Lombroso and Ferrero spoke of 'the extreme trustfulness' of occasional female criminals 'towards their advocates, especially if young and good-looking',[70] and Blake's relationship with Kircaldy was indeed beginning to show something of this attribute. One does not know, of course, whether Blake placed herself at Kircaldy's mercy in response to her own feelings, or as a way of flattering the male ego. Certainly Lombroso and Ferrero consistently underestimated female agency, especially the process whereby many women were educated to be manipulative, to use sexual appeal and helplessness as tools to gain influence. Blake wasn't planning to add new information to her testimony in court, but her surrender of the files, the laudanum, the note, and perhaps her eventual writing of an autobiography said to Kircaldy, in case he had forgotten, that even if they were opponents, the principal dance still consisted of the police chief and the young domestic. What opened as a 'masculine' gambit for escape moved towards a 'feminine' denouement.

Blake's note in his possession, Kircaldy paid a second, less polite call to Stripp's home early in November and asked her to come down to the police station for questioning, though his primary interest, he said, was to gather information for Blake's trial. He asked her whether she had taken any letters from Blake to others outside the jail. She again denied it. He then read Blake's note aloud and asked Stripp if she knew what 'things' Blake was referring to. 'No', she repeated. When Kircaldy showed her the bottle of laudanum he had been given by Blake, Stripp became very nervous.[71] Finally she broke down and said, 'Yes Chief, I'll tell the truth, I did take those things in.' She also admitted carrying letters to someone outside the jail only in an attempt to pacify Blake, who, she said, had led her to believe that the chief knew all about the files and the laudanum.

In the end, no evidence against Robert Lane or anybody else came forward at Blake's formal trial in November, and Blake's refusal to name the 'wicked and dishonorable' recipient of her letter began to make her appear self-sacrificial, as a true woman should be. But Noxon and Kircaldy were not much moved. They charged Emma Stripp with attempting to aid Blake's escape and replaced her with a new matron, Mrs Newton, who would prove less susceptible to Blake's management.[72]

11

A Man Coldly Impervious to
the Emotional

*. . . a brilliant man with a legal mind of scholarliness,
keenness and precision, a man coldly impervious to the
emotional in his long career as a judge.*

—obituary for A.C. Killam, *Winnipeg Tribune*, 14 June 1930

In the last years of the nineteenth century, the authority of the Canadian state was exercised decorously in the courtroom. Unpleasant denouements happened later, behind closed doors and before a small, usually professional, audience. A case in point: on 18 February 1892, a man named Bryce, having been convicted of indecent assault on a 10-year-old, was stripped to the waist at the Brandon jail and thrashed repeatedly with a 12-corded whip. The public did not need to know. Only the chance sighting of the Winnipeg jailer—he had conveyed the whip to Brandon—activated the curious press.[1]

Such reticence showed the growing influence of demands that the justice system put aside retribution in favour of measured punishment and moral redemption. Concern that physical punishments and state killings might brutalize the innocent observer had forestalled public access to punishments, while press descriptions were increasingly conveyed in bland—and untruthful—euphemism. Some reformers remained dissatisfied, insisting that the state must shed all barbarous tendencies. Why should the death penalty be retained, asked one writer, when there was ample evidence that the fear of capital punishment did not prevent murder?[2]

Although no woman could be whipped, whipping and hanging continued to be deployed. The Hobbesian argument that a stable civil order was possible only in the presence of 'a common power to feare'[3] remained persuasive to those who shaped Canada's 1892 Criminal Code. Criticism of the existing patchwork of statute and common law led to Parliament's approval of the 1892 Code, but it was more a product of state formation than a concession to reformers. Rather than put together an integrated version of criminal statutes approved by colonial legislatures before Confederation, centralists in 1869 followed the Criminal Law Consolidation Acts approved by the British Parliament eight years earlier, ensuring that exclusive jurisdiction over the criminal law remained with the federal government.[4]

Despite the growing preoccupation of the state with male sexual predation and the victimization of young women,[5] the 1892 Code and judicial practice continued to be grounded in patriarchal assumptions, a fact profoundly frustrating for women since they could not serve on juries, act as lawyers, or be appointed to the bench. Legal education for women was denied until the late 1890s, when Clara Martin Brett, an Ontario woman, became the first full-fledged lawyer in the British Empire.[6] The *Canadian Law Journal* reflected prevailing attitudes towards women and the law, supporting the opposition mounted by the Benchers of the Law Society of Upper Canada against the admission of women to the profession in the early 1890s:

> There is some reason for the Admission of women to the medical profession, but we know of no public advantage to be gained by their being admitted to the Bar. . . . As a matter of taste it is rather a surprise to most men to see a woman seeking a profession where she is bound to meet such that would offend the natural modesty of her sex.[7]

Such arguments for the exclusion of women were rooted in idealized notions of femininity; a respectable woman ought to stand above the kind of disorder and unseemly conflict that a court would consider. In the masculine terrain of the courtroom, it was highly unusual for a woman to appear, even as a spectator.[8] Those who appeared either as defendants or plaintiffs in cases involving sexuality or even romance were placed in circumstances that made their evidence personally embarrassing, and sometimes damaging to their cases. 'The Victorian doctrine of female passionlessness and purity increased the stakes for women; it meant they had further to fall.'[9] Most women were thus reluctant to disclose intimate personal lives before a courtroom of strange men. In such cases, justice could be driven by the perceived moral status of the women involved. This was not always a disadvantage if the woman's moral status was high. Depending on the situation, women could be the subjects of chivalric condescension or of moral reproof.

What might Blake expect before the courts? In England in the nineteenth century not many women were executed for murder. From 1843 to 1890 only 49 British women were put to death. The majority 'were miserably poor', and not one of the five middle-class women convicted of murder during that period was executed. The principal motivation for the murders committed by women arose out of sexual triangles.[10] In Canada, the pattern was remarkably similar. While the paradigm of the virtuous, altruistic, and moral woman was increasingly contested in both fiction and real life, it was still true that in late nineteenth-century Canada, as elsewhere, women rarely murdered, and almost never murdered other women.[11] The murder and manslaughter victims of Canadian women, aside from their own unwanted babies, were almost always men, frequently the women's husbands. Setting aside the Blake case, six of the 12 other murder convictions of women in Canada between 1867 and 1899 involved love triangles and the murder of a husband. The other motives were varied: the disposal of an unwanted baby, a failed abortion, a response to physical abuse, robbery, and insanity (twice).

Canadian legal authorities, like their British counterparts, were beginning to avoid executing women. Before 1874, two of the three women convicted of murdering their husbands had been executed, but during the 50 years that followed, only two women—Cordelia Viau and Blake—were executed, both in 1899. Before the Blake case, six women either had their sentences commuted or were acquitted following a new trial ordered by cabinet, even though judges and juries sometimes did not recommend mercy. Women who could not be dismissed as hopelessly atavistic tended to have their sentences commuted. None of the cases was really comparable to the Blake case, because only Susan Kennedy, whose sentence was commuted on the basis of insanity, had murdered another woman, and Kennedy's 1879 case was very different from Blake's. The muscular Kennedy had beaten another woman, Mary Gallagher, to death with a mallet. Gallagher's head and a severed hand were found in a pail in Kennedy's blood-stained kitchen, for Kennedy had apparently intended to dispose of the body by cutting it into pieces. The prosecution characterized the murder as the end of a drunken brawl over a man, while the defence blamed an aberrant mental condition, domestic troubles, and drink.[12]

Then, late in 1897, after 24 years during which no woman was executed, Cordelia Viau and her lover, Sam Parslow, were accused of the murder of Viau's husband. He had been attacked a year and a half earlier while asleep: had been repeatedly stabbed and had had his throat slit from ear to ear. In a memorandum prepared for the Minister of Justice when the case was reviewed by cabinet, the deputy minister asserted that 'the impression left upon my mind by reading the evidence is that the woman was the master-mind in the crime. The evidence given on Parslow's behalf shows him to have been a soft and pliant disposition and easily influenced.'[13] Viau confessed only after Parslow had done so, but their statements clashed: Parslow affirming that Viau had been present when her husband was killed and had urged the murder, Viau denying it. After both were convicted, it hardly seemed possible to execute Parslow and not Viau. Cabinet directed that the death sentence be carried out, and in 1899—four months before Blake killed Mary Lane—it finally was.

Given these precedents, Blake could expect that the revelation of a sexual affair would bring a heavy disgrace, and that she would not be spared death simply because she was a woman—though if there were extenuating circumstances or questions of mental competence, her sentence might well be commuted.

*

On Tuesday, 15 November, she finally came to formal trial. The 1899 Fall Assizes in Brandon were unusual and disquieting because two women—Blake and Agnes Glendenning—faced murder charges. In its presentment, the grand jury of the Western Judicial District spoke regretfully: 'the criminal docket, although not a long one, is of a very serious nature. The indictment of two women on the charge of murder is a new and startling event in the history of the province.'[14] Male sexual and emotional roles in both of these 'startling' cases were not commented upon.

Blake's judge, the 50-year-old A.C. Killam of the Manitoba Court of Queen's Bench, was no stranger to her, for in 1889 he had presided over the legal wrangling between A.P. Stewart and Mary Rex about Blake's guardianship. A native of Yarmouth, Nova Scotia, Killam had arrived in Manitoba in 1879 following a brief (two-year) legal career in Ontario. His contemporaries called him 'a many-sided genius' and 'a slave to duty'. He had been elected to the provincial legislature in 1883 as a Liberal and had become a vocal member of the opposition. Within two years Prime Minister John A. Macdonald, departing from the usual patronage practices, appointed him to the Court of Queen's

Bench.[15] Conservatives had little to fear ideologically from his judge-
ments. In his first year on the bench he upheld the conviction of Louis
Riel, and in 1890 he upheld Liberal Premier Thomas Greenway's
decision to abolish financial support for denominational schools.
Nevertheless, he was reputed to be incorruptible, meting out the same
justice to enemy and friend. He spoke very little on the bench, and
spectators were unable to tell which way he was leaning until he
delivered his verdict. By April 1899, three months before the Lane
murder, the charming and urbane, though unemotional, Killam was
already Chief Justice of the Court of Queen's Bench, and four years
after the case he ascended to the Supreme Court of Canada as the first
western member.

In dealing with Agnes Glendenning, Killam did not appear to be
'coldly impervious', as he was later described in his obituary as having been.[16] As she had no counsel, Killam appointed a defence attorney. After conferring with the attorney, she plea-bargained, offering a
guilty plea for a reduction of the charge from murder to manslaughter.
The Crown consented, and in his decision Killam agreed with the recommendation. While Glendenning had intentionally subjected her
child to a terrible ordeal by leaving it on the prairie, alone and uncom-
forted, British courts for decades had treated such cases as something
less than cold-blooded murder, recognizing that the women were act-
ing under emotional duress and that the fathers of unwanted children
shared at least a moral, though not legal, responsibility. The trend was
similar in Canada. Constance Backhouse reports that between 1840
and 1900 in Ontario, only 7.4 per cent of those who caused the deaths
of their own children were convicted of murder, while 66.7 per cent
were acquitted and 22.2 per cent were allowed to plead guilty to a
reduced charge of 'concealment of birth'.[17] Killam's agreement to
accept a guilty plea to the reduced charge of manslaughter was, therefore, not simply a bending to emotion but a decision quite consistent
with contemporaneous trends. Glendenning was overjoyed at the
smallness of her sentence.[18]

Something of Killam's approach to Blake may also be drawn from
his stern and precise—but again, not 'coldly impervious'—handling
of Philip Hill during the Brandon Fall Assizes six years earlier. Hill,
only 13 years old, had been charged with murder following the death
of Albert Greaves, apparently from strychnine poisoning. Circumstantial evidence linked Hill to the death. In the course of the trial,
defence lawyers demonstrated that Hill had received no education or
moral instruction and that he, like Blake, had been sent out to work at
10 years of age. Moreover, his mother and the man with whom she

was living were indifferent to the boy's fate, for they had neither visited him in jail nor taken the trouble to secure a legal defence for him. The *Winnipeg Morning Telegram* was quick to condemn Hill as a Barnardo boy. Hill's background did not surprise Killam, but he felt that the boy's social disadvantages were ultimately irrelevant. In advising the jury, Killam set out his unemotional attitude about the role of extenuating circumstances in the application of law:

> I have no doubt you all see this as a painful case. The lad has had no education, none of that care and attention so necessary to a young child. He, poor waif, appears to have been left to drift anywhere of his own free will. The consequence is, that he stands today charged with the most heinous crime in the calendar. And we see him as friendless with no one to comfort him, left completely on his own resources in the dock today. Just such a poor waif as one might expect to be brought up on such a charge. Try to banish all this from your minds, do not from this judge him guilty, or do not extend to him too much pity. He is not on trial for being a liar or thief, but on a charge of murder.[19]

Though the jury returned a verdict of guilty in the case, the fact that he was convicted on rather tenuous circumstantial evidence led the jury to recommend mercy. As the law required, Killam sentenced Philip Hill to death, but agreed, in his report to the federal Minister of Justice, with the jury's recommendation of mercy. The Privy Council commuted Hill's sentence to life in prison.[20]

Like that of Philip Hill, Blake's was a 'painful case'. She had had little of the care and attention that Killam acknowledged were necessary to a young child. 'Friendless', 'a poor waif', Blake had drifted for nearly as long as Hill had, though for different reasons and at a different stage in her life. Now she, too, stood before Killam, 'not on trial for being a liar or thief' but charged with 'the most heinous crime in the calendar'.[21] Her guilt was confessed, not just circumstantial, and if a 13-year-old had reached the age of accountability, how much more a 21-year-old? As in the Glendenning case, there were hints that a man might share some of the moral responsibility, but unlike Glendenning, Blake could not easily argue that her crime had been unpremeditated.

The trial was brief. Jailer Noxon and Rev. McLaurin accompanied the 'pretty, modest-looking prisoner' into the male terrain of the courtroom. 'She was neatly dressed', this time in a brown velvet dress, and 'the picture of health', though one account added that she looked 'a trifle pale'.[22] Like Glendenning, Blake had not retained legal counsel. A

number of lawyers, including Joseph Singer, who now practised law in
Virden, had offered themselves as counsel at no cost, but Blake had
declined. Killam asked her if she wanted someone to speak for her, and
again she declined. As he had done for Glendenning, Killam adjourned
proceedings to insist that Blake speak with a court-appointed counsel.
He proposed G.R. Coldwell, a devout member of St Matthew's—Mary
Lane's church—and, like Killam, familiar to Blake from the child-
abduction litigation 10 years earlier. In the Stewart-Rex custody case
Coldwell had acted for Mary Rex and had explained to Blake her
rights and responsibilities in Rex's guardianship. Now he was a pillar
of the community, a lawyer on the verge of becoming Crown prosecutor,[23] an alderman on the verge of beginning a successful 20-year
career as a Conservative MPP (and eventually Minister of Education in
R.P. Roblin's cabinet), a lover of gardening and shooting. Although he
would soon defend the Dakota chief Wanduta for his role in a banned
Grass Dance, Coldwell was no innovator in social matters, saying as
late as 1914 that 'Women's suffrage [is] not at present needed.' No
weak-kneed philanthropist either, he scolded the poor in 1900 for
abusing the city's generosity during the previous year—'the city had to
pay large sums for prescriptions filled and filled again.'[24]

His advice in 1889 had not given Blake the kind of home she
wanted, and this time she refused to co-operate. Coldwell told her
that a guilty plea to first-degree murder would force the court to issue
a death sentence, but she took no heed. Killam, in his notes, described
the scene in the following way:

> Prisoner being brought in, I ask her if she has no legal advice. She
> says not. I ask her if she wishes some & she says no. I then ask Mr.
> Coldwell to advise with her & urge her to consult with him before
> arraignment. She retires with him. After about 15 minutes prisoner
> returns & Mr. Coldwell announces that prisoner is fully deter-
> mined not to be advised by counsel & he can do nothing.[25]

Once the court resumed proceedings, Blake said 'guilty' in a firm
voice, but as soon as she was conducted out of the courtroom she broke
down, sobbing violently and losing all consciousness of feeling.[26]

*

Such a plea and such behaviour could do her no good legally, though
it could do her good in other ways. Legally, a guilty plea substituted
for a *story* of guilt or innocence: section 690 of the Criminal Code
allowed the Crown to dispense with the proof of any fact that the
accused was willing to admit.[27] Once a guilty plea was entered, there

was no legal obligation for the court to present further evidence. Yet in cases involving the death penalty, a prudent judge might insist on the presentation in open court of sufficient facts to ensure that a defendant such as Blake understood both the exact nature of the charge and exactly what she was doing by pleading guilty. Neither the Crown prosecutor, R.M. Matheson, nor Judge Killam insisted on the presentation of any evidence other than Blake's plea. Nevertheless, Chief Kircaldy would acknowledge later that long after Blake's confession he was still looking for 'evidence on Mrs. Lane's murder', and hoped to get the evidence from Blake's letters to a person outside the jail.[28] Killam almost certainly had to consider the possibility that Blake was involved in a love triangle, but he got no help from Blake, and speculations about Lane's involvement were, of course, matters of life and death.

Arguably, Blake's only hope of securing a sympathetic hearing from the court required that she describe her affair with Robert Lane in detail. Blake would have had to convince the court that she was the victim of seduction by a sexual predator and that her subsequent depravity demonstrated what one writer has termed 'the workings of the "slippery slope" theory of fallen womanhood, in which primary sexual agency was placed in the hands of men and men only, but in which woman, once fallen, could only continue to fall.'[29] Blake refused such a defence. To admit to premarital or extramarital sex was to admit to a sin worse than violence. Women could anticipate moral outrage, while men—whose sexuality was reputed to be rampant and difficult to control—did not suffer under the same rigour. If an illicit or immoral relationship developed between a man and a woman, the woman was far more likely to be a target of moral censure. More was expected of her: she was required to act both as the moral guardian of her own character and as a brake on the unbridled sexuality of the male. If, as seems probable, the Blake/Lane affair was consensual and Lane had no role in his wife's murder, then a disclosure of an affair would not really help her case but would only deepen her public disgrace. She would be revealed as someone who had despised 'the natural modesty of her sex'.

Blake's guilty plea and her behaviour could, on the other hand, partially recuperate for her the image of the moral woman, the feminine sphere she had lost after the murder. Expectations about feminine conduct were sometimes impossibly high:

> If she can, without observation, slip the burnt roll or undercrust on her plate, it is done. If some one must stay at home when there is a

day's outing, she tells, with music in every tone, how glad she will be to be left quietly behind and have time all to herself to do ever so many things she has in mind. . . . Is a harsh round of judgment started by some ill-advised criticism, she deftly and tenderly drops the gentlest, the sweetest possible word for the criticised one, and switches the conversation to other topics. Do we not all recognize this 'angel'? We call her mother, wife, sister. In the glory-land they will call her saint.[30]

Violent women like Blake, unless they had used violence to defend their honour, could obviously not lay claim to respectable womanhood, never mind sainthood. However, by refusing to name Robert Lane publicly, while privately hinting that he was responsible, she could appear sympathetic—a romantic heroine—since she would confirm the stereotype that Woman was 'defined by love'. She could put on the image of the sacrificial woman, 'the languishing, despairing female who chooses', as a woman ought, 'to take her own life'[31] rather than destroy another. In the Christian mythos, as in Romantic abjection, the worthiness of the beloved is quite beside the point. People knew that she had killed Mary Lane; still, she was remorseful and had asked for 'the severest punishment'. People heard rumours that she had engaged in extramarital sex; those rumours might be untrue. Even if they were true, was she not now behaving out of a selfless love that could no longer hope for sexual consummation? Even for those people who saw her as solely responsible, her unwillingness to claim extenuating circumstances could put her on a higher moral ground, as an eleventh-hour conversion to full and courageous femininity. And the image of the sacrificial woman did have an effect: it helped seed a campaign to save Blake from the gallows.

According to Carolyn Strange, not only did Victorian murderesses internalize prevailing images of women as fundamentally pacific and moral, but also 'judges, both inside and outside the courtrooms, were mesmerized by the popular stereotypes'—with the result that public sympathy was accorded the murderess. Premising their defences on the vulnerability and weakness of women, defence lawyers could, and did, as the Carrie Davies/Charles Massey case shows, effectively frame their pleas to judge and jury in the language of chivalry. The central dynamic at play has been described in the following way: 'While men were to be brave and decisive, women were expected to be pure and submissive. Thus for the nineteenth century gentleman to realize his subjectivity, the "true woman" had also to play her part.'[32] Blake's patrician attitude, her 'courageous' refusal to implicate Lane, her unwillingness to claim extenuating circumstances, her firm guilty plea, and her fainting afterwards would make her a prime candidate for such chivalry.

But a judge actuated by chivalry would inevitably come up against the body of Mary Lane. Unlike Agnes Glendenning, Blake wasn't so clearly the victim of a man and of her own biology. Blake wasn't the protagonist of a story in which a man preying upon a vulnerable woman had received his just deserts: she hadn't shot a seducer or an abusive husband but a respectable middle-class woman. Nor was Blake a wife defending her home against her husband's philandering. A middle-class wife driven to protect her family by killing her husband's mistress could expect sympathy while a mistress murdering a wife could not—'some kinds of jealousy were worthy more than others.'[33] Under these circumstances, the chivalric ideal would condemn rather than serve Blake, no matter what her demeanour. And the case provided an opportunity simultaneously to affirm both the rule of law and the probity of the existing order, because actual guilt matched class intuitions about guilt. If the courtroom was a male terrain centred on conceptions of male rationality and the protection of women, then even a man sensitive to emotion would feel chivalric sympathy for Mary Lane rather than for Blake. A man 'coldly impervious to emotion' would have no doubt where his duty lay.

One day after the trial, Killam rendered judgement: 'The sentence of the court is that you shall be taken from this place to the place from whence you came, and there remain until the 27th day of December, and then taken to the yard of the Brandon jail, and there hanged until you are dead; and may the Lord have mercy on your soul.'[34] Since she had pled guilty, the jury could not render a verdict and, therefore, could not recommend mercy. Killam explained that it was his duty to refer her case to the federal cabinet for review; nevertheless, repeating the words that judges conventionally used when they decided not to recommend mercy, he said he could hold out no hope of having her sentence commuted.[35]

PART III

12

Whene'er a Wrong Is Done

*Women suffer from this injustice all their lives, but its hideous-
ness becomes apparent in all its baldness when we see one
throttled to death in obedience to a law which neither the
criminal nor any other woman had any voice in framing.*

—Dr Amelia Yeomans,
Manitoba Morning Free Press, 21 Dec. 1899

The ominous tolling of 'there hanged until you are dead' brought
about an unlikely and important side-episode in Blake's story. Two
very different women, who would not otherwise have met, crossed
paths: one, orphaned, a servant grasping awkwardly for status, was
now a murderess condemned; the other, canny and highly educated,
was both a doctor who could presume to speak with authority about
female criminals and a Woman's Christian Temperance Union leader
planning the strategy that would eventually give Manitoba women the
provincial vote (not just an occasional municipal vote) before women
anywhere else in Canada.

The meeting between Blake and Dr Amelia Yeomans of the
Winnipeg WCTU occurred on 25 November, 10 days after the trial, as
Yeomans made a Friday evening trip 120 miles west to Brandon,
planning to spend several days 'for the spiritual benefit of Hilda
Blake'.[1] But she only met with Blake for an hour and a half on Saturday. Clearly disappointed with Blake's response, Yeomans, nevertheless, did not fail to put the interview to use in her suffrage campaign,
and her role did introduce Brandon to broader crises in Victorian

gender relations. She had clear political goals and knew that during the agitation for the female vote and the right to help make laws, the spectre of a pretty and youthful woman condemned by a law she had no voice in framing could be powerful. Within a couple of weeks, Yeomans would frame a petition seeking a stay of Blake's execution.

Yeomans was one of the first female medical doctors in Canada, a dedicated advocate of social purity, president of the Manitoba WCTU in 1896–7, and one of the leading maternal feminists of her generation.[2] Coming from a well-educated and highly motivated family, she did not begin her medical career until she was 38. Even though Dr Edward H. Clarke (formerly on the medical staff at Harvard) warned, in *Sex and Education, or a Fair Chance for Girls*, that women who pursued higher education could expect 'neuralgia, uterine disease, hysteria and other derangements of the nervous system',[3] Yeomans, after the death of her husband, followed her daughter Lillian into the study of medicine at the University of Michigan. Yeomans graduated in 1883, a year after her daughter. 'They had a definite character, those Michigan women graduates of the '70s and '80s', says Dorothy McGuigan, 'independent, determined, a bit audacious, and with it all, those lofty Victorian "moral ideals".'[4] Like her daughter, Yeomans opened a medical practice (initially unlicensed) in Winnipeg, specializing in the treatment of women and children. During the course of her work, she explored slum conditions in Winnipeg's North End and became an advocate of reform, arguing that the 'white slave trade' must be stopped and that conditions must be improved in prisons and in clothing factories.

Her emancipation work arose from her reformist hopes: the serpent in her time, she said, was the liquor traffic, and for woman's seed to bruise the serpent's head, as God had commanded in Genesis, she must be given the vote.[5] The famous temperance advocate Letitia Youmans wrote about 'the right of every woman to have a comfortable home', and therefore concluded, 'it is, to my mind, as much of a duty to vote as to pray.'[6] By 1893 Amelia Yeomans had begun to argue publicly that it was unacceptable for women to have no say in the laws by which they were governed. Not only were women outside the state, but their efforts to influence those who controlled the state had to be pursued without the vote. In February 1893 the Winnipeg WCTU had staged a mock parliament to debate the question of 'the ballot for women', Yeomans taking the role of Premier. In her speech she argued that 'Women, at home and in the workplace, had no say in the laws which affected their lives and were powerless in the hands of their oppressors. . . . For the sake of both justice and expediency this had to be altered; women had to be given the vote.'[7] About 20 MPPs showed up to watch the women, giving them some hope that change was around the corner. Almost immediately, Yeomans was made president of the Dominion Women's Enfranchisement Association, and in the next year she helped to create a Manitoba chapter of the Equal Franchise Association.[8] But that same year she also witnessed the humiliating failure of the first suffrage bill, when its promoter, Mr Ironside, withdrew it prior to second reading. Nevertheless, Edith Luke said that 'if we had in every city in Canada as enthusiastic a suffrage club as that which exists in Winnipeg, we should not be long in gaining the point for which we are striving.'[9]

Yeomans's medical job and her public role in the franchise associations were symptomatic of a crisis in the affairs of the WCTU, a crisis rooted in the WCTU's ideology of domesticity. Initially the WCTU had avoided the question of women's rights and stressed the protection of home and children through temperance activities and petitions to government calling for prohibition. The Brandon WCTU distributed temperance literature (some of which the *Brandon Mail* published on its front page), convened prayer meetings, visited prison inmates, and, in conjunction with the ministers of the Anglican and Methodist churches, operated a coffee and reading room. WCTU membership, as in Ontario, was Protestant and middle class. However, the failure to bring about temperance at a political level, and the feminine powerlessness that this failure emphatically declared, moved leading members of the organization to demand the right to vote. As Mrs Jacob Spence, the first superintendent of the Ontario WCTU's Franchise Department, explained, the vote was required to allow women 'to protect the home against the licensed evil which is the enemy of the home, and also to aid in our efforts to advance God's kingdom beyond the bounds of our homes.'[10] The broader involvement of women in public life and the agitation for women's rights were thus justified on the basis of the domestic ideal, the very ideal that, by working now in the public sphere, these maternal feminists must in practice renounce.

The domestic ideal, combined with an evangelical zeal for God's work, also moved the WCTU and Yeomans in an ameliorative direction: young girls and women, particularly those girls who did not have the advantages of a decent home life, must be protected, and their difficult circumstances must be ameliorated. Young women without decent homes, it was believed, were frequently ignorant of the basic facts of life and especially vulnerable to sin and sexual danger presented by men: 'man was the seducer, women his victim, and

The Equal Franchise Association at the unveiling of a portrait of American abolitionist and feminist Lucy Stone, c. 1900. Seated on the far right is founder Dr Amelia Yeomans, who made a quick psychological diagnosis of Blake and petitioned for a stay of execution. (Provincial Archives of Manitoba N10675)

unfortunately, the law favored the former.' Speaking about late nine-teenth-century British society, Judith Walkowitz et al. observe that women's public speech about sexual passion and sexual danger allowed 'middle-class women's forceful entry into the world of publicity and politics'.[11]

Among those entering forcefully into the public world through open (and not easily dismissed) speech about sexuality was Yeomans, who campaigned against prostitution and spoke explicitly about the dangers of venereal disease.[12] She wrote a pamphlet warning young women about the perils of city life, attracting censure from other women for being too outspoken.[13] A witty speaker, she also made domesticity and the reputed saintliness of women into a weapon: 'If men spent more time at home . . . they would be more fitted to remedy the social evils of their national home. But as things [stand] at present, it [is] women who [are] most suited to govern the nation, because women [are] at home more and therefore [have] a more godly and philanthropic approach to life.'[14] Ngaire Naffine, summing up sociological studies that show that feminism is *inversely* related to delinquency, describes the ideal feminist, a description that fits Yeomans: 'She may believe in the equality of the sexes, she may be strong and assertive, but she may nevertheless take seriously her social duties.'[15] After her medical degree Yeomans was no longer passive and private enough to qualify fully for the position of 'domestic angel', but neither was she a 'New Woman'. She imagined and lived a public career that counted on the moral capital of the domestic angel, but that also traded it on the public exchange.

In a men-only public lecture at the Selkirk Hotel, a little more than a year after her meeting with Blake, Yeomans spoke in terms that explain her philanthropic sympathy for, but also her distance from, Blake. Yeomans referred to a visit to a city hospital where she saw 'young girls made to suffer through the wickedness of men, their young lives ruined, while their betrayers moved untarnished in any rank of society.' She held up the life of the Saviour as a model for the men at the Selkirk Hotel to imitate. Some of Yeomans's contemporaries might feel offended by her frankness, but they could not claim that she had forgotten her place as a Christian or a woman—and they could not argue that prostitution or extramarital sex had no repercussions in the domestic sphere. The lecture was well received: 'she didn't berate the men for their licentious behavior. She appealed to their chivalry and begged them to protect innocent young maidens as they would their own daughters.'[16]

To her November 1899 interview with Blake, Yeomans brought all these things: her medical training, her ameliorist hopes, her feminism, her political activism, her sense of religious and moral superiority, and perhaps also her knowledge that she might be classed among the 'sob sisters',[17] the 'silly and hysterical women of various societies, sisterhoods and churches' who were always 'petting and making a fuss over notorious criminals'.[18] Yeomans, having moved from a strong feminine base to roles beyond the scope of traditional femininity, was the least likely to be overwhelmed or charmed by Blake, a woman who tried hard, not always successfully, to meet traditional feminine expectations. Yeomans would be sympathetic towards Blake's plight, but at the same time would not be sympathetic to elements in Blake's character—coyness or sexual freedom, for example—that might compromise the feminist enterprise by asking for apparently immoral liberties. Because Blake was young, orphaned, of the working class, and a woman, she initially called out a sympathetic response in Yeomans, but it was a complex and strained sympathy.

Yeomans's calling suggests that the ascendancy of the middle class derived from more than its capacity to work hard, to display itself architecturally, or to discipline others to its will.[19] Growing out of Enlightenment rationalism and evangelical Christianity, middle-class culture changed attitudes: education, not just birth, became the sign of a cultivated sensibility, while new understandings of body and mind placed great emphasis on the importance of sensibility as the basis of thought and morality. These understandings also elicited a new consciousness of social obligation and community, so that empathy towards the poorer classes became a measure of intelligence and morality. In practical terms, this new social consciousness was evident in expressions of new bonds of social and personal obligation: to empathize with those who suffered and to strive to relieve suffering through benevolent works were the marks of the cultivated person.[20] The tears of the policemen at Blake's farewell to the Lane children, of court spectators during Blake's preliminary hearing, and, now, of maternal feminists hoping to get a pardon for Blake all suggest the character of this sensibility. One ought not, however, to overstate the reach of such altruism: Yeomans had her own political and personal reasons for coming to Blake's aid.

To the interview Yeomans also came flush with success in the work of the heart. Seven months earlier she had been the spiritual adviser to a condemned Winnipeg man, Wasyl Guszczak, who had, bless his conformity to Canadian mores, preferred 'her religious administrations to those of a Galician priest'. While another man on death row, Simeon Czuby, raved about his innocence and scorned spiritual advice, Guszczak had become 'rather buoyant' prior to his 27 May execution: 'he professes to have made his peace with God, and is prepared to die.' Credit went to Yeomans.[21] She was doing, and doing well, what political moderates had suggested for women in the workforce: 'there would be a natural function for women in providing the psychological analysis that would classify offenders'; if women were entering non-traditional areas of the workforce they could find an appropriately feminine place by performing the 'work of the heart'.[22]

*

'I spent perhaps an hour and a half with Miss Blake . . . having gone . . . to bring her to a saving knowledge of Jesus Christ',[23] Yeomans reported. According to the *Manitoba Morning Free Press*, Yeomans talked with Blake about spiritual matters, moved her to tears, and then Blake refused to see Yeomans again.[24] But Blake wasn't nearly as co-operative as the *Free Press* suggested. Yeomans's own account is considerably less dramatic—no hot, repentant tears, just a distance between the socially responsible, evangelizing feminist and the young domestic not so eager to be saved. Blake did not drive away 'venerable' spiritual counsellors 'of her own persuasion' as Simeon Czuby and Dickens's Fagin had,[25] but neither did she entirely accede to their ministrations as Wasyl Guszczak had. Yeomans said, 'I observed her closely, and found myself face to face with the problem of how to reach something in her, necessary to my work, but which seemed absent.'[26] It may be that Blake, who was more receptive to McLaurin's spiritual overtures, sensed condescension on Yeomans's part, or perhaps Blake recognized that Yeomans had not come 'to drop', *pace* 'Moralist', 'the chaste tear of sympathy'.

Admitting that her brief assessment would not allow 'scientifically, for a positive conclusion', still Yeomans said, 'Miss Blake is an abnormal product, the result probably of a baleful heredity and does not possess the moral responsibility which alone would justify her execution.'[27] Yeomans found Blake mentally bright, but lacking both 'concentration of thought' and 'logical sequence in her ideas'. Blake's moral faculties were 'so far below the normal standard as to exert little or no inhibitory power on conduct'. She was, in the language of Victorian alienists, 'morally insane', 'a moral lunatic', and the Lanes and McIlvrides would afterwards emphasize the possibility that Blake's infatuation with Robert Lane was the result of mental problems rather than of a sexual relationship. 'The girl was a bit dim-witted', said one family member.

Yeomans found no evidence of dim-wittedness. According to her, the separation between moral and intellectual faculties was a feature of all criminals to some degree, but when the moral faculties no longer inhibited conduct, then alienists could justifiably speak of moral insanity. A moral lunatic, Yeomans explained, was not 'immoral' but '*unmoral*'. This did not mean that one was safe near Blake: 'an unmoral yet reasoning lunatic is more dangerous than any other, because he or she is able cleverly to plan evil while the absence of an inhibitory moral sense leads to it being recklessly carried out.'[28] Like others before her, Yeomans commented on Blake's lack of honesty, even in situations where the truth could be more advantageous than a lie:

> I gather that she has been a constant puzzle, even to those most anxious to befriend her, this on account of repeated, apparently motiveless disregard of truth, and other wrong-doing to her own constant disadvantage. Her refusal to have counsel I regard as an

insane freak, having its root in a most irrational self-importance of which she seemed to be full when I saw her.[29]

At the same time, the limits of Yeomans's diagnosis appear when we address the question of 'moral idiocy'. Of all the categories of mental illness in the nineteenth and early twentieth centuries, 'moral idiocy' was, and, despite changes in terminology, still *is*, the most slippery. It was defined by James Prichard in the mid-nineteenth century as 'madness consisting in a morbid perversion of the natural feelings, affections, inclinations, temper, habits, moral dispositions and natural impulses, without any remarkable defect in the intellect or knowing and reasoning faculties.'[30] Although there were major disagreements within the medical community as to whether 'moral insanity' described an actual condition (especially since it was linked with the increasingly discredited science of phrenology), doctors continued to make such a diagnosis.[31] The term was applied to what contemporary psychiatry would call an 'anti-social personality disorder'—someone (formerly called a 'sociopath' or a 'psychopath') who is unable to identify at least partially with the physical pain he or she is inflicting upon a victim. Thus, remorseless violence or the torturing of animals, for example, was taken as a symptom of moral insanity.[32] Even if we could be sure that this was the sense in which Yeomans used the term, we would have no way of knowing whether she based the diagnosis on something she perceived in the interview or simply on Blake's crime. On the other hand, 'moral insanity' in its loosest definition meant an inability to distinguish between right and wrong,[33] so that lying, profanity, high temper, and sexual 'perversions' (from masturbation to sexual assault to actions 'unthinkable, much less printable') were each, at different times, taken to be symptoms of moral insanity.[34] And reformers sometimes used 'moral lunacy' or 'moral degeneracy' indiscriminately to describe women who killed.[35]

Some physicians believed that hysteria, moral insanity, and sexual desire were linked. A 'disordered state of the digestive or uterine organs, producing irritation of some part of the ganglionic system, causes hysteria, which is followed by irritation of the cerebellum, producing moral insanity, which develops itself in strong sexual desire, in time this irritation spreads to the cells of the cerebrum, and the consequence is violent mania.'[36] Accounts of mental illness in Britain suggest that gentleman callers could be scandalized by women uttering obscenities or demonstrating sexual promiscuity, and that Victorian women were occasionally treated not for debilitating illnesses but for ignoring the highly decorous and confining roles assigned to them.[37]

If Blake regretted the murder of Mary but not the extramarital sexual relationship with Lane, then her moral sense, Yeomans would have felt, was improperly developed. Maternal feminists fought for many kinds of female agency, but not for female sexual agency.

The wide variety of symptoms and opinions about those symptoms made 'moral insanity' a catch-all term. Where a criminal motive could not be explained as the result of a medical condition, as a desire for material gain, or as the enactment of vengeance, it could be put down to the criminal's lack of a moral sense. Yeomans could thus have relied on 'symptoms' that are not credible today as signs of mental illness. A poorly constructed lie; a lack of repentance of a sexual affair; a story about files, bananas, and fishing poles; the singing of a 'coon song' when one's condition was so serious: each of these singly or in combination could have led Yeomans to conclude that Blake did not perceive the gravity of her moral condition. And again: less credibly, the same diagnosis could have been made simply on the basis of Blake's crime or as a consequence of information supplied to Yeomans by Blake's warders. As a result of the terminological slipperiness, Singer and Krohn, for example, make it clear that in the early twentieth century 'moral insanity' was still a parvenu—at least where courts were concerned—and that true insanity consisted not in immorality nor even in 'the commission of an unnatural and atrocious crime', but in 'a more or less prolonged deviation from [one's] normal method of behavior', making one either incapable of managing one's own affairs or a danger to others.[38]

Yet despite the brevity of the interview, the lack of understanding between the two women, and the slipperiness of 'moral insanity', one cannot entirely dismiss Yeomans's assessment; more than anyone, she was in a position to move beyond male stereotypes of the fallen woman—to see Blake neither as the personification of evil nor as a beautiful and sentimental heroine to whom chivalry was due. Certain themes that we have found elsewhere reappear directly and indirectly in Yeomans's assessment, and we may therefore give them weight: Blake had equivocal feelings about 'salvation', desiring it at certain times (especially when McLaurin was nearby), yet often resisting demands upon her; she regarded truth as an interpersonal game; her intelligence lay not in the anticipation of logical outcomes but in impressive rhetorical flourishes; she maintained a theatrical sense of her own importance. Except for Kircaldy's and Noxon's comments about her lies, these themes were ones that none of the men involved in her case, from McLaurin to Governor-General Minto, commented upon—perhaps due to reticence, but possibly also because of a male-female sexual dynamic that would grant a high degree of indulgence (though not legal immunity, of course) to an attractive young woman.

Thus, even if we see no hard kernel of *medical* evidence at the centre of Yeomans's psychopathological assessment, we may expect that an observer as astute as Yeomans would have taken into account all the evidence—anything gleaned from the actual interview, anything offered by the newspapers and by Blake's warders, anything offered by the crime and confession, anything she had learned in medical school or on the job. And some aspects of Blake's case do indeed cohere with nineteenth- and early twentieth-century definitions of moral insanity offered by Prichard and others:

> In moral imbeciles of middle-grade, the absence of altruism and the constant invasion of the rights of others is a noted characteristic. They delight in mischievous pranks, and enjoy beyond measure the excitement consequent upon attracting attention to themselves; because they are 'egomaniacs.' They spend their spare time in plotting and planning mischief, and, easily influenced— especially for evil—are the victims or the tools of others of stronger mentality.[39]

The prevalence of lying and sexual promiscuity in almost every one of Barr and Maloney's case studies suggests that 'mischief' had a predictable, if expandable content,[40] but one ought not to dismiss quickly this as the prudery of an earlier age. While in a post-Freudian age we might wink at 'the absence of altruism' and while we can no longer be sure that such symptoms coalesce into an 'illness', named or not, we may nevertheless approach Yeomans's diagnosis as an educated guess about what things went together in human beings. The absence of behaviour that seemed 'altruistic', she felt, went together with a theatrical sense of self-display. A theatrical sense of self-display went with a propensity towards mischief—including lying and sexual promiscuity. Mischief involved a readiness to disregard social codes and the well-being of others.

This is not at all to suggest a syllogistic progression but simply to argue that certain associations were *not* arbitrary constructions; rather, they comprised a language, quite unscientific to contemporary eyes, but a language nevertheless, whereby one could speak about people who injured other people. The patient was not simply dishonest and therefore dangerous, or promiscuous and therefore dangerous, but (to invert Foucault) was dangerous (having killed or assaulted) and must therefore be anatomized. A diagnosis of 'moral insanity' was Yeomans's way of saying, 'there's something wrong with Blake; I'm not sure what. The murder of Mary Lane is not a freak or simply the result of social conditions, but somehow connected to the way Blake behaves. Yet I'm not sure that Blake fully understands what she has done.' Or to use Yeomans's own words: 'mentally [Blake] appears bright enough, though lacking, to some extent, concentration of thought, and logical sequence in her ideas. There is, in my opinion, a lack of co-ordination between the intellectual and moral faculties.'[41]

Yeomans's practical conclusions were twofold: that it would be barbaric to see 'one throttled to death in obedience to a law which neither the criminal nor any other woman had any voice in framing', and that if Blake didn't possess moral responsibility, her execution could not be justified.[42] Coming from one who blamed Blake for lacking 'logical sequence in her ideas', the first conclusion sounds rather cavalier in its leap from Blake's case to general principles of the suffragette movement, and the conclusion shows clearly that Yeomans used Blake to further her own political goals. 'Throttled to death in obedience to a law which she has no voice in framing': the phrase has the pithy and graphic appeal of a slogan, and one can see why Yeomans, constantly fighting male prejudice and power, would have found the slogan irresistible. Politicians who had to respond to campaigns such as the one eventually initiated by Yeomans and the WCTU on behalf of Blake could sleep easily, knowing that progressive women did not vote and that pressure from men could much more directly inflict political damage. The injustice of political muteness intruded into the lives of women from birth to death, but, as Yeomans sensed, only in capital cases could enough emotion be mustered to decry this inequality. However, while there would have been a great deal of logic in applying Yeomans's phrase to reproductive cases such as Glendenning's or McCabe's, it is difficult to see why women needed to help frame murder law in order to condemn a woman who murdered her mistress. Yeomans's first conclusion was emotionally powerful, but unless it could be shown that someone had urged Blake to murder Mary Lane, the conclusion could only remain a polemical addendum, having little to do with the diagnosis.

The second conclusion—that Blake should have been allowed the insanity defence—arose more logically from Yeomans's assessment, and, if convincing, could have pushed Prime Minister Sir Wilfrid Laurier to commute Blake's death sentence. People who were morally insane should not be executed but be studied, argued Yeomans, so that science could learn more about the nature of degeneracy. The murderess herself might be beyond treatment, but knowledge gained from her case could benefit others in the future. In the emphasis on 'baleful heredity', Yeomans followed the biological determinism of Lombroso and Ferrero. For the two criminologists, who sometimes linked moral lunacy with epilepsy and sometimes with all crime,[43] delinquency depended much less on social experience and personal circumstance than on cranial capacity. Anti-social or criminal acts were atavistic 'throwbacks from an earlier evolutionary stage in human development'[44]—'blood with the taint of Cain', so to speak—and the capacity to murder was a genetic adaptation to an earlier, more hostile environment, an adaptation that was no longer beneficial.

In this theoretical framework women, like children, were less developed than ordinary adult males: 'Women have many traits in common with children; that their moral sense is deficient; that they are revengeful, jealous, inclined to vengeances of a refined cruelty. In ordinary cases these defects are neutralized by piety, maternity, want of passion, sexual coldness, by weakness and an undeveloped intelligence.'[45] Speaking therefore of the female 'born criminal', the category from which Blake had taken pains to dissociate herself, Lombroso and Ferrero quoted Rykère: 'Female criminality . . . is more cynical, more depraved, and more terrible than the criminality of the male.'[46] Yet only rarely was the female offender a born criminal, Lombroso and Ferrero consoled their readers, holding out much hope for the occasional female criminal's reform. But it seems clear from Yeomans's language—'baleful heredity' and (in the petition) 'vicious heredity'—that she classed Blake as someone with a basic physiological defect. Unlike Wasyl Guszczak, whom Yeomans had been able to counsel towards penitence, the more distant Blake must be missing some crucial moral organ.

Yeomans concluded the diagnosis with the following unattributed lines of poetry:

Whene'er a wrong is done
To the humblest and the weakest
    'neath the all-beholding sun
That wrong is surely done to us and
    we are slaves most base
Whose love of right is for ourselves,
And not for all the race.

The agenda of middle-class progressives like Yeomans, looking down upon the humble and the weak, reflected both the ruling class's preoccupation with an efficient social order and with reforms for the underclasses. Through initiatives like that of Yeomans, the deviant were classified for purposes of amelioration, co-option, or suppression. If the morally insane Blake should not exactly be freed, at least she could live in comfortable detention and contribute to the advancement of knowledge.

But Blake, neither the humblest nor the weakest of the race, refused to play along with Yeomans's 'love of right' and would not consent to any attempt to save her.[47] While Blake probably did not know the terms 'born female criminal' and 'occasional female criminal', she certainly understood the concepts, and she may have recognized during the interview that Yeomans's sense of inbred fatality would not reflect well on her own attempts to portray herself as essentially a good and feminine woman. Certainly she did not want a life in jail.

The meeting between the two women was perhaps destined to end unsatisfactorily for other reasons, too, for the terms each lived by clashed so directly against the other's. Yeomans was resolutely ameliorist and comic in outlook. Relatively powerful, she was a small part of a larger community striving, with qualified success, towards the betterment of conditions for women. Endemic social blight was an affront to her Victorian liberal commitment to progress, yet she never seems to have considered the possibility that Blake's predicament was the result of a wish to move upward. Her own experience of personal success and acclaim in almost every endeavour, despite opposition, allowed her to expect that every problem had a solution.

Blake's sensibility in jail, on the other hand, alternated between tragic melodrama, in which powerful forces (both within and without) were arrayed against her, and an almost postmodern (or at least Wildean) sense that life consisted of a series of game roles, 'that Truth is entirely and absolutely a matter of style.'[48] During her melodramatic and introspective moods, she was more likely—in keeping with the genre—to appeal to male chivalry than to female solidarity. During her Wildean moods, she was not likely to worry overmuch about the state of her soul, even though counsellors like Yeomans wanted her to worry. In both moods she by now felt relatively powerless, because even when she had acted decisively, she had lost. She could only compensate for that lack of power with a rich imaginative life that expressed itself in 'a most irrational self-importance'.

*

And, briefly, she was important. In Brandon, the legal firm of Clement & Clement drafted, and several philanthropic societies sponsored, a petition seeking a delay of the execution. It was already circulating by 13 December; the first to sign was R.M. Matheson, the about to be superannuated Crown prosecutor[49] who had secured her conviction, and many prominent citizens followed suit. 'Many are refusing to sign,' the *Sun* observed, 'but the majority appear to desire her to escape the gallows.'[50] Yeomans's Winnipeg petition materialized three days later.

Commutation campaigns such as Blake's were frequent. Condemned men, and especially women, were almost always the inspiration for campaigns of reprieve, commutation, or retrial. Since early in the nineteenth century, in Britain at least, no subject incited male benevolence and feminist oppositional thought more dramatically than that of the wronged woman, particularly if she was young, attractive, and vulnerable to male wiles. Two of the most extraordinary appeal campaigns were initiated on behalf of young female servants. One of these servants, Sarah Lloyd, was hanged for stealing from her mistress; a second, Eliza Fenning, was hanged in 1825 for attempting to murder her master's family by poisoning their dumplings with arsenic. Unprecedented campaigns to save these commoners or rehabilitate their reputations incorporated long-standing critiques of *ancien regime* law.[51]

A decade before Blake's case, broad popular sympathy emerged in 1889 for Florence Maybrick, an American woman in Britain who had been convicted on circumstantial evidence of poisoning her husband. After public pressure, her sentence was commuted, and a campaign continued to have her released from jail. Canadian public pressure had failed to get a commutation for Sarnia's Elizabeth Workman in 1873, but did get a new trial (and acquittal) in 1897 for Olive Sternaman in Cayuga, Ontario. Workman had killed a man who had abused her for years. Many people, including the jury that convicted her, urged that her sentence be commuted. Workman's hanging was marked by public lament rather than a sense of justice done, but since she was poor, working class, and hardly 'respectable', the political repercussions were minimal. Nevertheless, the campaign must have made a difference, because for 26 years after Workman was put to death, no woman was executed in Canada, even though the women who murdered did so under much less provocation than Workman had experienced. Of the seven women sentenced to death in Canada after Workman, six had their sentences commuted, while public pressure brought about a new trial for the seventh—Sternaman—despite strong evidence that she had poisoned her husband in order to pursue an illicit love affair. When at the second trial the defence raised doubts about the circumstantial evidence, Sternaman was acquitted. Women who killed women, on the other hand, found little support. Mary

Wheeler Pearcey, a British woman who had bludgeoned to death the wife of her lover in 1890, was executed in London without popular expressions of regret.[52]

In Brandon, the evidence disclosed during Emma Stripp's preliminary hearing on 10 December helped to throw popular support behind the movement to save Blake. Stripp's case raised new speculation that Blake had not acted alone. One did not have to cause the death of another person directly to be guilty of murder. Under the doctrine of 'constructive murder', Robert Lane could be convicted of murder if he knew or ought to have known that his words or actions might cause his wife's death.[53] Legal authorities had to decide whether or not to prefer charges against Lane, and Manitoba's Attorney General therefore wrote to the federal Minister of Justice on 14 December for a deferral of the execution until the investigation of Lane was completed.

Rev. McLaurin told the press that the movement to save Blake was the product 'of a dissatisfied public'. On many occasions he had been approached to do something, but he had been unable because Blake's was a clear case of first-degree murder. Efforts to prevent her execution had also been frustrated by the fact that Blake was 'friendless' and had no family members who would take up her cause. Of course, Blake, for her part, had refused free legal counsel, had blocked every effort to bring her case to trial, and had insisted that she would rather die than spend years in prison. On 14 December, 'My Downfall', with its broad hints that Robert Lane might be responsible for Blake's fall, was published in the *Western Sun*, along with the interview in which Rev. McLaurin sympathetically revealed some of Blake's feelings about her life. There were rumours that she had also written an autobiography, which, the *Western Sun* later said, would 'hardly stand publication',[54] presumably because the material it contained was potentially libellous.

On the 15th, Winnipeg newspaper readers first saw Yeomans's report of her interview with Blake, and on the 16th Yeomans's petition appeared, supported by her authority as a doctor and addressed to Governor-General Minto:

> The petition of the undersigned citizens of the city of Winnipeg, humbly showeth:
> That one Hilda Blake, a young woman of unknown parentage, from the first a waif cast on public charity, is confined in jail in the City of Brandon, Manitoba under sentence of death, and awaiting execution on the 27th of this month (December).
> Your petitioners would earnestly ask that

Whereas no defense has been made in the case of said Hilda Blake, she having declined such assistance, and

Whereas, her probably vicious heredity, and the facts of her life as known to those who have been associated with her, might throw some doubt on her moral responsibility in the commission of the crime to which she has confessed, and

Whereas, light on the case for the defence has been utterly excluded by the course taken, and

Whereas, with full inquiry, much reason might have appeared for a mitigation of her sentence, and it is manifestly unjust to execute the death penalty in the absence of such inquiry.

Therefore we, your petitioners, urgently ask for a stay of execution, and a thorough examination both of the prisoner herself, as regards her mental and moral responsibility, and of her past actions and history, as these may, in their measure, account for and throw light upon her commission of the crime.

Blank forms of petitions were put in the *Free Press* business office, and in Mitchell's, Inman's, and Gordon's drug stores.[55] While the petition to save was spearheaded by women, it found broad community support in Winnipeg. Signatories included A.J. Andrews, the mayor of Winnipeg who later played such a prominent role in the suppression of the 1919 Winnipeg General Strike; Horace Wilson, mayor-elect; Rodmond P. Roblin, who within a few months would replace Hugh John MacDonald as the Conservative Premier of Manitoba; Georgina Stewart, provincial president of the WCTU; as well as prominent businessmen, professionals, and churchmen.[56] By 20 December 487 people had signed. That number may seem small in comparison with petitions for middle-class women such as Olive Sternaman, but the *Winnipeg Daily Tribune* said 'the number is thought large considering the short time, three or four days, the petition has been before the public.'[57] According to the *Western Sun*, the Blake case generated more interest in Winnipeg than in Brandon.[58]

By this time the campaign to save her did not really need Blake's approval, for after she was sentenced to hang, the image of 'the orphan' resurfaced from its 10-year slumber, and, in echo of the child-savers who had sent her to Canada, people now strove to save the 'friendless' girl from the gallows. The patriarchal family, presided over by men but shaped by the nurturing of women, was supposed to be an oasis of safety and morality, but the shadow of the middle-class family was the orphan child. Some people, like Melita's 'Moralist', classified the orphan among the dirty and vicious industrial working class (whatever her actual origins). Yeomans's analysis of Hilda as a congenital deviant similarly confirmed the widely held stereotype of British pauper children as a threat to Canadian social purity. But the orphan, without parents, could also appear to exist without social context, so one could perceive her in the way that some middle-class reformers did: as a child very nearly like one's own children. The Victorian image of 'the child' gazed out from the frontispiece of the *Child's Bible*: large serious eyes, preternatural whiteness, and pre-Raphaelite beauty.[59] Who would not want to aid such a child? Here were the middle and upper classes at their most innocent, seemingly prior (though clothing and whiteness declared otherwise) to the acquisition of wealth. To comfort such a child was reason enough for material acquisition.

One letter to the editor in support of commutation pointed to the murder as the culmination of Blake's orphanhood:

> The fact that she was reared in a workhouse, departed from her native land at a tender age to eke out an existence as a drudge among strangers, good, bad, or indifferent as the case might be, to the girl's welfare tells the whole pitiable story. It was shown that her environments since youth were not conducive to the expression and cultivation of her higher nature. Who knows of the struggles going on in this girl's soul in her battle with unjust conditions that, alas, only too often surround a girl of her class. The broodings of an undisciplined spirit over imagined or imposed wrongs in most cases stultifies and perverts the character. Naturally weak in moral stamina, she was thrown like a thing of chance upon the ocean of life and shipwrecked. And we, as a community are now ready to hurl this misguided soul into eternity, aye, before it ever had a chance of knowing or realizing the full meaning and purpose of life, nor awakened to the divine possibilities of her being.[60]

The sexuality of female orphans adrift in the world and vulnerable to sexual predators gave lives like Blake's an additional pathos. Sympathy for Blake was rooted in the notion that men bore responsibility for the tragedy of fallen women, because men exploited the lack of self-control of young women, particularly of orphans.[61] Lombroso and Ferrero argued that the 'natural form of [atavistic] regression in women was prostitution',[62] very different from the male regression into violence. Blake's letters to a man outside the prison, revealed at Stripp's preliminary hearing, suggested that Blake's case might be so

explained—as a combination of baleful heredity, adverse social conditions, and male sexual desire. Supporters of commutation hinted at
this point: 'My plea for the girl's temporary respite from death is
based on the impression that there is another or others implicated in
the murder.' [63]

The newspapers and letters to the editor reflected community support for a pardon, generally using Yeomans's reformist and social-
ameliorist language. Some writers urged that capital punishment was
inherently immoral, and especially so in this case. According to one
writer, the futility of capital punishment was evident from years of
study of 'penology and social economics'; capital punishment was a
'relic of barbarism, a blot upon the civilization that [claimed] to be
Christian'. According to another, 'the treatment of the weak, the ignorant and the vicious is one of the greatest problems of the age.' The real
issue raised by the Blake case was said to be 'the reformation of the
criminal, the aiding and assisting him toward a higher development—
a development of the soul'. It was essential that steps be taken to prevent 'judicial murder'.[64] In the *Western Sun*, 'Citizen' could find no
explanation for the murder, and followed Yeomans in saying that public opinion would 'be shocked if something was not done to establish
the sanity and the full responsibility of the poor creature.' Others
agreed, noting that Blake's trial had lasted only five minutes and that
the court had not taken the trouble to establish the facts of the case
prior to sentencing.[65]

Some who called for a review of the sentence urged that Blake's
own guilty plea not be used as the sole basis for execution. 'A Daughter of England' invoked 'British justice' in support of a reconsideration. Of Blake's brief trial, she wrote, 'surely in the nineteenth
century we do not call that justice.' She noted that the prisoner was an
Englishwoman like herself, and concluded that Blake's execution
'would be the first time in the annals of British justice, they are hanging a woman on her own word, without taking the trouble to prove her
guilty.'[66] People had been known to use the courts as a way of committing suicide, claimed 'Caritas', and it appeared that Blake was
determined to die. While her guilt seemed clear given the circumstantial evidence, Blake's testimony against herself should still be set
aside and the case more thoroughly investigated in a full trial whether
Blake wished it or not. In short, before the state took a life it had an
obligation to prove a case against the accused in open court.[67]

One writer drew direct comparisons between Blake and Florence
Maybrick, bringing in considerations of class and gender. Maybrick's
British husband of seven years, a cotton merchant some years older

than she, had died suddenly. Maybrick acknowledged involvement in an extramarital sexual relationship, a disclosure that came to figure prominently in the trial—the Crown arguing that Maybrick had poisoned her husband in order to be free to pursue the affair. The judge, Sir James Fitzjames Stephen, was an outspoken advocate of moral neutrality in the administration of the criminal law. Responding to defence claims that men and women were held to different standards of private conduct (Maybrick's husband, too, had had a mistress), Stephen began his charge to the jury neutrally:

> we have not to determine any moral question at all, but simply look at the matter as it comes before us, and with reference to the well-established rules of conduct. There is one thing in this matter upon which there can be no doubt whatever; in fact, we have it now stated by Mrs. Maybrick herself, that she did . . . carry on an adulterous intercourse with this man Brierly.

But then Stephen condemned the affair as 'disgraceful', and began, in the eyes of Maybrick's supporters, to prejudge her on the basis of her sexual reputation rather than on the facts of the murder:

> You must remember the intrigue which she carried on with this man Brierly, and the feelings—it seems horrible to comparatively ordinary decent people—a horrible and incredible thought that a woman should be plotting the death of her husband in order that she might be left at liberty to follow her own degrading vices. . . . There is no doubt that the propensities which lead persons to vices of that kind kill all the more tender, all the more manly, or all the more womanly feelings of the human mind. . . . I will not say anything about it, except that is easy enough to conceive how a horrible woman, in so terrible a position, might be assailed by some fearful and terrible temptation.[68]

Many people were outraged, both by Stephen's gender partiality and, more broadly, by the difficulties placed before women who sought divorce. Following her conviction, Maybrick's supporters successfully appealed to public opinion and the British Home Secretary to commute her death sentence.[69]

Maybrick was of the middle class; those who had advocated on her behalf were also middle class. Writing to the *Free Press*, 'Sympathizer' emphasized the role of class in sentence commutations:

> What is the difference between [Blake's] case and Mrs. Maybrick? One took the life of a woman, the other the life of a man, yet one is

condemned to death, the other to life imprisonment: the latter a woman with friends, position, money, consequently appeal after appeal has been made for her freedom, not from death, but from the less terrible punishment.

'Sympathizer' concluded that Blake would eventually be executed simply because she was 'nobody, a servant girl friendless and alone'.[70] 'A Daughter of England' echoed this: 'she is only a servant girl, and so I suppose that entitles her to be hanged.'[71]

One western newspaper pressed for a more diligent examination of the case. The *Regina Standard* editorialized (mistakenly) that in Brandon, the 'city of churches', no one other than Emma Jane Stripp had moved a finger on Blake's behalf. The *Standard* also noted that while women in the United States clamoured for the absolute release of Maybrick, Blake's plight had failed 'to arouse the sympathies of the women of Canada even to the extent of pleading with the Minister of Justice to substitute life imprisonment for the revolting and ignominious death to which she stands condemned.'[72] The *Standard* acknowledged that initially Blake had lied about her involvement in Lane's death. Still, Blake had not provided a convincing explanation of her motive. She had declined defence counsel, and, with 'stoical indifference', had heard the death sentence pronounced on her. Although 'rumours which gossiping tongues set afloat' had not been substantiated, nothing apart from the murder had been shown against her character. These circumstances demanded delay and further investigation:

> the mystery of the murder has not been unraveled. . . . Let the mystery of motive be penetrated and the girl's mental condition be ascertained, before we deprive a fellow creature of the God-given life which no legal process can restore.[73]

The *Western Sun* reprinted the editorial for Brandonites.

Not everyone was sympathetic. The *Brandon Times*, a Conservative Party organ, suggested that there were people in Brandon and Winnipeg 'working overtime in an attempt to make the Hilda Blake affair as sensational as possible'. The *Times* believed that Brandon was 'pretty tired of the newspaper twaddle in reference to the condemned woman, which for some weeks now has been pretty generally supplied by the yellow journals of the province.'[74] Such a reaction was not surprising, since the *Times* had painted the original murder scene in broad strokes of pathos:

> It was a pitiful sight to see the three little children crying over the mother gasping out her life the victim of a fiend's dastardly act.

Those who witnessed this pathetic little scene turned away with swelling hearts and tearful eyes and with a prayer on their lips to the Friend of Little Children.[75]

The sensibility and morality, the capacity for emotional identification with the sorrow of others that tears disclosed,[76] were best spent upon the Lane children, not upon a murderous servant. Even the WCTU was not unanimous in its call for commutation. When a petition was circulated requesting that the sentence be commuted to life imprisonment, some members of the Brandon WCTU rose and left the meeting in protest.[77] Blake had certainly placed herself outside of the domestic ideal, and there was a current in 1890s reformist thinking that sought the abolition of capital punishment, but without sympathy for the criminal.[78]

As well, organized labour took little interest in Blake's case, despite the letter writers who blamed Blake's sentence on social class. In Ontario, the federal Minister of Justice credited the Knights of Labor for convincing him to legislate against seduction in the workplace. Labour in Hamilton, again under the auspices of the Knights, lobbied the federal cabinet on behalf of Maria McCabe in 1883, arguing that the murder of her child showed 'the vulnerable position of working-class women'.[79] In the West, however, craft unions devoted to advancing the interests of groups of skilled male workers—of British and Canadian railway workmen in Brandon[80]— generally ignored the circumstances of unskilled workers. The problems of women workers in particular stood outside of, and in some cases were perceived as a threat to, the interests of male workers. As late as 1919, the Brandon Trades and Labour Council refused to accept women delegates named to the Council by the recently organized sanitarium workers union in the city.[81] These workers laboured within the categories of liberal capitalism and accepted its basic legitimacy while advancing the corporatist interests of workers within the established order. More simply, some union members felt that Blake was guilty. The Winnipeg labour newspaper, *The Voice*, found it ironic that with the Boer crisis in South Africa Manitobans were 'yelling for war and shuddering at a prospective hanging'. Like 'A Daughter of England', *The Voice* invoked British justice, but for very different purposes: Blake was clearly guilty, the crime was premeditated, and petitions to sway the public could only cloud the issue, substituting, as petitions always did, sentiment for law.[82]

Nevertheless, on the day of the publication of 'My Downfall' (with its renewed emphasis on the orphan child) the *Free Press* commented that public sympathy for Blake was increasing as the execution date approached and that those who knew Blake well described her as a very sensitive person. One of her former employers reported that he 'never knew a better girl or one so affectionate with children. His children almost worshipped her, she was so kind to them.'[83] The newspaper urged reconsideration of her death penalty. And despite internal opposition, the WCTU determined to circulate the petition. The principal argument advanced by the petitioners was that Glendenning, who had left her child to die of exposure, had received a five-year sentence, while Blake had been sentenced to death.[84] Petitions were 'being largely signed, very few refusals being given'. Many people believed that had she offered the court some reasonable explanation for the murder, her case would have been dealt with more leniently: 'that there were extenuating circumstances seems more than probable, the story that she was influenced to commit the horrible deed through love of the murdered woman's children being too silly to deserve credence.'[85]

Two people from Blake's past resurfaced and also took an interest. Alfred Broadhurst, who had taken the Blake children over to Canada, remembered the small girl and responded to her now pitiable condition; he tried to contact her by letter and hoped to ameliorate her condition if possible.[86] As well, A.P. Stewart, still mourning his wife's recent death, visited his former ward in jail and showed a conciliatory attitude.[87] Stewart's visits seemed to move Blake more than that of Yeomans had, the enfranchisement of women touching Blake less directly than did sympathy from her once inflexible guardian.

13

Novels, Poems, and Coon Songs

You will flop your snow-white wings and try to fly;
I know the angels they will giggle
When I do that awful wiggle,
When I do the hoochy coochy in de sky!

—Gussie Davis (1894)

While people in the streets argued about the petitions, Blake spent her time in solitary pursuits: she read novels and devotional literature, wrote poetry and letters, prayed and sang 'coon songs'. One report suggests that she was not even kept informed of the petitions.[1] For a time she was in possession of the laudanum that Stripp had brought her and she could have attempted suicide, but did not. Her state of mind is not very easy to reconstruct, yet the hints that have been preserved suggest that she lived a complex inner life in prison, as she must have while still free. She alternated between regret and defiance, serious reflection and comic forgetfulness. In a conversation with Matheson, the Crown prosecutor, just days before her execution, Blake said, 'I seem to be possessed of two natures, one good and one very bad, and they seem to control me at different times. I am either good or very bad. You cannot think me altogether bad?'[2] This was the best Blake could do to describe the various currents of her being, yet the statement is a dramatic oversimplification, since her goodness could not always be separated from her theatrical sense of self, and the evil she had done had roots in something other than bald perversity.

As she awaited execution, newspapers like the *Independence* portrayed an unreflective woman, one careless about the state of her mortal soul:

> During the time she has lain under sentence she has betrayed no anxiety, but read trashy novels and sung nigger songs; though the Rev. Mr. McLaurin spent much time with her and without doubt impressed her with the awful possibilities of her position.[3]

More specific was the *Sun*:

> She has occupied her time in reading useless novels, cared but little until the last day or so, for such reading as would prepare her for another life, has chafed at the apparent coldness of the world, and chided the public that never before took an interest in her moral welfare; she has delighted in playing practical jokes, and it is said that within forty-eight hours of her death had an evident pleasure in singing 'Coon songs.'

The *Sun* writer dismissed her as 'a character difficult to understand',[4] but to other eyes, this portrait, together with what we have seen so far, suggests a woman split between a moral middle-class language, which she thought worth imitating, and a seemingly lower-class language that she found pleasurable. One language might effect her pardon, but the other was more easeful, not obsessed with good and evil.

The domestic servant's life, Ella Sykes had warned, 'is that of a drudge . . . and the woman who undertakes it becomes a drudge',[5] but in prison, domestic duties laid aside, Blake flowered. For her reading, she preferred 'Scott, Dickens, and other high class novels'.[6] In nineteenth-century North America, novels were often considered useless, a distraction from the earnest business of saving one's soul, on the one hand, and the equally earnest business of getting and spending on the other. Dangerously for the health of society, novels enlisted one's sympathy for women of dubious morality, and for the New Woman.[7] They could, potentially, induce hysteria, and certainly cause young women to lose their chastity.[8] Moralists such as Rev. Bernard O'Reilly, author of *The Mirror of True Womanhood*, warned especially women away from novels:

> Akin to the fatal passion for dress is the still more fatal and no less general passion for light reading. . . . Whereas conscientious druggists will give what is healthful to all, they will only deal out what is poisonous in small quantities and to responsible and properly authorized persons;—while libraries and librarians have no

conscience, and let the innocent child take away and devour what kills purity, innocence, and conscience forever.[9]

Yet novels, so long as they displayed appropriate morals, were also signs of culture. In 1885, Canadian literary critic Graeme Mercer Adam longed for 'the good old romantic and imaginative novel of our grandmothers' time'; and in the 1890s, Blake's beloved Scott, in particular, was praised as a novelist who created 'fresh wholesome romance, free from soul-harrowing incidents'. Both Scott and Dickens were praised in 1889 for their idealism—their striving for 'beauty and virtue', [10] and after her arrest Blake fantasized about the high sentiments that even criminals in Scott's work demonstrated. She would have read excerpts from novels by Dickens and especially Scott in the *Victorian Readers* that had been authorized for schools by the Advisory Board of Manitoba.[11] As well, Brandon had at least two bookstores in the 1890s: Christie's, which called itself 'The Largest Bookstore in the Canadian West', and Ye Famous and Fashionable Book Shop, which promised to fill mail orders promptly.[12] Library accession records at Brandon College (now Brandon University), which began life as a Baptist seminary, show that a number of Scott novels were acquired in the first few years of the institution's existence.[13] The Brandon Local Council of Women even planned, in 1896, to open a reading room and library in Brandon. President Jessie McEwen argued that 'Good books and bright magazines are as needful as bodily food and clothing.'[14]

Blake certainly read *Jane Eyre*; we may guess that of Dickens and Scott she probably read the shorter and more popular works. The orphan Pip's haunting discovery in *Great Expectations* that the source of his education and fine clothes was the convict Magwitch, and not the upper-class Miss Havisham, might have stirred Blake, but Pip's situation wasn't hers, and irony was not quite her line. Yet the abandoned children—Magwitch, Estella—and other poorly treated children 'growing up to be hanged' would have struck a nerve. Blake may also have seen portents of her own situation in that of Mr Jaggers's housekeeper, who went to trial for murdering another woman, while the man in the case, Magwitch, 'kept himself dark . . . out of the way of the trial, and was only vaguely talked about.'[15] If Blake managed to struggle through the massive *Our Mutual Friend*, she would have seen that even a 'mercenary' beauty like Bella Wilfer could be made sympathetic via love, and especially that Lizzy Hexam's hopeless love for a gentleman cad was very nearly the highest emotion to which the female breast could aspire. Blake would have recognized the orphan's fantasy about childless and wealthy people (Miss Potter-son, Mr and Mrs Boffin) who were ever so eager to adopt an orphan, particularly a good-looking one.[16] *Jane Eyre* and *Rob Roy* would have probably felt nearer to her situation and would have allowed her to fantasize about how a friendless orphan might have succeeded: in *Rob Roy* the motherless Diana Vernon Beauchamp, 'alone in the world, left to her own guidance and protection', laments that God sent most people into the world 'to enjoy, and *her* to suffer'.[17] Still, she, like Jane Eyre, gets a good man and a fine station in the end.

Fictional orphans like Jane Eyre experienced an independence and agency 'denied to most young women' of Blake's era. If she read more contemporary novels, Blake would have seen the sentimentality and vulnerability of the orphan convention's early form give way, par-ticularly among women writers at century's end, to 'radical comment, capable of providing alternative behaviour and roles to the domestic ideal without directly threatening the structure of the family'. By means of the orphan convention, novelists throughout the nineteenth century questioned issues of class and women's roles.[18]

But stirring above all would have been the early and sentimental *Oliver Twist*. Dickens 'wished to show, in little Oliver, the principle of Good surviving through every adverse circumstance, and triumph-ing at last.' How could Blake not become enamoured of an author who was contemptuous of the respectable and of their tendency to exaggerate narrow little virtues at the expense of downtrodden women such as the prostitute Nancy?

> [An] allusion to Nancy's doubtful character, raised a vast quantity of chaste wrath in the bosoms of four housemaids, who remarked, with great fervour, that the creature was a disgrace to her sex; and strongly advocated her being thrown, ruthlessly, into the kennel.

Of the workhouse orphan Oliver, Mr Grimwig prophesies, 'I know that boy will be hung', words now familiar and piercing to Blake, and Oliver nearly, through no fault of his own, fulfils the prophecy.

With *Oliver Twist*, Blake could have it both ways: she could enter an alternate world in which orphans accused of hanging crimes did not, in the end, hang; at the same time, through the guilty but good-hearted prostitute, Nancy, Blake could ponder her own approaching death. Nancy refused to be 'saved', even by the sympathetic Rose Maylie, because 'salvation' had to be bought at the price of the scoundrel Bill Sikes's neck. Nancy's refusal-of-salvation speech must have echoed deep in Blake, who had written a passionate note to her own 'wicked and dishonorable' man:

When ladies as young, and good, and beautiful as you are . . . give away your hearts, love will carry you all lengths—even such as you, who have home, friends, other admirers, everything, to fill them. When such as I, who have no certain roof but the coffin-lid, and no friend in sickness or death but the hospital nurse, set our rotten hearts on any man, and let him fill the place that has been a blank through all our wretched lives, who can hope to cure us? Pity us, lady—pity us for having only one feeling of the woman left, and for having that turned, by a heavy judgement, from a comfort and a pride, into a new means of violence and suffering.[19]

Thackeray, having observed a few young prostitutes, called Nancy 'the most unreal fantastical personage possible. . . . [Dickens] dare not tell the truth concerning such young ladies.'[20] But for Blake, whose note to a man outside of the prison implied that love could reconcile her to the gallows, Nancy was an ideal worth imitating.

Some in Dickens's middle-class audience objected to the sentimental portrait of the criminal and lower-class Nancy. Reading novels had once been a class divider, an important distinction between the literate master and the uneducated servant, but by the 1890s even servants could use libraries or buy cheap editions of British and American novels.[21] Those with less liberal views than Jessie McEwen still argued in Blake's day that novel-reading for servants was a highly questionable practice, and in magazine articles of the time one finds arguments for and against allowing servants anything other than devotional reading material. An employer from Rapid City, near Brandon, advised incoming domestics in 1886 to 'Bring . . . sufficient good sense to avoid all romantic ideas of accepting the first offer of marriage on arriving here; also frivolous notions about dress, reading novels, and the like.'[22] While good reading might improve the mind,[23] the reading of novels by servants was unproductive at best; at worst it could give them ideas above their station. As the winking reference to Blake's interest in 'other high class novels' indicates, the 1899 newspapers too could be ironic about murderous servants who pretended to fine literature. And of course, so the *Sun* preached, the novels that Blake was reading would not prepare her for the next life.

*

Yet entertainments that seemed lower class were even less appropriate, and Blake's partiality to 'coon songs' made the issue of her leisure time that much clearer. Coon songs arose in the post-Civil War United States out of the earlier blackface minstrelsy, mixing infectious early ragtime syncopation with racist stereotypes of American blacks. Both whites and blacks—usually in separate companies—wrote and performed the songs, so that the coon song phenomenon brought financial and artistic success to black performers, at the same time justifying segregation and turning America's tragic apartheid into comedy.[24] For black performers, the coon song provided a way of getting noticed by a broad portion of the North American public, usually at the price of insulting one's own race. The comic image of the coon sublimated the fear of a racial threat, excused past white crimes, and made segregation seem like an appropriate response to racial difference.[25] Occasionally coon songs could contain subtle satire against white attitudes,[26] but the vast majority of the songs were clearly insulting to blacks. When the black musician Ernest Hogan brought out 'All Coons Look Alike to Me' in 1896, whites sang along while blacks raged, and all his life Hogan regretted writing the song. Its content was much less incendiary than its title; nevertheless, for whites to whistle it was construed as a racial slur and started fist fights.[27]

If the coon song wasn't precisely a lower-class entertainment, it certainly felt like one. It licensed risqué humour and broached all sorts of taboo subjects—sexuality in particular—to the point that, according to the black composer Gussie Davis, some respectable people shunned what they saw as the coon song's moral taint: '[Women] cannot sing a minstrel or Negro song in the parlour, and refined people would not allow it in the house.'[28] The coon songs that Blake sang also licensed slang, bad grammar, and dialect, mixing the vernacular with the formal,[29] releasing one from the verbal decorum of Victorian culture. 'Don't use slangy words; they are vulgar', Grandma Nichols had cautioned. 'Don't use profane words; they are sinful and foolish. . . . Your conduct on the street should always be modest and dignified. Ladies', she urged, 'should carefully avoid all loud and boisterous conversation or laughter and all undue liveliness in public'[30]—though perhaps Grandma Nichols didn't have jail in mind as a public place where a lady might appear.

Like the 'coon' in 'I Guess I'll Have to Telegraph My Baby' (George M. Cohan, 1898),[31] Blake knew what it was like to languish in jail, but she was certainly not alone in her taste. Coon songs were the craze all over North America in the 1890s among all social classes, with over 600 coon songs published in that decade, some selling in the millions of copies.[32] When in early December the 'Coontown 400' were advertised as coming to Brandon, the *Sun* hastened to quell any potential outrage by asserting that the show put on by the 15 coloured actors and actresses would be, despite expectations to the

contrary, clean and refined.[33] A review of the Coontown 400's performance allows, reluctantly, that there may be a place for such entertainments: 'It cannot be said that there is anything instructive about
the programme, yet it is full of harmless flowery jokes, sayings, and
songs.' More appropriate, one gathers, for well-to-do citizens than for
penitent criminals. Despite (or shall we say because of?) the program's lack of moral instruction, it 'brought the house down'.[34] The
music was good, and for British Canadians eager to assert their social
ascendancy in an increasingly polyglot West, coon songs could clarify
their position as the privileged race.

By means of coon songs and practical jokes, Blake could be the
Artful Dodger, defying the authorities who were going to punish her.
But what did she see in the songs? It may simply be that the songs
provided her with an escape, a time during which she could be
momentarily free of the knowledge of what lay ahead, and also free
of the patrician dignity that she liked to affect. Yet such songs provided a very particular kind of escape. Like *Oliver Twist*, coon songs
allowed Blake to ponder her position obliquely, through the pop-cul-
ture image of the 'coon'. In an unconscious and playful manner, the
songs could 'explain' her society's (and her own) feelings of where
the cardinal points of conflict, suffering, and joy lay for the modern
individual. She was *not* a coon; as a white person of British descent
she could look down on the coon from a far superior position. At the
same time, she *was* a coon: although she would have been completely
unconscious of the social hurdles placed before anyone who had
black skin, nevertheless the stereotype of the lower-class outsider, the
lying, stealing, usurping, and occasionally murderous coon echoed
some of the images of herself that Blake saw in the newspapers.

Given the heavy reliance on crude racial stereotypes, coon songs
tell one very little about black American culture, but a lot—cir-
cuitously and metaphorically—about the inner world of the coon
song's audience: what it felt like to be white and young and modern
in the 1890s. The songs expressed attitudes to which Blake and many
young people of the 1890s unconsciously assented in their actions.
White musician Harry von Tilzer's 'I'd Leave Ma Happy Home for
You' was a big coon-song hit in 1899, in contrast to other 1890s songs
about 'the sanctity of the nuptial promise'.[35] Sentiment, particularly
love, was often secondary in coon songs to material considerations.
'I'm Always Glad to See You When You'll Buy' by George Totten
Smith (1899) and 'All Coons Look Alike to Me' depict the coon's
'ladyfriend' as mercenary and hard-hearted. In serious popular songs,
women who left the domestic sphere were prey to corruption, likely

Sheet music cover for 'I Don't Want No Yellow Coon', 1899. Blake loved 'coon songs', probably because they dealt with things like extramarital relationships and social class more directly than did 'proper' forms of entertainment. (Brown University Library.)

to 'fall', and could redeem themselves only by rejecting the material gain they received as 'kept' women.[36] The coon song therefore felt like a more realistic account of relations between the sexes, especially to a person like Blake, who wanted to climb socially.

Coon songs not only portrayed city life, but arguably enacted (and, by means of the laughable coon, defused) the conflict 'between the new urban culture and the cultures of older elites'.[37] Skin colour expressed a 'natural' boundary, so whites could indirectly address class conflict *within* white society and could at the same time believe that satire against the social pretensions of coloured people was incisive, as in John Queen's 'Got Your Habits On' (1899):

> And when dey learn how to read and write,
> Why most of dem niggers just think they're white.

In songs like Irving Jones's 'Let Me Bring My Clothes Back Home' (1897), women spoke bluntly about wishing to change their racial—and thereby their class—status:

> His wife said, "Honey, I'm tired o' coon,
> I goin' to pass for white."

The young mulatto mistress in Hogan's 'No More Will I Ever be Your Baby' (*c.* 1897) changes her persona to match her new uptown address:

> She wants all the nigs to let her alone,
> She looks on them with a frown . . .
> She won't have anything to do with coons any more. . . .
> She says she's got money and she's goin' to pass for white.[38]

Although the attitudes of such women were certainly not lauded, the coon song's sly humour could undermine satire or broaden it to white audiences by hinting at racial and class miscegenation.

> My gal is a high born lady,
> She's black, but not too shady

went Barney Fagan's 1896 song, 'she is not colored, she was born that way.' That the singer was sometimes in blackface, singing to a woman whose 'blackness' was more the result of a particular legal code than of her nearly white physical appearance, made the song's message rather ambivalent.[39] Fagan's satire would also be understood ambivalently by one who had her own pretensions to culture, her beauty and her Britishness letting her 'pass' as one of the ascendant class.

Even if Blake was not directly conscious of such conflicts, satire was in any case a relaxation from the more idealized female images in

serious popular songs. Some interpreters of American slavery go so
far as to suggest that, socially, blackness came to represent the 'former
selves' of the Anglo-American bourgeoisie, the repressed life that had
to be laid aside when white America adopted 'an ethos that attacked
holidays, spurned contact with nature, saved time, bridled sexuality,
separated work from the rest of life and postponed gratification.'[40]
Such an explanation certainly helps explain the lure of the coon song
for Blake and her society. The sexual innuendo and the depictions of
shifting, temporary sexual liaisons in coon songs[41] went out to, and
helped create, sympathetic listeners in the 1890s, 'predicting' the
growth of the divorce rate in the early twentieth century. 'Smutty'
shows like 'Gay Paris', featuring 'a liberal display of the female
form', were popular in Brandon despite the *Western Sun*'s scolding:
'the dirtier the story, the more vociferous was the applause.'[42] And in
coon songs such as W.S. Gilbert's 'The Cannibal and the Missionary'
(1889), sexually aggressive women as well as racially and socially
improbable sexual unions became possible, comically so:

> A Cannibal maiden loved too well,
> A missionary good!
> And he loved her but dare not tell his love,
> For this is how it stood:
> A clergyman he, and a cannibal she,
> And their creeds were wide apart,
> And how could he take for sentiment's sake
> A cannibal to his heart?
> Oh! 'twas a problem vexing, very,
> For the cannibal maid and the missionary. . . .
>
> This cannibal maiden's love grew bold,
> For she was a simple thing.
> And thus her love to her love she told:
> "Oh, marry me, be my king!
> For I love you my sweet, well enough, oh, to eat,
> It's a terrible thing, I know,
> But I must be your bride, or devour you fried,
> Oh, I must, for I love you so!"
>
> . . . .
>
> They were wed on that day, for 'tis ever the way,
> That passion must conquer creed;
> And a happier pair, it's remarkably rare,
> To discover it is indeed.[43]

Heat and warmth were traditional coon song codes for sex,[44] exaggerated here by the business of eating. Women who initiated courtship occasionally appeared outside of the coon song, though more elegantly, in calculated swoons,[45] and never with sexually compromising language. If Dickens couldn't tell the truth about girls like Nancy, the coon song could, obliquely.

Sexual innuendo would have been enough for Blake's observers to feel that the coon song was an inappropriate entertainment for a condemned woman. Irreverent portrayals of the afterlife in songs like Gussie Davis's 'When I Do The Hoochy-Coochy in De Sky' (1894) would not have done much to change minds:

> You will flop your snow-white wings and try to fly;
> I know the angels they will giggle
> When I do that awful wiggle,
> When I do the hoochy coochy in de sky!
>
> . . . .
>
> I will raise a big sensation with the white population,
> When I do the hoochy coochy in de sky![46]

Those who knew of gallows mishaps in which the condemned person was not killed instantaneously, and of the awful wiggles that ensued as the victim struggled for breath, would not have thought it edifying for Blake to laugh alongside Gussie Davis. Less metaphorically, such frivolities could not have impressed Rev. McLaurin either, who in a sermon of his later years complained that dancing and card playing were turning young people away from serious matters in order to gratify the flesh.[47]

*

Yet amid frivolities and romantic fantasies, Blake found time to make a confession to McLaurin, the content of which he refused to divulge to the newspapers,[48] and she wrote the veiled autobiographical poem, 'My Downfall', which he did divulge. She wrote more poems,[49] but they are no longer extant, and it was 'My Downfall' that she gave to McLaurin to pass on to the *Sun*. Other thoughts, more explicitly accusatory, she wrote down (perhaps with Jane Eyre as a model)[50] in an autobiography and handed the work over to the authorities. It was many pages in length, well-written and expressive, but Blake didn't intend it to be published; she wrote that it was 'for the Chief's perusal, and not for the newspaper'.[51]

According to Lombroso and Ferrero, 'the confession of her sins' was a characteristic document of female crime. Not only the occasional female criminal but also the born female criminal was full of religious feeling, and while that religiosity might lack depth, it did not lack truthfulness. 'The guilty woman', especially if she is only an occasional criminal, 'is more easily moved to penitence than men, recovers lost ground more quickly and relapses into crime less frequently.' Such a woman, Lombroso and Ferrero maintained, was readily influenced by sentimental religious advisers.[52] This is not surprising, since the pressure to conform to the ideal was so much stronger for women than for men, and we have already seen in Blake the impulse to conform. But against Lombroso and Ferrero's knowing irony (smiling as they do at the distance between the criminal's deeds and her religious profession), and against Mr Wemmick's assessment in *Great Expectations* that 'manuscript confessions written under condemnation' are 'every one of 'em Lies, sir',[53] we must counterpoint Blake's spiritual yearning—the wish to live a 'spiritual' life—as it was expressed in the Sunday school tracts she saved and in her poem.

It seems that towards the end of her imprisonment some of the people she knew from First Baptist did try to encourage her, possibly at the suggestion of McLaurin. 'That dear, kind Mr. Brown' (probably Robert Brown, a 49-year-old Baptist caretaker) wrote her 'the kindest, most loving, brotherly letter' and offered to do 'anything in this mortal world' to get Blake out of her predicament.[54] Zena Harper, a 52-year-old Baptist nurse who had been widowed, occasionally came to see Blake. It is not clear whether she came in an official or a private capacity, but she did mail letters on Blake's behalf.[55] And it may be that McLaurin had a hand in recommending the prison matron—Mrs Newton—who replaced Emma Stripp. The only Mrs Newton listed in the 1901 census was Mary Newton, a widowed Baptist housekeeper who lived with her well-to-do brother, Israel Scott. With Scott's farm income listed at $1,000 a year and her own at $400, Newton could choose what kind of job was beneath her and what kind of job was worthwhile, either economically or for reasons of ministry.

McLaurin and the Baptists may have been fascinated by the liminal experience Blake was about to undergo. She was coming near to that unnerving moment when 'the social' would no longer exist, the moment when 'faith' was supposed to become 'sight'. This moment, theoretically able to make or break the Christian meaning upon which the social order was built, could only, despite its centrality, be approached and approached and approached, but never met. In Brandon at that time only one person—Hilda Blake—was sure of going 'beyond' faith, and at a set hour she might see the substance of what McLaurin could merely hope for. If she died a holy death, she would be his surrogate, indeed, a surrogate for an entire society professing a faith in the next world.

In whatever way the Baptist visitors encouraged Blake, the dissonances between her love of coon songs and her own serious Christian poem remain striking. Yet an orphan, too, could have a conscience, even if, like Pip's in *Great Expectations*, it were not quite as tender as that of regular folks, and even if Blake's poetic turn sounds a bit like Compeyson's tendency to misdirect judges by showing up 'wi' verses in his speech'.[56] If we look at 'My Downfall' this time as a snapshot of Blake's thoughts in December 1899 and less as the story of her life, we see a variety of currents—some consistent with McLaurin's Baptist views, some going in rather different directions.

The poem's images of confinement are expected and obvious: the 'lonely cell', the 'awful wall' that separates Blake from her youth. More importantly, despite the newspapers, which portrayed her as careless of her soul and of 'the awful possibilities of her position', she was evidently thinking much about death. The several poetic references to her position at the brink of a river (twice), upon 'sinking sand' (twice), and in the middle of a leap 'into hell' make it clear that she was thinking corporeally about what would happen to her on the gallows.

The Christian elements are also clear, and it is neither surprising nor ironic that McLaurin should have been the agent who saw to the poem's publication. Her life a battle between good and evil, her situation a result of giving in to temptation: with the gallows in sight, Blake was prepared to interpret her situation using McLaurin's terms of personal responsibility and to portray herself as a repentant Magdalene, even if her character had a few rough edges. The image of the repentant Magdalene often resolved the dialectical opposition of good women and bad women in fiction and in real-life investigations by British journalist W.T. Stead, by the rescuer of 'ruined' women, Josephine Butler, and by their Canadian equivalents.[57] Blake, emphasizing how she fell to a male tempter and that she now regretted that fall, could count on her youth and beauty to complete the image.

While the Magdalene image was originally a focus of moral condemnation and rejection, by the late nineteenth century her guilt was transferred to the society that had caused her suffering.[58] Blake, too, had begun to see her position in jail as part of a larger social problem:

You hypocrites, pleading religion,
    You inquisitive seekers of fame,

> Ready now with your good advice
>> When I've drunk of the sorrow and shame;
> You gave me no timely warning,
>> You held out no helping hand,—
> Why didn't you see me sinking
>> As I stepped on this treacherous sand?

Hard words in Brandon, the 'city of churches', where pious spires rose from the prairie and where lay the headquarters of Methodist and Baptist missionary activities in the Northwest. The 'hypocrites' probably included Amelia Yeomans and, more generally, those Christians who were interested in Blake only after she was convicted, Christians like the benevolent souls in *Great Expectations* who give Pip a tract depicting a malevolent young man in fetters, a tract entitled 'TO BE READ IN MY CELL'.[59] Whatever the identity of the 'hypocrites', Blake intimated that Christians should aid servants and the lower classes. Certainly the *Sun* reporter felt the sting of Blake's words, since he attacked her for wasting her time with novels and yet having the gall to criticize the public for its lack of interest in her moral welfare.

Blake's accusation reflected the traditional discourses of Christian charity and philanthropic social amelioration, but also signified the growing emphasis on the social gospel in western Canada, challenging, to a small degree, the sobriety, respectability, dogged perseverance, and individualism that dominated the city's official evangelical ethos. McLaurin would have agreed with Blake's sermon. As the only one who had visited Blake before the murder, McLaurin knew that he could not be among those now accused of hypocrisy. Describing himself in the third person in his history of western Canadian Baptists, McLaurin perhaps idealized his feelings, but he did accurately depict his habit of visiting his congregants:

> He did not want a desk; he was not particularly fond of a study; he always liked to meet people, new people, and could tramp all day, visiting, without feeling weary. . . . Every hardship endured or difficulty met was a joy to him. He never had an unpleasant experience or an unhappy hour that he would have avoided, if possible.[60]

Near the end of his life McLaurin would fear that he was not well-read enough,[61] but the desire for a life of study had not been what drew him to the ministry and to missions. Rather, he wanted a life in which social pleasure could be combined with spiritual purpose, and so he went about his work with an evangelistic zeal that brought him into contact with such as Blake. Perhaps he saw to the publication of

'My Downfall' because he felt that Blake would awaken among the laity something of his own passion for souls; perhaps, as well, he thought that Blake's sad case would serve as a Christian warning to others contemplating crime; perhaps he even agreed with the signatories to the petitions: that justice had not entirely been done.

If McLaurin was speaking through Blake's own poetic cadences in 'My Downfall' and moralizing her case, nevertheless her reference in the poem to the role of 'Fortune' in her downfall was less in keeping with McLaurin's views. The reference was not just a poetic cliché. For an 'evangelical' document, the poem ends remarkably without any convincing hope of conversion: although Blake implores pity from God, her emphasis on hell, weariness, and loneliness in the last four stanzas suggests that by the middle of December she had lost faith in her own agency and did not really sense God's agency replacing her own. The poem ends with biblical offers of forgiveness, but without any feeling that the *speaker* has been able to fasten onto these offers. Such an ending placed rather too much into the hands of chance, and its despair could hardly have been what the optimistic McLaurin would have wished for.

'My Downfall' was, of course, primarily a self-dramatization. It demonstrated to Brandon that ill-used as Blake was, she carried a gentle soul and an artistic sensibility. Despite the metrical awkwardness of stanzas 2 and 10, Brandonites conceded that Blake's writing showed 'no little literary merit'.[62] The poem was Blake's way of saying what Rose Maylie said of Oliver Twist: 'But even if he has been wicked . . . think how young he is; think that he may never have known a mother's love, or the comfort of a home; that ill-usage and blows, or the want of bread, may have driven him to herd with men who have forced him to guilt.'[63] While the poem did nothing to justify the murder of Mary Lane, it did fuel speculation that someone else was also implicated, and it did engender sympathy for Blake. Readers of the *Sun* extracted from 'My Downfall' an admission that Blake had fallen into an intimate relationship with Robert Lane at his urging. The poem's language, while necessarily full of euphemism, was unmistakable. It made Blake the victim of a predatory male and echoed those feminist and social purity discourses that de-emphasized female sexual agency.

Why was Blake hinting at her relationship with Lane in December when she had not done so from July to November? Throughout the fall she had refused to do anything to avoid the gallows, and her change of heart in December seems best explicable as a reaction to the feeling that Lane had betrayed her, or else as a means to avoid the

gallows. If an agreement of some kind existed between Lane and
Blake in the summer of 1899, she must have concluded, after Stripp's
removal, that Lane had deserted her.

The poem highlights several shifts in Blake: abandoning her earlier statement—'I am guilty, and I want you to inflict the severest
punishment upon me that is all'—she now hinted that someone else
bore partial responsibility; abandoning the unconvincing motive of a
fit of domestic jealousy, she now hinted at the more visceral motive of
sexual desire. Governor-General Minto's correspondence to Prime
Minister Laurier shows that these new assertions were made more
explicitly in her autobiography:

> To execute her would appear I should have thought logically to
> compel his execution too. . . . According to her confession it was
> Lane's influence that was answerable for the murder & it seems to
> have been a shabby mean influence, evidently intended to save
> himself, while she is bent on saving him.[64]

Given Blake's tendency to strew red herrings, it is certainly possible
that she invented the affair, that the letters she wrote from prison to
Lane were elaborate ruses. Just before her death Kircaldy, as if he
were beginning to doubt her new story, asked whether she wanted to
retract anything that might injure others, 'to which she firmly replied
that she had nothing to retract.'[65] Some sort of a relationship with
Lane seems more likely than an elaborate ruse: it seems probable that
after sending her affectionate letters—to which she had responded, 'I
feel as if I can submit to my fate again'—he had avoided further contact. Blake disclosed the relationship only when she felt that Lane no
longer deserved her continued loyalty. Once the beloved, he was now
transformed in her eyes into the devil.

*

Blake alternated, she said, between fits of rebelliousness against her
fate and moments of submissiveness.[66] The way she passed her time
in jail confirms this. 'My Downfall' contains both submission and
rebellion. Her interviews with McLaurin and the novels she read suggest that she thought seriously about the future, but her 'calm look of
indifference' (upon which visitors remarked)[67] and the coon songs
she sang imply that over the long haul she could not maintain a fully
serious approach—neither to please God nor to sway Fortune.
Although she had kept up a 'modest and dignified' mien in court
instead of thrilling the audience with repartee and *bons mots* as the
Artful Dodger had done, now, at least, she could loosen up.

Just before Christmas she received 'dear, kind' Mr Brown's letter and earlier letters from Mr Thomas Smart and Mrs Corbett, the latter two dated 14 and 27 November.[68] Blake replied to Mr Brown 'and thanked him, and . . . saw him weeping great big tears' over the letter.[69] She wondered why the Smart and Corbett letters had been kept from her so long; she would have at least replied to Mrs Corbett, an old friend, had she received the letters earlier. Thomas Smart was a 42-year-old feed store clerk making very small wages at $200 a year. In 1891 he had been a farmer and a Presbyterian, but by 1901 he listed his religion as 'Ch. Ho. Mo.', short for the 'Holiness Movement Church', an 1890s Methodist splinter group also called the 'Hornerites' after founder Ralph Horner. With 'excessively emotional conduct' in its services, the new movement was frowned upon by more traditional Methodists,[70] and whether Blake had no wish to reply to him because Smart was proselytizing, or simply because she did not know him personally, is not clear. Corbett is not listed in the 1901 census.

With her married sister in England Blake had been allowed to exchange letters, and in a last bit of resistance against the future she begged everyone not to write to that sister, to a brother in England, or to Tommy in the West. Instead, Blake wrote a final letter, saying to her sister, 'if you do not hear from me for a long time, don't be alarmed.'[71] Such self-dramatization one would expect at the end of a novel or a song. It declared again both her resistance—in the refusal to acknowledge her upcoming execution to her sister—and her shame (that she, a lady, could be associated with the gallows). Did she happen to wear her shame publicly by publishing a poem and by revealing her letters to the press? So be it.

14

Duty to the Public

It is certainly one of the most painful duties which I have had to perform since I have occupied the position of chief advisor of the crown in this country, but notwithstanding all the sympathy which one must feel for the poor girl, the crime remains an abominable one.

—Laurier to Minto, 26 December 1899

Blake's audience in Ottawa was not as innocent as her Brandon audience. Less likely to scold her for listening to coon songs and at the same time less likely to weep 'great big tears' with her in her repentant moods, the politicians in Laurier's government had recently been through long debates about the sexual mores and moral responsibilities of young women. They also understood the nuances of political praise and blame that could attach to such a case. Killam's decision not to recommend clemency boded ill for Blake's chances of avoiding execution, but her fate now rested with the 'Governor-General in Council': in other words, Prime Minister Laurier along with the federal cabinet would review the grounds for clemency and instruct Governor-General Minto whether the sentence should be commuted or delayed.

A number of options were available. Section 11 of the Criminal Code specified that no one could be convicted of a crime while 'labouring under natural imbecility, or disease of the mind'.[1] Commissions were therefore frequently appointed to decide on the accused's mental state,[2] and one could have been appointed for Blake if cabinet found merit in Yeomans's diagnosis of Blake.

Second, under section 748, Justice Minister David Mills could order a new trial if new evidence came to light, as he had done for Olive Sternaman in January 1898.[3] Sternaman was subsequently found innocent and released. Some MPs objected to the minister having such authority.[4] Defending the power to order new trials, Mills's cabinet colleague, Sir Louis Davies, invoked the still controversial Maybrick case: 'There are many people of the highest judicial standing, amongst them the Lord Chief Justice of England, who have avowed their belief in the woman's innocence, but there is no power in the English Act, as there is in our Act, if grave doubts are expressed . . . as to the proper conviction of that woman.' '*Festina lente*,' Davies urged, 'make haste slowly.'[5]

Finally and most commonly, section 967 of the 1892 Criminal Code allowed the Prime Minister and his cabinet to commute any death sentence. Generally, the Laurier administration liked to emphasize the rule of law and a limited role for government. The Laurier government's anti-statism followed the rhetoric of liberal individualism embraced by Canada's middle-class élite: the state should merely set and enforce the ground rules under which, as Douglas Owram has explained, 'man must be free to seek his own improvement and be responsible for his own destiny.'[6] Mills, who taught constitutional law, had a finely tuned sense of how cabinet and Parliament were bound to legal obligations and customary practices. Yet, despite the Liberals' 'rule of law' ideology, Mills was quite prepared to defend some types of arbitrary authority. In particular, he felt that pardons should not be routinely debated in Parliament. In March 1900, employing the royal 'We', he told the Senate that 'We, of course, deprecate the discussion of the exercise of the power of pardon. . . . it would lead to very great embarrassment in the administration of justice and in the exercise of the power of pardon if the subject was made on every occasion, or indeed, frequently made, the subject of parliamentary inquiry.' He was happy to appeal to 'executive discretion', and contended that only in the case of 'a great error of judgement' should Parliament stick its nose into cabinet prerogatives.[7]

A judge could recommend a pardon if he believed that the sentence he was required to impose under statute law was too severe, or if he believed that there was some doubt as to guilt. If a judge called for mercy, cabinet could not disregard his recommendation. 'Settled usage' demanded that cabinet could go *further* than the judge in granting mercy, but could 'not go a *lesser* distance': cabinet could show mercy even if a judge wanted the full sentence carried out, but could not demand that the full sentence be carried out if the judge

urged a less severe punishment.'[8] Killam, of course, had not recommended a pardon. Mills personally felt that the Conservative government in power before 1896 had allowed far too many executions,[9] but
he was clearly referring to the executions of men, who made up the
bulk of the cases, not to women. In the 32 years since Confederation
the federal cabinet had intervened more often than not when women
were sentenced to hang, perhaps recognizing that women's crimes
were frequently mitigated by extenuating circumstances. Between
January 1874 and December 1922, only two of the 24 condemned
women were actually executed, while a full 52 per cent or 311 of the
599 condemned men paid the full penalty. After 1873, Cordelia Viau
and Blake were the only women executed, until Florence Lassandro
suffered the same end in 1923.

In the area of sexual consent and, more broadly, gender relations,
the rule of law had congealed around sections 181–90 of the 1892
Criminal Code (incorporating most of the earlier Charlton Seduction
Act). By making it a crime to seduce a previously chaste girl between
the ages of 12 and 16, and a crime for men over 21 to seduce with a
promise of marriage a previously chaste woman under 21, lawmakers
implied that women over 16 were responsible for defending their
'virtue', and that women over 21 were mature enough to fend off any
advances couched in false promises. The division of women into the
chaste and the dissolute was supposed to safeguard innocent men
from designing women.

In 1898 and 1899, supported by the WCTU of every province,
Epworth League Societies, the National Council of Women, the
YWCA, branches of Christian Endeavour, the Presbyterian and
Methodist general conferences, 'a deluge of petitions', and even
Prime Minister Laurier, John Charlton, the Liberal MP for Norfolk
North, campaigned again to raise the age of consent from 16 to 18
years of age.[10] Men engaging in sexual relations with 16- or 17-year-
old women would be liable to criminal prosecution. At the same time,
Charlton also wanted section 648c amended. Section 648c required
that for prosecution under sections 181 to 190, corroborative evidence must be produced.

As Charlton's proposals were not dealt with along party lines, MPs
spoke freely. Advocates of the amendments complained that very few
seducers were ever prosecuted under sections 181 to 190 because corroborative evidence was hard to come by:

There are cases of girls who are obliged to go out to service, their
parents are poor and they let their daughters go out to service at an

early age. A girl goes into a house and is seduced by her master. There is no doubt of the girl's previously chaste character . . . there is no doubt about the improper intimacy of the girl with some man because pregnancy follows, and the offence according to the girl's own statement, has been committed by the person in whose employment she was, and in his house.

Nevertheless, judges, relying on the Criminal Code, demanded cor- roborative evidence.[11] Opponents of the amendment applauded this judicial practice, contending that anybody familiar with the criminal courts knew that many prosecutions under the Charlton Seduction Act were 'instigated not from the best of motives', but for extortion and blackmail: 'if you change the law that makes it necessary for two witnesses to the commission of the offence . . . you will open wide the door to crimes worse than those provided for in the *Criminal Code*— fraud, attempts to extort money, and attempts to blackmail.' Innocent men needed a parliamentary shield.

Charlton's efforts in 1898 were unsuccessful, but in the spring of 1899 he came back with a watered-down proposal—dropping the challenge to section 648c and hoping merely to raise the age of con- sent. Arguing contra, one MP said, 'If a woman who has reached six- teen years of age is not capable of taking care of her own virtue, she ought to suffer the consequences, because she arrived at an age when she knows what consent means.' Laurier's Solicitor General, Charles Fitzpatrick, agreed: 'This thing of making good morals by an Act of Parliament may be overdone a bit.' Sir Charles Tupper, the Conserva- tive leader, doubted the wisdom of setting the age of consent even at 16: 'I may say I have never heard the objection which was raised by the late Sir John Macdonald answered—the difficulty, that this puts blackmail into the hands of abandoned and absolutely dissolute women, an extraordinary engine of blackmail.' In Tupper's view, such an amendment 'would involve a very serious danger to the most respectable citizens of the land and put a weapon in the hands of a very dangerous class in every community.'[12] Of course, Tupper may not have been the most objective arbiter of such matters; his womanizing reputation, back in his Nova Scotia days, had tagged him with the nickname, 'the Ram of Cumberland'.[13]

Charlton countered that he did not hope to make people moral:

but it is possible, by law to restrain immorality, to restrain vicious tendencies, and to do that, among other ways, by the punishment of those who transgress moral obligation. We punish thieves, we punish forgers, we punish murderers; we do not enact these laws

primarily for the purpose of making these men moral by legislation, but we enact these laws for the purpose of punishing these
men who transgress law, and for the purpose of holding them up as
culprits, and as a deterrent in the case of others.

He dismissed the blackmail scenario as a 'stock argument' that placed
'poor, innocent defenceless men at the mercy of designing women'.
His amendment would shield 'that class of society who have otherwise no defence', secure 'morality and public virtue', and protect
young women 'from the wiles of seducers'.[14]
    One MP who supported Charlton asked whether young women
under the age of 18 understood much about sex. Indeed, D.C. Fraser
argued, 'up to the time they marry, many of these young women have
very little knowledge of the world. To these women this law will be a
protection. I am not afraid of very many young women in the country
blackmailing the young men.' More pointedly, Fraser hinted that it
was not young men who feared the legislation, but philandering
middle-aged and middle-class parliamentarians: 'The experience of
every man in this House and out of it is that if he conducts himself
properly, there are very few chances of his being blackmailed.' In
99 per cent of the cases, 'the man has been to blame and not the
women', Fraser said.[15]
    The reactions to Charlton's proposal showed how divergent even
cabinet views were on the sexual and moral relations between men
and women. Of the six cabinet members who voted, three—Charles
Fitzpatrick, Andrew Blair, and Sir Louis Davies—voted against the
measure, while three—Sir Henry Joly de Lotbinière, W.S. Fielding,
and Laurier—voted in favour. Charlton's amendment squeaked by. In
effect, Parliament was prepared to make the smaller concession
(about the age of consent) to moral crusaders, but was not prepared to
challenge the gender orthodoxy that demanded chaste character of
young women and winked at the philandering of middle-class men as
long as they restricted themselves to 'ruined' women. This is not surprising. With only one exception, Laurier's cabinet was made up
entirely of men over 50, many of them presiding over large families.
With, again, one exception, all were professionals, mostly lawyers:
three had been premiers, and three would go on to either the Ontario
Supreme Court or to the Supreme Court of Canada. Laurier rarely
imposed his will on them.
    Justice Minister Mills—in the Senate at this point—stood among
those who wanted to strike 'of previously chaste character' from section 181 of the Code. The protection of young girls under 16 should

be absolute, he argued: 'between 14 and 16 I do not think there is such
a maturity of mind and judgement that a girl ought to depend wholly
on herself for the protection of her virtue.'[16] He was also sympathetic
to the proposal approved by the House of Commons to raise the age of
consent to 18, though he did not feel that the seduction of a girl
between 16 and 18 was as much of a crime as seducing a girl between
14 and 16.[17] On the opposite side, Senator William J. Almon followed
Sir Charles Tupper in objecting to the very concept of an 'age of consent', arguing that the way a woman was raised and not her age was
the best protection. A girl who was allowed 'to stroll about in the
streets in the evening', buy alcohol, and listen to 'ribald conversation'
was more likely to be corrupt at age five than a properly raised girl at
18. To verify his point he quoted, with minor alterations, from Robert
Burns's cantata, 'The Jolly Beggars'—'I once was a maid; but I dinna
mind when'—and proposed to fix the age of consent at 45. Mills
responded with uncharacteristic humour that the bill was designed
'for the protection of youth and not second childhood'.[18]

Yet on one question Mills eventually sided with Almon against
Charlton's reformist position. In 1897, then Justice Minister Oliver
Mowat had sought to include domestic servants under the protection of
the seduction laws: 'A man has a greater opportunity to corrupt a girl
who is employed as a domestic servant than in any of the other cases.'
In debate, senators generally supported the inclusion of girls employed
in 'shop or store' but several objected adamantly to the inclusion of
domestic servants. Senator Drummond said, 'I do not know any person
in the world that would not be open to blackmail if you put in the words
"domestic servant". . . . How could a man, in the clutches of a designing or bad woman, ever prove his innocence if the woman is a domestic servant in his employ?' Senator James Lougheed added:

> Invariably, a woman however unchaste she may be, will in court
> swear to her chastity. It is not necessary to point out the influence
> that a woman of that kind very often has upon a jury and even
> upon the judge, because a judge is possessed of human sympathy
> and is appealed to very often by a pathetic tale which is always, in
> cases of this character, told with telling effect.

Mowat responded that the girl's testimony would of course have to be
corroborated. 'We all know it is the female that is seduced in probably 999 cases out of 1,000', he claimed, to which several honourable
members cried 'No, no.' Mowat quickly revised his figures downward to 900 of 1,000, but the falsely maligned kept up the chorus of
'No, no.'

When in June of 1899 Senate discussion returned to sections 181–3 of the Code, dealing with the seduction of wards or employees 'of previously chaste character', Mills agreed to delete 'domestic servants' from among the protected classes of women. He insisted that protection should cover young women in factories, mills, workshops, shops or stores, but admitted that 'a domestic servant stands in a different position' and said that he 'did not intend that a domestic servant should be included in the bill.' While he never explained what he meant by 'in a different position', he obviously gave weight to the blackmail scenarios that parliamentarians in 1897 and 1899 put forth with what one might call 'telling effect'.

*

The federal cabinet's deliberations on the Blake case also took place in the context of a highly charged political atmosphere. A federal election would be called in less than a year, and the results of a Manitoba provincial election two weeks earlier, on 7 December 1899, bluntly told the Liberals that they were in trouble in Manitoba. Premier Thomas Greenway's provincial Liberals had unexpectedly gone down to defeat.[19] Mary Lane's friend, Charles Adams, the Liberal incumbent from Brandon, had lost to the Conservative Dr S.W. McInnis by eight votes—569 to 561—despite help from Brandon's federal MP, Clifford Sifton, the pre-eminent Liberal in the West and the principal agent of the West's transformation. Helping McInnis win was Robert Lane's partner, Alexander McIlvride, who canvassed on behalf of the Conservatives and had the unenviable task of persuading foreign voters in the North End to vote for the party that labelled them 'a mongrel breed'.[20]

The December 1899 defeat of the Greenway Liberals was 'an acutely embarrassing reverse for Sifton . . . . He was supposed to be the political strongman of the West, the master of Manitoba, and he had been defeated in his first serious contest.'[21] Sifton did not have to be told, as he was in January 1900, that given what had happened to Adams, his own federal seat was no longer safe, that he 'could not be re-elected tomorrow' if an election were held. As late as August 1900, the race still looked like a dead heat: Sifton was advised that 'outside Brandon City there were 3,472 Liberal voters, 3,379 Conservative voters, 778 "Liberal Doubtful," and 852 "Conservative Doubtful." '[22]

Because the Conservatives pounded on Sifton's aggressive immigration policy, and because beliefs about class and race had such weight, particularly among rural voters, the disposition of the Blake case could have had electoral implications. The provincial election had been focused as much on the federal Liberals and Sifton as on the

Minister of the Interior Clifford Sifton, c. 1901. Soon to face a largely rural male electorate, Sifton approached the Blake case within the boundaries of gender and class prejudices. (Provincial Archives of Manitoba, N19971.)

local Liberals. Hugh John Macdonald and the provincial Conservatives, bolstered by support from federal politicians such as Charles
Hibbert Tupper, had attacked on many fronts, including Sifton's
immigration policy.

The day after Mary Lane was killed, one of Macdonald's campaign
sheets laid the murder at the feet of the Galician Peter German, and thus
at the feet of Clifford Sifton, the man whose policies brought such murderous foreigners to Canada. 'We are to submit to have our nearest and
dearest butchered on our doorsteps', Macdonald cried.[23] When the
murderer turned out to be a British maidservant, Macdonald was forced
to retract, and the Liberal newspapers crowed loudly. Nevertheless, the
Conservatives understood the province well enough not to change their
immigration platform and continued to seek for Manitoba 'her share of
a desirable class of European immigrants as well as those from the
older parts of Canada and the United States', while regretting 'the
wholesale importation of undesirable immigrants from southern
Europe'.[24] Macdonald elaborated that 'He did not want to have a mongrel breed in this portion of Canada. He did not want Slavs introduced
among us, whether from Austria, Poland or Russia, men who are practically serfs and slaves. . . . He wanted men of the same race as ourselves.'[25] The Conservative *Brandon Times* also castigated Sifton's
policy as a grand 'round-up of European freaks and hoboes'.[26] Although the two parties were nearly even in the popular vote, Macdonald
carried the province with 23 seats to 15 for the Greenway Liberals.[27]
There were other causes for the Liberal defeat, but Macdonald's racist
rhetoric certainly did not hurt the Conservatives.

While Macdonald's attacks in 1899 were directed mostly at Eastern
European immigrants, not at the British lower class, Conservative
objections to Sifton's immigration policy were based on social
Darwinist notions about heredity—notions shared even by reformers
such as Amelia Yeomans and that could potentially be used against the
British poor. With the growing number of destitute children sent to
Canada by charitable or philanthropic organizations, the public perception of these children during the late 1880s and early 1890s grew
increasingly negative despite their British nationality, and their presence was attacked as a threat to the stability and health of Canadian
society. Dr C. Ferguson, MP for Wellington, told the House of Commons Standing Committee on Agriculture and Colonization in 1888
that such children were the 'offal of the most depraved characters in the
cities of the old country'. In 1890, Ontario's Royal Commission on the
Prison and Reformatory System was told that, in addition to threatening the economic security of Canadian workers, many of the orphans

'went wrong through hereditary traits', and that they corrupted others
with whom they associated, putting them up to 'all sort of evil habits'.
The Commission concluded that unless considerable care were exercised in the selection of such children, immigration practices threatened 'to swell the ranks of the criminal classes in this country'.[28]

Similar biologically determinist concerns about a class of immigrants, 'rumoured all over the West to be villainous and criminal',
were expressed in southwestern Manitoba.[29] During the Assizes in
Brandon in the fall of 1893 the grand jury of the Western Judicial District complained to Chief Justice Killam about the 'birds of passage'
arriving in Canada.[30] An alleged increase in the level of crime in the
district prompted the grand jury to point at the British pauper immigrants and to ask authorities to prevent 'the further importation of
boys from the slums of the large cities of the Old World'. 'We need not
state', jury members explained, 'that we refer more particularly to the
class of youth which has been brought to the "Barnardo Home" from
the old country.'[31] Because many of the orphans sent to Canada were
children of impoverished British workers or agricultural labourers, the
orphans were thought to be congenitally lazy, ignorant, and immoral,
their presence a threat to the social order and purity of Canadian society. To his credit, Killam rejected the claims that growth in crime could
be blamed mainly on impoverished orphans.

When the Canadian boy Philip Hill, 13 years old and neglected by
his parents, was sentenced to death by Killam in 1893, the mistaken
perception that he was a pauper child immigrant caused the *Manitoba
Morning Free Press* to publish an editorial to set the record straight. Yet,
as Kenneth Bagnell laments, 'the prejudice was hard and set forever.
For years afterward the papers would carry articles and letters that portrayed immigrant children in dark and villainous ways.'[32] Even the progressive J.S. Woodsworth, who was raised in Portage La Prairie and
Brandon (but who was in Oxford at the time of Blake's execution)
learned such prejudices. In his study of Canadian immigration,
Strangers Within Our Gates, published in 1908, Woodsworth followed
a crude biological determinism, asserting that English orphan children
and paupers with 'inherited tendencies to evil' were 'a very doubtful
acquisition to Canada' and 'any large immigration of this class must
lead to a degeneration of our Canadian people.' Others inveighed more
bitterly and more colloquially against British 'charity', which sent the
lower classes to the colonies: 'Another stumbling-block is the "charity" still too often encountered, which delights to send imbeciles and
ne'er-do-weels [sic] to turn over a new leaf in "the Colonies," and this
has a great deal to answer for.'[33] Young women of questionable social

origins were portrayed just as negatively. Lombroso and Ferrero taught that 'women who committed crimes [were] . . . closer to the primitive condition than even male criminals.'[34] Yeomans's petition and newspaper references to Blake's time in the Heckingham Workhouse identified Blake with the complaints.

Sifton also had to contend with the Manitoba newspapers. He understood the power of news reports and was convinced that news columns had more influence in shaping views than any number of editorials:

> What actually injures the Government is some carefully concocted piece of alleged news . . . that the Government has done something very offensive to the reader, it is not given as an attack upon the Government, it is simply given as an item of news. The simple-minded farmer swallows it, and a great many people who are not farmers and who ought to know better.[35]

Naturally, Sifton therefore sought every opportunity to control the regional press through careful management. To ensure that the reading public was kept correctly informed, he supervised the production of slanted news reports to be published in newspapers under his influence, and he used much-sought-after government patronage to secure favourable coverage of Laurier government policy.[36] Sifton could be sure that the *Western Sun*, which he owned, would take a positive view of cabinet actions whatever the final decision about Blake. The *Sun* habitually printed notes like the one that appeared around the time of Yeomans's visit with Blake: 'the grand jury at the Winnipeg assizes commented on the absence of crime among foreign immigrants.'[37]

Sifton could not, of course, count on the city's two Conservative papers, the *Brandon Times* and the *Brandon Independence*. If the federal Liberals chose to commute Blake's sentence, or worse, to order a new trial, the *Times* would hold Sifton personally responsible for an outrage against the family, public morality, and the memory of Mary Lane. The *Brandon Independence* would likely do the same. It had a smaller circulation, but made up for it by the virulence of its attacks. W.G. King, the disgruntled former employee of the Immigration Department who published the paper, accused Liberals at both the provincial and federal levels of attracting to Manitoba immigrants King described as 'pampered paupers', 'foreign scum', and 'barbarians'.[38] The popularity of the *Independence* was clearly on the rise, because after the Conservatives won the provincial election, government advertisers preferred the upstart *Independence* to the establishment *Times* in six out of nine municipalities.[39]

In Winnipeg, the *Manitoba Morning Free Press* was safe. Owned and controlled by Sifton, it often circulated news copy and editorial direction to small rural newspapers. However, the *Winnipeg Morning Telegram*, a Conservative paper, would be sure to take political advantage of the Blake case if a way could be found. Like Hugh John Macdonald, the *Telegram* had tried to take advantage of the Mary Lane murder when it had initially seemed that 'Another Siftonian Tragedy' could be blamed on a Galician tramp, a symbol of 'the vicious foreign scum [Mr Sifton] is dumping down on the prairies'.[40] Also like Macdonald, the *Telegram* had to retreat before Blake's English heredity, but could potentially turn to the attack again on the basis of her class, orphanhood, and workhouse stay. Most of all, Sifton feared the influence of the *Winnipeg Daily Tribune*, an independent Liberal paper but one that viewed Sifton as a villain.[41] The *Tribune* let it be known that Blake should be executed.

The movement to commute Blake's sentence was principally urban and female, but women did not run newspapers and did not vote.[42] In Melita, a strategic rural centre in Sifton's constituency, he could use the unaligned *Melita Enterprise* as a barometer of rural opinion. The *Enterprise*—under the banner 'Devoted to the Interests of Province, not Party'—usually took an independent and critical view of Sifton's activities as an MP and cabinet minister. Through the biological-determinist letter from 'Moralist' on the front page, the newspaper announced that Mary Lane was the latest victim of an undiscriminating immigration policy:

> The propriety of draining Europen [sic] slums, under the inviting sobriquet of immigration, into this fair Canada of our [sic] is a much discussed question, but in the face of these frequent horrors surely it is laid. . . . Britain can buy or acquire everything else she fancies, then why not secure some habitable islands away from the 'haunts of men' and colonize them with this waste material? And only consider what a paradise this would be for the ardent enthusiastic immigrant missionary!—the missionary of Equal Rights and universal Brotherhood of love profession! . . . Britain does not encourage the transportation of her men of wealth and influence, only this scum which is, of course, good enough for Canada. Let her clean her sewers at her own expense. Canada will do well to look to her own.[43]

Because soaring hopes of unlimited western expansion and the rather unrealistic expectation that 10 million pioneers would soon arrive jarred against the reality of life on an often stagnant agricultural frontier,[44] it was easy to complain about the federal government. While the *Enterprise* did not speak for all of rural Manitoba, it showed an important current of opinion among the farmers that Sifton ridiculed but could not ignore. In fact, Sifton had recently spent $300 of his own money to found a competing paper in Melita, the *Western Progress*.[45]

Admittedly, the danger was not all on one side. Among some men, including the prominent Conservatives R.P. Roblin and A.J. Andrews, there was support for commutation or at least for a delay until the facts were clearer. Yet the dangers of intervention were becoming self-evident. If Blake were pardoned, hard-nosed Conservatives like Macdonald would accuse Sifton of coddling criminals and immigrants. If, however, the Laurier government let the execution take place, Sifton would not necessarily suffer: he could, potentially, gain a few 'Conservative Doubtful' voters; at the same time, reform-minded people knew that a Conservative government would have been even less likely to commute the sentence.

In any case, there was the more pressing question of tariff liberalization. It is quite possible that Sifton paid little attention to Blake until late in December. The Boer War, particularly during the 'Black Week' of 10–15 December, and the provincial election had occupied all politicians for some time, so that Sifton was in a state of near exhaustion by late December. But possibly by 12 December, when the *Manitoba Morning Free Press* began to editorialize against a commutation, and certainly by Christmas, when Laurier and the cabinet deliberated the case, Sifton could no longer ignore the issue.

*

Though Blake had been sentenced on 17 November, Justice Minister Mills did not begin to deal with the case until mid-December. Trial documents and some early petitions began to arrive in Ottawa by 14 December. In the documents, Blake alleged that 'a certain man who wronged her promised to marry her if she murdered her mistress, Mrs. Lane.' The story had initially been disbelieved, but Blake claimed to have evidence in the form of letters from 'the man in question' and these were being forwarded to Ottawa.[46] Blake's claims raised the spectre of a seduction prosecution or, depending on how the evidence was interpreted, a murder prosecution against Robert Lane.[47]

Even though Blake had no corroborating evidence of seduction, and even though her age placed her beyond the range of the 1892 Criminal Code, there was some support for prosecuting Lane. Full documentation arrived in Ottawa on 19 December, only days before the scheduled execution.[48] Through the week ending Friday, 22 December, the federal cabinet conferred three times, considering Killam's report, copies of the depositions, and other proceedings on the preliminary investigation of the case before the police magistrate, as well as copies of certain written statements made by the prisoner and certain letters written by her, together with other correspondence.[49]

An indication of the arguments advanced in cabinet appears in the correspondence of William Mulock, the federal Postmaster General, to Laurier. Just before Christmas, Mulock explained to Laurier, 'My impression derived from a perusal of the prisoner's statements—as contained in her auto-biography and copies of letters said to have been sent to Lane—is that little if any credence can be given to her evidence, but that is a question for the jury.'[50] Mulock's assessment of Blake's story may have turned partly on his view of women's position in society. Evidence from Mulock's later role as a judge (he presided over the case of Carrie Davies, for example) suggests that those women who conducted themselves in a manner appropriate to their gender and class—in the case of domestics, this meant preserving one's chastity and obeying one's mistress—could expect a sympathetic hearing.[51] Those who, like Blake, flouted conventions could expect the reverse. Nevertheless, Mulock recommended that the execution be deferred, not commuted, because of a request from the Attorney General of Manitoba for a month's respite. Mulock thought that Macdonald's new Conservative government in Manitoba should have the opportunity to charge Lane or not and that the law should be allowed to 'take its course only after it became clear her evidence was not required' for Lane's prosecution. Such a delay would deflect criticism that cabinet had rushed to judgement. In particular, Mulock feared that on the scaffold Blake might make public accusations and embarrass the government.

Safely above partisan politics, Governor-General Minto, on the other hand, wrote to Laurier that Robert Lane bore some responsibility for his wife's death:

> The case certainly seems a very hard one. Of course the murder itself could not be worse—but the girl is apparently convicted on her own confession, & if her confession is accepted against herself, that confession lays bare the most horrible story I have ever read against Lane—if her story against herself is true it is completely intertwined with the story of Lane, & to execute her would appear I should have thought logically to compel his execution too. The confession tells the story of herself and Lane, & if it is true enough to condemn her it must be true enough to condemn him.

Governor-General Minto and his dog. Minto, against the unanimous opinion of the federal cabinet, joined with voices from Brandon, Winnipeg, and Regina calling for a more thorough investigation of Mary Lane's murder. (National Archives of Canada, PA28065.)

The letter of the Attorney General of Dec. 14th seems to throw out a suggestion that 'her youth, sex and circumstances of her early training can be taken into consideration'—it certainly appears to me an exceptional case in which they might be considered, & also that during a respite of two months, evidence might be forthcoming as to Lane which might alter the appearance of the case. Judging from the girl's letter it may be almost a mercy to execute her, but, I cannot help feeling that condemned as she is on her own confession, the case in the interest of Justice has not been sufficiently threshed out as regards Lane. The poor girl suffered enough in her youth to account for much that is unaccountable otherwise in her career.[52]

Minto's tone of chivalry is pronounced. He does not dismiss Blake's responsibility for the murder, but he does blame her fall on Lane's passion and on Blake's loyalty to him. Minto clearly felt that Lane's agency mattered more than Blake's.

Unfortunately, neither the correspondence from the provincial Attorney General nor Blake's autobiography and putative correspondence with Lane are extant—the entire capital case file for Blake disappeared after Lord Minto sent it back to Joseph Pope, secretary of the cabinet.[53] Despite that, reporters in the East, and one from the *Western Sun*, Sifton's paper, claimed to have seen the autobiography.[54] Someone, either in the cabinet or in the Department of Justice, leaked salient details from the Blake file. None of the recipients of the information quoted directly from the autobiography or said *when* they had seen it. And they did not, of course, disclose how they came by their leisure reading.

Minto's faith in Blake's story may have reflected his own personal circumstances. Rumour had it in 1899 that he had begun an extramarital affair with Lola Powell, known unofficially as 'Minto's Folly'. Her father, William F. Powell, having been a member of the Ontario legislature and sheriff of Carleton County, she was no domestic, but belonged to 'Old Ottawa' society. She was only in her early twenties—half Minto's age—and he was, as Sandra Gwyn puts it, 'blazingly indiscreet' about the affair. For her part, Powell, like Blake, was a person of the 1890s: Hilda Blake's upper-class double, one might say, a theatrical woman who subscribed to a 'modern' sensibility and who played coon songs such as 'All Coons Look Alike to Me' and 'Come Back My Honey' on the piano at parties. While Minto's constant companionship with Powell evidently angered Lady Minto at first, the two spouses seem to have come to some sort of an

Lola Powell, c. 1901. Governor-General Minto's Canadian diary is filled with references to time spent with 'Miss Lola', an Ottawa debutante. For Minto, Blake's allegations against Robert Lane were refracted through his own relationship with Powell. (National Archives of Canada, PA138386.)

understanding (in the manner of British aristocracy) and the affair continued until Minto left Canada five years later.

The application of logic to the business of government was not Minto's strong point; he was a 'huntin'-fishin'-shootin' aristocrat' and had little patience for 'clever people', who, he said, 'are generally so damned silly.' On the other hand, Minto was broad-minded, also a person of the nineties. Long before his appointment as Governor-General, he had helped put down the North-West Rebellion, but he had felt that Riel should not hang and had been appalled by General Lansdowne's 'sneering reception of Poundmaker'. One might expect that Minto's interpretation of the Blake case was not founded on a careful analysis of where exactly the truth lay, but upon his instincts: that it was neither surprising nor offensive for a successful man to take a mistress; that, nevertheless, there was a big difference between taking a mistress and encouraging the murder of one's wife; that one ought to take a mistress from one's own class; that the powerless—the Native, the domestic, the woman—should be treated with solicitation;

that (in particular) one should treat one's mistress handsomely. Given Minto's personal circumstances, his interpretation of the Blake case implicitly distinguished between his own benign (he felt) affair with Lola Powell and Lane's obviously less benign affair with Blake. Minto could congratulate himself that he and his wife no longer fought over Powell, and that Powell was far from a compromised domestic servant but remained an independent woman (who would later give papers on Lady Mary Wortley Montagu, an exceptionally independent eighteenth-century writer, and would receive an expensive gift from Minto upon marriage). Vis-à-vis Blake, Minto could take a clearly benevolent and chivalrous role, defending feminine vulnerability against male villainy and compensating somewhat for the criticism that in Ottawa followed around the edges of his own affair.[55]

Laurier was much less inclined than Minto to feel lenient towards a woman like Blake. Perhaps Laurier sensed that Mulock's suggestion for a delay would merely allow pressure to build for a commutation, and perhaps Laurier's personal circumstances, like Minto's, had some bearing. A few observers thought that Laurier, too, had a mistress: Emilie Lavergne. Nevertheless, to all evidence their relationship was platonic and intellectual rather than sexual—in fact, he and Emilie both judged harshly those whose relationships were governed by physical desire.[56] Notwithstanding Minto's views, Laurier politely and firmly reiterated the position taken by cabinet on 22 December:

> I am really sorry to have to give to Your Excellency an advice which is so repugnant to Your Excellency's sense of humanity. It is certainly one of the most painful duties which I have had to perform since I have occupied the position of chief advisor of the crown in this country, but notwithstanding all the sympathy which one must feel for the poor girl, the crime remains an abominable one. Giving full weight to all that can be said in the girl's behalf, the reasons for the carrying out the sentence remain dominant. It is certainly a most painful duty to perform, this carrying out of this sentence of death, & of all times at Christmas time.[57]

With the assent of cabinet, Laurier and Mills decided neither to appoint a commission to inquire into Blake's mental health nor to order a new trial. Mills wrote that he was 'unable to recommend any Executive interference with the due course of the law.'[58] To proceed with the execution, cabinet had to dismiss the delay request from the Attorney General of Manitoba and reject petitions from Winnipeg and Brandon. But there was no corroborative evidence of Blake's claims against Robert Lane, and Mills may have viewed Lane as a man 'in the clutches of a designing . . . woman' spinning 'a pathetic tale'.[59] The federal cabinet may also have allowed Blake's execution to proceed so as not to expose Sifton and the Liberals to political danger by rescuing someone who could at best be portrayed as a congenital deviant and at worst be associated (though she immigrated during Sir John A. Macdonald's tenure) with a too-permissive immigration system. Mills had recently come under fire for undue leniency in the disposition of murder cases, including the case of Winnipeg's Paul Brown, whose sentence had been commuted on the grounds of insanity.[60] Laurier did not reveal the tone of cabinet deliberations and his letter to Minto is silent about Blake's autobiography, and does not comment on whether she had falsely accused Lane or whether Lane bore responsibility in the murder.

Laurier asked Minto to return at the earliest possible moment the signed Order-in-Council directing that the execution proceed. Minto's overarching tendency as a Governor-General had always been to assert himself when he came up against something 'detrimental to Imperial interests', but to be accommodating when dealing with internal Canadian matters. On the Blake case, he retreated: 'I have only expressed my opinion as strongly as I could, simply as my opinion, for what it was worth.'[61] Laurier's PC 2140 C directed that 'the law be allowed to take its course'. Minto signed. In reply to Laurier's decision, Minto admitted, 'there can . . . be absolutely no doubt as to the crime', and he quoted the Prime Minister's own words: 'as you said to me the duty towards the public has to be considered.' 'It is', Minto concluded, 'a terribly sad story.'[62]

15

The Interests of Province,
Not Party

*The scene in the last act of Brandon's tragedy was
indescribably sad. It was one of the most dreaded enactments
humanity is compelled to resort to for self-protection.*

—*Winnipeg Daily Tribune,* 27 December 1899

During the late nineteenth century the press figured centrally in state executions, and so, before we approach Blake's final hours, we turn first to the press's response after the execution. The day after Hilda Blake was executed, the *Montreal Gazette* summed up the record of state killings in Canada for the last year of the nineteenth century: Blake became the second woman and the fourteenth person hanged in 1899. From the perspective of the *Gazette*'s editors, these were remarkable numbers, especially so for a country with a small population of generally law-abiding citizens. If there was any consolation for readers amid such carnage, it was that 'four of the law's victims were Indians and two Galicians newly arrived in the country.'[1] In the *Gazette*'s Malthusian-like assessment, 'Indians' and 'Galicians' were expendable: they stood beyond the 'deep, horizontal comradeship' of bona fide Canadians.[2]

The *Gazette*'s mordant intervention on the question of capital punishment could be read as a kind of public meditation on the state of the nation. For Canada's daily press, ruminations about state executions (particularly those fresh in the public imagination) provided opportunities to clarify and reaffirm the bonds of society while evoking in the minds of respectable readers of all classes 'the image of their communion' as Canadians.[3] State killings thus triggered a consideration of first principles among a people generally disinclined to abstraction. At the same time, the press could and did underscore the immorality, malevolence, and pathos of the hanged. The state killing of a young domestic for the murder of her mistress offered fertile ground for commentary on the sanctity of the Victorian home, the virtues of family life, and the obligations of social subordinates.

Executions and the sad stories behind them always demanded much more than a factual rendering, always demanded a narrative that could legitimate the state's power to kill its citizens.[4] Accounts of state executions were thus inevitably political: by implication, every word written about an execution could either assault or defend the government's political conduct and, more broadly, the legitimacy of the state itself. Journalistic responses to a murder were partly unconscious—gut responses to the crime—and partly conscious because reporters understood that they had a role to fill, both generally with respect to the social order and more specifically with respect to the newspaper's partisan stance. Even murders could have political implications and were therefore sometimes exploited for political advantage or journalistically tailored to diminish the risk of political cost. In either the logical (though hardly impartial) 'report' or the more melodramatic 'story', editors could slant the news.[5]

Of course, didactic commentary had to share space with other preoccupations. Readers dictated that stories of crime and punishment must involve the audience emotionally, and so newspapers in Manitoba, like newspapers everywhere, chased scandal and tragedy. Headlines were dramatic, the language and description of the stories evocative.[6] On issues less clear-cut than tariff policy or government financial mismanagement, journalists could be caught between the dual functions of telling a good story and defending a political party. Domestic murder promised nothing less than a feast, and Sifton's *Western Sun* had from the beginning made the most of the Blake case. Despite editorializing in favour of the execution, the *Sun*, by mid-December, had gone so far as to publish 'My Downfall', her veiled advertisement of grievance against Robert Lane.

Editorial comment and submerged editorial comment in reports, stories, and headlines about the Blake case began before the execution and continued afterwards. The Conservative and the Liberal papers were almost unanimous in finding the servant girl's death a fitting, if not actually desirable, conclusion. This did not necessarily mean, however, that the papers had risen above party interest. The execution allowed Conservative papers to feel comfortable in a hierarchical and traditionalist discourse. Meanwhile the Liberal papers, more given to lament, had displayed a variety of opinions about the murder in the months leading up to the execution, but as the government leash was shortened the Liberal papers, too, justified the execution. In reporting the execution, the press converted Hilda Blake's tragic life and singular death into a series of ideological representations designed to reaffirm the moral and social verities of late Victorian Canada.

*

Conservative ideological preoccupations guided the coverage of the *Brandon Times* from the outset. For the *Times*, the Blake case was a clear matter of domestic treason. The *Times* dismissed reports of the case in other newspapers as yellow journalistic scandal-mongering and objected to the printing of material like 'My Downfall'. While the *Times* had, of course, given space to the murder, it had protested that it did so reluctantly and had scolded other papers for reporting on the case. The *Times* consistently spent more time moralizing on Blake than reporting the details of the case and, indeed, refused to print letters to the editor calling for a more thorough investigation or a commutation.

The *Times* headed its execution story 'Hilda Blake Hanged' and, making clear that the ensuing narrative would satisfy justice, added a subheading, 'The Penalty for Her Awful Crime'. The ensuing story— underlining the paper's preoccupation with class relations—presented the execution as the final scene 'in one of the most horrible and cold-blooded tragedies in the history of Canada'. Although in fact both women had cared for the children, with the heavier load probably falling on Blake, the *Times* imagined the two women in dialectical opposition: mother against assassin. 'One of Brandon's most estimable and highly respected women' had been struck down by 'the hand of an assassin . . . without a moment's notice. . . . Four little children, all too young to realize their irreparable loss, were shorn of a mother, a husband of a devoted wife, and a great and happy home of the one who contributed more than any other to the happiness of the family.' Chivalry and the cult of domesticity figured prominently in the condemnation of Blake, for her crime was not just the murder of another human being but a sin against the sanctity of the home, woman's inviolable private space. In such an idiom, the case could seem, at least in the late nineteenth century, to be beyond politics.

All this the *Times* observed from on high. Given servants' complaints about 'loneliness in a house full of people', about their considerable share in the work of the house but lack of share 'in the pleasures and delights of a home',[7] the language of *noblesse oblige* resonates ironically:

> the enormity of the crime becomes apparent when it is remembered that it was committed beneath the roof of the very home and by one who had been befriended by her victim, who had been accorded every privilege of that home, and had shared every happiness with those who were called upon to bear that terrible affliction brought upon them by the awful act of a heartless woman who appeared to know not the meaning of gratitude or honor.[8]

The social hierarchy was confirmed, since honour so clearly belonged to the upper middle-class woman whose only purpose in hiring a servant must have been philanthropy, while dishonour and lack of gratitude belonged to the faithless serving classes. Blake's enormous crime had a twofold social resonance: through the violence done to Mary Lane, a young woman had transgressed Victorian notions of femininity; through the murder of her mistress, an insurgent domestic had betrayed her social betters, those to whom she owed fidelity.

As well, for the newspaper's readership, one's own home, however unhappy, must now take on a nearly golden aura in the light of the melodramatic murder and suffering among the Lanes. And melodrama required a fitting conclusion. Through the execution, a step towards the deterrence of similar crimes was taken and an ethical balance was restored, good triumphing in the last chapter. One need not, and the *Times* did not, ask about motives—villains were bad because they were bad. Certainly the *Times* would have been outraged had the state done anything but execute.

The *Winnipeg Morning Telegram* struck a more neutral and more dramatic note, without forgetting crime and punishment: 'THE FATAL DAY—EXECUTION AT BRANDON THIS MORNING . . . Hilda Blake to Suffer Extreme Penalty of the Law for the Murder of Mrs. Lane . . . Startling Revelations Expected'. The next day's heading confirmed the event—'Paid the Penalty'—and added a bit of piquancy: 'Hilda Blake's Last Words—She Walks to the Scaffold Unaided—Story of Her Crime and Efforts to Effect Escape'. Two weeks earlier, the *Telegram* had publicized Amelia Yeomans's petition to commute the sentence, but the *Telegram*, as a Conservative paper, could hardly protest against a strenuous application of the law. The paper, therefore, simultaneously justified the execution and (more subtly) the chivalry of commutation supporters like Conservative leader R.P. Roblin, arguing that, 'although a strong feeling of sympathy existed for the girl, the ends of justice had to be met and Hilda Blake a young, prepossessing girl, just budding into womanhood, has paid the penalty of her awful crime on the gallows.' The *Telegram* reported that Blake, 'a trusted servant', attempted to shield herself by implicating a tramp and tried to escape by filing her prison bars—the escape foiled only by what was now (memories being short) seen as the 'prompt action' of Chief Kircaldy.

The question of a miscarriage of justice the *Telegram* left open, noting that 'an opinion which many seemed to hold was that the murderess was either mentally or morally insane', mentioning again that commutation petitions had been circulated, and hinting that 'the young girl was not the only one connected with the crime.' Without the Liberal newspapers' evident access to Blake's autobiography from her capital case file, and perhaps unwilling to print hearsay against a prominent businessman, the *Telegram* presumed that, in the final analysis, Ottawa could take no other course: 'If Hilda Blake has had an accomplice, she has most faithfully screened such person, and has carried her secret to the grave.' Her body, the *Telegram* said— putting her under the eye of omniscience—'shot downward and her soul into eternity to answer for her horrible sin.'[9] Although in comparison with the *Brandon Times*, the *Telegram* was rhetorically subdued, its reference to the 'trusted servant' and her 'horrible sin' may suggest an implicit agreement with the defence of the Victorian middle-class home presented by the *Times*. The state had imposed a just price. Others in Blake's position should take heed.

The Liberal *Tribune*, though independent and always ready to attack Sifton, supported the execution immediately. The order to hang had been a decision of the full cabinet, and the *Tribune* followed the party line. 'Generous-minded citizens' had tried to get a commutation, but the *Tribune* argued, as it had before the hanging, that to have pardoned Blake under the circumstances would have established a dangerous precedent and brought the administration of justice into contempt: 'if hanging can be justified in any case it certainly can in Hilda Blake's case, and we therefore believe the right and proper course was followed in sending her to the scaffold this morning.'

Having settled the question of the state's obligations to civil society, the *Tribune* turned to matters of greater import. From the *Tribune*'s perspective, while an ordinary hanging was repulsive and ghastly enough, there was something extraordinarily ignominious in the death of a young woman 'in the very prime and flower of her life'. 'Is human nature more pitiful than just?' the *Tribune* asked, and then answered: 'The sympathetic eyes that riveted their gaze on Hilda Blake and followed her from her prison cell to the scaffold seemed to answer "yes" ':

The life that was about to be taken was in its youth of freshness. It once had promised well, for it possessed natural faculties for usefulness, which, under proper control, might have been average; it was a life which under different surroundings and circumstances might have been happy, cherished and loved by many, and ending amid sorrow, respect and esteem. The scene in the last act of Brandon's tragedy was indescribably sad. It was one of the most dreaded enactments humanity is compelled to resort to for self-protection.

The gloomy thoughts of those within the scaffold's precincts were reflected on their faces, and the eyes of some otherwise stern-looking men glimmered with tears, the awfulness of the crime for the moment being probably forgotten. Did Hilda Blake ever know a mother's love? Was she ever dandled on the knee of a proud father? Was her progress through childhood to the maturity of womanhood watched and hopefully marked by fond parents' eyes, and was her own mind ever capable of the honorable maidenly imaginings of the future? These and a hundred other thoughts would press themselves upon the minds of the spectators.

As she stood there on the scaffold, notwithstanding all the surroundings, her appearance might have answered a 'yes' to these questions. But what a mighty negative answer—what a dreadful contradiction will the story of her crime imply. Hilda Blake offended against the law of humanity as deeply as she could have done; the legal penalty for her offence was death, the law has sent her to eternity and her earthly debt is paid.

This imaginative reconstruction of Blake's life was designed to make her misfortune intelligible and to evoke sympathy for her suffering in life and death.

Yet a more fundamental point was also made. The *Tribune*'s assessment served as a platform upon which to preach the value of bourgeois order, in particular, the middle-class family as the heart of a social order and as the basis for moral direction and safety. Marrying the Bible and Thomas Hobbes, the *Tribune* editorial argued that there was 'abundant scriptural warrant' for capital punishment and that 'murderers are not hanged from any spirit of revenge. Society has banded itself together for self-protection and it is deemed to be in the best interest of society, and to make for its better protection that murderers should be hanged.'[10] Again the image was one of closing ranks, of a province-wide ritual not dictated by party. For many Manitobans, Blake's death constituted a tragic yet integral feature of her kind of life, a cautionary tale to those who might follow in her path. The *Tribune* did make one major criticism, a criticism that could be laid at the feet of Brandon authorities but not at the feet of the Liberals generally: the reporter found it a matter of some surprise that as many as 25 people were allowed into the jail grounds for the execution, 'morbid curiosity prompting more than half who should not have been allowed in at all'.

Not unexpectedly, the Sifton-owned papers—the *Western Sun* and the *Manitoba Morning Free Press*—came down decidedly for the state. Despite generally opposing capital punishment and freely covering the Lane murder early on, the *Sun*, like the Conservative papers, set its execution report within a stricter moral economy: 'THE PENALTY PAID . . . The Death of Mrs. Robert Lane Has Been Avenged'. While the subheadings admitted that Blake 'Displayed Wonderful Nerve', they weren't about to let the reader forget who she was: 'Hilda Blake the Girl Murderess'. Of the case's subterranean currents, the *Sun* said only that 'Hilda Blake Did Not Make Any Statement'.

The *Sun* was determined to justify the execution. Gliding quickly past motives, the paper used language that, heightening the pathos of Mary Lane's death and appealing to chivalry and domesticity, sounded very much like the opposition *Times* in reaching for interests beyond those of party: 'guided by an instinct that no reasoning or evidence seems to have been able to discover the trusted domestic places a pistol muzzle at the back of her mistress and pulling the trigger takes the life of the most devoted of wives, and the fondest of mothers.' By cataloguing Blake's useless reading and love of coon songs, the *Sun* emphasized her lack of proper contrition, and though her last hours seemed to sober her up a little, she still did not properly realize that she would soon be meeting the 'Great Judge'. Tactfully forgetting that it was Blake who had exonerated the 'tramp' Peter German, the *Sun* noted that 'for a few hours it looked as if the guilty would escape, and that an innocent man would suffer at the hands of the infuriated mob, but clever as was the girl she could not hide from the law her guilt.' 'Even so,' the *Sun* added, hinting at a divine comedy, 'she was not yet that hardened in crime that her conscience was but a cipher. . . . She confessed all.' The *Sun* remembered to defend Sifton's immigration policies, making it clear that if Blake was guilty, the 'infuriated mob' that had prejudged the foreigner's guilt was not much better. As well, the *Sun* spoke in an official voice, taking pains to answer charges that too many people had witnessed the execution: the crowd that gathered outside the jail fence was 'disappointed', the *Sun* insisted, since 'those who had in charge the carrying out of the law, permitted but the presence [in the jailyard] of those absolutely necessary.'[11]

In similar fashion the other Sifton paper, the *Manitoba Morning Free Press*, announced the triumph of an impartial justice with 'HILDA BLAKE IS HANGED', and went on in by-now familiar terms: 'The Murderess of Mrs Robert Lane Pays the Penalty of Her Crime on the Scaffold'. Another subheading promised 'Final Interview With Chief Kircaldy—The Prisoner's Dress'. The *Free Press* did say that 'a great many details have been wanting', and did, like the *Sun*, emphasize her self-possession: 'She Was Ashy Pale, But Completely Composed and Plucky to the End'. Nevertheless, the crime was 'one of the most deliberate and cold blooded that has ever occurred in the West', and there were 'no extenuating circumstances'. Besides reviewing the entire case (and, again, skewing the Peter German affair by insisting that Blake had been *unable* to identify him), the *Free Press* reported Blake's letter to Kircaldy, a letter in which she finally resigned herself to death and felt 'an indescribable peace' come over her.[12] This sense of closure was not surprising, because back on 12 and 15 December the *Free Press* had already revealed where it stood. The editor had agreed to print Yeomans's petition, but had also, possibly under Sifton's direction, insisted that Yeomans's grounds for commutation were not strong enough. According to the editor, there was no basis for Blake's implication of others in the murder, and the Minister of Justice would ask for 'some much better ground' than the inability to resist murder.[13]

Only the independent newspapers came down strongly against the execution. The *Melita Enterprise*, having spoken so aggressively against Blake at the time of the murder, could not very well argue against the sentence now, but the *Brandon Independence*, the *Minnedosa Tribune*, and the *Regina Standard* all roundly criticized the powers that be. The *Independence* asserted that public opinion had opposed the execution. Thoroughly Tory but less staid and less worried about consistency than the officially Conservative *Times*, the *Independence* wanted to exploit any possible dissatisfaction with the state's handling of the case as a means of damaging Sifton and the Liberals. Arguing from both sides of the issue, the *Independence* implied that the government was both too soft on crime and too hard on Blake. Blake had been executed for murder, the *Independence* said, while at the same time Agnes Glendenning, who had murdered her infant, had been allowed to plead guilty to a reduced charge and had been given a light prison term. Of even greater concern, the *Independence* worried—and in this it disclosed growing public skepticism about Blake's 'confession' at the trial—was that Blake had been 'convicted on her own confession only and no motive [had] been assigned for the crime.' The *Independence* believed that had she been sent to the penitentiary, the real cause of the crime might have been ultimately discovered.[14] Such accusations, it was hoped, would convey to readers that Sifton and the Liberals had failed in their obligation to ensure an even-handed justice. Yet, had the federal cabinet commuted Blake's sentence, the *Independence* probably would have found different reasons for dissatisfaction.

The *Minnedosa Tribune* began somewhat differently, saying that 'it is poor use to put a human being to, dangling it at the end of a rope. It neither deters the living, nor restores the dead.' Yet, the *Tribune* followed the *Independence* in finding something fundamentally wrong with a legal system 'when a woman of mature years deliberately abandons her baby on the prairie to suffer unutterable pangs before death, and is only punished by a few years imprisonment, while a younger woman did not seem so heinous, whose crime may have been committed in a fit of temporary insanity and which was not proved against her except for her confession, has to suffer the death penalty.'[15]

The most vociferous condemnation of the execution came from the *Regina Standard*. Unaffiliated politically, the *Standard* was owned and edited by J.K. McInnis, a native of Prince Edward Island who had come west in the 1880s to teach school in Manitoba, and who eventually transformed the *Regina Journal* into the pungent *Standard*. McInnis—described by one writer as tactless, impolite, and stubborn—denounced the Blake sentence as a miscarriage of justice. On 3 January the *Standard* carried the headline 'Lawfully Murdered . . . the Orphan Executed', and the subheadings, 'Went to the Gallows Without Trial or Examination as to Her Mental Condition . . . The Official Killer an Expert'. McInnis's anger at the execution was rooted in the belief that the state had not taken the trouble to get to the bottom of the case. He insisted that Brandon was full of rumours that at least one other person bore responsibility for the murder. Morally void, the execution was lawful only because the state had sanctioned it.[16]

*

Apart from the *Standard*, the *Minnedosa Tribune*, and the *Independence*, however, most Manitoba papers were prepared to condone if not support the execution as an appropriate way of putting the scandal to rest. Two *Western Sun* articles in early January replied to some of the criticisms by the independents and served as a calming epilogue to the case. On 4 January the *Sun* reported that Blake had asked Kircaldy to deliver a letter to a Brandon 'gentleman' just prior to her execution,

Blake forgiving the receiver and expecting that 'death would greatly relieve.' Without explanation, the *Sun* moved from the letter to Blake's autobiography: 'the auto-biography takes up many pages of paper. It is well worded and written, but will hardly stand publication.'[17]

While the story could potentially fan rumours about Robert Lane's involvement and thereby discredit justice, the *Sun* was probably making a pre-emptive strike against Blake's autobiography from her capital case file, news of which had been coming out in eastern newspapers and filtering into western papers like the *Standard*. The *Ottawa Journal* had noted that 'it is said she committed the crime because she was in love with Mrs. Lane's husband',[18] while the *Toronto Globe* had reported as early as 18 December that, according to Blake, 'a certain man who wronged her promised to marry her if she murdered her mistress, Mrs. Lane.'[19]

The *Sun*'s brief reply could do three things: it could discount rumours that the federal cabinet had ignored the possible role of Robert Lane; it could reiterate that the scandalous information was only hearsay; and it could remind readers that Blake had accepted moral responsibility for the murder. Blake was, the story insisted, prepared to forgive the man who had wronged her and to embrace death as a means of repentance for her crime. In walking the line between protecting the vulnerable Liberals on one side and following the scent of scandal on the other, the *Sun* ultimately chose to hint at, but not pursue, the alternate account of the murder—not so much to protect Robert Lane as to ensure that the execution continued to be perceived as just. If society had required that Blake pay on a corporeal level the penalty for Mary Lane's death with her own, the *Sun* now strongly implied that on a higher level Blake's taking of responsibility for the murder brought proper spiritual closure to the case and to Blake's life. The subheading—'Hilda Blake's Last Writing on Earth is one of Forgiveness'—reminded readers that eternal salvation was at stake, that to assign guilt elsewhere at this late stage would make a mockery of Divine Grace. A brief reprint, careful to emphasize Minto's role over the real powers vested in the Laurier cabinet, assured readers that,

> In spite of the number who signed a petition for the commutation of Hilda Blake's sentence, there seems to be a general approval of the course pursued by the governor in council, in allowing the law to take its course.[20]

On 8 January, the *Sun* again addressed the Blake case, this time answering, it said, the 'more or less hysterical articles' that had appeared 'in a large number of Canadian and American newspapers'. One searches in vain for this widespread and hysterical comment.[21] In fact, the 'large number' of hysterical newspapers probably included only the *Brandon Independence*, the *Minnedosa Tribune*, and the *Regina Standard*. To answer the charges of a miscarriage of justice, the *Sun* did not go into the details of Blake's autobiography, but recast the debate simply as an abstract question of whether women should be executed. The *Sun* explained that while the hysterical newspapers admitted 'that the woman deserved the severest penalty of the law . . . they consider it inhuman to subject the weaker sex to capital punishment.' In keeping with earlier letters that the *Sun* had printed, letters calling for a liberalization of the death penalty, the *Sun* advocated the position set out by the *Chicago Journal*:

> Is society the better for having legally killed a woman? Do we feel that Manitoba has made a forward stride by its stern enforcement of the law against one of the weaker sex? Most men will feel rather that it was a backward step, that humanity and the age alike are disgraced by the act. . . . But the people say, if a woman commits as black a crime as a man is capable of, she should suffer as a man would. Perhaps this is true. If so, it is not an argument for the hanging of women, but for the abolition of the death penalty.

Only days after confirming the justice of Blake's execution, the *Sun* thus reverted to the notion that capital punishment should be abolished for both men and women, since 'in the better age to which all things irresistibly tend we shall hold that the state itself should set the example for holding life too sacred to be taken away by the act of man.'[22] By advancing such an argument, the *Sun* ran little risk of inflaming its readers with a sense of injustice. Instead, the *Sun* was signalling that under the terms of the present law, no other verdict, no other cabinet decision, could have been reached; at the same time, with the soil on Blake's grave still fresh, the *Sun* was ready to resume its reform-oriented, 'liberal' rhetoric to distinguish itself from the heartless Conservatives. Some time in the future, during the ceaseless happy progress that would mark the twentieth century, the bountiful state would no longer demand blood.

16

Come Ye That Are Weary

Oh Friend of all Friends who rules earth and sea,
  Look down with a pitying eye upon me;
  Thou'll forgive my transgressions, says the book that is best—
Come ye that are weary, and I'll give you rest.

—Hilda Blake, 'My Downfall'

Liberal reformers did have rather graphic reasons to feel disenchanted with the death penalty. Prior to the 1870s the gallows, that destination of so many Victorian novels, was a scene of public strangulation, the victim's bound legs kicking as he or she struggled for air. Usually, the victim choked to death over a period of minutes. Contrary to popular belief, the introduction of the Newgate drop in 1783 and calculations of ratios between body weight and drop did not make hanging any less gruesome or less prone to misadventure. In 1894, A.S. Taylor said that 'in hanging . . . death takes place either by asphyxia or apoplexy, or by both.' The long drop, which was designed to break the spinal cord, sometimes failed to achieve its purpose, and the victim could remain conscious for minutes while the heart still beat. If the drop was too long, the victim could be decapitated. Even in 'successful' executions, the corpse always expressed the nature of the experience:

> lividity and swelling of the face, especially of the ears and lips, which appear distorted: the eyelids swollen, and a blueish colour; the eyes red, projecting forwards, and sometimes partially forced out of their cavities . . . a bloody froth or frothy mucus sometimes

escaping from the lips and nostrils. . . . The fingers are generally much contracted or firmly clenched. . . . The urine and faeces are sometimes involuntarily expelled at the moment of death.[1]

Historically, state killings were viewed as a deterrent to crime, and until the late nineteenth century execution was accompanied by beheading, burning, and boiling. Until 1790, women hanged for counterfeiting or the murder of their husbands were also publicly burnt after the hanging,[2] a kind of surcharge on an already expensive fine. Public executions spectacularly enforced the morality of the state and displayed its lethal authority.[3] For the 1838 and 1839 executions of rebels in the second Lower Canadian rebellion, the gallows were placed on a wall facing a large street, the executions were all held on market days, and the victims were invited to make speeches.[4]

The 1886 Fort Battleford, NWT, executions of eight Aboriginal participants in the North-West Rebellion—Iron Body, The Fast Runner, Wandering Spirit, Bad Arrows, Miserable Man, Man Without Blood, Round the Sky, and Little Bear—were also highly public:

Erected in the open square of the stockade . . . the scaffold consisted of a platform about twenty feet high with four heavy posts, one at each corner, and two higher posts in the centre with a crossbeam. This had the effect of giving an uninterrupted view from all sides of everything that went on, both on and under the scaffold. Hundreds of Indians from the many reserves surrounding Battleford were gathered to witness the execution, and I am sure that very few of the surrounding settlers failed to be present.[5]

These Rebellion executions publicized the Anglo-Canadian myth of a spreading tide of civilized order, made possible by the British Empire. In most cases, however, executions were not burdened with such weighty political freight. Canadian women especially, confined to the private sphere, did not threaten the state and only infrequently provoked its lethal power.

Public executions could furnish a pleasant and inexpensive morning's diversion for the masses, including women and children. Spectators could watch the operation of real power over real bodies, and, with a joke, could demonstrate their fearlessness at liminal moments. 'How much sound humour does one hear bandied about from one to another!' said Thackeray of a hanging in 1840. 'This hideous debauchery . . . is more exciting than sleep, or than wine, or the last new ballet, or any other amusement they can have.' Intending mainly to express the disgracefulness of executions, Thackeray also testified

to the communal and democratic *pleasures* of the hanging event: gentlemen could mingle with the lower classes in what amounted to a carnival and could enjoy a wider social intercourse than was their use.[6]

Canada had executed 147 people since Confederation. By the late
nineteenth century the long list of crimes for which a person might be
executed had been trimmed to include only the most serious crimes—
rape, piracy, treason, intent to murder, and murder. By 1886 it was
only murder that brought the death sentence in Canada. Following
British practice, the Canadian Parliament in 1869 had banned *public*
executions. In response to the perceived need to uplift popular sentiment and morals in an increasingly democratic age, it was argued that
'privacy in executions was better for the right state of mind of the
criminal himself in his last moments . . . and better also . . . by avoiding the injurious consequences which result from immense crowds
gathered together to witness such exhibitions.'[7] Legislation required
that executions take place within the walls of the prison in which the
offender was confined, though moral sentiment wasn't so strong that
exceptions couldn't be made for Riel and for Native rebels. The 1869
Act also restricted access to executions: only the jailer, a priest, a
physician, and a few others invited by the sheriff were supposed to
witness executions. In 1888, after William Webb's hanging, the
Brandon Mail had spoken against both capital punishment and the
practice of allowing spectators: 'This was Brandon's first execution
and for the sake of humanity we hope it will be the last one during the
existence of the present generation. To our mind these executions are
a relic of barbarism, and do nothing towards abating crime, if indeed
they do not dull the sensibilities of those who witness them.'[8]

Less than a year before Blake was executed, the revelry during
Cordelia Viau's execution at St Scholastique (just outside of Montreal) had provoked criticism by reformers. The fact that Viau was a
woman and that she and Sam Parslow, her lover, were to be executed
back-to-back had made the event sensational. There had initially been
no public outcry since the two were clearly guilty and the murder had
been brutal. Someone, almost certainly Viau, had slit the victim's
throat from ear to ear after he was dead.

Because the law demanded that the execution be done in private, a
black cloth was draped around the lower part of the scaffold, to
sequester the bodies of Parslow and Viau away from the audience.
But that ambivalent fork in the narrative of moral education—one
ought to *show* the execution in order to warn; one ought to *hide* the
execution in order to preserve citizens from harmful effects—had the
habit of turning executions into tumultuous affairs. On 9 March 1899,

the day before the execution, a throng descended on the small village of St Scholastique. The train from Montreal, which brought members of the provincial police and six guards from a Montreal prison to ensure order, also carried an army of determined spectators, who pressed officials for permits to enter the jail grounds the next morning. The sheer numbers of arrivals ensured that many who hoped for access would be disappointed. Hotels in town overflowed and late-comers couldn't find rooms. No matter; during the night 'high revel was being kept.'[9]

The next morning, the conduct of the 2,000 men, women, and children assembled for the execution was, reported the *Montreal Gazette*, 'disgraceful' and 'far from reflecting credit upon a civilized people'. Those who couldn't get into the jailyard took up positions in trees, on snowbanks, or at any point that allowed vision over the 12- to 15-foot stone wall that surrounded the jail. One man even tried to scale the wall, and persisted until police fired a warning shot, harrying him down, to the pleasure of the other spectators. Those who couldn't get a good vantage point crowded around the prison and turned into a 'howling cosmopolitan mob', which attempted to break down the large door leading into the jailyard. Order was restored only when the police drew their revolvers again and repeatedly fired warning shots into the air. When Canada's first professional hangman, John Robert Radclive, pulled the bolt to drop Viau and Parslow through the trap doors, the crowd cheered, continuing to 'surge and sway long after the law had been satisfied'.

Inside the jailyard the scene was hardly more decorous. There, more than 600 spectators likewise cheered when Viau and Parslow plunged downward. The privileged 600 then rushed forward, ignoring the admonishments of the authorities, tore aside the black cloth, and exposed 'two limp lumps of humanity'—hooded in black caps and hanging back to back. The priest, Rev. Father Meloche, ran around the scaffold shouting '*Honte, honte*; shame, shame; for decency's sake. Have you no decency?' and attempted to restrain the crowd without success.[10] Afterwards, reformers objected not so much to the execution itself as to the crowd's complete lack of propriety and to the scandalous spectacle of the veil being torn aside. Letters to the press and to Laurier denounced the scene, while a *Gazette* editorial called for a change in the law to prevent a repetition of St Scholastique.[11]

*

Nine months later, Brandon looked forward to Blake's execution with excitement, too, and the sheriff's office was besieged with requests for tickets of admission—pleasure and curiosity evidently outweighing the fear of harmful moral effects. Considerable interest was generated by press reports suggesting that Blake would make 'startling incriminating statements' on the scaffold.[12] Newspapermen tried to get interviews with her, but were refused by Kircaldy. Wanting to forestall a scene such as that at St Scholastique, Brandon authorities only distributed 25 tickets of admission into the jailyard. Recipients included Sheriff Clement, Jailer Noxon, guards, policemen, jurymen, Dr McDiarmid (who had attended Annie and Mary Lane in death, and who had recently been acclaimed as Brandon's mayor), Dr Hurdman, Dr Fraser, the coroner, press representatives, and a few others, including Robert Lane's business partner, Alexander McIlvride.

The hangman, the Englishman John Robert Radclive, arrived at the Brunswick Hotel a few days before the execution. Radclive had learned his trade first as a sailor in the British navy and then as an apprentice to the official British hangman, William Marwood.[13] As a common seaman he had sometimes been detailed to hang Chinese pirates from the yardarm: 'I was sorry for the poor blighters, they used to struggle and suffer so, so I figured out 'ow to do it quick and mercifullike.' When he was hard up in Canada he took a hanging job, and although he also tried to work as a steward under an assumed name, the disclosure of his identity made it impossible for him to hold any job other than his $700-a-year position as hangman. Many of his relatives, vexed by his notoriety, had begged him to resign the position, but to no avail. Claiming that it was no harder on him 'to perform his duty on the weaker sex', he had hanged Cordelia Viau, and boasted that although he had hanged 80 people, he had never had an accident: 'If there 'as to be 'angings the only merciful thing is to do 'em right!'[14] Nevertheless, after the chaos of the Viau and Parslow hangings, his habitual drinking became more serious.[15]

In Brandon he supervised the building of a wooden scaffold. On the east side of the jail just outside the courthouse, the scaffold stood 20 feet high, with a five-foot-square trap door; eight feet above the trap Radclive secured a cross beam from which the hemp rope would hang. A flight of rough steps led from the low platform at the north door of the prison to the stage at the top of the scaffold. The structure was only finished at 10:00 p.m. on the night before the execution, when the lever required for the mechanical apparatus arrived. With the exception of a small doorway on its south side, the scaffold was boarded up from bottom to top so that not even the rope was visible to those standing in the yard. If morbidly curious Brandonites wanted to repeat the scene at St Scholastique and look closely on death, they would have to tear aside more than a curtain; they would have to pry apart nailed board from nailed board with their bare hands.

In the meantime, Blake was winding up her earthly affairs and agonizing. With the hour of death fast approaching, Blake's society insisted that she should turn to devotional literature and prayer. At times she did. According to Lombroso and Ferrero, the occasional female criminal's 'intermittent goodness' explained 'the facility with which these women listen to sentimental suggestions, and the behavior of the most ferocious among them in the presence of the scaffold, which to ordinary observers seems so heroically Christian and resigned as to appear a miracle worked by God for the redemption of a lost soul.'[16] However, for Blake to turn to devotion and to behave with fortitude on the scaffold was not only to class herself as fully feminine or admit that one needed to repent certain acts—and Blake did repent—but also to acquiesce in the justness of the punishment. If the criminal repented under the threat of hanging then she would be plucked as a brand out of the flames of hell, an inquisitorial salvation to be sure, but salvation nonetheless. Salvation might even commend the gallows for producing, as some newspapers hinted, a divine comedy. Yet if one did not repent, then hanging was also justified, though of course in a different way: how could an unrepentant prisoner, calloused about the state of her soul, be safely reintroduced into feminine roles that required tenderness and devotion? In fact, repentance aside, Blake was no longer eager for 'the severest punishment', as she had claimed to be during the inquest, but instead asked for a stay of proceedings of a week or so. It wasn't granted.[17]

On Saturday, 23 December, Kircaldy arrived with paper, urging Blake to write out her confession. Probably beginning to sense in her bones that the death sentence really would be carried out after all, and beginning to see the void at the centre of her little drama, she refused, rudely it seems. But the mood did not last long. Later in the afternoon of the same day she sent for Crown prosecutor Matheson, who had earlier supported her commutation and who now hurried to the jail expecting a statement from her. However, in better humour and laughing, she wasn't terribly interested in last statements and instead resumed her starring role in the drama. When the conversation turned to the execution, she bantered in an arch and yet revealing way: ' "Am I not brave? I seem to be possessed of two natures, one good and one very bad, and they seem to control me at different times. I am either good or very bad. You cannot think me altogether bad?" she asked pointedly.'[18]

The next day, Christmas Eve, she set to work winning back Kircaldy's approval by presenting herself as weak and pitiable and sentimental:

> Dear Chief Kirkaldy [*sic*], I hardly know what to make of myself. The last two or three days have been the most terrible, but today I feel so rested, such an indescribable peace came over me all yesterday, and this morning I feel [*sic*] so rebellious it seemed as if I could not submit. This afternoon it is all gone and I feel almost happy. One reason is I think I have tired myself out. My brain feels so weary that it is almost too much to think. I feel as if I could sit quietly down and await my fate. I have never felt like this before, although I have pretended to be submissive, and I am getting alarmed about myself. I wonder if I am going crazy.

Her descriptions of turmoil suggest that she was far less peaceful about the end than she claimed to be. However, more to the point than self-revelation was her wish to continue her friendship with Kircaldy on whatever terms he dictated. In the most extravagant terms she made it clear that she would never defy him, and she called him back to her side:

> I have complied with your request and written a confession. I did it yesterday and I do wish you had it for I have to guard it so zealously. If anything prevents you coming up here tomorrow, I shall destroy it. I had intended sending this to the post this afternoon, but the opportunity has gone. I shall go on writing anyway and you can read it when you are up. I am trying to make up for being so rude to you on Saturday by showing you that I do want your paper and I am going to use every scrap of it.

Of course, it was too late for any confession to save her. She told Kircaldy that she planned to use his paper as well to reply to other letters she had received, and she said, 'you will need all your pockets empty when you come up as I intend writing for the rest of the day, and you shall mail them for me.'

In order to be respected by Kircaldy, she must have also felt that she should somehow reassert her honour and her femininity. She professed to be quite appalled by her situation: 'To think this is Christmas day and Hilda Blake spending it in jail, and worse than that is the thought of it being my last.' Her femininity she emphasized by expressing much tenderness about the kindness that had been shown to her. The tensions between the heroic feminine image she wanted to portray and the gnawing of a death's head are apparent in her prose, yet the world, she now insisted, was a good place:

> Every one is so nice to-day, I just feel like loving Mr. Noxon. Even Mr. Stewart, who I thought quite unmoveable, has been particularly kind. And that dear, kind Mr. Brown, what do you think he did for me? He wrote me the kindest, most loving, brotherly letter and offered to do anything in this mortal world that I could suggest to get me out of this. Oh, if he had only been here two months ago. But it is too late now. I wrote back and thanked him, and I saw him weeping great big tears over my letter. A little while ago I thought this such a hard cruel world. I don't know how I can be so ungrateful when I see sympathetic hearts aching for me.[19]

She was evidently ready, at least for the benefit of Kircaldy, to repudiate the concluding lines in 'My Downfall', in which two weeks ago she had berated people for coming too late to her aid. By renouncing the slight aggressiveness of 'My Downfall', and by emphasizing to Kircaldy that she was the object of much solicitousness, she could again seem worthy of his chivalry.

And behind a façade of dog-like devotion to one's master, Blake prostrated herself in a romantic way before the Chief of Police and vice-president of the Kennel Club. Fleeing the married Mr Rochester, out in the fields with no place to go, Jane Eyre had cried out in extremity, 'I would fain at the moment have become bee or lizard that I might have found fitting nutriment, permanent shelter here. But I was a human being, and had a human being's wants.'[20] Possibly with help from *Jane Eyre*, Blake's thoughts just before her execution went in a similar direction, though her phrasing was much less formal—more suggestive of a coon song than of high tragedy, yet plaintive enough in its own way: 'I wish the Hindoos were correct in their belief that when our spirit leaves this body we turn into an animal. Then I should wish to be your chicken dog. Wouldn't that be nice?'[21]

Thackeray, writing in the 1840s, explained the condemned person's (not just the 'occasional female criminal's') good behaviour in a less reductive way than did Lombroso and Ferrero in the 1890s: 'As the day of the convict's death draws nigh, it is painful to see how he fastens upon everybody who approaches him, how pitifully he clings to them and loves them.'[22] Such terms make sense of Blake, who could no longer expect to rise to the Canadian upper classes but only wish she were a faithful servant to their pleasures, begging love as a viaticum for the coming journey, a fire by which to warm herself during the night ahead.

*

The evening before her scheduled execution, while the Coontown 400 played to 'a large and appreciative audience',[23] Blake spent 'a season' in prayer and hymn-singing with Rev. McLaurin. She also had a long talk with Kircaldy and retired around midnight. Those in charge of her reported that her sleep was 'fitful and restless'. Between five and six the next morning, long before sun-up, she was awakened and again dressed herself in the 'neat and becoming' brown velvet dress she had worn at the trial.[24] She ate heartily at breakfast and spent the balance of the early morning in more prayer and conversation again with McLaurin, while those with tickets to the execution gathered, after their first taste of 'gallows-shock', to warm themselves in the jail hallways. Sheriff Clement came in with the final word from Ottawa—that 'the law must take its course.'

Wednesday, 27 December, dawned −18° Celsius and clear.[25] The morning sun rose low over the prairie in the southeast, and only a cloud or two disturbed one of those Manitoba winter days when a slight mist surrounds everything but it's still possible to see for miles. There would be no repeat of St Scholastique, though even before sunrise a motley procession had begun clustering up the hills towards the rise of ground at the top of what is presently Rideau Park, where stood the courthouse (part of a seniors complex now), the jail, and the scaffold. Among the crowd wishing for a glimpse of the last act there were, the *Western Sun* was scandalized to learn, two women.[26] No one in Brandon could forget even for a moment what was about to happen; between 7:45 and 8:15 the fire bell rang every 30 seconds,[27] forcing Brandonites to think as Thackeray did when he heard the clock sound: what is *she* doing now? has *she* heard it in her room in the Provincial Gaol yonder?[28]

Despite the weak sun outside, the Provincial Gaol was a tomb. 'The stillness of death was everywhere in the great building; the air of the corridors seemed to be stifling; with the feeling of the impending act, the officials moved about with silent footsteps and spoke in hushed tones.' During her last few minutes Blake asked yet again to see Kircaldy. She begged that there would be no surprises awaiting her. She was willing to die, she said, but wanted to know when the end was coming. He reassured her, and then returned to her allegations, presumably against Lane. Telling her that she had only a short time to live, Kircaldy asked whether she wanted to retract anything 'that might injure others'. Blake replied that she 'had nothing to retract.'[29] Instead, she asked him to deliver a letter she was writing, a letter that one might say 'completed' her femininity and her repentance by offering forgiveness to an unnamed recipient. Since she had given Kircaldy the confession he had asked for, he agreed to deliver the letter.[30]

To the consternation of jail officials, 8:00 a.m. came around without the arrival of Radclive. Officials scurried about, but nothing could be done until 8:15 when he finally showed up, a rope in his valise. Later he declared that he had stalled on purpose, because 'he never expected that his services would be required', anticipating a pardon from Ottawa at the eleventh hour.[31]

Radclive tested the equipment of death and told police to clear away the curious who had gathered outside the jail fence. Finally at 8:30 Noxon shepherded the 25 official ticket holders out into the bracing cold. In the hallway he formed a procession—himself leading; Blake next, her elbows pinned tightly to her sides by two of Radclive's leather straps; Rev. McLaurin and Radclive following. When Noxon appeared at the north entrance of the prison before the official gallery, the scene assumed 'an intense and oppressive stillness'.

Blake knew, especially from fiction, that for honour's sake one ought to meet death with proud indifference. In Scott's *Waverley*, Fergus jokes before his execution, shedding no tears; in *Ivanhoe* the sympathetic Rebecca is able to face, after a brief shudder, the instruments of death even though she has been falsely accused; and the real-enough Cordelia Viau had managed to walk without faltering to the gallows in St Scholastique.[32] With a flair for the theatrical, Blake also knew her role in the ceremony. At this point there were no more ruses whereby the individual could shield herself from the fulfilment of the ritual; she could only put on a brave front and make a good show of the few prescribed movements she had left. And indeed, though torn between the image she wanted to present and her fear of death, she put on a brave-enough show, which was interpreted variously as remarkable fortitude or as the unconsciousness of one who did not fully grasp that she was about to meet God. The *Telegram* reported that 'Hilda Blake passed through the hall with a firm steady tread, her head erect and her bearing that of a young lady going to an evening party, rather than the gallows.' Her tread, added the *Independence*, was 'the tread of a girl in a ballroom'.[33]

According to most reports, Blake arrived at the foot of the scaffold ashy pale though completely composed. Despite Radclive's hand on her shoulder, guiding her to the stairs, she did stop and kiss someone. It may have been her guard or it may have been, as the *Independence* claimed, her former guardian, Mr Stewart. With tears rolling down his face as Blake stretched out her hand to him, Stewart 'remained firm on the steps, although ordered back by the hangman.' Blake's voice almost broke as she said 'Good-bye' and kissed him.[34] Another report depicted her near the point of breaking down and her eyes filling with tears before she, 'by a supreme effort',[35] regained her strength. After asking Radclive to hold her skirt so that it would not catch on the first step, she climbed partway up to the platform. Then she stopped, turned, and 'looked searchingly into the faces of those below', evidently looking for someone who wasn't there.[36]

Radclive urged her forward. 'I'm going', she replied, climbing the rest of the 16 steps without the weak knees that Radclive frequently observed during last ascents,[37] and stepping out into a large vista; a prairie landscape in muted colours. Even today, with the city grown around the old courthouse and stately elms guarding so many streets, on that hill one still gets a sense of the expansiveness of the Assiniboine River valley and all the territory beyond. Unusually, in December 1899 no snow covered Brandon's roofs and gables, huddled together to Blake's left. Straight ahead, she could see the Assiniboine, curling from west to east through the valley below her, and the straighter line of the CPR following the river off into the horizon on her right, the railway on which she had come west 11 years before. All along the river stood trees and bushes without their summer foliage but not yet graced with white: sparse and barren and grey. And north beyond the river, the miles and miles of newly opened farmland, also grey.

On the gallows Blake prudently stepped around the trap door. She walked to the front of the gallows and said, 'I think Mr. McIlvride wants to say something to me, may I see him?' Some observers felt that she was merely trying to delay the inevitable, because when McIlvride ascended the scaffold, all she said was, 'Do not think too hardly of me. Good-bye.' She may have hoped that McIlvride carried a message from his business partner and her former employer, but that was not the case. To the audience it was growing clear that she would make no startling disclosures after all.

'Step over here', Radclive motioned, and this time Blake stepped onto the trap door without hesitation. She asked Rev. McLaurin to kiss her goodbye. With tears in his eyes, he did so. Then, while Radclive buckled the straps around her body and her feet, Blake cast one look upward, smiling briefly at the noose. He pulled the black cap tightly over her head. She didn't cry out.

When the noose was tightened around her neck, Blake twitched. But despite that and her stalling, Radclive would later report that 'Hilda Blake displayed more nerve than any of the many he has hanged.'[38] Then the voice of McLaurin could be heard, raised in the Lord's Prayer. Many handkerchiefs could be seen. When McLaurin reached 'forgive us our sins', a grating noise announced the opening of the trap doors, and Blake began her long drop.

I wish the Hindoos were correct in their belief that when our spirit leaves this body we turn into an animal. Then I should wish to be your chicken dog.

Wouldn't that be nice?

Aftermath

The world did not pause long. Radclive returned to the Brunswick Hotel and got a few hours of sleep.[1] In the afternoon, a number of citizens made a point of calling upon Mr Willis of the Coontown 400 and convincing him to return to Brandon in two weeks 'to give another of their creditable performances'.[2] Predictably, the hall was again packed to the doors when they did return. The day after the hanging, the First Baptist Sunday school held its Christmas entertainment, for which the children had been busily training,[3] and on New Year's Day the Brandon Gun Club, which contrary to rumour 'had not died a natural death', returned with a spectacular pigeon shoot, featuring 300 live birds.[4]

Rev. McLaurin announced that on 14 January he would be speaking on 'A sigh heard in a prison cell'. Not unexpectedly, there was a very large attendance at the Baptist church that Sunday.[5] Such a title so soon after the hanging, and after McLaurin's prominent role in it, held the promise of revelations. But as a minister who had earlier refused to give information about Blake's confession, McLaurin could hardly liven his sermon with too many specific details. In later years, after 16 years as superintendent of Baptist Missions in Alberta and after having a Grande Prairie church named in his honour, he reminisced, 'Occasionally I was tempted to announce a sensational topic, which to my surprise brought a crowd. When they discovered that I had in my display windows what I did not have in my shop, they did not come again. It requires a genius to hold an audience by eloquence, learning or sensation. Few of us are equal to it. But if you give the Bread of Life, from that inexhaustible supply, the hungry will come.'[6] Although he preached many sermons over his long career, it

is possible that the memory of his involvement with a young domestic in Brandon caused him to reminisce in this way. By the end of January 1900, McLaurin had set aside sensational titles and was giving a
somewhat less titillating series of lectures entitled 'The Tabernacle',
with illustrations.[7]

Only after the potential jailbreaker Hilda Blake was safely out of
this world was Emma Stripp incarcerated in the Brandon Provincial
Gaol. She was jailed on 10 January and went to trial eight days later,
pleading not guilty to the charge of attempting to aid Blake's escape.
Two successful businessmen—hotel owners Peter Payne and David
W. Beaubier (who declared his profession to be 'Gentleman')[8]—had
put up $150 each for Stripp's bail bond when she was first charged. A
Salvation Army friend who worked in a bonding house, E. Gooding,
and the successful retail merchant and prominent Liberal, A.C.
Fraser, provided character references. But such support availed little,
for Stripp was found guilty and sentenced to two months in prison.[9]
When she heard the verdict, she broke down: 'The scene . . . was a
most pitiful one. Seldom if ever has a prisoner taken a sentence
harder. She . . . was almost hysterical for some time, and even the
lawyers and law officials could not help but feel kindly towards the
aged lady who had made a mistake.' The *Sun* believed that Stripp's
sentence 'would have the desired effect'.[10] It did. No Stripps appear in
the 1901 census for Brandon.[11]

Newspaper interest diminished shortly after the execution, though
on 4 January, right beside the article describing Hilda Blake's last
letter of forgiveness to an unnamed party, a sly editor placed the successful tenders for wood delivery to the courthouse and jail—
'McIlvride and Lane'—as well as to the Brandon Asylum—
'McIlvride and Lane' again. Tongue-in-cheek, the *Sun* had also
reported that 'A book agent in North Dakota writes . . . to secure
agency for the sale of Hilda Blake's autobiography which he understands we are publishing.'[12] But these were only subtle hints. A Liberal newspaper, whatever the private leanings of the editor, would not
want to damage the feeling that justice had been done. The Liberals
won the looming Canadian election in November 1900, and Sifton
easily retained his Brandon seat, 5,011 to 4,342, over Hugh John
Macdonald, who had resigned as Premier of Manitoba to challenge
Sifton federally.

James Kircaldy, skilled detective and chivalrous man, continued to
rise in the estimation of Brandonites, taking a central part in the AOUW
lodge's next meeting on 3 January.[13] In the two-man debate,
'Resolved that Britain is justified in her war in the Transvaal', he did

not harm his reputation by taking the affirmative.[14] He continued as chief constable until 1905, when, after 13 years of police work, he resigned to 'try his hand at hotel-keeping and real estate'. He successively ran the Empire Hotel, worked as a city assessor, and as a liquor store employee. Serving with distinction and wounded three times in World War I, he rose to the rank of Brigadier General by war's end, in command of the 12th Canadian Infantry Brigade. Though he failed to get elected to the provincial legislature in 1920 as a Conservative candidate, he did spend 16 years as a Brandon alderman. When he was 85 he said, during a banquet in his honour at the Prince Edward Hotel, 'I have enjoyed all the years of my earthly existence.'[15]

John Robinson, Mary Lane's father who had been living with Mary and Robert, died of an illness in late January 1900, a month after Blake was hanged.[16] His wife, Annie, did not remain with Robert, but went back to Birtle to live with her daughter, Lucy Murdoch. In contrast to his in-laws, Robert himself remained in Brandon for the rest of his life. But not as a widower: within a month he began courting Jessie McIlvride, his 22-year-old bookkeeper (and the sister of his partner Alexander McIlvride). She had come to Brandon from Guelph in 1898 to keep house for her brothers and to look for a husband.[17] According to McIlvride family stories, Alexander had a friend whom he hoped Jessie would marry, but she saw Robert Lane and fell in love at first sight. Alexander, still an alderman, abruptly dissolved his business partnership with Robert in early February of 1900—shortly after the hanging and in the middle of the courtship of Robert and Jessie. After the provincial Tory victory, McIlvride angled for the position of bursar at the Brandon Asylum, but he did not get it. He farmed near Brandon for a time and then moved to Victoria about 1914. He left Brandon early enough in 1901 for the city to call a by-election to fill his unexpired term as alderman.[18] Although the McIlvride clan continued to associate with the Lanes,[19] by the time of the 'quiet wedding' on 9 September 1900 in the home of E.A. Henry, a Presbyterian minister, Robert was known as the senior member of Lane & Elviss, transfer, coal, and wood merchants.[20]

Lane eventually fathered twelve children altogether, five with Mary (including the first-born, Annie, who died in infancy) and seven with Jessie. The two sets of children were together without distinction; Jessie was spoken of highly and was accepted among the Robinsons, who, like the McIlvrides, continued to associate with the Lanes. That the wound opened by Mary's death was beginning to heal is suggested by a relaxed photograph of the extended Lane family—mostly women—picnicking at Lake Clementi in 1903.[21]

Robert Lane's company continued to expand. By 1912 he directed 35 horses and a proportionate number of wagons from his office at 735 Rosser Avenue, and claimed to have the largest market share in his fields of business. His Crystal Ice Company vowed that its ice, cut at a rate of 12,000 tons a year from the Assiniboine River, had been 'repeatedly analyzed' and was 'declared to be clear and pure and much better than the water that comes from the river. It gives a softer water when melted and is palatable as well as healthful.' Exactly how the river water was transmogrified, the advertising supplement did not mention. Lane also owned the biggest share of stocks in the Brandon Cartage and Warehousing Company, employing 30 people, and had exclusive privileges to deal with the Canadian Pacific, Great Northern, and Canadian Northern railroads. Through his transfer company, he continued to sell fuel—hard coal, soft coals from the US and western Canada, charcoal, long and short wood[22]— and some of his money he invested in real estate, buying land around Wapella. The novelist and suffragette Nellie McClung became a friend of the family, and Jessie is said to have helped organize a parade for her.

In June of 1924, Robert Lane took ill, recovered to the point that he was able to go back to work, but then suffered a serious relapse and went to the hospital, apparently for a gall bladder operation. According to his obituary, his condition 'baffled all medical skill, and in a comatose state he passed out of this life'—which may mean that he did not survive the anaesthetic. The obituary described him as 'a man of quiet demeanor and a good-hearted fellow whose death will be regretted by his fellow citizens'.[23] On one side of Mary Lane's large tombstone is Robert's epitaph: 'The Day Thou Gavest Lord Is Ended'. Thomas Lane, decorated in the war, eventually took over his father's business, although it was declining. The Lane family, and Thomas in particular, talked very little about the murder. Some family members first heard the story in school or from their cousins in the Robinson family. Family stories and stories reported in the *Birtle Eye-Witness* (the Lane hometown newspaper) tended to metamorphose the events from the dynamite of sexuality and class into more acceptable passions like theft or a quarrel between mistress and servant.[24] Such motives would have much simplified Brandon's reaction to the murder, but no such motives were ever reported in court documents or in the newspapers outside of Birtle. One family story even sanitized Blake's 'chicken dog' wish: instead of abasing herself before Kircaldy, Blake is said to have wished that she could come back as a dog so that she could follow around the Lane *children*.

The monument to Mary Lane eventually became the tombstone of Robert and then of Jessie Lane: 'The Day Thou Gavest Lord Is Ended'. (Authors' collection.)

*

Hilda Blake, who would have turned 22 late in January of 1900, was buried in the gravelly soil of the jail's courtyard beside William Webb, the wife-murderer who had been executed when Blake was 10 and still lived with the Stewarts.[25] Historically, there had been 'moments when hanged bodies were overtly politicized, converted into emblems of injustice, and carried off to fine funerals in parodic inversion of the executioner's intended significance', so the Criminal Code required burial on the jail grounds.[26] But in Brandon in 1899, the body of a domestic servant was not a political body, and the precise location of her grave was soon forgotten. Although Blake fantasized about a trip back to her sister, only a small news item made the round trip, appearing in the *Norfolk Chronicle*. The item was quite inaccurate, but is curiously evocative, even today, of the young orphan who left a British workhouse and crossed the seas to be 'adopted' by a Canadian family: 'Emily Blake, a servant girl who went to Ottawa from London last year, was hanged on Tuesday morning for the murder of her mistress. She became passionately fond of her mistress's babies, and therefore killed her, so that she might adopt the children herself.' [27]

Despite the deaths of Mary Lane and Hilda Blake, Brandon assessment rolls show that by 1900 there were, once again, seven people in the Lane household. Jessie McIlvride, of course, had joined Lane, taking charge of Mary's four children. The seventh person? Henrietta Adams, a 20-year-old Scottish Presbyterian woman with a purple birthmark on one side of her face.[28] Her position? Domestic servant. Her first job? Finish hanging the curtains.

Writing about Hilda Blake:
A Note on Sources

Walk Towards the Gallows: The Tragedy of Hilda Blake, Hanged 1899 began as 'history from above' in an article by Tom Mitchell (published in the *Journal of Canadian Studies*) explaining why the state executed Hilda Blake at a time when the death sentences of women were almost always commuted. Our book-length treatment of the Blake case, however, slowly turned into an account of Blake's life both 'from above' and 'from below'. Traditional historical methods and sources were adequate to the former but not to the latter. A simple constructed narrative based on state documents and newspaper reports would tell a story of state action but could neither approach the less explicit levels of culture nor probe human subjectivity.

Writing a history that did not ignore Blake's subjectivity required a historical 'reading' of a wide range of sources, some of them traditional tools for the historian, some less traditional. British censuses, Heckingham & Clavering Workhouse records, materials in the Norfolk Record Office, Self-Help Emigration Society records in the National Archives of Canada, and the University of Victoria's cache of materials on Norfolk, England, allowed us to introduce Blake at the beginning of her journey. Various records of the Western Judicial District (Brandon), rich in detail, helped us flesh out both Blake's early encounter with life on Canada's agricultural frontier and also the contest to claim the youthful Blake's labour. Small-town Manitoba newspapers, as well as those in Winnipeg, Regina, Toronto, and Ottawa, were essential sources, mixing factual information with sensationalism and political opportunism, rumours with actual words from the principal figures in the drama.

Brandon's Victorian streetscape and domestic architecture gave us important clues to the 'imagined' world of the late nineteenth century. As backgrounds to our pointillist study of Blake's life, we found Joy Parr's *Labouring Children*, Phyllis Harrison's *The Home Children*, Claudette Lacelle's *Urban Domestic Servants in Nineteenth Century Canada*, Susan Jackel's *A Flannel Shirt and Liberty*, and Ann-Louise Shapiro's *Breaking the Codes* invaluable; as background to her death, V.A.C. Gatrell's *The Hanging Tree*. The many excellent books and articles on women's history by Leonore Davidoff, Karen Dubinsky, Carolyn Strange, Joan Sangster, and Constance Backhouse allowed us to orient ourselves in the Canadian history of gender. For our attempt at 'thick description' we turned to a wide variety of nine- teenth-century sources, such as manners books like Grandma Nichols's *The Great Nineteenth Century Household Guide*, as well as academic works like Lucy Salmon's *Domestic Service* and Cesare Lombroso and Guglielmo Ferrero's *The Female Offender*. These were enriched by texts on immigration, gender, manners, and social reform made available through Early Canadiana Online by the Canadian Institute for Historical Microreproductions (CIHM). The *Canadian Magazine* helped us immensely with its late Victorian examinations of neglected children, women's roles, female suffrage, and fads, while parliamentary and Senate debates on seduction revealed nineteenth- century understandings of class and gender.

Immigration and land settlement records, Canadian censuses, birth and death records, and local histories (published with the financial assistance of the Manitoba provincial government after Manitoba's centennial in 1970) were valuable in dealing with family histories of the Stewarts, Rexes, and Lanes. Several members of the Robinson and Lane families spoke confidentially, telling family stories, often in defence of Robert Lane. A trip to the former Church of the Advent in Kola took us to Stewart family gravestones and to a scrapbook of church history still kept in the deserted church. For material on Rev. C.C. McLaurin we relied on the Canadian Baptist Archives at McMaster University and on the Glenbow Archives in Calgary.

Less obviously, once we discovered that Blake had read Charlotte Brontë, Walter Scott, and Charles Dickens, and had enjoyed 'coon songs', we realized that Blake's reading could give us a window into her desires. Sam Dennison's *Scandalize My Name* proved to be the best source for 'coon songs', though the 'African-American Sheet Music, 1850–1920' Internet site at Brown University helped as well. The problem, of course, was not to *find* novels and songs, but to know how to use them, since they are not much used in conventional history. Here Carlo Ginzburg's micro-history, *The Cheese and the Worms: The Cosmos of a Sixteenth-Century Miller*, proved seminal. Ginzburg's ability to open up the past by means of a close reading of documents has shown historians how much is lost when documents—literary and otherwise—are used only as evidence of larger historical patterns. In a more general sense, the theoretical foundations laid by Antonio Gramsci and Hayden White guided us: Gramsci's consistent refusal to dismiss the superstructure as a merely secondary growth upon material relations, his readiness to allow resistance and desire a variety of languages and cultural clothes; White's insistence that *all* historiography (not just narrative history) depends on plot, that *all* historiography enacts some form of desire.

Clearly, one of the ways in which a small city achieves 'historicity' is for the past to become seen: mythical and mysterious and real. Both the serious historian and the 'true crime' writer agree that a spectacular and specular murder is often the point at which the local suddenly becomes the universal, the point at which human bodies and fates become urgent expressions of larger social patterns.

Notes

Introduction

1. *Winnipeg Daily Tribune*, 6 July 1899; *Winnipeg Morning Telegram*, 6 July 1899. Neither Brandon papers nor the *Manitoba Free Press* (which had a Brandon correspondent) mentions this rather significant detail.
2. *Manitoba Morning Free Press*, 6 July 1899.
3. *Brandon Times*, 6 July 1899.
4. *Western Sun*, 6 July 1899.
5. *Brandon Times*, 6, 13 July 1899.
6. Ibid., 6 July 1899.
7. Ibid.
8. Walter Gordon was executed in 1902, Harry Green in 1915. *Brandon Sun*, 7 June 1985.
9. Ibid.
10. Our correspondence with the Manitoba Department of Culture, Heritage and Tourism suggests that the government has no record of where Hilda Blake was buried. Personal correspondence, Judith Baldwin, special assistant to the Honourable Diane McGifford, to Tom Mitchell, n.d.
11. J.L. Granatstein, *Who Killed Canadian History?* (Toronto, 1998), 73.
12. Joan Sangster, 'Beyond Dichotomies—Re-Assessing Gender History and Women's History in Canada', *Left History* 3, 1 (Spring-Summer 1995): 118. She cites Joan Kelly, *Women, History, Theory* (Chicago, 1984).
13. See Carlo Ginzburg, *The Cheese and the Worms: The Cosmos of a Sixteenth-Century Miller (Il formaggio e I vermin: Il cosmo di un mugnaio del '500)*, trans. John and Anne Tedeschi (Baltimore, 1980); Peter Brown, *Augustine of Hippo: A Biography* (London, 1967).
14. See Ngaire Naffine, *Female Crime* (North Sydney, Australia, 1987), 24, 90.

15. For a thoughtful examination of these trends, see Neville Kirk, 'History, Language, Ideas, and Postmodernism: A Materialist View', *Social History* 19, 2 (May 1994): 221–40.

16. Catherine Belsey, 'Constructing the Subject: Deconstructing the Text', in Judith Newton and Deborah Rosenfelt, eds, *Feminist Criticism and Social Change: Sex, Class, and Race in Literature and Culture* (Andover, 1985), reprinted in Robert Con Davis and Ronald Schleifer, eds, *Contemporary Literary Criticism*, 4th edn (New York, 1998), 382.

17. David Mayfield and Susan Thorne, 'Social History and its Discontents', *Social History* 17, 2 (1992): 165–88.

18. Karl Marx, *The Eighteenth Brumaire of Louis Napoleon Bonaparte*, in Robert C. Tucker, ed., *The Marx-Engels Reader* (New York, 1972), 437.

19. This is Leonore Davidoff's quotation of Lövgren and Frykman, *Worlds Between: Historical Perspectives on Gender and Class* (New York, 1995), 2.

20. Tom Mitchell began work on this book long before the 1996 publication of *Alias Grace*. For an early assessment of the Blake case, see Tom Mitchell, ' "Blood with the Taint of Cain": Immigrant Labouring Children, Manitoba Politics, and the Execution of Emily Hilda Blake', *Journal of Canadian Studies* 28, 4 (Winter 1993–4): 49–71.

21. Margaret Atwood, *Alias Grace* (Toronto, 1996).

22. Or (least likely of all) was the seance a scheme cooked up by the itinerant Jeremiah? The 'unknowable' comment—phrased as a statement, not a question—comes from Margaret Atwood, *In Search of Alias Grace* (Ottawa, 1996), 37.

23. Early on, Atwood attempted to use Susanna Moodie's account of Grace Marks's guilt; later, Atwood rejected that guilt in favour of a more twentieth-century thesis about the indeterminacy of certain past events. See *In Search of Alias Grace*, 29–37.

24. The double bind: if Grace is too improper we will blame the novelist for not really leaving the twentieth century, but if she is too proper we will blame the novelist for relying on twentieth-century stereotypes about the nineteenth century. Nevertheless, a moment of silence is long overdue for all the post-1960s trivializations of mental illness as a trope—from R.D. Laing to Deleuze and Guattari.

Chapter 1

1. Ernest R. Suffling, *The Land of the Broads* (London, 1887), 54; *Who's Who 1902* (London, 1902), 133.

2. Reginald Beauchamp to A.P. Stewart, 17 Apr. 1889, Provincial Archives of Manitoba (PAM), Surrogate Court of the Western Judicial District, Emily Hilda Blake, GR 5338, file no. 108, 1889.

3. *1881 Census*, FHL film 1341473, PRO ref RG11, piece 1963, folio 51, p. 3, Norfolk Studies Library. The eldest daughter's identity is something of a puzzle, since she does not appear in this census. Given the ages of the parents, it could be that Sarah Ann had given birth at 16 and that her daughter was out of the home—either married or working out—by the time she, too, was 16. It is also possible that the eldest daughter was Hilda's stepsister and resided with another parent.

4. The *1881 Census* lists his occupation as 'police constable'.

5. Personal letter from Superintendent Kirkham of the Norfolk Constabulary to Christina Crease, 29 Feb. 2000.

6. Henry Alfred Barrett to Tommy and Hilda Blake, 6 Aug. 1888, *Queen v. Mary Rex* (1889), PAM, Court of Queen's Bench (Brandon) filings, A 0088, GR 363, L–11–4–14.

7. Constance Beauchamp to Mrs Stewart, 19 Mar. 1888, *Queen v. Mary Rex* (1889).

8. Heckingham Workhouse, *Loddon and Clavering Union Admission and Discharge Book*, 1891, Norfolk Record Office.

9. Self-Help Emigration Society, *Report for the Year 1892*, National Archives of Canada (NAC), Immigration Branch, RG 76, vol. 72, file 3440, 30.

10. Heckingham Workhouse (Loddon and Clavering Union), *Guardians' Minute Book*, 1887–9 (C/GP 12/123), 16 Apr. 1888, Norfolk Record Office.

11. Gerald Friesen, *The Canadian Prairies: A History* (Toronto, 1987), 251. The only legislation existing in Manitoba at the time of Blake's arrival affecting orphaned or abandoned children was the 1877 Apprentices and Minors Act modelled on the Ontario legislation of 1874. Under this legislation, mayors, magistrates, or charitable institutions could make arrangements for the indenture of orphaned or abandoned children. Not until the passage of the Child Immigration Act of 1897 was provision made in Manitoba to regulate and monitor the conditions upon which children were settled in the province as immigrants. For a detailed discussion of this legislative framework, see Jan Ursel, *Private Lives, Public Policy: 100 Years of State Intervention in the Family* (Toronto, 1992), 111–24.

12. Ivy Pinchbeck and Margaret Hewitt, *Children in English Society*, vol. 2 (London, 1973), 555.

13. Reginald Beauchamp to A.P. Stewart, 17 Apr. 1889, Surrogate Court of the Western Judicial District, Emily Hilda Blake, 1889.

14. Scrapbook at the Church of the Advent, Kola, article taken from the *Virden Empire Advance*, 1962. Stewart's age is listed in Margaret Goodman et al., *Index to the 1901 Census of Manitoba for Brandon* (South

West Branch, Manitoba Genealogical Society, 1998), 15, 34. Letitia Stewart's gravestone shows that she was about 12 years older than Alfred Stewart.

15. Surrogate Court of the Western Judicial District, PAM, GR 5338, file 108, 1889.
16. Self-Help Emigration Society, *Report for the Year 1892*, 2; *Report for the Year 1893*, 19.
17. Constance Beauchamp to Mrs Stewart, 19 Mar. 1888, *Queen v. Mary Rex* (1889).
18. Charles Dickens, *Oliver Twist* (Harmondsworth, UK, 1966 [1837]), 61.
19. William White, *White's Norfolk* (Newton Abbot, 1969), 16.
20. *Melita Enterprise*, 21 July 1899.
21. *Western Sun*, 14 Dec. 1899.
22. Kimberly Reynolds and Nicola Humble, *Victorian Heroines: Representations of Femininity in Nineteenth-Century Literature and Art* (New York, 1993), 24.
23. John Reed, *Victorian Conventions* (Athens, Ohio, 1975), 254.
24. Michael McKeon, *The Origins of the English Novel, 1600–1740* (Baltimore, 1987).
25. Constance Beauchamp to Mrs Stewart, 19 Mar. 1888, *Queen v. Mary Rex* (1889).
26. Letters of 6 Nov. 1894 and 28 Aug. 1895 from Lyndwode Pereira, Assistant Secretary to the London High Commissioner for Canada, speak of a $2 per capita bonus being paid to the Self-Help Emigration Society. Self-Help Emigration Society, NAC, Immigration Branch, RG 76, vol. 72, file 3440.
27. Self-Help Emigration Society, *Report for the Year 1892*, 4, 27.
28. Reginald Beauchamp to A.P. Stewart, 17 Apr. 1889, Surrogate Court of the Western Judicial District, Emily Hilda Blake, file 108, 1889.
29. 'No. 12 Annual Report of Winnipeg Immigration Agent', *Sessional Papers* 5 (1889): 89–90.
30. Elkhorn and District Historical Society, *Steel and Grass Roots: History of Elkhorn 1882–1982* (Elkhorn, Man., 1982), 80.
31. PAM, NR 0215, Natural Resources Lands Branch, Homestead files, reel 1110 (hereafter Lands Branch, reel 1110).
32. *Virden Advance*, 12 Oct. 1899.
33. Dickens, *Oliver Twist*, 54.
34. Paul D. Steinhauer, *The Least Detrimental Alternative: A Systematic Guide to Case Planning and Decision Making for Children in Care* (Toronto, 1991), 27, 33, 353.
35. Henry Alfred Barrett to Mrs Stewart, 6 Aug. 1888, *Queen v. Mary Rex* (1889).

36. Henry Alfred Barrett to Tommy and Hilda Blake, 6 Aug. 1888, *Queen v. Mary Rex* (1889).
37. Romans 8:17 (King James Version).
38. Joy Parr, ' "Transplanting from Dens of Iniquity": Theology and Child Emigration', in Linda Kealey, ed., *A Not Unreasonable Claim: Women and Reform in Canada, 1880s–1920s* (Toronto, 1979), 176.
39. Ibid., 177.
40. Elkhorn and District Historical Society, *Steel and Grass Roots*, 68; *Elkhorn Mercury*, 11 Apr. 1911.
41. Ibid.
42. G.M. Marshall to S. Carsley, President, Society for the Protection of Women and Children, 15 Feb. 1896; Edward Wilson Gates to the Minister of the Interior, 16 Jan. 1896, NAC, Immigration Branch, RG 76, vol. 72, file 3440.
43. Phyllis Harrison, ed., *The Home Children: Their Personal Stories* (Winnipeg, 1979), 22.
44. Parr, ' "Transplanting from Dens of Iniquity" ', 173.

Chapter 2

1. *Western Sun*, 14 Dec. 1899.
2. 'It is marvelous that anyone finds their way on the prairie', says Mrs Cecil Hall about those early days. Hall, *A Lady's Life on a Farm in Manitoba* (London, 1884), 123.
3. Hilda Blake's submission, Surrogate Court of the Western Judicial District, Emily Hilda Blake, PAM, GR 5338, file 108, 1889.
4. Harrison, ed., *The Home Children*, 20. Joy Parr, *Labouring Children: British Immigrant Apprentices to Canada, 1869–1924* (Montreal and Kingston, 1980), 109.
5. See, for example, Self-Help Emigration Society, *Report for the Year 1892*, 16.
6. *Virden Advance*, 14 Mar. 1899.
7. Rex probably was not held in the Provincial Gaol at Brandon because a 7 Mar. 1899 *Western Sun* story made light of the fact that Jailer Noxon had no customers. Who would work Noxon's potato garden? the reporter wanted to know.
8. *Mary Rex v. A.P. Stewart* (1889), Court of Queen's Bench (Brandon), PAM, GR 360, ATG 0062–6, no. 39, TB 8. See also *Rex v. Stewart* (1889), *Manitoba Law Reports* 6 (1889): 257–68.
9. Surrogate Court of the Western Judicial District, Emily Hilda Blake, 1889.
10. *Rex v. Stewart* (1889).

11. 'Formation of Parish', Scrapbook at the Church of the Advent, Kola. When the 'Sentence of Consecration' was passed on 22 September 1895, the second signatory, after the incumbent minister, was that of A.P. Stewart. Among the 13 subsequent names is that of H.J. Rex.

12. Reginald P. Beauchamp to A.P. Stewart, 17 Apr. 1889, Surrogate Court of the Western Judicial District, Emily Hilda Blake, 1889.

13. Surrogate Court of the Western Judicial District, Emily Hilda Blake, file 108, 1889.

14. Ibid.

15. Ibid. Tommy Blake apparently remained with the Stewarts until his departure for Alberta in the mid-1890s.

16. Ibid.

17. H.J. Rex to the Minister of the Interior, 19 Nov. 1883, Lands Branch, reel 1110, PAM.

18. *Virden Advance*, 11 July 1889.

19. Herbert's shanty was 12 x 12 feet. Mary Rex's land patent statement said that in 1884 she broke four acres. In 1885 she cropped four and broke 14; in 1886 she cropped 18 and broke 15; in 1887 she cropped 33. Stewart's land patent statement says that in 1884 he broke 10 acres and cropped them. In 1885 he cropped 10 and broke 40; in 1886 and 1887 he cropped 50. Lands Branch, reel 1110, PAM.

20. *Elkhorn Advocate*, 13 July 1899.

21. *Virden Advance*, 13 June 1889.

22. That statement may not be strictly accurate, since in 1887 Stewart witnessed to the accuracy of Rex's homestead patent application, though it is possible that the process was handled through the Dominion Lands inspector. Stewart testified that Rex's answers on the patent application were correct, but he did get a little barb in: he estimated her stables as worth $60 while she had valued them at $150. Lands Branch, reel 1110, PAM.

23. Mary Rex's deposition, 6 Mar. 1889.

24. See Parr, *Labouring Children*, 106–7.

25. Mary Rex to Messrs Daly and Coldwell, 8 June 1889, Surrogate Court of the Western Judicial District, Emily Hilda Blake, file 108, 1889.

26. *Brandon Independence*, 5 Oct. 1899; *Virden Advance*, 5 Oct. 1899. The reference must be to Robert Burn Singer, whom we will encounter shortly. The rumour of Blake's involvement appears to have been untrue. Of the three papers in Brandon at the time, the *Independence* was least reliable, for example, calling Mary Lane 'Mrs John Lane'. On 20 July 1899, the *Western Sun* discounted rumours 'connecting the name of Emily Hilda Blake with two sudden deaths occurring in families where she was working'. Rev. C.C. McLaurin, who probably knew Blake best, also discounted the rumour because Blake was living in Springfield (just

east of Winnipeg) at the time and because the dead Stewart's 'brother' (Joseph Singer, who became a lawyer) offered to defend Blake after the Lane murder. *Western Sun*, 14 Dec. 1899. On the other hand, McLaurin would have had to rely on Blake's own account in speaking of Blake's whereabouts in the years prior to their meeting, and the rumour was also reported in the *Elkhorn Advocate*, 5 Oct. 1899, much closer to where the events were supposed to have transpired.

27. Letitia Stewart was probably Capt. Singer's wife, but, curiously, she is not named on Robert Burn's gravestone. As well, Constance Beauchamp, in one of her letters to 'Mrs Stewart', refers to a cheque from 'Mrs Singer', as if there were two women. Constance Beauchamp to Mrs Stewart, 5 May 1888. This could have simply been Beauchamp's error. The *1891 Census* (District of Selkirk, Subdistrict Municipality of Wallace) lists the four Singer children as having an English mother and an Irish father. Letitia was born in England, having a Scottish father and Irish mother. The most likely permutation would make Letitia the mother of the Singer children. The *Manitoba Morning Free Press*, 28 Dec. 1899, said that Blake had resided with a family named Singer.

28. Joseph Singer file, Archives of the Manitoba Legal-Judicial History, P1329, PAM; *Index to the 1901 Census of Manitoba for the Rural Municipality of Wallace* (Southwest Branch of the Manitoba Genealogical Society, 1999). The 24 Jan. 1883 survey for Township 10 shows land for a J. Singer on Section 18. It couldn't have been our Joseph Singer (who was 13 at the time), but was likely a relative.

29. Letter to the Minister of the Interior, 31 Mar. 1886, Lands Branch, reel 1110, PAM.

30. The holdings of Stewart, Singer, and 'Thomas Blake' can be found in the 'Dominion Land Grants' database available through ArchiviaNet, National Archives of Canada:
www.archives.ca/exec/naweb.dll?fs&020111&e&top&0

31. *Rex v. Singer et al.* (29–30 May 1889), County Judges' Criminal Court (Brandon), PAM, GR 360, ATG 0062–6, file 71.

32. See Pinchbeck and Hewitt, *Children in English Society*, 575.

33. Several land grants were made to 'Thomas Blake', but we have no way of knowing whether the so-named person was Hilda's brother.

34. The results of this survey are reported in Veronica Strong-Boag, 'Pulling in Double Harness or Hauling a Double Load: Women, Work and Feminism on the Canadian Prairie', *Journal of Canadian Studies* 21, 3 (Fall 1986): 37–8.

35. This is an oft-repeated complaint. See, for example, Ella C. Sykes, *A Home-Help in Canada* (London, 1912), 143, 221. Although Sykes's book is based on the year 1911, many of her experiences echo those of

servants in the 1890s, and one of her placements was in Newton, Manitoba—not far from Brandon. She often seems more forthright than other writers who wanted to encourage immigration to Canada.

36. Theresa Richardson, 'Ambiguities in the Lives of Children: Postmodern Views on the History and Historiography of Childhood in English Canada', *Postmodern History* 22, 2 (1996): 374.

37. See, for example, Harrison, ed., *The Home Children*, 38–9; Parr, *Labouring Children*, 109–10; Kenneth Bagnell, *The Little Immigrants* (Toronto, 1980), 46.

38. Elkhorn and District Historical Society, *Steel and Grass Roots*, 81–2, 92.

39. See Parr, *Labouring Children*, 82–3. Davidoff, *Worlds Between*, 15, drawing her evidence from Britain, says that 'in the hierarchy of domestic service it was often the youngest (and overwhelmingly female) servants who did the heaviest work.' Standards may have been different for members of the family than for servants.

40. Frank E. Huggett, *Life Below Stairs: Domestic Servants in England from Victorian Times* (London, 1977), 113, cites the adage. Pip, in *Great Expectations*, gets money from mysterious sources, but until he does, he expects nothing from the sister who adopted him. Charles Dickens, *Great Expectations* (Harmondsworth, UK, 1965 [1860–1]), 74.

41. Davidoff, *Worlds Between*, 3.

42. Parr, *Labouring Children*, 84–5, 82.

43. *Manitoba Morning Free Press*, 28 Dec. 1899.

44. Dickens, *Great Expectations*, 79.

45. *Western Sun*, 14 Dec. 1899.

46. It was possible in 1893 to use the word 'abuse' to refer to sexual abuse, but the fact that the *Oxford English Dictionary* did not give sexual interference as one of the meanings of 'abuse' until its 1993 on-line *Supplement* suggests that the usage was not common until the 1980s. http://dictionary.oed.com

47. *Queen v. Singer et al.* (1889). The offence of stealing children under 14 is described in section 284 of the 1892 Criminal Code.

48. According to Joseph Singer, Hilda was returned to the Stewarts in May 1889, ran away again to a family north of Elkhorn, and then left for Winnipeg in 1890. Thus, she would have been only 12 years old when she was first on her own. *Elkhorn Advocate*, 27 July 1899. The *1891 Census*, however, still lists Hilda as living on the Stewart farm. Singer or the *Elkhorn Advocate* may have mistaken the chronology, or the Stewarts, as guardians, may have kept up the fiction that Hilda still belonged to them and was simply 'working out'. The latter seems most likely since Singer's information is in other respects accurate. In any case, Hilda was on her own at a very young age.

49. We will later show how her poem, 'My Downfall', echoes a ballad that appeared in *Jane Eyre*.
50. Charlotte Brontë, *Jane Eyre* (New York, 1981 [1847]), 7, 48, 50. In Dickens, *Great Expectations*, 92, Pip, another orphan, complains about the injustice of his upbringing.
51. From *The Quarterly Review*, quoted in Sandra M. Gilbert and Susan Gubar, *The Madwoman in the Attic* (New Haven, 1979), 338.
52. Otto Rank, *The Myth of the Birth of the Hero*, trans. F. Robbins and Smith Ely Jelliffe (New York, 1959 [1914]), 69, 84. Rank was born in 1884, six years after Blake. Someone with knowledge of nineteenth-century German fiction or of German translations of English fiction might well be able to argue that Rank's initial ideas came not from mythology, but from his reading of contemporaneous literature.
53. Information and complaint of Mary Rex, 28 May 1889, *Rex v. Stewart* (1889).
54. *Manitoba Morning Free Press*, 21 Dec. 1899.
55. Steinhauer, *The Least Detrimental Alternative*, 35, 39, 62, 64–70, 74, 335.
56. For examples of romance narratives in adoption accounts, see H. David Kirk, *Shared Fate: A Theory of Adoption and Mental Health* (New York, 1964), 163, 165. In one case a young girl fastened onto the story of Cinderella, in another, a young boy told his parents 'You stole me.' Kirk often cites the mourning that accompanies adoption. Clare Marcus, *Adopted? A Canadian Guide for Adopted Adults in Search of Their Origins* (Vancouver, 1979), 57, cites the case of a girl who was separated at a young age from her sister, and whose reunion at adulthood proved disappointing, since she expected the sister to be rich and popular. Marcus, *Who Is My Mother? Birth Parents, Adoptive Parents and Adoptees Talk about Living with Adoption and the Search for Lost Family* (Toronto, 1981), 123, reviews studies, concluding that expectations of reunions are often high and unrealistic and that adoptees are often unable to acknowledge the needs of either birth parents or adoptive parents.
57. Brontë, *Jane Eyre*, 146; Dickens, *Oliver Twist*, 476.
58. *Brandon Independence*, 5 Oct. 1899, reports the rumour that Blake wrote these things to Mrs Stewart in a letter. Since the rumour occurs in the same article that describes a letter in which Blake admitted murdering young Stewart, the rumour may not be reliable. However, one might also compare other home children's fantasies of a return to England and other orphans' creation of fictional brothers and sisters in Britain. Parr, *Labouring Children*, 75, 77.
59. *Virden Advance*, 14, 28 Nov. 1899.
60. Tombstone of Robert Burn Singer, Church of the Advent, now Kola Anglican Church.

61. *Virden Advance*, 12 Oct. 1899.
62. *Elkhorn Advocate*, 4 Nov. 1894.
63. A.P. Stewart posted a $400 bond to ensure that Joseph, as a student, would fulfil all the regulations of the Law Society of Manitoba. Joseph Singer file, Archives of the Manitoba Legal-Judicial History, P1329, PAM.
64. *Virden Advance*, 12 Oct. 1899.
65. *Elkhorn Advocate*, 7 Dec. 1899.
66. *Manitoba Morning Free Press*, 28 Dec. 1899.
67. We can say, however, that the intimacy of the parent-child bond is 'strongly and inversely related to delinquency'. Naffine, *Female Crime*, 65.

Chapter 3

1. John Hudson, *Plains Country Towns* (Minneapolis, 1985), 15, quoted in Donald G. Wetherell and Irene R.A. Kmet, *Town Life: Main Street and the Evolution of Small Town Alberta, 1880–1947* (Edmonton, 1995), 2.
2. *Brandon Daily Sun*, 30 June 1924.
3. Douglas Owram, *Promise of Eden: The Canadian Expansionist Movement and the Idea of the West 1856–1900* (Toronto, 1980), 193.
4. Friesen, *The Canadian Prairies*, 105. For an extended discussion of these writers, see Irene Spry, 'Early Visitors to the Canadian Prairies', in Brian W. Blouet and Merlin P. Lawson, eds, *Images of the Plains: The Role of Human Nature in Settlement* (Lincoln, Neb., 1975), 165–80.
5. *Church Missionary Record* 13, 1 (Jan. 1841): 11, quoted in Owram, *Promise of Eden*, 24. Despite her satirical streak, Kate Hayes, too, calls the West Eden. Kate E. Hayes (pseud. of Mary Markwell), *Prairie Potpourri* (Winnipeg, 1895), 14.
6. The phrase is taken from the title of C.B. Macpherson, *The Political Theory of Possessive Individualism: Hobbes to Locke* (Oxford, 1962).
7. S.J.R. Noel, *Patrons, Clients, Brokers: Ontario Society and Politics 1791–1896* (Toronto, 1990), 28–9.
8. George Bryce, *The Romantic Settlement of Lord Selkirk's Colonists* (Toronto, 1909), 277; Owram, *Promise of Eden*, 212.
9. C.C. McLaurin, 'Introduction', in McLaurin, *Pioneering in Western Canada: A Story of the Baptists* (Calgary, 1939), n.p.
10. See also Rev. (Capt.) Wellington Bridgman, *Breaking Prairie Sod: The Story of a Pioneer Preacher in the Eighties with a Discussion of the Burning Question of Today, Shall the Alien Go?* (Toronto, 1920) ; Ralph Connor (pseud. of Charles W. Gordon), *To Him that Hath: A Novel of the West of Today* (New York, 1921); M. Vipond, 'Blessed Are the Peacemakers: The Labour Question in Canadian Social Gospel Fiction', *Journal of*

Canadian Studies 10, 3 (Aug. 1975): 32–41; John MacLean, 13 June 1919, 'General Diary 1917–19', NAC, MG29 D65.

11. Bridgman, *Breaking Prairie Sod*, 34.

12. Jessie McEwen, 'Home Life in the West', *Women of Canada: Their Life and Work* (1900?), 31.

13. *Western Sun*, 30 Mar., 27 Apr., 11, 18 May 1899.

14. *Winnipeg Morning Telegram*, 9 Dec. 1907. Those not in the advertising business had less exalted notions: 'O the prairie! I cannot describe to you our first impression. It's vastness, dreariness, and loneliness is appalling.' Hall, *A Lady's Life*, 24.

15. Bridgman, *Breaking Prairie Sod*, 33.

16. 'No. 12 Annual Report of Winnipeg Immigration Agent', *Sessional Papers* 5 (1889): 88. See also C.L. Johnstone, *Winter and Summer Excursions in Canada* (London, 1894?), 155. The volunteers wounded in the North-West Rebellion recovered very quickly, it was claimed, because of the purity of the western air. Major C.A. Boulton, *Reminiscences of the North-West Rebellion, with a record of the raising of her Majesty's 100th Regiment in Canada, and a chapter on Canadian social and political life* (Toronto, 1886), 296.

17. Quoted in Marion W. Abra, comp., *A View of the Birdtail: A History of the Municipality of Birtle, the Town of Birtle and the Villages of Foxwarren and Solsgirth 1878–1974* (Birtle, Man., 1974), 115.

18. E.J. Wilson, *Birtle's Beginning* (Birtle, Man., 1967 [1934]), 12–13.

19. Abra, comp., *A View of the Birdtail*, 56, 409–10; *Brandon Daily Sun*, 30 June 1924. John Lane may have been a councillor in Birtle, 1895–6. There was another John Lane in the Birtle area at the time, but he seems to have been in his early twenties and less likely, therefore, to be on council. As well, there is some question about Robert Lane's birthdate. His obituary implies that he was born in September 1862, while the *1901 Census* gives 21 September 1863 as the date.

20. Rev. A. Sutherland, *A Summer in Prairie-Land: Notes of a Tour through the North-West Territory*, 2nd edn (Toronto, 1882), 170.

21. *Canadian Methodist Magazine* 14 (Dec. 1881): 564, quoted in Owram, *Promise of Eden*, 135.

22. Boulton, *Reminiscences*, 201–3, 212–13, 226–7, 243–4, 281–92, 297–301, 351, 359–60, 370–4, 496–7, 501.

23. On this theme, see R. Douglas Francis, 'Changing Images of the West', *Journal of Canadian Studies* 17, 3 (Fall 1982): 5–19.

24. Sykes, *A Home-Help in Canada*, 80.

25. Hayden White, *Metahistory* (Baltimore, 1973), 9.

26. The phrase is taken from Alexander McLachlan's famous 1874 poem, 'The Man Who Rose from Nothing', in Carole Gerson and Gwendolyn

Davies, eds, *Canadian Poetry: From the Beginnings Through the First World War* (Toronto, 1994), 96–7.

27. 'R. Lane', *Brandon Weekly Sun*, Harvest Edition, 7 Nov. 1912.
28. *Brandon Times*, 28 Dec. 1893.
29. *1891 Census of Canada*, Manitoba, District #9 Selkirk, West Half Brandon City, 39.
30. Ibid., District #7 Marquette, Birtle Municipality, 27.
31. *Western Sun*, 1 Feb. 1900.
32. G.F. Barker, *Brandon: A City 1881–1961* (Brandon, Man., 1977), 28.
33. Thomas was born on 15 May 1893 and baptized on 9 May 1894. *St. Matthew's Church Brandon Register #1, 1884–1899; Baptisms, Marriages, Deaths or Funeral Services*. Mary's sister, Lucy Robinson, is listed as godparent, along with Willbury T. Milton and, strangely, Robert Lane.
34. Grant MacEwan, *Blazing the Old Cattle Trail* (Saskatoon, 1975), 187, 190.
35. *Western Sun*, 15 Sept. 1898.
36. *Assessment Roll for the City of Brandon*, 1900.
37. *Winnipeg Morning Telegram*, 6 July 1899. Calling oneself 'drayman' seems to have been less dignified than to say one ran a 'transfer' company; 'transfer', the more recent term, has greater cachet, and Lane appears to have vacillated between the two terms. Under Lane's occupation on the *1899 Assessment Roll for the City of Brandon* is listed 'drayman'. The 1900 assessment roll lists 'transfer', though the *1901 Census* has 'drayman' again.
38. 'Out of respect for Mr. Robert Lane who is treasurer of the Gun club, there will be no shoot to-night', *Western Sun*, 13 July 1899. For McIlvride on council, see the *Western Sun*, 14 Dec. 1899; *Brandon Daily Sun*, 20 July 1907.
39. MacDonald Coleman, *The Face of Yesterday: The Story of Brandon, Manitoba, 1883–1956* (Brandon, Man., 1957), 68–9.
40. *Manitoba Morning Free Press*, 30 Mar. 1899; *Western Sun*, 7 Sept., 21 Dec. 1899. Already in 1890, sportsmen were complaining that they couldn't get within sight of prairie chickens, they were so wild. A good chicken dog was, therefore, essential. *Western Sun*, 6 Nov. 1890.
41. Coleman, *The Face of Yesterday*, 44; Fred McGuinness, *The Wheat City: A Pictorial History of Brandon* (Saskatoon, 1988), 72. In 1901 a North Ender appealed for 'more light', complaining that it was easy for people with 'pull' in the wealthier areas of the city to get lighting but that the North End was too dark, even at railway crossings. *Daily Sun*, 25 Apr. 1902. According to Elizabeth Minnie, the house did not have a fireplace until her father put one in.

42. Claudette Lacelle, *Urban Domestic Servants in 19th Century Canada*, trans. Department of the Secretary of State (Hull, Que., 1987), 138.

43. *Western Sun*, 11 May 1899.

44. Ibid., 18 May 1899.

45. Ibid., 13 Apr. 1899.

46. Jeffrey Weekes, *Sex, Politics and Society* (London, 1981), 28.

47. Neil Semple, *The Lord's Dominion: The History of Canadian Methodism* (Montreal and Kingston, 1996), 63.

48. *Christian Guardian*, 2 Oct. 1833, quoted ibid., 63.

49. *Western Sun*, 30 Mar. 1899. See also J.J. Kelso, 'Neglected and Friendless Children', *The Canadian Magazine* 2, 3 (Jan. 1894): 213–16.

50. *Western Sun*, 25 May 1900.

51. Weekes, *Sex, Politics and Society*, 29.

52. Peter Ward, 'Courtship and Social Space in Nineteenth-Century English Canada', *Canadian Historical Review* 68, 1 (1987): 36.

53. *Christian Guardian*, 28 Nov. 1829, quoted in Semple, *The Lord's Dominion*, 64.

54. Semple, *The Lord's Dominion*, 64.

55. Alison Prentice et al., *Canadian Women in History* (Toronto, 1996), 156.

56. *Christian Guardian*, 28 Nov. 1829; quoted in Semple, *The Lord's Dominion*, 63–4.

57. Wendy Mitchinson, *The Nature of Their Bodies* (Toronto, 1991), 33, quotes a Victorian adviser of women who contended that for a married woman, children 'are as necessary to her happiness as the food she eats and as the air she breathes'.

58. Ibid., 15.

59. *Western Sun*, 2 Mar. 1899.

60. Ibid., 11 May 1899.

61. Ward, 'Courtship and Social Space', 57.

62. The phrase is drawn from Anne Z. Mickelson, *Thomas Hardy's Women and Men: The Defeat of Nature* (Metuchen, NJ, 1976), 7.

63. For earlier Victorian expressions of the home as 'a place apart, a walled garden', and of woman as (in Charles Kingsley's words) 'divine guide, purifier, inspirer of the man', see Walter Houghton, *The Victorian Frame of Mind: 1830–1870* (New Haven, 1957), 343, 351–3.

64. One of the two rooms on the third storey was Mrs Lane's sewing room, says Ron Godfrey, who has lived in the Lane home since 1949. Godfrey married a daughter of the veterinarian, Dr Ross, who bought the house from Robert Lane.

65. *Winnipeg Daily Tribune*, 27 Dec. 1899.

66. *Western Sun*, 28 Dec. 1899.

67. Davidoff, *Worlds Between*, 5.

68. Andrée Lévesque, *Making and Breaking the Rules: Women in Quebec, 1919–1939* (Toronto, 1994), 18.
69. Robert John Coates, 'St. Matthew's Anglican Cathedral, Brandon', Isabelle Heeney, interviewer, 19 Apr. 1982, Oral History Collection OH025Coa, Western Manitoba Regional Library.
70. *Western Sun*, 14 Dec. 1899; *Virden Advance*, 14 Dec. 1899. The new St Matthew's was consecrated at the beginning of December 1899.
71. *The Year Book of the Brandon Local Council of Women 1895–1923*, McKee Archives, Brandon University, 37–9. There were cases for the Council to be concerned about in 1899. During the Spring Assizes in March 1899 Stewart McKay was acquitted on the charge of carnally knowing a girl, 14-year-old Eva Lennox. After she broke down in tears three times during her attempt to witness against McKay, the judge concluded that no evidence was forthcoming and released the suspect. *Western Sun*, 30 Mar. 1899.
72. *The Canadian Magazine* (Sept. 1900): 471.
73. *Winnipeg Daily Tribune*, 6 July 1899.
74. J.A. Gemmill, ed., *The Canadian Parliamentary Companion, 1897* (Ottawa, 1897), 352.
75. *Winnipeg Morning Telegram*, 6 July 1899; *Winnipeg Daily Tribune*, 6 July 1899.
76. *Winnipeg Daily Tribune*, 27 Dec. 1899.
77. *Elkhorn Advocate*, 13 July 1899.
78. *Birtle Eye-Witness*, 11 July 1899

Chapter 4

1. *Elkhorn Advocate*, 27 July 1899.
2. *Winnipeg Morning Telegram*, 10 July 1899.
3. Private letter, Olive Andrews to Jim Forsythe, 27 Dec. 1999.
4. *Winnipeg Daily Tribune*, 10 July 1899; W. Leland Clark, *Brandon's Politics and Politicians* (Brandon, Man., 1981), 36; *Western Sun*, 8 Dec. 1899.
5. Susan Jackel, ed., *A Flannel Shirt and Liberty: British Emigrant Gentlewomen in the Canadian West, 1880–1914* (Vancouver, 1982), 58–9; Parr, *Labouring Children*, 126.
6. Emily Stowe, 1889, quoted in Constance Backhouse, *Petticoats and Prejudice: Women and Law in Nineteenth-Century Canada* (Toronto, 1991), 151; Lucy Maynard Salmon, *Domestic Service* (New York, 1897), 109; Lacelle, *Urban Domestic Servants*, 98, 192–3. When two bellhops plotted to resign together if their working conditions didn't improve, an Englishwoman found their behaviour 'quite anarchical'. Sykes, A *Home-Help in Canada*, 78.

7. See Christopher Hill, *The World Turned Upside Down: Radical Ideas During the English Revolution* (Harmondsworth, UK, 1972).
8. *Winnipeg Morning Telegram*, 10 July 1899.
9. *Manitoba Morning Free Press*, 28 Dec. 1899.
10. Parr, *Labouring Children*, 128.
11. Jean Thomson Scott, *The Conditions of Female Labour in Ontario* (Toronto, 1892), 19. For complaints about the word 'servant', see Salmon, *Domestic Service*, 155.
12. Salmon, *Domestic Service*, 88, 93, 101, 103, 113. Without much avail, sermons published in newspapers and proclaimed from the pulpit constantly reminded shopgirls and sewing women of how much better off they would be in domestic service. Ibid., 139.
13. Magda Fahrni, ' "Ruffled" Mistresses and "Discontented" Maids: Respectability and the Case of Domestic Service, 1880–1914', *Labour/Le Travail* 39 (Spring 1996): 82.
14. *Winnipeg Morning Telegram*, 10 July 1899.
15. Parr, *Labouring Children*, 108.
16. Quoted in Jackel, *A Flannel Shirt and Liberty*, 56.
17. McEwen, 'Home Life in the West', 32.
18. 'No. 12 Annual Report of Winnipeg Immigration Agent', *Sessional Papers* 7 (1892): 108.
19. Marilyn Barber, 'The Women Ontario Welcomed: Immigrant Domestics for Ontario Homes, 1870–1930', *Ontario History* 72, 3 (Sept. 1980): 148. For an example of such solicitation, see *English Tenant Farmers on the Agricultural Resources of Canada: The Reports of Mr. Reuben Shelton [and others] on Their Visit to Canada in 1893* (London, 1894), 91.
20. Self-Help Emigration Society, *Report for 1893*, 22.
21. *1901 Census of Canada*. See also 'No. 9 Annual Report of Brandon, Man., Immigration Agent (Mr. T. Bennett)', *Sessional Papers* 5 (1889): 53–4. In an 1886 CPR pamphlet the over 80 women who are cited generally pegged the monthly rate somewhat lower: at £1 to £3 ($5–$15). Mrs S.J. Carrigan of Whitemouth said that girls in her area could get $6–$20 per month, while she remembered paying girls only $4 a month in Ontario. Mrs C.H. Freeman of Elkhorn said that farm helps could get £2–£4 ($10–$20). The Freeman citation is taken directly from *What Women Say of the Canadian North West* (Montreal, 1886), 34, since Jackel's transcription, in *A Flannel Shirt and Liberty*, confuses Freeman of Elkhorn with Duensing of Emerson. Near the time of Blake's execution, the *Western Sun*, 21 Dec. 1899, carried an advertisement offering $15 per month for a general farm servant. Male wages could be three times as much, according to Jackel, ed., *A Flannel Shirt and Liberty*, 54–65. Scott, *Conditions of Female Labour*, 19, reports wages of $8–$14 per month. Wages

evidently did not change much over the next decade, since Fahrni, ' "Ruffled" Mistresses', 71, reports that in 1901 the average wage nationally was
$120; and Laura Goodman Salverson reports that in the early 1900s she
worked for $10 a month in the northern US. Salverson, *Confessions of an
Immigrant's Daughter* (Toronto, 1981 [1939]), 327. Ella Sykes received
£2 as an unskilled domestic in 1911, though others got £3–£5 per month.
Sykes, *A Home-Help in Canada*, x, 21, 24, 39, 43, 201. The *1901 Census*
reports servant wages as low as $12 a year, but that is likely for part-time
work, since most of the women made in the range of $100–$150. See also
Mary Kinnear, *A Female Economy: Women's Work in a Prairie Province,
1870–1970* (Montreal and Kingston, 1998), 105–8.

22. *Manitoba Morning Free Press*, 10 July 1899.
23. Private letter, Olive Andrews to Jim Forsythe, 27 Dec. 1999.
24. *Western Sun*, 20 July 1899; 'Death Certificate', Clifford Ward Crozier,
    Elton Municipal Records.
25. Elton Historical Committee, *Homesteaders and Homemakers: A History
    of Elton Municipality in its First Century* (1973), 254. Sparling Ceme-
    tery, Row C, #3.
26. *Western Sun*, 13 July 1899.
27. *Manitoba Morning Free Press*, 16 Dec. 1899.
28. Lacelle, *Urban Domestic Servants*, 109. Advising employers to make ser-
    vants' rooms cozy, Grandma Nichols says, 'A very little money and pains
    make all the difference between a dull, uninviting den and a dainty, pleas-
    ant chamber—curtains and carpets past their wear in the lower rooms, or
    if newly furnishing, why, cheap drugget and a bit of cheap muslin, make
    them homelike. A few cheap pictures, perhaps a shelf for a bright inno-
    cent novel or two and last month's magazine.' Grandma Nichols, *The
    Great Nineteenth Century Household Guide* (Toronto, 1978 [1894]), 17.
29. An eagle-eyed employer, such as the one who discovered that the rungs
    on the dining-room chairs hadn't been dusted, could be a sore trial. The
    'House of Bondage', Ella Sykes called that particular placement. Sykes,
    A Home-Help in Canada, 211–12. Backhouse, *Petticoats and Prejudice*,
    59.
30. Sykes, *A Home-Help in Canada*, 215, 178. Sykes, who in 1911 expected
    that domestic servants in Canada could partake of varied social distrac-
    tions such as tennis, driving, and dances, was sorely disappointed.
31. Marilyn Barber, 'The Servant Problem in Manitoba, 1896–1930', in
    Mary Kinnear, ed., *First Days, Fighting Days: Women in Manitoba
    History* (Regina, 1987), 113; Lacelle, *Urban Domestic Servants*, 98,
    100; Linda Rasmussen et al., *A Harvest Yet to Reap: A History of Prairie
    Women* (Toronto, 1976), 102; Scott, *Conditions of Female Labour*, 19–20;
    Salmon, *Domestic Service*, 134. In the US, 75 per cent of domestics

worked 10 hours or more per day. Ibid., 143. If employers slept late and ate a late breakfast, the servant might miss her outing to church as well. Sykes, *A Home-Help in Canada*, 214.

32. Lacelle, *Urban Domestic Servants*, 93, 103, 138. See ibid., 155–8, for British and French day plans for domestics.
33. Ibid., 119–20.
34. *Virden Advance*, 16 Oct. 1889.
35. Arthur E. Copping, *The Golden Land: The True Story and Experiences of British Settlers in Canada* (London, 1911), 248. For a description of the quality of life experienced by live-in domestic servants, see Barber, 'The Women Ontario Welcomed', 151–2.
36. Sykes, *A Home-Help in Canada*, 177. Calling a servant by her Christian name ('Ellen', more proper than the diminutive 'Ella' but not as proper as 'Miss Sykes'), using a bell to summon the servant, and having the servant eat separately in the kitchen are some of the British practices that Sykes detested. Ibid., 203, 206.
37. One thinks of the Pocket household in Dickens, *Great Expectations*, 213.
38. Lacelle, *Urban Domestic Servants*, 125. See also Mrs Burnett-Smith (pseud. of Annie S. Swan), *Courtship and Marriage and the Gentle Art of Home-making* (Toronto, 1893?), 132.
39. Burnett-Smith, *Courtship and Marriage*, 131, 135.
40. Aline Raymond, 'Maîtres et serviteurs', *La Revue canadienne* 41 (Feb. 1904), reprinted in Lacelle, *Urban Domestic Servants*, 166–8. Rev. Bernard O'Reilly echoed such sentiments in *The Mirror of True Womanhood; a Book of Instruction for Women in the World*, 14th edn (New York, 1880), 305–19.
41. Quoted in Salmon, *Domestic Service*, 151; Sykes, *A Home-Help in Canada*, 221. Sykes also narrates an incident in which her employer asked stiffly if she would like to sit with the family in the parlour, hoping fervently for a 'no'. When guests came, the servant was often ignored. In one place, Sykes spoke to no one except her mistress. Ibid., 175–6, 204.
42. Ibid., 225–6.
43. Salverson, *Confessions of an Immigrant's Daughter*, 323.
44. Quoted in Salmon, *Domestic Service*, 152. Some employers granted servants the use of the dining room or a sitting room to receive visitors, and a few employers did not restrict the types of visitors. Ibid., 133–4. See also Helen Campbell, *Home Economics: A Course of Lectures in the School of Economics of the University of Wisconsin*, 2nd edn (New York, 1898), 220–1; Self-Help Emigration Society, *Report for the Year 1893*, 17.
45. Services were at 11 a.m. and 7 p.m. on Sundays, with Bible classes at 3 p.m. *Brandon Times*, 28 Dec. 1893.

46. *What Women Say of the Canadian North West*, 34. The same advice appears in *Jane Eyre*: 'I remembered that strangers who arrive at a place where they have no friends, and who want employment, sometimes apply to the clergyman for introduction and aid.' Brontë, *Jane Eyre*, 312.

47. The main pastimes for servants were chatting, walking, dancing, sewing, reading, and churchgoing. Lacelle, *Urban Domestic Servants*, 119.

48. C.C. McLaurin, 'Our Dominion as a Mission Field', Commencement Oration at the Canadian Literary Institute, 17 Apr. 1877, Glenbow Archives, M6072, box 3, folder 41.

49. *Western Sun*, 1 Mar. 1900.

50. McLaurin, 'Our Dominion as a Mission Field'.

51. Four years after Blake's death, the First Baptist congregation finished building a stately new church on the corner of Lorne and 11th, while the church that Blake had attended was conscripted first as a Union (Methodist and Presbyterian) mission on Van Horne, and then, a few years later, as an East End mission on Russell and Lorne. After this second move it remained put. It still stands there today, as St Andrew's Presbyterian.

52. Most of the information here comes from the papers deposited in the Canadian Baptist Archives at McMaster Divinity College, Hamilton. The papers include an article by M.L. Orchard, 'Rev. C.C. McLaurin, D.D.: A Master Missionary in Western Canada', and a couple of autobiographical accounts written by McLaurin: a pamphlet, *Sixty Years in the Ministry* (Edmonton, 1937), and personal reflections on 'My Old Home Church in Rural Ontario' (*c.* 1937). The eulogy was given by Rev. W.C. Smalley and appeared in an Edmonton publication, *The Western Baptist* 33, 11 (Mar. 1941): 2–3. For an overview of his career, see McLaurin, *Pioneering in Western Canada*.

53. Barker, *Brandon*, 10; *Western Sun*, 25 May, 14 Dec. 1899.

54. Little can be deduced from her decision to attend a Baptist rather than an Anglican church, since judging by Constance Beauchamp's letter the Stewarts were probably more evangelical than the name 'Anglican' at first suggests, and judging by McLaurin's book, *Pioneering in Western Canada: A Story of the Baptists*, he was more formal than the name 'Baptist' at first suggests. Denominational lines were often drawn loosely in the nineteenth-century Canadian West, where different congregations might use the same houses of worship. Although he characterized Roman Catholics as 'image-worshipers' and warned of 'Romish schemes' to power, McLaurin certainly had little use for denominational exclusivity within Protestantism: 'Behold how soon is "Christianity in Earnest" degraded to "Methodism in Earnest"! And what church is entirely free from this spirit?' McLaurin, 1877, Glenbow Archives, box 3, folder 38.

55. Ibid.
56. Bridgman, *Breaking Prairie Sod*, 20.
57. *Manitoba Morning Free Press*, 27 Dec. 1899.
58. *Western Sun*, 14 Dec. 1899.
59. Campbell, *Home Economics*, 222; Burnett-Smith, *Courtship and Marriage*, 130–1.
60. Some handbooks did advise employers to allow servants to entertain lovers in the evening, also advising domestics not to meet the lover in the street or to smuggle him into the kitchen. Nichols, *Household Guide*, 14.
61. Fahrni, ' "Ruffled" Mistresses', 85; Sykes, *A Home-Help in Canada*, 226. Campbell, *Home Economics*, 220, criticizes domestic service as 'essentially a celibate system'.
62. For example, Salverson, *Confessions of an Immigrant's Daughter*, 330, tried not to let her beau see her in a maid's uniform. She didn't think that his affection could survive the shock. See also Sykes, *A Home-Help in Canada*, 226.
63. Lacelle, *Urban Domestic Servants*, 128. In an 1896 American survey that asked domestics why more women do not choose housework as regular employment, 29 per cent gave reasons related to social status, 28 per cent reasons related to pay and working conditions, 23 per cent reasons related to confinement and loneliness, and 14 per cent reasons related to independence. Salmon, *Domestic Service*, 141.
64. For information on the few attempts at unionization, see Fahrni, ' "Ruffled" Mistresses', 84.
65. This is taken from an 1863 British book on domestic service, and is found in Lacelle, *Urban Domestic Servants*, 137. O'Reilly, *The Mirror of True Womanhood*, 451, says: 'True humility consists in obeying a harsh order or in doing what is irksome, and that for a person who evidently dislikes you or is disagreeable in many ways.'
66. *Western Sun*, 6 Apr. 1899.
67. See Fahrni, ' "Ruffled" Mistresses', 73, for pronouncements against women's work in hotel bars and laundries.
68. Strong-Boag, 'Pulling in Double Harness', 45.
69. *What Women Say of the Canadian North West*, 34.
70. Salmon, *Domestic Service*, 105.
71. Parr, *Labouring Children*, 127.
72. *Manitoba Morning Free Press*, 10 July 1899.
73. *Western Sun*, 14 Dec.1899.
74. Lacelle, *Urban Domestic Servants*, 100.
75. Naffine, *Female Crime*, 8.
76. Lacelle, *Urban Domestic Servants*, 132.
77. *Manitoba Morning Free Press*, 28 Dec. 1899.

78. Ibid., 13 Nov. 1899.
79. *Western Sun*, 6 Oct. 1892.
80. See Ann-Louise Shapiro, *Breaking the Codes: Female Criminality in Fin-de-Siècle Paris* (Stanford, 1996), 34.
81. Genevieve Leslie, 'Domestic Service in Canada', in Janice Acton et al., eds, *Women at Work 1850–1930* (Toronto, 1974), 83.
82. The case of Charlene, a child who lost both her parents in a car accident, is perhaps instructive, as the following exchange in Steinhauer, *The Least Detrimental Alternative*, 48, shows:

    Therapist: If a girl is feeling sad, is it all right for her to cry, or is it better for her to pretend she's not sad?

    Charlene: She shouldn't cry if she's drawing.

    Therapist: Why not?

    Charlene: Because if she did, it would splash all over the paper. No, it's better to pretend you're happy. Even when you're sad, you pretend you're happy.

Chapter 5

1. Prentice et al., *Canadian Women in History*, 129. See also Fahrni, ' "Ruffled" Mistresses', 85. A disproportionately high percentage of unwed mothers in the nineteenth century were domestics. Lacelle, *Urban Domestic Servants*, 121. Salverson, *Confessions of an Immigrant's Daughter*, 336, gives an example of unwanted sexual advances from the son of her employer:

    'See here, can't you be a bit friendly to a loving young man?' he demanded, wearing his most fetching expression. 'You can't be such an icicle', he pursued, improving upon invention in fine, histrionic style.

    Oh well, a sturdy, bovine stare is more effective than a million words. The loving creature dropped his arms, and off I went about my business.
2. *Winnipeg Daily Tribune*, 10 July 1899. Many newspaper reports describe her as 'good-looking'.
3. Backhouse, *Petticoats and Prejudice*, 113. See also Carolyn Strange's description of the Mary Dolan case in 'Stories of Their Lives: The Historian and the Capital Case File', in Franca Iacovetta and Wendy Mitchinson, eds, *On the Case: Explorations in Social History* (Toronto, 1998).
4. James G. Snell, ' "The White Life for Two": The Defence of Marriage and Sexual Morality in Canada, 1890–1914', *Histoire Sociale/Social History* 16, 31 (May 1983): 112.
5. See Fahrni, ' "Ruffled" Mistresses', 85–6, 92–3.
6. *Regina v. McCabe*, RG 13, vol. 1438, series 307, file 614, NAC.

7. Ibid., W.H. Sutcliffe to the Minister of Justice, 18 Oct. 1883.

8. *Regina v. McCabe*, NAC.

9. A. Power to J.H. Thompson, Minister of Justice, 1 May 1889, *Regina v. McCabe*.

10. *Winnipeg Free Press*, 9 Feb. 1915.

11. Ibid., 10 Feb. 1915.

12. Ibid.

13. Ibid., 16 Feb. 1915.

14. Ibid., 27 Feb. 1915.

15. Carolyn Strange, 'Wounded Womanhood and Dead Men: Chivalry and the Trials of Clara Ford and Carrie Davies', in Franca Iacovetta and Mariana Valverde, eds, *Gender Conflicts: New Essays in Women's History* (Toronto, 1992), 170.

16. *Winnipeg Free Press*, 1 Mar. 1915.

17. The words are from the Englishman F.W. Newman's 'Remedies for the Great Social Evil' (1869), quoted in Houghton, *The Victorian Frame of Mind*, 365–6.

18. For another example, see the account of the trial of Alexis de Roussell, accused by Susannah Eliza Davis of rape, in Lacelle, *Urban Domestic Servants*, 143ff.

19. 'Some ten years ago Hilda Blake was hanged in Brandon shortly after her child was born. Her crime was the carefully prepared murder of an expectant mother.' *The Voice*, 14 July 1911. Records at the Brandon General Hospital and Brandon Mental Health Centre contain no reference to Hilda Blake giving birth to a baby during the period September to December 1899. Nor is there any evidence that Blake gave birth to a child while confined in the Brandon Gaol. In the 1870s, common-law procedure still allowed a pregnant woman to 'plead the belly' and thereby escape execution. James C. Oldham, 'On Pleading the Belly: A History of the Jury of Matrons', *Criminal Justice History* 6 (1985): 16.

20. Other situations, while not quite as similar to her own and while sometimes touched with irony, would also insist that love ought to defy caste: in his suit for Flora Mac-Ivor, the sister of a 'highborn Highland beggar', Edward Waverley argues that his family would look only to 'birth and personal qualities . . . in such a connection'. By the time he instead asks for Rose Bradwardine's hand in marriage, she, too, is a high-born beggar. Sir Walter Scott, *Waverley* (London, n.d. [1814]), 143, 335.

21. Brontë, *Jane Eyre*, 146.

22. Ibid., 15.

23. The man standing 'beside a dark stream' in 'My Downfall' could also have come from many sources, but may echo a poetic moment in *Jane Eyre*: 'And I shall see it again,' he said aloud, 'in dreams, when I sleep by

the Ganges; and again, in a more remote hour—when another slumber
overcomes me, on the shore of a darker stream.' Ibid., 383.

24. T.J. Lears, 'The Concept of Cultural Hegemony: Problems and Possibilities', *American Historical Review* 90, 3 (June 1985): 573.

25. W. Peter Ward, 'Unwed Motherhood in Nineteenth-Century English
Canada', Canadian Historical Association, *Historical Papers* (1981): 34.

26. Judith R. Walkowitz, *City of Dreadful Delight: Narratives of Sexual
Danger in Late-Victorian London* (Chicago, 1992), 87.

27. Jon W. Finson, *The Voices That Are Gone: Themes in Nineteenth-
Century American Popular Song* (New York, 1994), 54.

28. 'Did I forbid myself to think of him in any other light than as a paymas-
ter? Blasphemy against nature!' Although *Jane Eyre* will not live as Mr
Rochester's mistress, the portrait of St John Rivers suggests that Brontë
is not overly critical when Jane places Mr Rochester between herself and
'every thought of religion'. Brontë, *Jane Eyre*, 164, 260.

29. Of the many portraits of such censorship, despite a high instance of prostitution in Victorian England, Walter Houghton's is perhaps the most
instructive: 'Thackeray might satirize prudery, but he was ready enough to
praise *Punch* because it contained nothing unfit for little boys at school to
read, or for women to enjoy without blushing: "We like that our matrons
and girls should be pure."' Houghton, *The Victorian Frame of Mind*, 358.

30. Brontë, *Jane Eyre*, 175.

31. Angus McLaren and Arlene Tigar McLaren, *The Bedroom and the State:
The Changing Practices and Politics of Contraception and Abortion in
Canada, 1880–1997*, 2nd edn (Toronto, 1997), 21.

32. See Karen Dubinsky, ' "Maidenly Girls" or "Designing Women"? The
Crime of Seduction in Turn-of-the-Century Ontario', in Iacovetta and
Valverde, eds, *Gender Conflicts*, 42.

33. *Statutes of Canada*, 1892 Criminal Code, Victoria, 2 June 1886, section
183, 81, makes it an offence for a man to seduce or have illicit connection with a ward, 'any woman or girl of previously chaste character and
under the age of twenty-one years who is in his employment in a factory,
mill or workshop'. For a full discussion of the law, see Chapter 14. See
also Constance Backhouse and Leah Cohen, *The Secret Oppression:
Sexual Harassment of Working Women* (Toronto, 1979), 53–70.

34. Feminist reinterpreters of Freud, for example, have convincingly argued
that much of the evidence of childhood sexual desire in his patients
stemmed from sexual abuse, not from libidinal fantasies.

35. Kali Israel, 'French Vices and British Liberties: Gender, Class and Narrative Competition in a Late Victorian Sex Scandal', *Social History* 22, 1
(Jan. 1997): 17, 52.

36. Strange, 'Wounded Womanhood and Dead Men', 177.

37. Parr, *Labouring Children*, 115. Parr also describes the case of a 12-year-old girl whose rape was treated lightly.

38. Leslie Savage, 'Perspectives on Illegitimacy: The Changing Role of the Sisters of Misericordia in Edmonton, 1900–1906', in Patricia T. Rooke and R.L. Schnell, eds, *Studies in Childhood History* (Calgary, 1982), 110.

39. Karen Dubinsky, *Improper Advances: Rape and Heterosexual Conflict in Ontario, 1880–1929* (Chicago, 1993), 52.

40. Rev. J.B. Wakeley, *Heroes of Methodism*, 11th edn (Toronto, 1855).

41. *Queen v. Strippe* (1899), Queen's Bench (Brandon), PAM, GR 363, ATG, box 31. Since Lane was considered genial and well liked by those around him, it is probable that wickedness and dishonour referred to his overstepping the bounds of legal sexuality.

42. Brontë, *Jane Eyre*, 301, 296.

43. Karen Dubinsky, 'Afterword: Telling Stories about Dead People', in Iacovetta and Mitchinson, eds, *On the Case*, 363–4.

44. See Alan Hustak, *They Were the Hanged* (Toronto, 1987). This claim is repeated in D. Owen Carrigan, *Crime and Punishment in Canada, A History* (Toronto, 1991), 260, probably because Carrigan relied on Hustak without checking the information.

45. Stories passed down through D. Jean Scott (née Mathie) and also through Henrietta Adams (later Henrietta Scott Woods), who replaced Hilda as maid after the murder, suggest the same interpretation: that Robert Lane was innocent of sexual impropriety and that Hilda believed she could entice Lane to marry her.

46. Governor-General Minto to Wilfrid Laurier, 23 Dec. 1899, Laurier Papers, NAC, Series A, C-771, 40180–5.

47. Dubinsky, ' "Maidenly Girls" or "Designing Women"?', 34. Backhouse, *Petticoats and Prejudice*, 74–7. For a discussion of how these laws came to be, see Chapter 14.

48. In 1905 a Citizen's League represented by Mrs S.E. Clement of the WCTU, Mr W.N. Finley, principal of Central School, and Dr A.R. McDiarmid, principal of Brandon College, confronted city council with demands that prostitution in the city's East End be extinguished. The headline in the *Sun* read, 'Is Brandon Bad as Alleged?' *Brandon Daily Sun*, 16 May 1905.

49. Snell, ' "The White Life for Two" ', 121.

50. Backhouse, *Petticoats and Prejudice*, 77.

51. Dubinsky, *Improper Advances*, 152

52. Nichols, *Household Guide*, 201.

53. Backhouse, *Petticoats and Prejudice*, 72–3.

54. Ibid., 65; Dubinsky, ' "Maidenly Girls" or "Designing Women"?', 34–6, 47. John Charlton, who introduced the bill, along with the Montreal

Society for the Protection of Women and Girls, argued that a woman's previously chaste character should not be taken into consideration.

55. Carolyn Strange and Tina Loo, *Making Good: Law and Moral Regulation in Canada, 1867–1939* (Toronto, 1997), 54.

56. Dubinsky, ' "Maidenly Girls" or "Designing Women"?', 42.

57. Ibid., 50.

58. Backhouse, *Petticoats and Prejudice*, 66–7.

59. Dubinsky, ' "Maidenly Girls" or "Designing Women"?', 30. The law could short-circuit the informal barter system in which a woman would trade sexual favours in return for the promise to marry, but the law could also enforce the barter.

60. *Brandon Daily Sun*, 30 June 1924.

61. *Winnipeg Morning Telegram*, 15 Dec.1899.

62. *Elkhorn Advocate*, 20 July 1899.

63. Steinhauer, *The Least Detrimental Alternative*, 36–7.

64. Elaine Showalter, 'Victorian Women and Insanity', *Victorian Studies* 23, 2 (Winter 1980): 162; Naffine, *Female Crime*, 18.

65. Dubinsky, ' "Maidenly Girls" or "Designing Women"?', 40

66. Shapiro, *Breaking the Codes*, 165, 178.

67. *Western Sun*, 11 May 1899.

68. *Manitoba Morning Free Press*, 12 June 1899.

69. *Winnipeg Daily Tribune*, 16 Nov. 1899. *Queen v. Glendenning*, Court of Queen's Bench, Criminal Pockets, ATG 0007, GR 273, 2/1009, PAM. A warden from the Regina Gaol informed Brandon Jailer Richard Noxon that Glendenning had served five years in Regina and was 'a natural born thief'. In *Names of Persons Committed to the Western Judicial District Jail*, Brandon Correctional Institute, 66, Glendenning's place of residence is listed as 'Alcorn', presumably a misspelling for 'Elkhorn'.

70. *Virden Advance*, 8 June 1899; *Queen v. Glendenning*.

71. *Manitoba Morning Free Press*, 10 July 1899.

72. The words are those of Paul Strauss, a French politician who in 1896 responded to a case of infanticide committed by a single mother. Quoted in Shapiro, *Breaking the Codes*, 167.

73. *Virden Advance*, 23 Nov. 1899.

74. *Winnipeg Daily Tribune*, 10 July 1899; *Manitoba Morning Free Press*, 10 July 1899.

75. Naffine, *Female Crime*, 19, 98–100.

76. *Winnipeg Daily Tribune*, 11 July 1899. According to Shapiro, *Breaking the Codes*, 210–11, the image of the 'feminist-criminal', particularly the one who bought a gun, 'was set in opposition to the real woman'.

77. John Sutherland, 'Introduction' in Sir Walter Scott, *Rob Roy* (London, 1995 [1817]), xxii.

78. Shapiro, *Breaking the Codes*, 33. Shapiro means to be ironic about how commentators in the nineteenth century blamed crimes (including adultery) on literary images: 'I have found virtually no references to men being led into adultery by novelistic suggestion.' Nevertheless, putting aside the naïve deterministic arguments that reading about crime predisposes one to criminal acts, and that women are more susceptible to literature than men, there still remains a symbiotic connection between crime and media. Popularly reported crimes constantly influence novelistic representation, and, conversely, novelistic representations sometimes influence the form that the criminal chooses.
79. Scott, *Rob Roy*, 357, 94, 119, 91, 93, 120, 320, 147.
80. E. Thompson, *Customs in Common: Studies in Traditional Popular Culture* (New York, 1993), 262–3.
81. *Western Sun*, 29 June 1899; *Manitoba Morning Free Press*, 24 June 1899.
82. *Manitoba Morning Free Press*, 6 June 1899.

Chapter 7

1. Peter Brooks, *The Melodramatic Imagination* (New Haven, 1976), 17, 20.
2. Sarah Carter, *Capturing Women: The Manipulation of Cultural Imagery in Canada's Prairie West* (Montreal and Kingston, 1997), xiii.
3. *Winnipeg Morning Telegram*, 18 Mar. 1905.
4. *Brandon Daily Sun*, 20 July 1927.
5. Ibid.
6. Quoted in Boulton, *Reminiscences*, 245–6. 'Mr. Murdock' is likely V. Murdoch, listed among the 91st Battalion. Ibid., 521. It's possible that he was a relative of James Murdoch, who later married Mary Lane's sister Lucy.
7. Coleman, *The Face of Yesterday*, 48.
8. *Annals of the Sisters Faithful Companions of Jesus* (Brandon, 1887).
9. Quoted in James M. Pitsula, 'The Treatment of Tramps in Late Nineteenth-Century Toronto', *Canadian Historical Association Papers* (1980): 117.
10. *Western Sun*, 4 Dec. 1890.
11. For example, the *Western Sun*, 27 Apr. 1899, criticized, but was careful not to name, a man prominent in church and business who cheated the Doukhobors by paying 35¢ for a woman and two men to scrub and wash his house for three days. For nine days' labour, the most poorly paid female domestic would be paid $2; a normal rate of payment would be $3.
12. Pitsula, 'The Treatment of Tramps', 116.
13. Ibid., 120, citing *Toronto World*, 31 Jan. 1890; *Toronto Globe*, 5 July 1881, 8 Nov. 1894.

14. See ibid., 119–20, which cites *Toronto World*, 31 Jan. 1890; *Toronto Star*, 12 Mar. 1895.
15. *Brandon Mail*, 19 Dec. 1882.
16. *Brandon Sun*, 12 June 1884.
17. *Western Sun*, 6 July 1899.
18. See ibid.; *Manitoba Morning Free Press*, 28 Dec. 1899.
19. *Winnipeg Daily Tribune*, 6 July 1899.
20. *Western Sun*, 13 July 1899.
21. This is suggested by the formulaic quality of judges' addresses in murder trials. See James Fulcher, 'Murder Reports: Formulaic Narrative and Cultural Context', *Journal of Popular Culture* 18, 4 (Spring 1985): 31–42.
22. Such isolation of unskilled workers was not unique to Brandon. See Daniel Hiebert, 'Class, Ethnicity and Residential Structure: The Social Geography of Winnipeg, 1901–1921', *Journal of Historical Geography* 17, 1 (1991): 56–86.
23. *Brandon Weekly Sun*, 5 June 1902.
24. During the Great War and until at least the tumultuous labour revolt of 1919, the immigrant population in Brandon remained isolated. By the end of 1915, Brandon's alien detention centre contained nearly 1,000 'enemy aliens'.
25. Barker, *Brandon*, 55–7; Clark, *Brandon's Politics*, 37. Attacks came in February and then in November, long after Blake's confession, so her guilty plea evidently did little to temper the *Independence*'s rhetoric. The *Independence* was run by a disgruntled former employee of the federal Immigration Department, hence the animus against Sifton. The tone of the paper was much less measured than the Conservative Party organ, the *Brandon Times*.
26. *Brandon Independence*, 1 June 1899. Even commentators such as Laura Goodman Salverson, more sympathetic to immigrants, described these refugees from Eastern Europe as 'a race of hairy monsters, stewing in their own reek, like the animals in a circus'. Salverson, *Confessions of an Immigrant's Daughter*, 43.
27. Bridgman, *Breaking Prairie Sod*, 161, 178–9. Bridgman also said that 'the Hun is at variance with everything that Jesus Christ taught'; that Eastern European immigrants were costly; that criminals were always dumped on the West; that 90 per cent of the criminal calendar in Winnipeg consisted of immigrants. Against the argument that cheap labour was a good reason to let the alien stay, he rejoined that we should pay more and let British citizens dig sewers. Bridgman made these points during the labour crisis after World War I, but his views were shaped much earlier in his 1899 Virden days and, before that, during his circuit-preaching days near Brandon. Ibid., 154, 161–2, 167, 201.

28. Barber, 'The Servant Problem in Manitoba', 101.
29. Copping, *The Golden Land*, 234; Sykes, *A Home-Help in Canada*, 54.
30. Sykes, *A Home-Help in Canada*, 54, also mentions that Galician servants are not preferred.
31. *Western Sun*, 6 July 1899.
32. *Brandon Times*, 6 July 1899. *Western Sun*, 13 July 1899, says that the leader was Capt. Clark.
33. *Manitoba Morning Free Press*, 6 July 1899.
34. *Winnipeg Morning Telegram*, 6 July 1899.
35. *Western Sun*, 6 July 1899.
36. *Virden Advance*, 6 July 1899.
37. Walkowitz, *City of Dreadful Delight*, 87.
38. *Virden Advance*, 2 Nov. 1899.
39. In a personal letter, dated 1 March 2000, and in a subsequent phone call, Lorraine Thurston detailed some oral history from her family. Her grandfather, Tom Woycheshen, stopped at a Brandon farmyard for a drink, was picked up by police, and was thrown in jail during his first year in Canada. At first he didn't know why he was in jail. He was soon released, and, according to the story, a maidservant was eventually hanged 'for killing her mistress because she loved the master of the house'.
40. *Western Sun*, 6 July 1899.
41. Ibid., 20 July 1899.
42. Ibid., 13 July 1899; *1901 Census of Canada*.
43. *Manitoba Morning Free Press*, 7 July 1899.
44. In the *Winnipeg Morning Telegram*'s 6 July 1899 account, the four Lane children saw the tramp running from their house, but that seems to have been a reporter's error, the reporter mixing up the boys who testified about German and the much younger Lane children who thought that they might have seen a man.
45. *Manitoba Morning Free Press*, 10 July 1899.
46. *Winnipeg Morning Telegram*, 11 July 1899.

Chapter 8

1. *Brandon Daily Sun*, 17 May 1951. Fred McGuinness, 'Rising through the ranks with Gen. Kircaldy', *Brandon Sun*, 22 Feb. 1996; *1901 Census of Canada*, Manitoba, District #6 Brandon, B³ Brandon City (between 6th and 7th Streets), 6; *Western Sun*, 6 Apr. 1899.
2. 'From the *Sun* 1897', *Brandon Daily Sun*, 20 July 1907; George Bryce, *A History of Manitoba: Its Resources and People* (Toronto, 1906), 551.
3. 'From the *Sun* 1897', *Brandon Daily Sun*, 20 July 1907.
4. Probably I.F. Talbutt, a middle-aged accountant.

5. *Winnipeg Morning Telegram*, 10 July 1899; *Western Sun*, 13 July 1899.
6. *Brandon Times*, 13 July 1899.
7. *Western Sun*, 13 July 1899.
8. *Brandon Times*, 13 July 1899.
9. Scott, *Rob Roy*, 354.
10. Investigators must have had the co-operation of Robert Lane.
11. *Winnipeg Daily Tribune*, 10 July 1899.
12. *Birtle Eye-Witness*, 11 July, 1 Aug. 1899.
13. *Winnipeg Morning Telegram*, 28 Dec. 1899.
14. *Brandon Times*, 13 July 1899.
15. *Manitoba Morning Free Press*, 10 July 1899. According to the *Winnipeg Daily Tribune*, 10 July 1899, Blake revealed this information herself. It could also have come from Kircaldy or from Robert Lane.
16. *Western Sun*, 13 July 1899.
17. Ibid.
18. Ibid.
19. Major Melville, who must arrest Edward Waverley, begins, 'Young gentleman, I am extremely sorry that this painful duty has fallen to my lot.' Scott, *Waverley*, 167. In *Our Mutual Friend*, Mr Inspector attempts to arrest John Rokesmith in a dignified manner—i.e., without using the word 'arrest' and without letting the ladies present know the nature of the crime. Charles Dickens, *Our Mutual Friend* (New York, 1990 [1865]), 742–3.
20. *Western Sun*, 8, 14 Dec. 1899.
21. *Winnipeg Daily Tribune*, 10 July 1899; *Manitoba Morning Free Press*, 10 July 1899. This account is the dominant one, though the less reliable *Brandon Independence*, 13 July 1899, reports that Blake was 'perfectly dry-eyed when seeing the weeping children for the last time . . . which is a sure sign of insanity'.
22. *Brandon Times*, 11 Apr. 1889.
23. *Winnipeg Daily Tribune*, 10 July 1899.
24. Quoted in Shapiro, *Breaking the Codes*, 174.
25. Ibid., 141–4. Shapiro's focus is late nineteenth-century France, but the parallels to the Blake case suggest that the image of extreme love was widely available.
26. *Western Sun*, 13 July 1899; *Manitoba Morning Free Press*, 10 July 1899.

Chapter 9

1. Letitia Youmans, *Campaign Echoes: The Autobiography of Mrs. Letitia Youmans, the Pioneer of the White Ribbon Movement in Canada* (Toronto, 1893), 70.

2. Antonio Gramsci, *Selections from the Prison Notebooks*, eds Q. Hoare and G. Nowell Smith (London, 1971), 260.
3. Benedict Anderson, *Imagined Communities: Reflections on the Origin and Spread of Nationalism* (London, 1983), 16.
4. *English Tenant Farmers on the Agricultural Resources of Canada*, Joseph Smith's Report, 82.
5. Copping, *The Golden Land*, 44. A waitress kicking open a door becomes an occasion for Copping to remark, 'Social conditions in Canada are, in truth, a delightful burlesque of those in England', where 'one has to plead and wait and scheme for opportunities to earn small wages.' Ibid., 38.
6. Hayes, *Prairie Pot-pourri*, 11.
7. See Johnstone, *Winter and Summer Excursions*, 156, for men who 'stooped to conquer'; or Copping, *The Golden Land*, 238, for an educated and cultured British lady, Miss R___, who said, 'Unfortunately . . . I had never learned to do anything useful', and who became a hotel maid, enjoying the way that everyone was treated as an equal and even learning to take pride in her work. Sykes, *A Home-Help in Canada*, 49, says 'in England I was looked upon as capable, but here . . . .'
8. Hall, *A Lady's Life*, 28, 73–4, 86, 127.
9. Hector W. Charlesworth, 'The Canadian Girl: An Appreciative Medley', *The Canadian Magazine* (May 1893): 189. Sykes, *A Home-Help in Canada*, 128 (emphasis added).
10. Copping, *The Golden Land*, 58. The efficient can 'make good', says Sykes, *A Home-Help in Canada*, 302.
11. For the ways in which the emphasis on sensibility in novels provided 'the middle-class readership with a fable for their own emergence', see Nancy Armstrong, *Desire and Domestic Fiction: A Political History of the Novel* (Oxford, 1987), 51.
12. *Western Sun*, 10 Mar. 1900; *Brandon Sun*, 9 Apr. 1977.
13. *Brandon Times*, 7 Dec. 1893.
14. *Western Sun*, 13 July 1899.
15. 'Whurrah! my boys! . . . Shure we'll all be jontlemen!' and 'Hout, man! hauld your clavers, we shall a' be lairds here' cry the labourers in Susanna Moodie's satire against lower-class pretensions. *Roughing It in the Bush* (Toronto, 1989 [1852]), 32, 40.
16. Canadians, especially in the West, did not make such nice distinctions as that (appearing in a Victorian etiquette book) between the 'great little' (professional and mercantile classes) and the 'little great' ('the old solid COUNTY PEOPLE . . . the Squirearchy'). Huggett, *Life Below Stairs*, 87.
17. Campbell, *Home Economics*, 29.
18. Henry Lefebvre, quoted in Don Mitchell, *The Lie of the Land: Migrant Workers and the California Landscape* (Minneapolis, 1966), 11.

19. Davidoff, *Worlds Between*, 18.
20. Cecil Logsdail, 'The Women of the United States', *The Canadian Magazine* (June 1893): 266–7.
21. *Western Sun*, 6 Apr. 1899.
22. *Brandon Weekly Sun*, 5 June 1902.
23. *Names of Persons Committed to the Western Judicial District Jail*, 64–9.
24. NAC, Capital Case File, William H. Webb, No. 231, 1888.
25. *Western Sun*, 18 May 1899.
26. Ibid., 7 Sept. 1899.
27. *Labour Gazette* 1 (Ottawa, 1902): 412.
28. Brontë, *Jane Eyre*, 152.
29. Ibid., 240. Gilbert and Gubar, *The Madwoman in the Attic*, 354, suggest that Brontë 'imagined a world in which the prince and Cinderella are democratically equal.'
30. Sykes, *A Home-Help in Canada*, 128.
31. Dickens, *Great Expectations*, 111.
32. Quoted in Salmon, *Domestic Service*, 154.
33. *Melita Enterprise*, 21 July 1899.
34. Richardson, 'Ambiquities in the Lives of Children', 380.
35. Dubinsky, *Improper Advances*, 90.
36. *Manitoba Morning Free Press*, 11 July 1899.
37. On the courtroom as theatre, see Paul Craven, 'Law and Ideology: The Toronto Police Court, 1850–1880', in David Flaherty, ed., *Essays in the History of Canadian Law*, vol. 2 (Toronto, 1983), 288.
38. *Winnipeg Morning Telegram*, 11 July 1899.
39. Surrogate Court of the Western Judicial District, Emily Hilda Blake, 1899.
40. *Manitoba Morning Free Press*, 11 July 1899.
41. 'She was an orphan like myself. . . . She was more noticeable, I thought, in respect of her extremities; for, her hair always wanted brushing, her hands always wanted washing, and her shoes always wanted mending and pulling up at heel.' Dickens, *Great Expectations*, 74.
42. Dickens, *Oliver Twist*, 47.
43. Dickens, *Great Expectations*, 365. Not until after the court cases, however, did Blake adopt Compeyson's other aristocratic expedient—the propensity to quote poetry.
44. Nichols, *Household Guide*, 206, 181. O'Reilly, *The Mirror of True Womanhood*, 198, 244, also attacks the passion for rich attire.
45. Fahrni, ' "Ruffled" Mistresses', 79, 87.
46. Aline Raymond quoted in Lacelle, *Urban Domestic Servants*, 167.
47. Shapiro, *Breaking the Codes*, 21, 171.
48. Ruth Campbell, 'Sentence of Death by Burning for Women', *Journal of Legal History* 5 (May 1984): 44–59.

49. Raymond Williams, 'Base and Superstructure in Marxist Cultural Theory', *New Left Review* 82 (Nov.-Dec. 1973): 12.

Chapter 10

1. *Western Sun*, 15 Feb. 1900.

2. Caesar [Cesare] Lombroso and William [Guglielmo] Ferrero, *The Female Offender* (*La donna delinquente*, 1895) (New York, 1958), 152, 159, 196, 202 (emphasis added).

3. Record of Capital Cases Since Confederation, NAC, RG 13, vol. 1404, file: Summaries 1867–1901.

4. Edward Stoddard, 'Conflicting Images: The Murderess and the English-Canadian Mind', MA thesis (Dalhousie University, 1991), 88–91, 121–3.

5. See Carolyn Strange, 'The Lottery of Death: Capital Punishment, 1867–1976', *Manitoba Law Journal* 23, 3 (Jan. 1995): 608.

6. Israel, 'French Vices and British Liberties', 1.

7. Reynolds and Humble, *Victorian Heroines*, 117.

8. Virginia Morris, *Double Jeopardy: Women Who Kill in Victorian Fiction* (Lexington, Ky, 1990), 88.

9. Thomas Hardy, 'Candour in English Fiction', *New Review*, 1 Jan. 1890, quoted in Carl J. Weber, 'Introduction', Thomas Hardy, *Tess of the D'Urbervilles—A Pure Woman* (New York, 1915), viii–ix.

10. 'Books and Authors', *The Canadian Magazine* (Nov. 1895): 98.

11. G. Mercer Adam, 'Recent Fiction in Britain', *The Canadian Magazine* 4, 3 (Jan. 1895): 219.

12. Thomas Hardy, 'Postscript' to the 1912 Edition, *Jude the Obscure* (New York, 1996 [1896]), 7.

13. David Christie Murray, 'My Contemporaries in Fiction', *The Canadian Magazine* (May 1897): 40.

14. Reginald Gourlay, 'A Decade of Fads', *The Canadian Magazine* (Nov. 1895): 71–2.

15. Susan S.M. Edwards, *Women on Trial: A Study of the Woman Suspect, Defendant and Offender in the Criminal Law and Criminal Justice System* (Manchester, 1984), 27.

16. Hargreave L. Adam, *Women and Crime* (London, 1914), 17, quoted in Morris, *Double Jeopardy*, 44.

17. For the New Woman's hatred of authority and her embracing of anarchism, see Gourlay, 'A Decade of Fads', 72–3.

18. Reynolds and Humble, *Victorian Heroines*, 19.

19. *Manitoba Morning Free Press*, 10 July 1899; *Elkhorn Advocate*, 20 July 1899.

20. Shapiro, *Breaking the Codes*, 205–6. Of the female 'born criminal', Lombroso says, her 'moral physiognomy' approximates that of the male. Her virility makes her 'excessively erotic, weak in maternal feeling, inclined to dissipation, astute and audacious'. She 'dominates weaker beings sometimes by suggestion, at others by muscular force'. Lombroso and Ferrero, *The Female Offender*, 187.

21. Feminist attitudes are inversely related to delinquency, while women with 'masculine' behaviour show no greater delinquency than those with 'feminine' behaviour. Naffine, *Female Crime*, 101–2, 43–63. However, girls who move away from traditional feminine expectations, but not towards masculine expectations, do show a greater incidence of delinquency. Ibid., 74. Besides the obvious difficulty in judging which actions of Blake's deserve the most weight, the data present serious problems, notably in the difficulty of defining what exactly constitutes 'masculinity' and 'femininity' and in the small sample of 'masculine' women.

22. *Melita Enterprise*, 21 July 1899.

23. Naffine, *Female Crime*, 100.

24. We do not assume that Blake's 'feminine' persona is entirely constructed—that her tearful goodbye to the children is simply inauthentic on a personal level, or that on a subconscious social level she is simply behaving how her society commanded the genders to behave. However, since she was able to turn some of her behaviours on and off, neither will we assume that she was behaving in an instinctual 'feminine' manner. Whatever duplicity did or did not exist at the core of her subjectivity, she wanted to be a 'woman'.

25. Helen Small, *Love's Madness: Medicine, the Novel, and Female Insanity 1800–1865* (Oxford, 1996).

26. Lombroso and Ferrero, *The Female Offender*, 245, 248.

27. Childless women were supposed to be especially susceptible to hysteria, but 'young vigorous girls—actively employed' were only rarely supposed to be susceptible. Mitchinson, *The Nature of Their Bodies*, 282, 284. In women, it was believed, 'instinctive responses predominated over intellectual ones.' Shapiro, *Breaking the Codes*, 32.

28. *Western Sun*, 13 July 1899.

29. *Brandon Independence*, 13 July 1899.

30. *Brandon Times*, 13 July 1899.

31. *Western Sun*, 13 July 1899.

32. *Brandon Independence*, 13 July 1899.

33. *Names of Persons Committed to the Western Judicial District Jail*, 66. Glendenning probably went on to Kingston Penitentiary eventually, because no women were incarcerated at Stony Mountain. *Western Sun*, 28 Nov. 1899.

34. William Middleton, Foreman of the Grand Jury, to Chief Justice Killam, 16 Nov. 1899, included with 28 Nov. 1899 letter from Robert Darrach, County Court Office Brandon, to Robert Watson, Minister of Public Works, PAM, RC18A2.
35. *Brandon Times*, 28 Dec. 1899.
36. *Queen v. Stripp* (1900), County Court Judges Criminal Court (Brandon), Judge's Notebook, 18 Jan. 1900, 314–35, PAM, G2109.
37. *Brandon Independence*, 23 Nov. 1899; *Virden Advance*, 8 June 1899. An earlier article in the *Independence*, 16 Nov. 1899, said that she was 'of rather forbidding appearance'. *Queen v. Glendenning*, Court of Queen's Bench, Criminal Pockets, ATG 0007, GR 273, 2/1009, PAM.
38. See Carolyn Strange, ' "The Criminal and Fallen of their Sex": The Establishment of Canada's First Women's Prison, 1874–1901', *Canadian Journal of Women and the Law* 1, 1 (1985): 79–92. The women selected for the Andrew Mercer Ontario Reformatory for Females 'retained enough self-respect to appreciate and desire a "better" life.' Obedient and well-deported women at the Massachusetts Reformatory Prison were rewarded with the fanciest uniforms and delicate china. Ibid., 86, 90.
39. Naffine, *Female Crime*, 86–7.
40. *Birtle Eye-Witness*, 25 July 1899.
41. *Western Sun*, 10 Aug. 1899.
42. *Virden Advance*, 17 Aug. 1899.
43. *Western Sun*, 10 Aug. 1899.
44. *Queen v. Stripp* (1899), Queen's Bench (Brandon), PAM, GR 363, ATG, box 31.
45. *Western Sun*, 25 Jan. 1900.
46. Strange, ' "The Criminal and Fallen of their Sex" ', 83, 81.
47. *Western Sun*, 9 Mar. 1899.
48. Strange, ' "The Criminal and Fallen of their Sex" ', 86.
49. *Queen v. Stripp* (1900).
50. Ibid. Jobb was a 50-year-old Ontario-Irish woman with six children. Her husband seems to have been a farmhand, and the family's religion is listed as Church of England. *1901 Census of Canada*, Manitoba, District #6 Brandon, A: Brandon City, East of 4th Street, 10.
51. *St. Matthew's Church, Brandon, Register #1, 1884–99 Baptisms, Marriages, Deaths or Funeral Services* describes him as a merchant in 1892 and a carpenter in 1894.
52. *Names of Persons Committed to the Western Judicial District Jail*, 69.
53. *Western Sun*, 14 Dec. 1899.
54. Dickens, *Great Expectations*, 37. As well, in Dickens, *Oliver Twist*, 160, if the unsentimental Mr Sykes were sentenced to death, he would rather have a file than any expression of undying devotion from his Nancy.

55. According to Kircaldy, Stripp's trial was the first time she mentioned the excuse of wanting to get a confession: 'I don't remember her saying that she did it to get a confession out of Hilda Blake, nothing was said about confessions.' *Queen v. Stripp* (1900).
56. This is according to Stripp. Kircaldy testified that he 'never knew Blake being hysterical in the jail', though it's hard to see how Kircaldy would know what went on at the jail in the night. Ibid.
57. Ibid.
58. *Western Sun*, 25 Jan. 1900.
59. *Brandon Independence*, 5 Oct. 1899.
60. Partially reported in *Queen v. Stripp* (1899). Full text in *Manitoba Morning Free Press*, 13 Dec. 1899; *Brandon Independence*, 21 Dec. 1899.
61. *Queen v. Stripp* (1900); *Queen v. Stripp* (1899).
62. The theories are cited and discounted in Naffine, *Female Crime*, 43.
63. *Western Sun*, 4 Jan. 1900. Newspaper accounts do not reveal whom the photograph depicted.
64. Shapiro, *Breaking the Codes*, 148, cites a study of cell graffiti. Male emotional life, also judging by graffiti, was dominated by pride and hatred.
65. Sir Walter Scott, *Ivanhoe* (New York, 1952 [1830]), 404.
66. *Brandon Daily Sun*, 18 June 1927.
67. *Queen v. Stripp* (1900).
68. *Debates of the Senate*, 20 June 1899, 402.
69. *Queen v. Stripp* (1899).
70. Lombroso and Ferrero, *The Female Offender*, 195.
71. *Western Sun*, 25 Jan. 1900
72. *Queen v. Stripp* (1900). The *Western Sun*, 25 Jan. 1900, calls her 'Mrs. Newcome', probably an error in the reporter's hearing.

Chapter 11

1. *Brandon Daily Sun*, 18 Feb. 1892.
2. John Ferguson, 'The Death Penalty', *The Canadian Magazine* 2, 5 (Mar. 1894): 470.
3. Thomas Hobbes, *Leviathan* (Harmondsworth, UK, 1968 [1651]), 187.
4. Desmond H. Brown, *The Birth of a Criminal Code: The Evolution of Canada's Justice System* (Toronto, 1995), 28.
5. Graham Parker, 'The Legal Regulation of Sexual Activity and the Protection of Females', *Osgoode Hall Law Journal* 21 (1983): 187–244.
6. Prentice et al., *Canadian Women in History*, 138.
7. *Canadian Law Journal* 32 (1896): 423, quoted in Richard A. Willie, *"These Legal Gentlemen": Lawyers in Manitoba: 1839–1900* (Winnipeg, 1994), 235.

8. Prentice et al., *Canadian Women in History*, 138.

9. Dubinsky, *Improper Advances*, 26.

10. Mary S. Hartman, *Victorian Murderesses: A True History of Thirteen Respectable French & English Women Accused of Unspeakable Crimes* (London, 1985), 5–6.

11. On the social construction of female sexuality, see Nancy F. Cott, 'Passionless: An Interpretation of Victorian Sexual Ideology, 1790–1850', *Signs* 4, 2 (1978): 219–36.

12. Stoddard, 'Conflicting Images', 79–88.

13. 'Memorandum for the Minister of Justice', Cordelia Poirier, Capital Case Files, RG 13, NAC, 4, quoted in Neil Boyd, *The Last Dance: Murder in Canada* (Scarborough, Ont., 1988), 93. In other records dealing with this case, Cordelia Poirier is referred to as Cordelia Viau.

14. Grand Jury of the Western Judicial District to Chief Justice A.C. Killam, Nov. 1899, RG 18 A2, Minister of Public Works, PAM; Middleton to Killam, 16 Nov. 1899.

15. The appointment was not entirely disinterested. The provincial Attorney General had resigned, and Premier John Norquay wanted to replace him with the Conservative lawyer and mayor of Winnipeg, C.E. Hamilton. By promoting the Liberal Killam from the South Winnipeg seat, and successfully running C.E. Hamilton in the subsequent by-election, Norquay was able to do just that.

16. *Winnipeg Tribune*, 14 June 1930; Albert Clements Killam, Biographical Files, Western Legal Archives, Law Library, University of Manitoba; Lee Gibson, 'Killam, Albert Clements', *Dictionary of Canadian Biography*, vol. 13 (Toronto, 1994), 542–4; Law Society Scrapbooks, Nov. 1907–Dec. 1908, P1273, PAM, 29–30.

17. There were 27 cases. In one case the verdict is unknown or unclear. Constance Backhouse, 'Desperate Women and Compassionate Courts: Infanticide in Nineteenth Century Canada', *University of Toronto Law Journal* 34 (1984): 462.

18. *Western Sun*, 28 Nov. 1899.

19. *Brandon Mail*, 23 Nov. 1893.

20. Ibid.

21. Ibid.

22. *Western Sun*, 23 Nov. 1899; *Brandon Independence*, 23 Nov. 1899; *Winnipeg Daily Tribune*, 27 Dec. 1899.

23. He was appointed as Crown prosecutor three months after Blake's trial. *Western Sun*, 8 Feb. 1900.

24. Clark, *Brandon's Politics*, 52; *Brandon Daily Sun*, 22 Jan. 1901; Constance Backhouse, *Colour-Coded: A Legal History of Racism in Canada 1900–1950* (Toronto, 1999), 82, 97–8.

25. PAM, Court of Queen's Bench, Judge's Notebooks, J0296, GR 2219, G2626, Chief Justice Killam No. 39, 12 Apr. to 17 Nov. 1899, 341.
26. *Brandon Independence*, 23 Nov. 1899; *Virden Advance*, 23 Nov. 1899.
27. See R.E. Salhany, *Canadian Criminal Procedure*, 5th edn (Aurora, Ont., 1989), 219.
28. *Queen v. Stripp* (1900).
29. Israel, 'French Vices and British Liberties', 8.
30. Nichols, *Household Guide*, 6.
31. The quotations are from Shapiro, *Breaking the Codes*, 150, 154. Recently, and by all accounts, sincerely, Karla Tucker recuperated the feminine sphere just before her February 1998 execution for murder in Texas. Her final statement, reported in the *Winnipeg Free Press*, 4 Feb. 1998, B1, included the following:

    Yes sir, I would like to say to all of you, the Thornton family and Jerry Dean's family that I am so sorry. I hope God will give you peace with this.

    Baby, I love you. Ron, give Peggy a hug for me. Everybody has been so good to me. I love all of you very much. I'm going to be face to face with Jesus now.

    Warden Baggett, thank all of you so much. You have been so good to me.

    I love all of you very much. I will see you all when you get there. I will wait for you.
32. Strange, 'Wounded Womanhood and Dead Men', 151.
33. Shapiro, *Breaking the Codes*, 163.
34. *Western Sun*, 28 Dec. 1899.
35. *Manitoba Morning Free Press*, 18 Nov. 1899.

Chapter 12

1. *Western Sun*, 29 Nov. 1899.
2. 'Dr. Amelia Yeomans', Manitoba Historic Resources Branch, 1985. For a discussion of early feminism in Canada, see Mariana Valverde, ' "When the Mother of the Race is Free": Race, Reproduction, and Sexuality in First-Wave Feminism', in Iacovetta and Valverde, eds, *Gender Conflicts*, 3–27.
3. Quoted in Dorothy Gies McGuigan, *A Dangerous Experiment: 100 Years of Women at the University of Michigan* (Ann Arbor, Mich., 1970), 54.
4. Ibid., 71, 73, 75. By 1880, 19.3 per cent of the medical graduates at Michigan were women. Yeomans went to Michigan at the same time as the first black women, and also at the same time as Lucy Salmon, whose

historical/economic work on domestic service, perhaps the first serious academic work on domestic service, underpins Chapter 3 of this book.

5. 'Dr. Amelia Yeomans', 5; Carlotta Hacker, *The Indomitable Lady Doctors* (Toronto, 1974), 90.
6. Youmans, *Campaign Echoes*, 128, 210.
7. 'Dr. Amelia Yeomans', 6.
8. The association expired from lack of leadership when Yeomans left the province. Catherine Cleverdon, *The Woman Suffrage Movement in Canada* (Toronto, 1950), 52.
9. Edith M. Luke, 'Woman Suffrage in Canada', *The Canadian Magazine* 5 (1895): 335.
10. Boyd, *The Last Dance*, 159.
11. Judith R. Walkowitz, Myra Jehlen, and Belle Chevigny, 'Patrolling the Borders: Feminist Historiography and the New Historicism', *Radical History Review* 43 (1989): 7, quoted in Israel, 'French Vices and British Liberties', 2.
12. 'Dr. Amelia Yeomans', 4.
13. Hacker, *The Indomitable Lady Doctors*, 90.
14. Ibid., 90–2.
15. Naffine, *Female Crime*, 132.
16. *Manitoba Morning Free Press*, 25 Mar. 1901.
17. Strange, 'Stories of Their Lives', 29.
18. Gourlay, 'A Decade of Fads', 69.
19. For Raymond Williams, such ascendancy, or hegemony, consists of 'a whole range of practices and expectations, over the whole of living: our senses and assignments of energy, our shaping perceptions of ourselves and our world. It is a lived system of meanings and values—constitutive and constituting—which as they are experienced as practices appear as reciprocally confirming.' Williams, *Marxism and Literature* (Oxford, 1977), 110.
20. See V.A.C. Gatrell's discussion of tears in *The Hanging Tree: Execution and the English People 1770–1868* (Oxford, 1994), 226.
21. *Manitoba Morning Free Press*, 28 Apr. 1899. A report of the execution, however, describes the ministrations of Rev. Fathers Kalavic and Woodcutter 'in the Galician tongue'. *Western Sun*, 1 June 1899. The *Sun* notes that the condemned men were convicted of murdering Wasyl Bojecko and his four children, and that Czuby walked to the gallows in a 'stooped, shambling stride' while Guszczak 'walked firmly' despite 'a decided look of fear on his face'. Both Guszczak and Czuby had been sentenced to death by Killam.
22. Shapiro, *Breaking the Codes*, 188.
23. *Winnipeg Morning Telegram*, 15 Dec. 1899.

24. *Manitoba Morning Free Press*, 16 Dec. 1899.
25. Dickens, *Oliver Twist*, 469.
26. *Winnipeg Morning Telegram*, 15 Dec. 1899.
27. Ibid., *Manitoba Morning Free Press*, 15 Dec. 1899.
28. Ibid.
29. *Winnipeg Morning Telegram*, 15 Dec. 1899.
30. James Cowles Prichard, *A Treatise on Insanity and other Disorders Affecting the Mind* (1847), quoted in Gregory Zilboorg, 'Legal Aspects of Psychiatry', in J.K. Hall, ed., *One Hundred Years of American Psychiatry* (New York, 1944), 197. Elsewhere, Prichard speaks of 'a form of mental derangement in which the intellectual faculties appear to have sustained little or no injury, while the disorder is manifested principally or alone, in the state of the feelings, temper or habits. In cases of this description the moral and active principles of the mind are strangely perverted and depraved; the power of self-government is lost or greatly impaired; and the individual is found to be incapable . . . of conducting himself with decency and propriety in the business of life.' Quoted in Anne Digby, *Madness, Morality and Medicine: A Study of the York Retreat, 1796–1914* (Cambridge, 1985), 93. This definition suggests a more thoroughgoing impairment.
31. Ruth B. Caplan, *Psychiatry and the Community in Nineteenth Century America* (New York, 1969), 120–4. Janet Colaizzi, *Homicidal Insanity, 1800–1985* (Tuscaloosa, Ala., 1989), 51–5, 77–8. Prichard's term was derived from Phillippe Pinel's 'manie sans délire' and Jean Esquirol's 'impulsive homicidal mania'. Prichard's term was immediately challenged by the prominent medical jurisprudent John Ordronzux, who commented dryly that 'Satan himself becomes converted into a simple moral lunatic.' Quoted ibid., 50. In the last half of the nineteenth century, the American medical profession was divided about whether 'moral insanity' was a verifiable clinical condition. John Gray, who, in conjunction with his followers, controlled the *American Journal of Insanity*, felt that 'moral insanity' was a deterministic and fatalistic label rather than an empirical malady, that only physical disease could cause insanity, and that a defence of 'moral insanity' was a way of avoiding responsibility for one's actions. In an 1881 trial at which Gray also testified, Dr A.E. MacDonald, a New York mental hospital superintendent and professor of medical jurisprudence at the University of New York, insisted that 'moral insanity' was another name for wickedness and had been invented at the time of the French Revolution to excuse the slaughter. Isaac Ray spoke for the minority position, holding that insanity could be present without a physical cause such as a brain lesion. See Zilboorg, 'Legal Aspects of Psychiatry', 550–7; Henry Alden Bunker, 'American Psychiatric Literature During the Past 100 Years', in Hall, ed., *One Hundred Years of*

American Psychiatry, 204–15. Medical superintendents were split about the existence of 'moral insanity'.

32. Colaizzi, *Homicidal Insanity*, 53; Martin W. Barr and E.F. Maloney, *Types of Mental Defectives* (Philadelphia, 1920), 101.

33. H. Douglas Singer and William O. Krohn, *Insanity and Law: A Treatise on Forensic Psychiatry* (Philadelphia, 1924), 220.

34. Ibid.; Barr and Maloney, *Types of Mental Defectives*, 91, 98, 101–2. Digby, *Madness, Morality and Medicine*, 95, lists some of the characteristics of patients who were diagnosed as morally insane in a nineteenth-century Quaker mental hospital: self-willed (8 cases), irritable (7), idle (7), unsuitable sexual behaviour, i.e., masturbation, overfamiliarity with the opposite sex, or the contracting of venereal disease (4), abusive (3), deceitful (2), violent (2), dirty (2), intemperate (2), sullen (2).

35. Stoddard, 'Conflicting Images', 121.

36. Thus Henry Howard, medical attendant to the Longue Point Lunatic Asylum, in 1878, quoted in Mitchinson, *The Nature of Their Bodies*, 289.

37. Showalter, 'Victorian Women and Insanity', 167. According to F.C. Skey in 1867, for example, typical hysterics were not women of weak mind, but women who exhibited 'more than usual force and decision of character, of strong resolution, fearless of danger, bold riders, having plenty of what is termed nerve'. Quoted ibid., 172. Digby, *Madness, Morality and Medicine*, 96, 279, mentions cases of 'moral insanity' that seem to have more to do with sexual discipline than with mental illness.

38. Singer and Krohn, *Insanity and Law*, 221.

39. Barr and Maloney, *Types of Mental Defectives*, 74.

40. One of the cases cited by Barr and Maloney makes an evocative, though hardly conclusive, echo of Blake: 'She always imagined that she was a long-lost princess and that some day wealthy people would come to claim her and carry her away in a coach and four. She was fairly well educated.' Ibid., 101.

41. *Winnipeg Morning Telegram*, 15 Dec. 1899. It must be emphasized that present-day psychiatry is not much farther ahead, trading the unfashionable word 'moral' for the sonorous 'anti-social personality disorder', but identifying most of the same behaviours as nineteenth- and early twentieth-century handbooks did and offering little hope for treatment. *Treatments of Psychiatric Disorders: A Task Force Report of the American Psychiatric Association*, vol. 3 (Washington, 1989), 2744–5. Under 'DSM-III-R Diagnostic Criteria for Antisocial Personality Disorder', the following childhood symptoms appeared, of which the patient must exhibit at least three: truancy, running away from home, assault, use of a weapon, sexual assault, cruelty to animals, cruelty to people, destruction of property, arson, lying, theft. Subsequently, the patient must exhibit four of the following symptoms

as an adult: inconsistent work behaviour, consistent illegal behaviour, assault, failure to honour financial obligations, lack of a fixed address, lying, recklessness about the safety of self or others, inability to care properly for children. By requiring three or four behaviours, psychiatrists clearly want to avoid tagging a person with anti-social personality disorder just because the person has one particular problem or because the person rebels against one or two aspects of societal control. While a person exhibiting these symptoms in combination clearly has problems, it is difficult to see a diagnostic coherence in the list. In effect, the list is a catch-all, a way of saying, 'there's something wrong with this person; I'm not sure what.'

42. *Winnipeg Morning Telegram*, 15 Dec. 1899.
43. Lombroso and Ferrero, *The Female Offender*, 154, 170.
44. Carol Smart, *Women, Crime and Criminology: A Feminist Critique* (London, 1976), 31.
45. Lombroso and Ferrero, *The Female Offender*, 151.
46. Ibid., 147.
47. Interview with McLaurin, *Western Sun*, 14 Dec. 1899.
48. Oscar Wilde, 'The Decay of Lying', *The Complete Works of Oscar Wilde* (London, 1966), 981.
49. *Western Sun*, 8 Feb. 1900.
50. Ibid., 14 Dec. 1899; *Manitoba Morning Free Press*, 13 Dec. 1899.
51. Gatrell, *The Hanging Tree*, 339.
52. Judith Knelman, *Twisting in the Wind: The Murderess and the English Press* (Toronto, 1998), 245.
53. *Statutes of Canada,* Criminal Code, ch. 29, 55–56 Vic., 1892, S.227.
54. *Western Sun*, 4 Jan. 1900.
55. *Manitoba Morning Free Press*, 19 Dec. 1899.
56. Ibid., 16 Dec. 1899. Among the names were J.C. Walker, pastor of Wesley Church; Joseph Hogg, pastor of St Andrew's Church; W. Redford Morlock, QC; S. Cleaver, pastor of Grace Church; O. Fortin, DD, rector of Holy Trinity, Archdeacon, Winnipeg; Georgina Stewart, provincial president, WCTU; T. Poyntz, druggist; R.Roblin; R.J. Campbell (Sutherland & Campbell); David Horne; W.A. Morgan; S. Nairn; J.M. Ross; S. Pink; Charles N. Bell; N. Bawlf; Thomas Ryan, wholesale merchant.
57. *Winnipeg Daily Tribune*, 20 Dec. 1899.
58. *Western Sun*, 21 Dec. 1899.
59. 'Samuel Praying. After Sir Joshua Reynolds', *Child's Bible* (n.p., n.d.), 'Donated to the Chapman Museum by Mrs. Marjorie Henry (Rivers)'.
60. *Manitoba Morning Free Press*, 12 Dec. 1899.
61. See Reed, *Victorian Conventions*, 58–64.
62. Lombroso and Ferrero, *The Female Offender*, 152.

63. *Manitoba Morning Free Press*, 13 Dec. 1899.
64. Ibid., 12 Dec. 1899.
65. *Western Sun*, 21 Dec. 1899.
66. Ibid.
67. Ibid., 15 Dec. 1899.
68. Morris, *Double Jeopardy*, 47, 132.
69. For a detailed account of the case, see H.B. Irving, ed., *The Trial of Mrs. Maybrick* (Edinburgh and London, 1912).
70. *Manitoba Morning Free Press*, 9 Dec. 1899.
71. Ibid., 12 Dec. 1899.
72. *Regina Standard*, quoted in *Western Sun*, 21 Dec. 1899.
73. Ibid.
74. *Brandon Times*, 21 Dec. 1899
75. Ibid., 6 July 1899.
76. Gatrell, *The Hanging Tree*, 230.
77. *Brandon Independence*, 14 Dec. 1899.
78. 'Our laws even have so far relaxed their terrors to evil doers, as to refrain from hanging a crimnal [*sic*] on every possible pretext. There can be no higher praise to this generation, than to say, which is true, that it has acknowledged the sweet quality of mercy; acknowledged that in wrong-doers there are possibilities of good, and that the "worst use" as Wilkes said, "that you can put a man to, is to hang him", and that even punish-ment should mean reform and not revenge. But directly from this very virtue has sprung the modern fad, beloved by weak-minded or cunning men in various churches, and by often well-meaning, but silly and hyster-ical women of various societies, sisterhoods and churches, of not only petting and making a fuss over notorious criminals, but of actually glori-fying unmitigated sinners, converted prize-fighters, (by far the best fel-lows in the collection), and very naughty people of both sexes, but lately repentant.' Gourlay, 'A Decade of Fads', 69
79. Dubinsky, ' "Maidenly Girls" or "Designing Women"?', 36.
80. *Labour Gazette* 2 (1901–2): 412.
81. Minutes of Sanitarium Attendants' Federal Union, No. 27, 27 Mar., 7, 20 Apr. 1919, in authors' possession. The Brandon Trades and Labour Council was organized in 1905.
82. *The Voice*, 21 Dec. 1899.
83. *Manitoba Morning Free Press*, 16 Dec. 1899.
84. *Brandon Independence*, 14 Dec. 1899.
85. *Manitoba Morning Free Press*, 16 Dec. 1899.
86. *Western Sun*, 14 Dec. 1899.
87. *Manitoba Morning Free Press*, 28 Dec. 1899.

Chapter 13

1. *Western Sun*, 28 Dec. 1899.
2. *Winnipeg Daily Tribune*, 27 Dec. 1899.
3. *Brandon Independence*, 28 Dec. 1899.
4. *Western Sun*, 28 Dec. 1899.
5. Sykes, *A Home-Help in Canada*, 143.
6. *Manitoba Morning Free Press*, 13 Nov. 1899.
7. Carole Gerson, *A Purer Taste: The Writing and Reading of Fiction in English in Nineteenth-Century Canada* (Toronto, 1989), 26, 29, citing an 1873 review of Wilkie Collins's *The New Magdalen* and an 1891 review of Emile Zola's *Money*.
8. Mitchinson, *The Nature of Their Bodies*, 290; Digby, *Madness, Morality and Medicine*, 92. *Debates of the Senate*, 1899, 350.
9. O'Reilly, *The Mirror of True Womanhood*, 247, 194.
10. Quoted in Gerson, *A Purer Taste*, 35, 75.
11. *Victorian Reader*, 4th and 5th Books (Toronto, 1898).
12. *Wheat City International Carnival* (Brandon, 1908).
13. *The Accession Catalogue* for Brandon College Library shows the following acquisitions in 1900–1: *Rob Roy, Waverley, Guy Mannering, The Antiquary, The Monastery, The Legend of Montrose*.
14. *What the National Council of Women of Canada has done: being a report of the proceedings of a public meeting, held in connection with the Local Council of Women of Ottawa, Feb., 1896* (Ottawa?, 1896), 9; McEwen, 'Home Life in the West', 33.
15. Dickens, *Great Expectations*, 361, 412, 418, 424.
16. Dickens, *Our Mutual Friend*, 311, 515–16, 66, 99.
17. Scott, *Rob Roy*, 119.
18. Reynolds and Humble, *Victorian Heroines*, 27.
19. Dickens, *Oliver Twist*, 33, 359, 58, 364–6.
20. William Thackeray, 'Going to See a Man Hanged', *The Works of William Makepeace Thackeray*, vol. 3 (London, 1898), 643.
21. 'Free libraries now dot the land. No poor boy can truthfully say that the best literature is beyond his reach.' 'Book Reviews', *The Canadian Magazine* (Sept. 1890): 476.
22. Jackel, ed., *A Flannel Shirt and Liberty*, 60.
23. 'Do not place a light estimate upon the arts of good reading and good expression; they will yield perpetual interest.' Nichols, *Household Guide*, 200.
24. LeRoi Jones [now Amiri Baraka], *Blues People: Negro Music in White America* (London, 1965), 83.
25. Ibid., 85; Arnold Shaw, *Black Popular Music in America* (New York, 1986), 68–9; Eileen Southern, *The Music of Black Americans: A History*,

2nd edn (New York, 1983), 298; James H. Dormon, 'Shaping the Popular Image of Post-Reconstruction American Blacks: The "Coon Song" Phenomenon of the Gilded Age', *American Quarterly* 40, 4 (Dec. 1988): 454–5, 465–7; Sam Dennison, *Scandalize My Name: Black Imagery in American Popular Music* (New York, 1982), 349.

26. Paul Oliver, *Songsters and Saints: Vocal Traditions on Race Records* (Cambridge, 1984), 102, 277.
27. Shaw, *Black Popular Music*, 30, 41–2.
28. Ibid., 31.
29. Philip Furia, *The Poets of Tin Pan Alley* (New York, 1990), 27–8.
30. Nichols, *Household Guide*, 206–7.
31. Paul Charosh and Robert A. Fremont, eds, *Song Hits from the Turn of the Century: Complete Original Sheet Music for 25 Songs* (New York, 1975), 39.
32. Dormon, 'Shaping the Popular Image', 450–71.
33. *Western Sun*, 8 Dec. 1899. The 'Coontown 400' may have been an imitation of the successful 'A Trip to Coontown', a black-produced variety show that toured the US in 1898. Southern, *The Music of Black Americans*, 297.
34. *Western Sun*, 18 Jan. 1900.
35. Isaac Goldberg, *Tin Pan Alley* (New York, 1930), 133, 137.
36. Finson, *The Voices That Are Gone*, 79.
37. Alexander Saxton, *The Rise and Fall of the White Republic: Class Politics and Mass Culture in Nineteenth-Century America* (New York, 1990), 170, 180.
38. Dormon, 'Shaping the Popular Image', 456–7, 459, 461–2; Oliver, *Songsters and Saints*, 55.
39. Charosh and Fremont, *Song Hits from the Turn of the Century*, 68; Furia, *Poets of Tin Pan Alley*, 27.
40. David R. Roediger, *The Wages of Whiteness: Race and the Making of the American Working Class* (London, 1991), 95.
41. Dormon, 'Shaping the Popular Image', 458; Dennison, *Scandalize My Name*, 409.
42. *Western Sun*, 1 Mar. 1900.
43. Dennison, *Scandalize My Name*, 413.
44. Furia, *Poets of Tin Pan Alley*, 29.
45. Finson, *The Voices That Are Gone*, 76.
46. Dennison, *Scandalize My Name*, 391.
47. C.C. McLaurin, 'Wilt Thou Not Revive Us Again?' n.d., Canadian Baptist Archives, McMaster Divinity College, Hamilton, Ont.
48. *Western Sun*, 13 July 1899.
49. *Manitoba Morning Free Press*, 16 Dec. 1899.

50. According to Shapiro, *Breaking the Codes*, 173, 'worried critics noted that some women flaunted their criminal acts, making themselves heroes of their own lives, refusing the role of victim, refusing even the required remorse. It seems that women who had acted on their anger found in the love discourse a narrative that legitimated their pain and urged them to revenge, but, even more invited them to tell their own stories.' Such a statement could have been made of Blake, except that she did seem to feel remorse. Perhaps Blake also remembered how in *Great Expectations* Jaggers undercut Mr Wopsle's dramatic murder recitation, with its easy presumptions of guilt: 'And now I ask you what you say to the conscience of that man who . . . can lay his head upon his pillow after having pronounced a fellow-creature guilty, unheard?' Dickens, *Great Expectations*, 162.
51. *Western Sun*, 4 Jan. 1900.
52. Lombroso and Ferrero, *The Female Offender*, 175, 192–3, 165, 168–9.
53. Dickens, *Great Expectations*, 231.
54. 'Mr Brown' could also have been James Brown, a 49-year-old Catholic brakeman on the railroad, or John Brown, a 55-year-old Anglican elevator man. 'J. Brown' was listed as one of the jurors at the inquest into Mary Lane's death. *Western Sun*, 13 July 1899.
55. *Manitoba Morning Free Press*, 28 Dec. 1899.
56. Dickens, *Great Expectations*, 365.
57. Walkowitz, *City of Dreadful Delight*, 10; Reed, *Victorian Conventions*, 475.
58. Reed, *Victorian Conventions*, 475.
59. Dickens, *Great Expectations*, 132.
60. McLaurin, *Pioneering in Western Canada*, 146.
61. McLaurin, *Sixty Years in the Ministry*, 12.
62. *Manitoba Morning Free Press*, 16 Dec. 1899.
63. Dickens, *Oliver Twist*, 268.
64. Minto to Laurier, 23 Dec. 1899.
65. *Brandon Independence*, 4 Jan. 1900.
66. *Manitoba Morning Free Press*, 28 Dec. 1899.
67. *Western Sun*, 28 Dec. 1899.
68. The names are cited ibid. as Thomas Smart and Mrs Haper; *Regina Standard*, 3 Jan.1900, has Thomas Stewart and Mrs Harper. Judging by the *1901 Census*, which contains no Haper or Stewart, the correct names must be Thomas Smart and Mrs Harper. Typographical errors and mistakes in reading handwriting probably account for the variation.
69. *Western Sun*, 28 Dec. 1899.
70. Semple, *The Lord's Dominion*, 221.
71. *Manitoba Morning Free Press*, 14 Dec. 1899

Chapter 14

1. *Statutes of Canada*, Criminal Code, 1892, 144.
2. *Debates of the Senate* (1900), 1136.
3. David Mills to His Excellency the Governor-General, 19 Jan. 1898, NAC, RG 13 c-1, vol. 1431, file 286-A, Olive Adele Sternaman.
4. *Debates of the House of Commons*, 61 Vic., 31 Mar. 1898, 1574.
5. Ibid., 2900, 2175–6.
6. Douglas Owram, *The Government Generation: Canadian Intellectuals and the State 1900–1945* (Toronto, 1986), 35
7. *Debates of the Senate*, 1 Mar. 1900, 112–13.
8. Mills to Laurier, 26 Sept. 1898, Laurier Papers, NAC, Series A, C-759, 26721–7 (emphasis added).
9. Donald J. McMurchy, 'David Mills—Nineteenth Century Canadian Liberal', Ph.D. thesis (University of Rochester, 1968), 533.
10. *Debates of the House of Commons*, 31 Mar. 1898, 2920, 2904.
11. Ibid., 2886–7.
12. Ibid., 2912–13, 2918, 2924.
13. Sandra Gwyn, *The Private Capital: Ambition and Love in the Age of Macdonald and Laurier* (Toronto, 1984), 65.
14. *Debates of the House of Commons*, 31 Mar. 1898, 2921–2.
15. Ibid., 2927.
16. *Debates of the Senate*, 20 June 1899, 403.
17. Ibid., 408.
18. Ibid., 9 June 1899, 350.
19. Clark, *Brandon's Politics*, 38; D.J. Hall, *Clifford Sifton: The Young Napoleon 1861–1900* (Vancouver, 1981), 296.
20. 'It is said Ald. McIlvride circulated a petition among the foreign vote to assist him in securing the position of bursar at the Asylum', the *Western Sun*, 8 Feb. 1900, commented sarcastically. Alexander's father, Andrew, was a Presbyterian elder and a staunch Conservative in Normanby, Ontario. Typed obituary in McIlvride family records, Aug. 1900.
21. Hall, *Clifford Sifton*, 281. For a discussion of the Manitoba provincial election of 1899 and Sifton's political problems, see Clark, *Brandon's Politics*, 36–8. Charles Adams's bid for re-election was not helped by the fact that he was in litigation with the City of Brandon about a sidewalk. The city felt that Adams was obligated to pay for the construction of a sidewalk, but Adams refused to pay. *Western Sun*, 8 Dec. 1899.
22. Hall, *Clifford Sifton*, 296.
23. *Manitoba Morning Free Press*, 17 July 1899.
24. Quoted ibid., 31 July 1899.
25. Ibid.

26. *Brandon Times*, 23 Nov. 1899.

27. Clark, *Brandon's Politics*, 37; Hall, *Clifford Sifton*, 279.

28. Neil Sutherland, *Children in English-Canadian Society: Framing the Twentieth-Century Consensus* (Toronto, 1976), 30–2.

29. Bagnell, *The Little Immigrants*, 169. Parr, *Labouring Children*, describes the experience of the children who emigrated to Canada's agricultural frontier in the late nineteenth century. Two recent studies concerned with themes of race and class—Angus McLaren, *Our Own Master Race: Eugenics in Canada, 1885–1945* (Toronto, 1990) and Mariana Valverde, *The Age of Light, Soap, and Water* (Toronto, 1991)—do not mention the criticisms of British pauper immigrants in Canada.

30. Sutherland, *Children in English-Canadian Society*, 30.

31. *Brandon Sun*, 30 Nov. 1893.

32. Bagnell, *The Little Immigrants*, 168–70; J.S. Woodsworth, *Strangers Within Our Gates* (Toronto, 1909), 12.

33. National Council of Women, *Women of Canada: Their Life and Work* (1900?), 412, cited at Early Canadiana Online Web site.

34. M. Elizabeth Langdon, 'Female Crime in Calgary, 1914–1941', 295, quoted in Louis Knafla, ed., *Law and Justice in a New Land: Essays in Western Canadian Legal History* (Toronto, 1986).

35. Hall, *Clifford Sifton*, 289.

36. Ibid., 222.

37. *Western Sun*, 29 Nov. 1899.

38. *Brandon Independence*, 20 Nov. 1899.

39. *Western Sun*, 1 Mar. 1900.

40. 'Gutter Journalism', *Western Sun*, 13 July 1899.

41. Paul Rutherford, *A Victorian Authority: The Daily Press in Late Nineteenth-Century Canada* (Toronto, 1982), 220–1.

42. The same held true for the temperance movement, as Sifton grasped. He thus gave lip service to his father's temperance ideals and mocked his opponents, Hugh John Macdonald and Sir Charles Hibbert Tupper, for their tippling, but he did not campaign directly for the Prohibitionist vote and did not promote the cause after elections. Hall, *Clifford Sifton*, 232; *Virden Advance*, 3 Aug. 1899.

43. *Melita Enterprise*, 21 July 1899.

44. Owram, *Promise of Eden*, 217–18. The prediction belongs to Thomas D'Arcy McGee.

45. Hall, *Clifford Sifton*, 290.

46. *Western Sun*, 21 Dec. 1899; *Toronto Globe*, 18 Dec. 1899.

47. See also Dubinsky, ' "Maidenly Girls" or "Designing Women"?', 39–51.

48. *Toronto Globe*, 18 Dec. 1899.

49. Order-in-Council 2140 C, NAC, RG 2, vol. 791, file 26, Dec. 1899, #2695.

50. Mulock to Laurier, 23 Dec. 1899, Laurier Papers, NAC, series A, C-771, 40197–200. For a more chivalrous Mulock, see Strange, 'Wounded Womanhood and Dead Men', 149.
51. Strange, 'Wounded Womanhood and Dead Men', 175.
52. Minto to Laurier, 23 Dec. 1899.
53. Although a Department of Justice code exists for the file, when Justice transferred capital case files to the National Archives it did not transfer a file for Blake. Correspondence between Minto and Joseph Pope, the Secretary to the Privy Council, makes it clear that Minto did return the documents related to the case in his possession. On 26 December 1899 Minto wrote Pope that he had sent the Blake papers directly to Pope's house. The papers apparently made it there, and Pope was supposed to return them to the Department of Justice. Minto to Pope, 26 Dec. 1899, Pope to Minto, 27 Dec. 1899, Minto to Pope, 27 Dec. 1899, Joseph Pope Papers, NAC, MG 30, E 86, vol. 10.
    Blake's is not the only missing file. From the total collection of 1,533 capital case files in the Department of Justice records, 30 are missing. Twenty-three of those files date from the nineteenth century, and archivists at the National Archives believe that the dated nature of the missing files rather than malevolence is the most obvious reason for their disappearance. Of the 58 women sentenced to death (11 of whom were actually executed) three capital case files are missing: those dealing with Genevieve Lafleur (1881), Felice Pasto (1899), and Blake. The death sentences of Lafleur and Pasto were both commuted. (Statistical information was kindly provided by Lorraine Gadoury of the National Archives.)
    As well, there are no references to Blake in the David Mills Papers or the Sifton Papers.
54. *Western Sun*, 4 Jan. 1900.
55. Gwyn, *The Private Capital*, 296–8, 303–7.
56. Marc LaTerreur, 'Correspondence Laurier-Mme. Joseph Lavergne, 1891–1893', *Canadian Historical Association Annual Report* (1964): 37–51; Gwyn, *The Private Capital*, 248–56; Joseph Schull, *Laurier: The First Canadian* (Toronto, 1965), 161–3, 276–80.
57. Laurier to Minto, 26 Dec. 1899, Minto Papers, NAC, MG 27, II, BI, vol. 5, 32–3.
58. Order-in-Council 2140 C.
59. *Debates of the Senate*, 1897, 485–6.
60. *Western Sun*, 30 Mar. 1899.
61. Minto to G.R. Parkin, quoted in Frank H. Underhill, 'Lord Minto on His Governor Generalship', *Canadian Historical Review* 40, 2 (1959): 124.
62. Minto to Laurier, 26 Dec. 1899, Laurier Papers, NAC, series A, C-177, 40245–7.

Chapter 15

1. *Montreal Gazette*, 28 Dec. 1899.
2. Benedict Anderson, *Imagined Communities* (London, 1983), 7.
3. Ibid., 15.
4. Graeme Patterson, 'An Enduring Canadian Myth: Responsible Government and the Family Compact', *Journal of Canadian Studies* (Spring 1977): 13–14, quoted in Rutherford, *A Victorian Authority*, 156.
5. Rutherford, *A Victorian Authority*, 141.
6. See Judith Knelman, 'Transatlantic Influences on the Reporting of Crime: England vs. America vs. Canada', *American Periodicals* 3 (1993): 1–8. According to Knelman, Canadian reports of the Blake case combined 'the American-inspired flair for drama and human interest and the British emphasis on completeness and decorum'.
7. Quoted in Salmon, *Domestic Service*, 151.
8. *Brandon Times*, 28 Dec. 1899.
9. *Winnipeg Morning Telegram*, 27, 28 Dec. 1899.
10. *Winnipeg Daily Tribune*, 27 Dec. 1899.
11. *Western Sun*, 28 Dec. 1899.
12. *Manitoba Morning Free Press*, 28 Dec. 1899.
13. Ibid., 12, 15 Dec. 1899.
14. *Brandon Independence*, 28 Dec. 1899.
15. *Minnedosa Tribune*, 4 Jan. 1900.
16. *Regina Standard*, 3 Jan. 1900.
17. *Western Sun*, 4 Jan. 1900.
18. *Ottawa Evening Journal*, 27 Dec. 1899.
19. *Toronto Globe*, 18 Dec. 1899.
20. *Western Sun*, 4 Jan. 1900.
21. A search for editorial comment from Canadian newspapers outside Manitoba and Regina in the North-West Territories in the days immediately following the execution of Blake proved generally fruitless.
22. *Western Sun*, 8 Jan. 1900.

Chapter 16

1. A.S. Taylor, *The Principles and Practice of Medical Jurisprudence*, 4th edn (1894), 34–6, 40, 44, quoted in Gatrell, *The Hanging Tree*, 46.
2. Gatrell, *The Hanging Tree*, 7.
3. Cyril Greenland, 'The Last Public Execution in Canada: Eight Skeletons in the Closet of the Canadian Justice System', *Criminal Law Quarterly* 29, 4 (1987): 415.
4. F. Murray Greenwood, 'The General Court Martial of 1838–39 in Lower Canada: An Abuse of Justice', in W. Wesley Pue and Barry Wright, eds,

Canadian Perspectives on Law and Society: Issues in Legal History (Ottawa, 1988), 263.

5. Charles Whitehead, 'A Day in Battleford, "Reveille" in December and Horse's Watering-hole Mile Away—Public Execution of Eight Indians while Chanting a Death Song', *Scarlet and Gold*, Fifth Annual, 1919, quoted in Greenland, 'The Last Public Execution', 419.

6. Thackeray, 'Going to See a Man Hanged', 638–43, 646.

7. Boyd, *The Last Dance*, 23. See also *Hansard's Parliamentary Debates* (London), 14 Feb. 1867, 5 Mar., 21 Apr. 1868.

8. *Brandon Mail*, 27 Dec. 1888.

9. All-night festivities were not unusual, regardless of the availability of rooms. Thackeray describes the habit of some English hanging aficionados: 'This gentleman was one of a party which had evidently not been to bed on Sunday night, but had passed it in some of these delectable night-houses in the neighbourhood of Covent Garden. The debauch was not over yet.' Thackeray, 'Going to See a Man Hanged', 641.

10. The *Gazette* actually quotes Rev. Father Meloche saying '*Houte, houte*', presumably a misprint.

11. *Montreal Gazette*, 11 Mar. 1899.

12. *Winnipeg Morning Telegram*, 27 Dec. 1899; *Western Sun*, 28 Dec. 1899.

13. Frank W. Anderson, *Hanging in Canada: Concise History of a Controversial Topic* (Surrey, BC, 1973), 32.

14. Hector Charlesworth, *Candid Chronicles* (Toronto, 1925), 216; Martin L. Friedland, *The Case of Valentine Shortis: A True Story of Crime and Politics in Canada* (Toronto, 1986), 135–6; *Western Sun*, 4 Jan. 1900.

15. Anderson, *Hanging in Canada*, 37. The not always reliable Howard Engel, *Lord High Executioner: An Unashamed Look at Hangmen, Headsmen, and Their Kind* (Toronto, 1996), 171, describes, without citing sources, Radclive's nightmares in which the ghosts of the hanged taunted him.

16. Lombroso and Ferrero, *The Female Offender*, 168.

17. *Winnipeg Morning Telegram*, 27 Dec. 1899; *Western Sun*, 28 Dec. 1899.

18. *Winnipeg Daily Tribune*, 27 Dec. 1899.

19. *Manitoba Morning Free Press*, 28 Dec. 1899.

20. Brontë, *Jane Eyre*, 309.

21. *Manitoba Morning Free Press*, 28 Dec. 1899.

22. Thackeray, 'Going to See a Man Hanged', 636.

23. *Western Sun*, 28 Dec. 1899.

24. *Manitoba Morning Free Press*, 28 Dec. 1899; *Winnipeg Morning Telegram*, 28 Dec. 1899; *Winnipeg Daily Tribune*, 27 Dec. 1899.

25. The overnight low was –23.3° Celsius, and the high was –10.6°.

26. *Western Sun*, 28 Dec. 1899.

27. *Winnipeg Morning Telegram*, 27 Dec. 1899.
28. Thackeray, 'Going to See a Man Hanged', 636.
29. *Manitoba Morning Free Press*, 28 Dec. 1899.
30. *Western Sun*, 4 Jan. 1900.
31. Ibid.
32. Scott, *Waverley*, 344, 347; Scott, *Ivanhoe*, 479.
33. *Brandon Independence*, 28 Dec. 1899.
34. Ibid., 4 Jan. 1900. This may be apocryphal, since only the *Independence* describes the scene with her former guardian, Mr Stewart. The other newspapers simply say that she kissed her guard. It is possible that the *Independence* embellished the story somewhat, but, given the amount of detail in the *Independence* version of the story, it is also possible that the other papers did not know the identity of the man whom she kissed.
35. *Winnipeg Morning Telegram*, 28 Dec. 1899.
36. *Manitoba Morning Free Press*, 28 Dec. 1899.
37. Engel, *Lord High Executioner*, 168, cites Radclive's views on weak knees.
38. *Western Sun*, 4 Jan. 1900.

Aftermath

1. *Western Sun*, 4 Jan. 1900.
2. Ibid., 28 Dec. 1899.
3. Ibid., 14 Dec. 1899.
4. Ibid., 4 Jan. 1900.
5. Ibid., 11 Jan. 1900.
6. McLaurin, *Sixty Years in the Ministry*, 9.
7. Sample titles in the series were 'The Altar of Innocence' and 'The Golden Candlestick'. *Western Sun*, 8 Feb. 1900.
8. *St. Matthew's Register: Births, Marriages and Deaths 1899–1905*; *Queen v. Stripp* (1899), Bail Bond, PAM, GR 363, box 31; 'From the *Sun* 1897', *Brandon Daily Sun*, 20 July 1907. Payne was also the president of the curling club. *Manitoba Morning Free Press*, 13 June 1899.
9. *Queen v. Stripp* (1900), County Court Judges Criminal Court (Brandon), Judge's Notebook, 18 Jan. 1900, 314–35, PAM, G2109.
10. *Western Sun*, 25 Jan. 1900.
11. Emma and Fred Sr moved away; Fred Stripp Jr and his wife, Alberta (Bertie), moved away; Frederick Robinson and his wife, Ella (née Stripp), moved away. (Ella, who was about 24 in 1901, is not to be confused with Ella Robinson, a 50-year-old seamstress.) *1901 Census*. See also *St. Matthew's Church Brandon Register #1 1884–1899: Baptisms, Marriages, Deaths or Funeral Services*.
12. *Western Sun*, 4 Jan. 1900.

13. The Ancient Order of United Workmen, despite its name, was not a labour organization, but an American-based association of progressive businessmen.

14. *Western Sun*, 28 Dec. 1899.

15. *Brandon Daily Sun*, 17 May 1951; Fred McGuinness, 'Rising through the ranks with Gen. Kircaldy', *Brandon Sun*, 22 Feb. 1996.

16. *Western Sun*, 1 Feb. 1900.

17. *Brandon Daily Sun*, 30 Dec. 1929. According to family stories, Alexander's wife had arthritis and eventually became a complete invalid.

18. *Western Sun*, 8 Feb. 1900; 'From the *Sun* 1897', *Brandon Daily Sun*, 20 July 1907. R.B. Cumming is listed as the bursar for 1901. *Journals of the Legislative Assembly of Manitoba, Session 1902* (Winnipeg, 1902), 399.

19. According to family stories, Robert hosted the Margaret McIlvride Gray family when they went west, and he arranged property for them near Wapella.

20. *Brandon Times*, 13 Sept. 1900. Elviss was a single 28-year-old Methodist. In the *1901 Census* he listed his relationship to the head of the household as 'partner', but no one else is listed as living in the same residence as Elviss. It is thus possible that he, like McIlvride before him, lived for a time with the Lanes.

21. Mary Hume, ed., *Brandon: A Prospect of a City* (Brandon, Man., 1981), 11.

22. 'R. Lane', *Brandon Weekly Sun Harvest Edition*, 7 Nov. 1912.

23. *Brandon Daily Sun*, 30 June 1924.

24. *Birtle Eye-Witness*, 11 July 1899. *The Eye-Witness* reported very little about the case, possibly out of consideration for Robert Lane's parents and brother in Birtle.

25. *Winnipeg Morning Telegram*, 28 Dec. 1899.

26. *Revised Statutes of Canada*, 1906, vol. 3 (Ottawa, 1906), 301. Gatrell, *The Hanging Tree*, 88. Rumours exist that Blake's body was subsequently removed from the jail grounds and placed in a grave in the Birtle region northwest of Brandon. It is claimed that the grave is marked with a large red gravestone. The story appears to be apocryphal.

27. *Norfolk Chronicle*, 30 Dec. 1899.

28. *1901 Census of Canada*, Manitoba, District #6 Brandon. B6: Brandon City Between 9th and 10th Streets, 4. The information about Henrietta's first job comes from her son, John Woods. Interview by the authors, 20 Nov. 2000.

Index

NOTE: page numbers in italic type refer to illustration captions.

THE CANADIAN SOCIAL HISTORY SERIES

Andrée Lévesque,
Making and Breaking the Rules:
Women in Quebec, 1919–1939, 1994.
ISBN 0–7710–5283–9

Cecilia Danysk,
Hired Hands: Labour and the
Development of Prairie Agriculture,
1880–1930, 1995.
ISBN 0–7710–2552–1

Kathryn McPherson,
Bedside Matters: The Transformation
of Canadian Nursing, 1900–1990, 1996.
ISBN 0–19–541219–2

Edith Burley,
Servants of the Honourable Company:
Work, Discipline, and Conflict in the
Hudson's Bay Company, 1770–1870,
1997.
ISBN 0–19–541296–6

Mercedes Steedman,
Angels of the Workplace: Women and the
Construction of Gender Relations in the
Canadian Clothing Industry, 1890–1940,
1997.
ISBN 0–19–541308–3

Angus McLaren and
Arlene Tigar McLaren,
The Bedroom and the State: The Chang-
ing Practices and Politics of Contracep-
tion and Abortion in Canada,
1880–1997, 1997.
ISBN 0–19–541318–0

Kathryn McPherson, Cecilia Morgan,
and Nancy M. Forestell, Editors,
Gendered Pasts: Historical Essays in
Femininity and Masculinity in Canada,
1999.
ISBN 0–19–541449–7

Gillian Creese,
Contracting Masculinity: Gender, Class,
and Race in a White-Collar Union,
1944–1994, 1999.
ISBN 0–19–541454–3

Geoffrey Reaume,
Remembrance of Patients Past: Patient
Life at the Toronto Hospital for the
Insane, 1870–1940, 2000.
ISBN 0–19–541538–8

Miriam Wright,
A Fishery for Modern Times: The State
and the Industrialization of the New-
foundland Fishery, 1934–1968, 2001.
ISBN 0–19–541620–1

Judy Fudge and Eric Tucker,
Labour Before the Law: The Regulation
of Workers' Collective Action in Canada,
1900–1948, 2001.
ISBN 0–19–541633–3

Mark Moss,
Manliness and Militarism: Educating
Young Boys in Ontario for War, 2001.
ISBN 0–19–541594–9

Joan Sangster,
Regulating Girls and Women: Sexuality,
Family, and the Law in Ontario
1920–1960, 2001.
ISBN 0–19–541663–5

Reinhold Kramer and Tom Mitchell,
Walk Towards the Gallows: The Tragedy
of Hilda Blake, Hanged 1899, 2002.
ISBN 0–19–541686–4